Principles of Retailing

Principles of Retailing

John Fernie
Suzanne Fernie
Christopher Moore

ELSEVIER
BUTTERWORTH
HEINEMANN

AMSTERDAM • BOSTON • HEIDELBERG • LONDON • NEW YORK • OXFORD
PARIS • SAN DIEGO • SAN FRANCISCO • SINGAPORE • SYDNEY • TOKYO

Butterworth-Heinemann
An imprint of Elsevier
Linacre House, Jordan Hill, Oxford OX2 8DP
200 Wheeler Road, Burlington, MA 01803

First published 2003
Reprinted 2004

Permissions may be sought directly from Elsevier's Science and Technology Rights
Department in Oxford, UK: phone: (+44) (0) 1865 843830; fax: (+44) (0) 1865 853333;
e-mail: permissions@elsevier.co.uk. You may also complete your request on-line via the
Elsevier homepage (www.elsevier.com), by selecting 'Customer Support' and
then 'Obtaining Permissions'

British Library Cataloguing in Publication Data
Fernie, John, 1948–
   Principles of retailing
   1. Retail trade   2. Retail trade – Management
   I. Title   II. Moore, Christopher   III. Fernie, Suzanne
   658.8'7

Library of Congress Cataloguing in Publication Data
A catalogue record for this book is available from the Library of Congress

ISBN 0 7506 4703 5

For information on all Butterworth-Heinemann publications visit our
website at: www.bh.com

Composition by Genesis Typesetting Limited, Rochester, Kent
Printed and bound in Italy

Contents

Preface

Principles of Retailing was conceived in 1998 when the authors lamented the lack of a good readable textbook in retailing to match the proliferation of equivalent works on Marketing. McGoldrick's *Retail Marketing*, the only notable text on the subject, was out of date and marketing-specific. The challenge was to produce a book which was readable to a wide audience, students and practitioners alike, but to have academic authority based on the teaching and research experience of the authors.

Although numerous texts have been published since the 'big idea', they continue to focus on Retail Marketing. *Principles of Retailing* offers four sections. Part 1 introduces the reader to the key retailers and the changing environment in which they operate. Theories of change are discussed and they provide a backcloth to retail strategy formulation – the planning process, strategic choices and the role of location in overall strategy.

Most books on this subject ignore the supply chain. This is not solely a problem with retailing texts but also in the general marketing area. This is surprising in that the key to success in retailing is the ability to buy well to meet customers' needs and co-ordinate the logistics to get these products to the shelf as efficiently as possible. Two of the authors are specialists in the fields of buying and logistics and Managing the Retail Supply Chain, Part 2, is therefore a core section of the book.

Part 3 deals with retail operations – customer service, selling, security and merchandising. The latter chapter is based on recent primary research and retail security is under represented in most textbooks. Finally, Part 4 deals with the future of internationalization and e-commerce. Again, a different approach is taken in these chapters. In the internationalization of retailers more focus lies on the impact of

Wal-Mart and other global players on retail markets than in other works, and in electronic commerce and retailing the problem of e-fulfilment and the so-called 'last mile' problem of home delivery receives considerable attention.

Hopefully we have provided a topical, readable, yet authoritative account of modern retailing today.

Part 1

The Changing Retail Environment

1

Introduction

Retailing impacts upon our lives. We all shop, albeit with different levels of enthusiasm! In terms of economic significance, the sector makes a major contribution to the Gross Domestic Product (GDP) of countries (around 10.5 per cent in the UK) and employs a large number of people (around 2.4 million in the UK). Moreover, retail organizations are no longer small-scale family-run concerns but powerful multi-national corporations. Wal-Mart is the largest corporation in the world, employing nearly 1 million 'associates'; Tesco, the largest UK company, employs 260 000 people. These corporations have global aspirations and have come a long way in a relatively short period of time. The vision of entrepreneurs such as Sam Walton (Wal-Mart) and Jack Cohen (Tesco) have transformed retail markets. Their stores are not unique, however, with Benetton, IKEA and Zara to name but a few successful companies which have benefited from strong entrepreneurial leadership. In 2002, for example, Stanley Kalms retired as chairman of Dixons, a company which has grown from a single photography shop in 1937 to Europe's leading electrical retailer. At the same time Ken Morrison, at the tender age of 71, continues to run one of the most successful grocery retail chains in the UK, Wm. Morrison, from a mere 114 stores. While illustrious corporations such as British Airways exit the prestigious FTSE 100, Wm. Morrison entered the top league table in 2001 and was ranked 65 in September 2002.

Because of the high-profile nature of retail corporations and their key management executives, the sector is prominent in the media. Retailing is therefore controversial. Headlines such as 'Rip-off Britain', 'Large stores lead to closure of small shops', 'the demise of city centres' and so on have promoted vigorous debate on the role of retailing in our society. Governments act as referees to ensure that a balance is struck between stimulating retail business yet protecting the consumer from anti-competitive practices and adverse environmental impacts of new developments.

The purpose of this introductory chapter is to give the reader an overview of a who's who in retailing. First of all we will attempt to identify the world's largest retailers by country of origin and discuss a series of performance measures to justify the ranking process. This will illustrate to the reader some of the difficulties in undertaking such a task because of definitional problems and 'missing' data. This is reinforced with a more detailed analysis of retailing in the UK, where 'official' retail categorizations have changed over time.

The world stage

In order to provide a global ranking of retailers, several key sources are invariably used by most academics and consultants. Each year the *Fortune* magazine publishes the Fortune 500, the largest companies based in the USA; similarly, *Asia Week* publishes a list of the 1000 largest corporations in Asia. The *Financial Times* and *Fortune* produce a global 500 – the world's largest corporations. If a more detailed assessment of international food retailers is required, Elsevier Food International publishes annually a ranking of the world's largest retailers.

Table 1.1 provides a list of the world's largest retailers in 2000 by market capitalization and sales. Caution should be used in interpreting this and any other 'ranking' tables. It is highly debatable that McDonald's would be classified as a retailer in most research. Market capitalization figures are based on publicly quoted companies and therefore exclude some notable privately owned companies such as Auchan, Aldi and C&A, for which sales data are available. Other important omissions from capitalization data sets are organizations with co-operative constitutions (prominent in Scandinavia and Switzerland) and voluntary trading groups such as ITM and Leclerc in France. Data are often not strictly comparable because of different financial year-ends, and conversion rates of currencies to one standard (the US dollar in Table 1.1) can distort figures in volatile currency markets.

Market capitalization figures are much more volatile than those of sales. This is particularly true since 2000, the base year for Table 1.1. The stock market has collapsed since then and the league table has changed (see Table 12.1). Stock market valuations are based on future income streams not existing sales, and therefore companies ranked by sales and market capitalization are not necessarily the same in each listing. In Table 1.1, Marks & Spencer, Walgreen and Boots perform much better with regard to stock market valuation than their sales

Table 1.1 Comparison of rankings of the world's largest retail companies

Rank	Ranked by capitalization			Ranked by revenues		
		Country of origin	$ billion		Country of origin	€ billion
1	Wal-Mart	US	123	Wal-Mart	US	163
2	Home Depot	US	58	Carrefour	France	52
3	McDonald's	US	41	Kroger	US	45
4	Seven 11	US	26	Metro	Germany	44
5	Carrefour	France	24	ITM	France	40
6	Safeway US	US	22	Home Depot	US	38
7	Walgreen	US	22	Albertson's	US	37
8	Marks & Spencer	UK	22	Sears Roebuck	US	37
9	Ito Yokado	Japan	20	K-Mart	US	36
10	Gap	US	20	Target	US	34
11	Metro	Germany	19	J C Penney	US	31
12	Tesco	UK	19	Ahold	The Netherlands	31
13	Ahold	The Netherlands	18	Safeway US	US	31
14	Sainsbury	UK	18	Rewe	Germany	30
15	Sears Roebuck	US	17	Tesco	UK	30
16	Pinault-Primtemps	France	17	Ito Yokado	Japan	30
17	Boots	UK	16	Edeka	Germany	30
18	Albertson's	US	13	Costco	US	27
19	Kroger	US	13	Tengelmann	Germany	26
20	Hennes & Mauritz	Sweden	13	Aldi	Germany	26

Source: Howard (2001).

would appear to indicate; conversely, K-Mart (now in liquidation), Costco and J C Penney generate high sales but rank lower in market value.

The largest retailers in the world tend to be those with large store formats offering grocery, general merchandise and household products. One half of the companies were US based, but with the exception of Gap and Wal-Mart, these retailers serve their domestic market. Hence size does not equate with internationalization; indeed, Wal-Mart's drive to international growth is a late 1990s phenomenon. European retailers, by contrast, have greater sales penetration in more international markets because of smaller domestic markets, greater regulation on store development and the opportunity to 'boundary hop' to adjacent countries.

Whilst Table 1.1 indicates which companies are the largest, we can also measure success in terms of a series of profitability measures. McGurr (2002) drew upon the year 2000 listings from the top 500 companies from Asia Week, the Fortune 500 and the European edition of the *Wall Street Journal* to form a data set of 117 retailers based in Asia,

Europe and the US. Tables 1.2–1.4 detail the data with a few indicators of retail performance. From this data, some key financial ratios can be computed:

$$\text{Net profit margin} = \frac{\text{profit after interest}}{\text{sales}}$$

$$\text{Return on total assets} = \frac{\text{net profit}}{\text{total assets}}$$

Net profit margin is a measure of profitability after all costs have been deducted. Return on total assets indicates a level of profitability from the assets deployed in the business. This will include fixed assets (land and property) and current assets (stock, debtors and cash) minus current liabilities, mainly creditors. McGurr also uses sales per employee as an indicator of employee productivity. He argues that Asian retailers show much greater employee productivity than either European or US retailers. This is not unexpected in that most Asian retailers in the sample are based in Japan, where land costs are high and sales densities are correspondingly high, leading to higher sales per employee. He also maintains that the converse is true for asset turnover, with US retailers showing greater efficiency in converting assets into sales.

The data from these tables illustrate some of the problems alluded to earlier in compiling rankings. The three different data sets have a variety of year-end dates. The classifications by main business are not consistent across the three categories, with the term 'retailing' used to describe some of the largest Asian retailers. Furthermore, some of the categorizations are questionable; for example, Metro as a grocer and Kingfisher as a drug/health and beauty retailer. Clearly, to make meaningful international comparisons of these financial ratios, like for like analogies have to be made. Thus, the food and drug stores in the US list can be compared with grocery retailers in Europe and supermarket chains in Asia.

The main problem with such classifications, however, is that the traditional categorizations of retail businesses are breaking down. Conventional grocery retailers seek to enhance their low net profit margins by moving into non-food lines, whilst Wal-Mart has developed a major food presence in the US through the building of supercentres to augment its discount development store offering. Nevertheless, the data from Tables 1.2–1.4 is useful in compiling rankings of the largest retailers by sales, profits and number of employees prior to undertaking analysis of financial ratios.

Table 1.2 Asia Week 1000 – retail firms

Retail rank	Rank in 1000	Company	Year end	Country	Main business	Sales ($ millions)	Net profit ($ millions)	Assets ($ millions)	Sales per $ assets	Employees (number)	Per employee Sales	Per employee Profits
1	27	Ito – Yokado	February 00	Japan	Retailing	28 302.2	418.1	18 464.8	1.53	116 636	242 654	3585
2	33	Daiei	February 00	Japan	Supermarkets	23 023.9	(192.6)	16 105.8	1.43	15 603	1 475 607	–12 344
3	36	Jusco	February 00	Japan	Supermarkets	22 162.7	(24.9)	16 091.9	1.38	34 375	644 733	–724
4	53	Mycal Corp.	February 00	Japan	Supermarkets	16 291.9	(51.9)	16 033.0	1.02	21 945	742 397	–2365
5	66	Coles Myer	July 99	Australia	Retailing	14 479.0	261.5	4971.1	2.91	157 440	91 965	1661
6	75	Woolworths	June 00	Australia	Retailing	13 271.3	190.7	3108.2	4.27	108 946	121 815	1750
7	111	Takashimaya	February 00	Japan	Department stores	10 189.6	56.4	7669.9	1.33	16 589	614 238	3400
8	112	UNY	February 00	Japan	Department stores	10 137.8	72.2	6904.4	1.47	6627	1529 772	10 895
9	124	Seiyu	February 00	Japan	Supermarkets	8954.6	(114.4)	7062.8	1.27	13 528	661 931	–8457
10	136	Mitsukoshi	February 00	Japan	Department stores	8403.3	58.6	4672.9	1.80	13 950	602 387	4201
11	168	Hutchison Whampoa[a]	December 99	Hong Kong	Retailing/telecom	7107.9	1166.1	48 156.5	0.15	42 510	167 205	27 431
12	171	Dalmaru	February 00	Japan	Department stores	6890.6	19.9	3466.1	1.99	13 046	528 177	1525
13	193	Dairy Farm	December 99	Hong Kong	Supermarkets	5917.9	37.3	2691.1	2.20	74 000	79 972	504
14	215	Selbu Dept Stores	February 00	Japan	Department stores	5057.8	2.9	5280.3	0.96	9602	526 744	302
15	217	Isetan	March 00	Japan	Department stores	5031.3	28.2	4218.0	1.19	5070	992 367	5562
16	247	Marui	January 00	Japan	Department stores	4580.8	152.3	5803.4	0.79	10 536	434 776	14 455
17	254	Tokyu Dept Store	January 00	Japan	Department stores	4491.5	129.8	4255.2	1.06	8774	511 910	14 794
18	298	Matsuzakaya	February 00	Japan	Department stores	3924.0	(94.2)	2167.1	1.81	4870	805 749	–19 343
19	331	Hankyu Dept Stores	March 00	Japan	Department stores	3537.9	25.3	2699.4	1.31	4802	736 756	5269
20	347	Life Corp.	February 00	Japan	Supermarkets	3365.7	8.9	1527.4	2.20	4180	805 191	2129
21	351	Izumlya	February 00	Japan	Supermarkets	3304.7	27.4	2556.0	1.29	14 053	235 160	1950
22	376	Nagasakiya	February 00	Japan	Clothes retailing	3110.2	3.7	3125.9	0.99	2624	1185 290	1410
23	394	Seven-Eleven Japan	February 00	Japan	Convenience stores	2961.0	630.6	6134.2	0.48	3660	809 016	172 295
24	395	Consumers Co-op Kobe	March 00	Japan	Supermarkets	2958.9	13.8	1830.1	1.62	15 888	186 235	869
25	399	Helwado	February 00	Japan	Supermarkets	2902.9	12.5	2413.0	1.20	3515	825 861	3556
26	400	Kotobukiya	February 00	Japan	Supermarkets	2889.1	10.8	2064.7	1.40	2549	1 133 425	4237
27	409	Maruetsu	February 00	Japan	Supermarkets	2863.9	(150.7)	1427.0	2.01	12 380	231 333	–12 173
28	420	Franklins	December 99	Australia	Supermarkets	2796.0	(18.5)	747.9	3.74	25 000	111 840	–740
29	434	Best Denki	February 00	Japan	Electronics retailing	2718.3	31.3	2053.6	1.32	4766	570 352	6567
30	454	Kintetsu Dept Stores	February 00	Japan	Department stores	2605.0	4.5	1570.9	1.66	4121	632 128	1092
31	463	Izumi	February 00	Japan	Supermarkets	2531.3	12.6	2078.7	1.22	6572	385 164	1917
32	464	Tokyu Store Chain	February 00	Japan	Supermarkets	2531.1	8.2	1277.1	1.98	2915	868 302	2813
33	498	Joshin Denki	March 00	Japan	Electronics retailing	2327.7	5.2	1334.0	1.74	2838	820 190	1832
34	499	Parco Co.	February 00	Japan	Fashion stores	2325.1	4.2	2102.0	1.11	2981	779 973	1409

[a] Net profit of Hutchison Whampoa reduced by $13 878 of gains on sales of businesses.

Source: McGurr (2002).

Table 1.3 The Europe 500 – retail firms

Retail rank	Rank in 500	Company	Year end	Country	Main business	Sales ($ millions)	Net profit ($ millions)	Assets ($ millions)	Sales per $ assets	Employees (number)	Per employee Sales	Per employee Profits
1	17	Metro	December 99	Germany	Grocery	44 113.6	367.1	19 116.1	2.31	216 475	203 781	1696
2	30	Carrefour	December 99	France	Grocery	37 621.9	760.5	23 049.7	1.63	144 412	260 518	5266
3	37	Ahold	December 99	Netherlands	Grocery	33 810.6	757.7	14 392.1	2.35	309 000	109 419	2452
4	54	Tesco	February 00[a]	Great Britain	Grocery	29 665.7	1063.8	15 576.2	1.90	80 650	367 833	13 190
5	56	Sainsbury	March 00[a]	Great Britain	Grocery	25 680.5	550.8	16 654.2	1.54	189 227	135 713	2911
6	67	Promodes[b]	December 99	France	Grocery	21 228.0	144.0	12 976.1	1.64	152 878	138 856	942
7	74	Pinault Printemps	December 99	France	Department store	19 042.0	630.0	20 514.8	0.93	78 510	242 542	8024
8	142[c]	Kingfisher	January 00[a]	Great Britain	Drugs and HBA	17 483.5	677.3	11 478.1	1.52	118 416	147 645	5720
9	85	Rallye	December 99	France	Grocery	16 374.0	215.0	12 622.7	1.30	89 981	181 972	2389
10	92	Casino Gulchard Perrachon	December 99	France	Grocery	15 747.7	296.6	10 662.1	1.48	73 468	214 348	4037
11	97	Karstadt Quelle	December 99	Germany	Department store	14 947.7	73.4	7980.9	1.87	89 920	166 233	816
12	102	Delhaize	December 99	Belgium	Grocery	14 691.3	232.4	5767.7	2.55	124 933	117 593	1860
13	125	Marks & Spencer	March 99	Great Britain	Department store	13 265.3	600.2	12 588.8	1.05	75 492	175 718	7951
14	140	Safeway	March 99	Great Britain	Grocery	13 018.8	392.3	7195.9	1.81	75 904	171 517	5168
15	166	Somerfield	April 99	Great Britain	Grocery	9502.1	255.4	2994.7	3.17	41 364	229 719	6174
16	176	Great Universal Stores	March 00[a]	Great Britain	Clothing	9007.0	437.9	8747.3	1.03	51 493	174 917	8504
17	194	Boots	March 99	Great Britain	Drugs and HBA	8136.9	38.6	5206.1	1.56	63 173	128 803	611
18	209	SPAR-Handels AG	December 99	Germany	Grocery	6735.9	(104.8)	1775.0	3.79	45 994	146 452	-2279
19	226	Kesko	December 99	Finland	Grocery	6153.5	85.5	2588.0	2.38	10 993	559 765	7778
20	280[c]	Dixons Group	April 00[a]	Great Britain	Electronics	6037.1	648.7	4335.7	1.39	29 571	204 156	21 937
21	244	Laurus	December 99	Netherlands	Grocery	5628.1	112.8	1393.7	4.04	39 625	142 035	2846
22	247	Galaries Lafayette	December 99	France	Department store	5589.7	83.0	3060.7	1.83	33 339	167 662	2490
23	288[c]	Rinascente	December 99	Italy	Grocery	5245.2	59.2	4439.0	1.18	27 947	187 684	2118
24	266	G.I.B Group	January 00[a]	Belgium	Building materials	5191.1	24.0	1951.0	2.66	32 679	176 964	734
25	339[c]	Morrison Supermarkets	January 00[a]	Great Britain	Grocery	4796.7	192.5	2394.2	2.00	22 000	189 682	8750
26	268[c]	AVA	December 99	Germany	Grocery	4530.2	58.3	1288.5	3.52	27 018	167 673	2158
27	306	Sonae SGPS	December 99	Portugal	Grocery	4349.2	67.5	5958.4	0.73	49 734	87 450	1357
28	470[c]	Vendex HKK	January 00[a]	Netherlands	Department store	4310.4	141.5	2131.9	2.02	54 100	50 959	2616
29	340	WH Smith	August 99	Great Britain	Booksellers	3770.3	145.9	1524.8	2.47	28 177	133 808	5178
30	337	Centros Commerc. Continente[d]	December 99	Spain	Grocery	3696.7	78.5	2030.1	1.82	19 135	193 190	4105
31	377	Jeronimo Martins	December 99	Portugal	Grocery	3303.0	48.3	2667.5	1.24	34 245	96 451	1411
32	378	Modelo Continente	December 99	Portugal	Grocery	3287.9	89.7	2858.9	1.15	38 066	86 372	2356
33	379	Hennes & Mauritz	November 99	Sweden	Clothing	3285.2	362.3	1672.5	1.96	17 652	186 109	20 525
34	382	Monoprix	December 99	France	Department store	3244.6	35.2	1372.1	2.36	14 551	222 978	158
35	384	Centros Commerc. Pryca[d]	December 99	Spain	Grocery	3225.4	121.8	1756.2	1.84	16 755	192 505	633
36	399	Castorama Dubois	January 00	France	Building materials	3105.6	345.4	3713.8	0.84	38 809	80 022	8900
37	464	Iceland Group	January 00	Great Britain	Grocery	3100.0	62.7	1210.4	2.56	20 272	152 920	3093
38	485	Arcadia Group	August 99	Great Britain	Clothing	2440.4	47.0	1868.9	1.31	24 140	101 094	1947
39	500	Douglas Holding	December 99	Germany	Specialty	2242.4	76.8	1140.1	1.97	18 699	119 921	4107

[a] Updated data obtained for more January–March 2000 fiscal year end. [b] Purchased by Carrefour in August 1999. [c] Rankings are from Europe 500; order of sales in US $ may differ due to translation and updated data. [d] Merged in January 2000 into Centros Comerciales Carrefour. *Source*: McGurr (2002).

Table 1.4 Fortune 500 – retail firms

Retail rank	Rank in 500	Company	Year end	Main business	Sales ($ millions)	Net profit ($ millions)	Assets ($ millions)	Sales per $ assets	Employees (number)	Per employee Sales	Per employee Profits
1	2	Wal-Mart Stores	January 00	General merchandise	166 809.0	5377.0	70 245.0	2.37	1 140 000	146 324	4717
2	14	Kroger	January 00	Food and drug stores	45 351.6	955.9	16 266.1	2.79	213 000	212 918	4488
3	16	Sears Roebuck	December 99	General merchandise	41 071.0	1453.0	36 954.0	1.11	326 000	125 985	4457
4	32	Home Depot	January 00	Specialty retailer	38 434.0	2320.0	17 081.0	2.25	201 000	191 214	11 542
5	24	Albertson's	January 00	Food and drug stores	37 478.1	404.1	15 700.9	2.39	235 000	159 481	1720
6	27	K-Mart	January 00	General merchandise	35 925.0	403.0	15 104.0	2.38	275 000	130 636	1465
7	32	Target	January 00	General merchandise	33 702.0	1144.0	17 143.0	1.97	182 650	184 517	6263
8	36	J C Penney	January 00	General merchandise	32 510.0	336.0	20 888.0	1.56	260 000	125 038	1292
9	40	Safeway	December 99	Food and drug stores	28 859.9	970.9	14 900.3	1.94	193 000	149 533	5031
10	44	Costco Wholesale	August 99	Specialty retailer	27 456.0	397.3	7505.0	3.66	52 500	522 971	7568
11	93	CVS	December 99	Food and drug stores	18 098.3	635.1	7275.4	2.49	100 000	180 983	6351
12	95	Walgreen	August 99	Food and drug stores	17 838.8	624.1	5906.7	3.02	75 000	237 851	8321
13	97	Federated Department Stores	January 00	General merchandise	17 716.0	795.0	17 692.0	1.00	133 300	132 903	5964
14	109	Lowe's	January 00	Specialty retailer	15 905.6	672.8	9012.3	1.76	80 000	198 820	8410
15	122	May Department Stores	January 00	General merchandise	14 224.0	927.0	10 935.0	1.30	134 000	106 149	6918
16	123	Winn-Dixie Stores	June 99	Food and drug stores	14 136.5	182.3	3149.1	4.49	94 500	149 593	1929
17	137	Publix Super Markets	December 99	Food and drug stores	13 068.9	462.4	4067.7	3.21	84 250	155 120	5488
18	142	Rite Aid	February 99	Food and drug stores	12 731.9	143.7	10 421.7	1.22	89 900	141 623	1598
19	148	Toys 'R' Us	January 00	Specialty retailer	11 862.0	279.0	8503.0	1.40	55 105	215 262	5063
20	152	Gap	January 00	Specialty retailer	11 635.4	1127.1	5188.8	2.24	140 000	83 110	8051
21	160	Circuit City Group	February 99	Specialty retailer	10 804.4	142.9	3445.3	3.14	54 430	198 501	2625
22	166	Office Depot	December 99	Specialty retailer	10 263.3	257.6	4276.2	2.40	40 687	252 250	6331
23	169	Best Buy	February 99	Specialty retailer	10 077.9	224.4	2512.5	4.01	33 500	300 833	6699
24	177	Limited	January 00	Specialty retailer	9723.3	460.8	4087.7	2.38	73 350	132 560	6282
25	192	Staples	January 00	Specialty retailer	8936.8	315.0	3846.1	2.32	27 573	324 114	11 424
26	193	Dillard's	January 00	General merchandise	8921.0	164.0	7918.0	1.13	54 921	162 433	2986
27	196	TJX	January 00	Specialty retailer	8795.3	521.7	2805.0	3.14	67 000	131 273	7787
28	270	Saks	January 00	General merchandise	6423.8	189.6	5090.1	1.26	60 000	107 063	3160
29	273	Compusa[a]	June 99	Specialty retailer	6321.4	(45.7)	1465.8	4.31	16 800	376 274	-2720
30	320	Nordstrom	January 00	General merchandise	5124.2	202.6	3265.1	1.57	40 000	128 105	5065
31	332	Officemax	January 00	Specialty retailer	4842.7	10.0	2275.0	2.13	29 015	166 903	345
32	344	Consolidated Stores	January 00	Specialty retailer	4700.2	96.1	2186.8	2.15	20 840	225 537	4611
33	346	Venator	January 00	Specialty retailer	4647.0	48.0	2515.0	1.85	49 151	94 545	977
34	352	Kohl's	January 00	General merchandise	4557.1	258.1	2914.7	1.56	27 260	167 172	9468
35	377	BJ's Wholesale Club	January 00	Specialty retailer	4206.2	111.1	1073.4	3.92	13 350	315 071	8322
36	382	Tandy	December 99	Specialty retailer	4126.2	297.9	2142.0	1.93	36 000	114 617	8275
37	385	Autozone	August 99	Specialty retailer	4116.4	244.8	3284.8	1.25	35 000	117 611	6994
38	413	Shopko Stores	January 00	General merchandise	3911.9	102.2	2083.3	1.88	21 000	186 281	4867
39	415	Dollar General	January 00	General merchandise	3888.0	219.4	1450.9	2.68	29 820	130 382	7357
40	416	Ames Department Stores	January 00	General merchandise	3878.5	17.1	1975.3	1.96	34 403	112 737	497
41	433	Supermarkets General	January 00	Food and drug stores	3698.1	(31.4)	835.0	4.43	18 200	203 192	-1725
42	435	Longs Drug Stores	January 00	Food and drug stores	3672.4	69.0	1270.3	2.89	20 400	180 020	3382
43	443	Barnes & Noble	January 00	Specialty retailer	3486.0	124.5	2413.8	1.44	22 500	154 933	5533
44	445	Hannaford Brothers	December 99	Food and drug stores	3462.9	98.0	1330.0	2.60	16 900	204 905	5799

[a] Purchased by Grupo Sanborns (Mexico), March 2000. *Source:* McGurr (2002).

UK retail rankings

The definitive listing of the major retail companies in the UK was compiled by Retail Intelligence in the 1990s, and more recently Retail Knowledge Bank with their Retail Week 500 in 2001 and 2002. Table 1.5 highlights the top ranked. The listing is dominated by grocery retailers and this has been the case for some time, in contrast to the US, where department stores tended to dominate rankings. Food retailers only became more prominent in the 1990s, with growth through acquisition and the competition from Wal-Mart and their supercentres (see Chapter 2).

The most recent figures in the UK (Table 1.5) conceal a slowing down and indeed a reversal of the consolidation trend at the top end of the market. In 1997 the top 10 retailers had a market share of 39.6 per cent, in 1999 this had risen to 43 per cent but by 2001, the figure had fallen to 41 per cent. The main reasons for these changes are increased competition in the market, with the subsequent pressure on price and

Table 1.5 The 20 largest retailers in the UK

Rank		Company	Retail sales	(£ million ex VAT)
			2001	2000
2001	2002			
1	1	Tesco	18 372	16 958
2	2	J Sainsbury	13 085	13 570
3	3	Asda Group	9 680	9 150
4	4	Safeway	8 151	7 659
5	5	Marks & Spencer	6 293	6 483
6	8	The Boots Company	4 696	4 667
7	7	Somerfield	4 613	5 466
8	6	Kingfisher	4 403	6 365
9	10	Dixons Group	3 960	3 553
10	9	GUS	3 927	3 791
11	11	John Lewis Partnership	3 720	3 374
12	13	Morrisons	3 500	2 970
13	14	Co-operative Group	2 586	3 060
14	–	Woolworths Group	2 199	1 960
15	14	Iceland Group	1 922	1 922
16	15	Littlewoods	1 894	1 902
17	16	Arcadia Group	1 801	1 851
18	17	Debenhams	1 613	1 398
19	20	Next	1 428	1 260
20	18	WH Smith	1 415	1 317

Source: Retail Knowledge Bank (2002).

profit margins. The conglomerates built up in the 1980s and 1990s are being demerged, for example the split up of the Burton Group into Arcadia and Debenhams, and more recently the demerger of Kingfisher by spinning off the General Merchandise division (Woolworths) and the sale of Superdrug. Also, other retailers have refocused their business through the sale of parts of the operation which are no longer part of the strategic vision of the future. Thus, Sainsbury's sale of Homebase and Boots' intended sale of Halfords in 2002.

Although these rankings are useful, they only represent *UK retail sales*. Tesco, with major international aspirations, is under-represented in Table 1.5 because these figures do not show group sales. Similarly, Kingfisher, Dixons and GUS have a strong international presence, whilst Boots and Marks & Spencer have withdrawn from international markets in recent years. Another difficulty with the retail rankings is comparing Table 1.5 with market capitalization data. ASDA is now owned by Wal-Mart and is not a listed British company; John Lewis Partnership and Littlewoods are private companies. Nevertheless, the top 10 publicly quoted companies have been the same for the last few years, so a comparison of Tables 1.5 and 1.6 provides a meaningful comparison of performance indicators.

As mentioned earlier with regard to the global rankings, some companies' stock market performance is considerably better than their retail sales ranking, notably Marks & Spencer, Morrison and Next. Safeway has over double the sales of Morrisons, but their stock market valuation is about the same. The other indicators used in Table 1.6 by researchers at the Oxford Institute of Retail Management attempt to

Table 1.6 Value creation by UK largest retailers

Company	Mcap (31/03/2001, £ billion)	VCQ	MVA (£ billion)	REV (%)	REV (£ million)
Tesco	17.4	2.2	7.7	10.2	613.5
Marks & Spencer	7.7	1.6	3.3	2.6	150.1
Sainsbury	7.4	1.3	1.5	6.9	389.5
Kingfisher	6.4	2.1	4.1	7.7	276.1
Boots	5.6	2.3	3.1	18.6	409.7
Dixons	5.3	3.2	3.8	24.6	360.0
GUS	5.0	1.4	1.5	8.7	302.7
Safeway	3.4	1.1	0.3	3.7	112.8
Morrison	3.0	2.4	1.2	14.1	129.0
Next	2.9	5.0	2.1	30.1	162.1

Source: Dragun and Knight (2001).

show the value created by British retailers (they have undertaken similar research for global companies). Market Value Added (MVA) is the difference between the combined market value of debt and equity *and* the total capital employed by the company. This measures the absolute wealth added to the existing capital base. The Value Creation Quotient (VCQ) is a ratio of the combined market value to capital employed in the business. A ratio of over 1 means that the company is adding value for shareholders. The Realized Economic Value (REV) is the difference between cash flows from operating activities and a capital charge inputed from these operations.

Overall, the companies in Table 1.6 perform well on all of these indicators; however, it is the smaller and non-food companies which perform better on VCQ, showing that for every pound of capital absorbed, the value in column 2 has been created. It is worth noting that Matalan, the discount clothing retailer, has the highest position in both the UK and global rankings for this indicator. In terms of generating cash in excess of the cost of capital, Next again performs the best of the top 10 companies, followed by Dixons and Boots.

Official statistics

Much of the discussion on retail rankings has been based on data derived from commercial organizations which have compiled financial statistics on retail corporations. Nevertheless, comprehensive data exists from a range of government agencies which compile statistics on retail businesses, their turnover, labour market trends and cost structures. Moir and Dawson (1992) detail the changes in classifications and the variety of sources of information pertaining to retailing until the early 1990s. 'As the structure of the industry has become more complex, so there has been a wide range of statistics to measure and chart the performance of the sector ... the balance between government and commercial agencies as providers of statistics has changed' (p. 30). They comment that the government has withdrawn from surveys, partly for cost reasons, and this void has been filled in some, but not all, cases by commercial organizations.

Much of the base data for retailing research in the post-war period until the mid-1970s was strongly derived from the Census of Distribution, especially the last full census in 1971, which gave the most comprehensive picture of British retailing we have ever had from official statistics. Data were provided on retail sales by different kinds of business and by floorspace in each shopping centre in towns with over 50 000 people around the country. As the 1970s experienced a boom in town centre redevelopment schemes, these data had a crucial influence on planning decisions pertaining to over- and underprovision of retailing in towns and cities.

Unfortunately this Census was the last of its kind and no national database with this level of detail on locational data has been updated. Government data on retailing since 1976 have been derived from a series of Retail Inquiries carried out by the Business Statistics Office.

During the last 30 years, it has often been difficult to monitor trends accurately over time because of classification changes. The Standard Industrial Classification (SIC), first introduced in 1948, has been revised in 1968, 1980 and 1992. Table 1.7 shows data of turnover, capital expenditure and employment costs for different kinds of business (KOB) derived from SIC, 1992, group 52 classification. The two largest groups (52.1 and 52.4) are companies formerly classified as large food retailers and mixed retail businesses. New categories in the 1992

Table 1.7 Total retail trade by broad kind of business, 1998 (£ million)

Kind of business (SIC codes in brackets)	Number of businesses	Employment costs	Total turnover (inc. VAT)	Capital expenditure (net)
Retail sales in non-specialized stores (52.1)	38 360	10 099	104 967	4 082
Retail sales of food, drink or tobacco in specialized stores (52.2)	50 435	1 246	13 794	228
Retail sales of pharmaceutical and medical goods, cosmetics and toilet articles in specialized stores (52.3)	7 383	803	7 952	130
Other sales of new goods in specialized stores (52.4)	98 847	9 585	80 948	2 405
Retail sales of second-hand goods (52.5)	6 105	114	2 063	19
Retail sales not in stores (52.6)	10 373	1 074	10 450	211
Repair of personal and household goods (52.7)	4 497	215	822	46
Total retail trade	216 000	23 136	220 998	7 121

Source: Broadbridge (2001).

classification are those pertaining to second-hand goods to reflect the rise in the number of charity shops and retail sales not in stores, an indication of the importance of Internet and other forms of remote shopping.

If the reader needs a comprehensive compilation of retail statistics from UK sources, both government and commercial, the Institute for Retail Studies publishes an annual statistical digest of key tables on the retail and wholesale trade in the UK. For those more interested in the grocery sector, the Institute of Grocery Distribution (IGD) is the authoritative trade body for members of the grocery supply chain, publishing a range of reports on this sector, including an annual market review of grocery retailing.

If researchers in the UK have experienced problems in working with comparative data sets over time, the problem in undertaking comparative analyses of international trends are fraught with more difficulties. We alluded to some of these issues when discussing Tables 1.1–1.4; however, if detailed research is needed on KOB categories or format development, definitions vary between countries. Thus, throughout the EU different size definitions exist for hypermarkets, superstores and supermarkets, not aided by the UK's use of square feet instead of square metres in some instances!

Summary

This chapter has provided a short introduction to retailing through a review of the world's largest retailers and the role of UK retailing within this context. Retailing is an important subject of study because of the rise of once small family businesses to the corporate giants of today. Wal-Mart is the world's largest company and leads the field of major retailers, most of whom are also US in origin. The very size of the US market has been responsible for the rankings in Table 1.1, although companies such as Ahold, Carrefour, Metro and Tesco are challenging US companies, particularly through their strong international presence.

In the UK, Tesco is by far the market leader; indeed, grocery retailers dominate the rankings. Nevertheless, when other performance indicators are taken into account, such as VCQ and REV, clothing retailers and other non-food companies achieve much better performances.

Much of this chapter provides the reader with a guide to data sources in retailing with a warning to treat statistics, whether from official or commercial organizations, with caution because of classification and other data comparability problems.

Review questions

1 Who are the world's major retailers?
2 What criteria were used to rank these retailers?
3 Analyse the performance of US retailers compared with those in Asia and Europe in Tables 1.2–1.4.
4 Discuss the problems in undertaking such an analysis.
5 Comment upon the UK retail rankings in Table 1.5.
6 Discuss the relative performance of the top 10 British retailers in Table 1.6.
7 Outline the key data sources for analysing retail trends in the UK and discuss some of the problems encountered in monitoring these trends over time.

References

Broadbridge, A. (2001). *Distributive Trade Profile, 1999–2000: A Statistical Digest*. Institute for Retail Studies, University of Stirling.

Dragun, D. and Knight, R. (2001). Value creation in the UK retail sector. *The European Retail Digest*, **30**, 45–52.

Howard, E. (2001). The globalisation of retailing: questions concerning the largest firms. 11th International Conference on Research in the Distributive Trades, Tilbury, June.

McGurr, P. J. (2002). The largest retail firms: a comparison of Asia, Europe and US-based retailers. *The International Journal of Retail Distribution Management*, **30**(3), 145–50.

Moir, C. and Dawson, J. (1992). *Distribution*. Chapman & Hall, London.

Retail Knowledge Bank (2002). *Retail Week Top 500*. Retail Knowledge Bank, London.

2

The retail environment

Introduction

> In essence, retail change has been driven in the past by the interaction of consumer, retailer and government: in the 1990s the role of technology is increasingly important as an agent of change.
>
> (Fernie, 1997, p. 384)

To understand the retail environment it is important to glean a knowledge of the inter-relationships between the factors illustrated in Figure 2.1. In this chapter, we will consider how changes in the consumer environment – demographic, socio-economic and lifestyle trends – have impacted upon retail change. At the same time, government has been a major agent of change. Retailers are regulated by an array of laws and ordinances which impinge on their operations. This can be on licences to operate, which goods to sell, hours of operation, health and safety matters through to planning ordinances on where to locate the business. The types of merchandise on sale and the formats developed are a response to such interactions; however, retailers *do* influence consumers and government on product choice and format development. For example, the UK slowdown of the introduction of GM foods has been driven by retailers' refusal to stock these products.

The role of technology is not discussed in length here as it embraces most chapters of the book, especially those on logistics and Internet

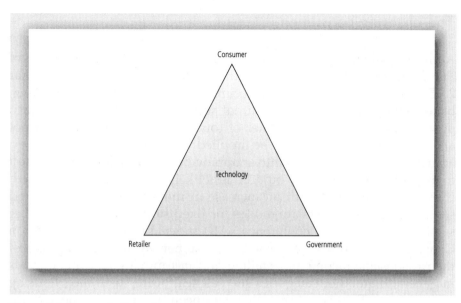

Figure 2.1 Factors influencing change.

retailing. It should be acknowledged here, however, that technology should be seen in its widest sense. For the consumer, technology has freed up time as capital goods replace labour in the home. Communications in both a physical and information sense have given access to wider geographical markets. Retailers embrace the IT revolution through sharing data with their suppliers and communicating with their customers, especially those with loyalty card schemes. New technologies have been applied throughout the supply chain to ensure that products can be designed/tested, manufactured and distributed through supply chains quicker and at a lower cost than ever before. Markets and companies have grown due to the links between innovation and technology. Take the case of chilled foods in UK supermarkets. Marks & Spencer's links with its main supplier, Northern Foods, goes back to a chance meeting of the current chairman, Christopher Hawkins, with an M&S executive on a flight to Northern Ireland. Initial dairy lines were introduced into M&S stores but a main catalyst for growth was the harnessing of BOC gases technology to distribute chilled and frozen products from warehouse to store. In response to the demand for ready meals, two businesses, Northern Foods and BOC Transhield, grew to supply M&S and latterly other supermarket chains with these product lines. It is perhaps appropriate that we now turn to the factors which have promoted change in the consumer environment.

The changing consumer

At the annual ECR Europe conference in May 2001, Maureen Johnson of The Store presented a picture of the changing consumer in the year 2015. 'Older, more affluent, insecure, discerning, more demanding, better educated and time pressured' were some of the terms used to describe the European consumer of tomorrow. Of course some, if not all, of these attributes can be applied to many consumers today. Translating these attributes into shopping behaviours, Johnson went on to argue that consumers would be less likely to shop in the 'planned' conventional method with an increase in more remote shopping and social, special or immediate modes for fixed store retailing. In another session at the same conference, Alexander Littner of the Boston Consulting Group showed that US consumers were spending less of their disposable income on retailing and fast-moving consumer goods in general than other categories such as healthcare, insurance, housing and utilities. This is a trend that has been apparent in the UK for decades as consumers find other avenues for their hard-earned cash rather than spending it on shopping.

In order to discuss the changing consumer in more depth we shall look at:

- demographic trends;
- socio-economic trends;
- lifestyle trends.

Demographic trends

The structure of a country's population and its rate of increase over time will impact upon the growth of the economy and the nature of a consumer's savings. Europe had been viewed as the battleground for retail competition because of the launch of the Euro and the potential enlargement of the EU to 25–30 members by 2010. This would mean an increase in the EU population from the 374 million of the 15 member states to 500–600 million by 2010. Despite the size of this market, the structure of the population in most European countries will experience dramatic changes in the next half century. Lower fertility rates and increased life expectancy will result in a 'greying population'. In 1997, around 23 per cent of the population in each member state was less than 20 years old (in Ireland it was 33 per cent) and the proportion of older people, those 60 and over, was 21 per cent and increasing. It is envisaged that, by 2030, the latter figure will increase to around 30 per cent for most countries.

The increasing number of old people is changing the nature of household composition. In 1996, 11 per cent of the EU population lived alone compared with 8 per cent in 1981. This is reflected in the increased number of single households across Europe and the number of people in a household declining in every EU country since the early 1980s. The classic image of a nuclear family of 2 plus 2.4 children in a household is the exception, not the rule. Independence is valued more and children leave the nest earlier than ever before. Also, divorce rates are at record levels, which have led to a breakdown of the traditional family household. On average, there are 2.5 people per household in the EU. In the UK, the figure is 2.3, a major decline from the 3.45 of 1951 (Table 2.1). Table 2.2 also gives a more detailed breakdown of housing types in England. This shows that married couples are the only category to experience decline in household numbers in the last 20 years.

Table 2.1 Declining size of households in the UK, 1951–2011

	1951	1961	1971	1981	1991	2001	2011
Average household size	3.45	3.2	2.8	2.7	2.4	2.3	2.25
Number of households (million)	15	17	17.5	19	22	24	26

Source: OPCS.

Table 2.2 Changing household types in England, 1981–2011 (thousands)

	1981	1991	2001	2011
Married couple	11 012	10 547	10 217	10 037
Co-habiting couple	500	1 222	1 446	1 549
Lone parent	626	981	1 202	1 259
Other multi-person	1 235	1 350	1 671	2 051
One person	3 932	5 115	6 509	7 875
All households	17 306	19 215	21 046	22 769

Source: Department of Environment, UK.

Socio-economic trends

Clearly there is a strong relationship between demographic trends and the labour market. Over a decade ago there were great fears that the changing structure of the population would lead to a demographic 'time bomb' producing labour shortages as numbers of 15- to 29-year-olds entering the labour market began to decline (historically, unemployment rates were highest within this age group).

In reality, the nature of the labour market had changed in line with the growth of high-tech 'sunrise' manufacturing industry and the service sector at the expense of traditional 'sunset' industries. This has seen the rise in female participation in the workforce, more part-time/casual working and the rise in self-employment, often as a result of early retirement or redundancy. In Europe, there has been a marked increase in the number of women in the labour force and there is no longer a significant fall in the rate after the age of 30, implying that women are not stopping work after having children. In the UK, women comprise a higher proportion of the labour force than men; they are flexible (often by necessity), are often better educated and have a wider range of skills for the service economy, of which retailing is a part. By contrast, men have seen their role in society change considerably, especially in areas of high unemployment, where 'light' industries and service jobs have replaced traditional male-dominated manufacturing work. The househusband is now common and the male head of household as the sole breadwinner is rapidly disappearing.

These trends in the labour market have occurred during a period of strong growth in most developed economies in the 1990s, which witnessed a period of low inflation and low unemployment levels. Cyclical changes in the economy have a major impact on discretionary purchases in that, in an upturn in the economy, consumers tend to spend more on non-essential purchases or those which can be deferred if uncertainty exists about employment opportunities or interest rates. In the UK, 'real' disposable incomes grew throughout the 1990s, although it is important to note that many of the factors which fuel consumer expenditure are unique to the UK. The main distinguishing features pertain more to the housing market and the size and structure of personal debt than households in other European countries. Much of this debt is mortgage debt, which tends to be short term and variable rated, exposing households to changes in short-term interest rates. The reason for the size of mortgage debt is that the rate of owner-occupancy in the UK is much greater (around 70 per cent) than in other countries; for example, the comparative figures for France and Germany are 55 and 50 per cent respectively. This also means that changes in house prices would impact on personal sector wealth and thus consumer demand to a much greater extent in the UK than elsewhere.

The combination of these factors in the housing market means that British homeowners are much more sensitive to changes in interest rates or tax relief on mortgages than their continental neighbours. Oxford Economic Forecasting (1998) estimates that a 1 per cent drop in short-term interest rates would lead to consumer expenditure growth of

0.5 per cent. Although UK interest rates are at historic low levels, the possibility of joining the Economic Monetary Union (EMU) would consolidate this trend to further fuel consumer expenditure.

Many of the trends discussed above are borne out by official UK government statistics on Retail Sales and Family Expenditure Surveys. For example, retail sales in the late 1990s account for around 37/38 per cent of total consumer expenditure compared with 40+ per cent a decade earlier. In terms of household expenditure, UK households now spend 16 per cent of their weekly expenditure on housing, 15 per cent on motoring and 12 per cent on leisure services. These all show increases over time compared with food, tobacco, clothing and footwear expenditure (Table 2.3). These figures indicate that the UK consumer is spending much more on 'services', rather than traditional retailing

Table 2.3 Pattern of household expenditure: average weekly expenditure (UK% shares)

Commodity	1960	1970	1980	1990	1998–9
Housing	9.3	12.6	15.0	18.0	16
Fuel, light and power	5.9	6.3	5.6	4.5	3
Food and non-alcoholic drinks	30.5	25.7	22.7	18.1	17
Alcoholic drink	3.2	4.5	4.8	4.1	4
Tobacco	5.9	4.8	3.0	1.9	2
Clothing and footwear	10.3	9.2	8.1	6.5	6
Durable household goods	6.3	6.5	7.0	–	–
Other goods	7.1	7.4	7.9	–	–
Transport and vehicles	12.2	13.7	14.6	–	–
Services	8.9	9.0	10.8	–	–
Household goods	–	–	–	8.1	8
Household services	–	–	–	5.0	5
Personal goods and services	–	–	–	3.8	4
Motoring expenditure	–	–	–	13.7	15
Fares and other travel costs	–	–	–	2.5	2
Leisure goods	–	–	–	4.6	5
Leisure services	–	0.3	–	8.7	12
Miscellaneous	–	–	0.4	0.6	0
Total	100.0	100.0	100.0	100.0	100.0
	£16.51	£28.57	£110.6	£247.16	£309.07
Average weekly expenditure per person	£5.43	£9.70	£40.75	£99.86	£148.90

The component/service groupings used to categorize FES expenditure have been revised to align with the categories recommended for the Retail Price Index (RPI) by the RPI Advisory Committee. The 11 Commodity groups have been extended to 14.
Source: Broadbridge (2001).

goods. The consumer is 'trading up', owning their own home, one or two cars and is taking more overseas vacations. Now around 72 per cent of all UK households have access to a car and are willing to be much more mobile in search of employment, retail and leisure opportunities. People seek better quality environments in which to live and work, and this is reflected in the general shift away from metropolitan to smaller-sized communities. Of course, this trend is evident in many developed economies, especially in North America, where suburbanization, urban sprawl and an automobile-orientated society alerted European planners to curbing the excesses of this type of development.

Lifestyle trends

The combination of demographic and socio-economic trends has resulted in a complex set of values associated with consumer behaviour. A range of paradoxes exists. We are a more affluent society than ever before, yet there is a growing underclass of poor people in the UK who are long-term unemployed and cannot be regarded as conventional consumers. The 'grey' consumer is not your austere customer of 20 years ago, but is likely to be relatively wealthy and 'young' in attitude to health, sport and fashion. But there is now a blurring of social activities so that people no longer perceive aspects of life in discrete compartments. Sport, fashion and music overlap so that, while the clothing market stagnates, the sports market grows, mainly by selling clothes.

Christopher Field in 1998 identified some characteristics of new consumers:

- they no longer conform to traditional stereotypes – they are demanding, fickle, disloyal, footloose, individual and easily bored;
- they are better informed and more sophisticated, and are prepared to complain when they get poor service;
- they have less time for shopping;
- they feel greater uncertainty about future personal prospects;
- they express a growing concern for the environment;
- they have lost faith in traditional institutions such as the police, church and state.

He illustrated the latter point from research undertaken by The Henley Centre to show how confidence in our established institutions has waned during the 1980s and 1990s (Table 2.4). The low turnout at the British General Election in 2001 after a lacklustre campaign illustrates this indifference. The decline in membership of 'collective' organizations from trade unions and religious bodies through to political parties is further evidence of the individualistic nature of today's consumer. Webb (1998) points out, however, that at the same time individuals express the need for security and solidarity by coming together in 'tribes'. He uses the examples of football supporters, local neighbourhood watches and PC users' clubs.

Table 2.4 The degree of confidence in established British 'institutions', 1983–1996

	1983	1993	1996
Armed forces	88	84	74
The police	83	70	58
The legal system	58	36	26
Parliament	58	36	26
The church	52	37	25
The civil service	46	36	14
The press	32	18	7
Trade unions	23	26	14
The monarchy	25	18	18

Source: Field (1998).

Although it is becoming increasingly difficult to segment consumers into discrete categories, this does not stop market researchers from producing segmentation models to categorize them. The younger generation has been the focus of much attention because of their influence on adult spending, their £1.5 billion spending power per annum and the fact that they have become 'consumers' much earlier than previous generations. Carat, the media buying agency, has analysed the post-children, young people generation. It identified eight subgroups of 15- to 34-year-olds based on data from 10 000 consumers. The groups are L-plate lads, disillusioned young mums, cross-roaders, progressive leaders, city boys, survivors, confident introverts and new traditionalists (see Table 2.5). The purpose of such a segmentation is to maximize the effectiveness of advertising campaigns to this age group. But while we can divide consumers into categories such as those above, it is often difficult to understand actual consumer behaviour. Webb (1998) quotes the managing director of New Look, a chain which targets clothes for teenage girls, as saying: 'a customer is as likely to buy a CD as one of our blouses. To be honest I've given up trying to fathom out why people buy what they do.'

Table 2.5 The younger generation (15–34 years old) market in the UK

Category	Characteristics
L-plate lads	Single, working class, living with parents. Started first job. Like lager, ladies, TV and sport. Spend money on beer, music and fast food.
Disillusioned young mums	Married or single parent, working class, lives in council flat. Possible part-time job. Low disposable income. Watch much TV.
Cross-roaders	Live with their parents. Ambitious, want to make money. Spend on designer labels, DVDs and like new 'gadgets'. Read trendy magazines.
Progressive leaders	Female graduates, renting with friends. Started first job. Go to gym, spend much on clothes. Read quality newspaper and magazines.
City boys	Married with children. Drive a BMW, thinking of setting up their own business. Work hard, play hard. Read 'right of centre' quality press.
Survivors	Older than disillusioned young mums, still renting, working part-time and tight budgets.
Confident introverts	Technology freaks. Spend hours on the Internet, which they use for news, games and shopping. Read 'right of centre' quality press.
New traditionalists	Married with children. Prematurely middle-aged with large mortgage and responsibilities. Interests are mainly 'domestic' in nature, reflected in their TV choices and magazine reading (gardening, food and drink).

The retail response

The retail response to these changes in consumer behaviour has made the retail sector one of the most dynamic in modern economies. Innovations in format development and operating practices have enabled retailers to compete or even survive in a changing retail environment.

Retail innovation

Many of these innovations emanate from the United States and ideas and 'know-how' have been borrowed from the US to other markets. For example, Marks & Spencer executives did fact-finding missions to the US in the 1920s and 1930s to refine operating practices at home. Similarly, Alan Sainsbury introduced self-service and the shopping basket into Sainsbury stores in the 1950s after sojourns to the US. More recently, formats such as warehouse clubs and factory outlet centres have reached these shores with varying degrees of success.

It is interesting to note that particular formats or operating practices are often associated with a company or country of origin. The hypermarket, developed in France in the 1960s, was the forerunner of 'big box' retailing, which is beginning to dominate the global retail scene today. The French began to restrict the development of the hypermarket at home in the 1970s in the wake of the Royer bill and companies such as Carrefour (crossroads in English) became synonymous with the international spread of the format. The Americans originally rejected this format in the 1970s and it only has been revived with the growth of Wal-Mart in the US and its development of the supercentre format in the 1990s.

Other innovative formats which have strong country of origin effects are 'hard' discounting and mail order in Germany. German mail order companies are world market leaders (Otto Versand and Quelle) and the German market is the largest in the world after the US. Why? The reason is historical. At the end of the Second World War there was a severe shortage of retail space in Germany and mail order provided an alternative form of retailing. Also, German consumers were relatively poor at this time and could receive goods on easy payment terms. This explains why home shopping is a major feature of German consumer behaviour (much of their frozen food is home delivered, for example) and why this form of retailing impinges upon a wider cross-section of society than in other countries. By contrast, in the UK, the big book catalogues were mainly targeted at lower socio-economic groups, invariably because it provided an avenue for cheap credit in the days before borrowing was so easy.

Not only do German consumers shop from home more readily than other European consumers, but they are very price conscious. It has often been stated that there are three marketing tools in Germany – price, price and price. Thus, an alternative to the hypermarket was developed – the limited-line, no-frills 'hard' discounter offering exceptionally low prices of frequently purchased packaged goods. This format, developed initially by Aldi and Lidl, has now spread internationally from its German base.

Again as a means of contrast, these discounters have been less successful in the UK market, where consumers have tended to polarize their grocery shop between a weekly trawl and a convenience 'top up'. Indeed, the main grocery multiples introduced their own limited-line offering to restrict defections of shoppers to Aldi, Lidl and Netto, the Danish discounter. Although Wal-Mart is changing the British consumers' store choice attributes with its every day low pricing (EDLP) strategy, the relatively unique emphasis on store brands has allowed the major companies to diversify into other sectors on the strength of this brand loyalty. As mentioned earlier, this has arisen because of the creation of new market segments, such as chilled foods, which spawned a new set of retailer–manufacturer relationships.

These formats are a response to the needs of specific country markets. The operation of retail formats also differ, however, because of different regulations and industry structures in such markets. For example, retailing in North America is not subjected to the same degree of government intervention as in Europe *and* there is more development land and cheaper fuel costs. Thus, retailers in North America can trade successfully on much lower sales per square metre ratios than their European or Japanese counterparts. This also explains the evolution of logistical support networks to stores in these markets. It is not surprising that the British, Dutch and Japanese have embraced just-in-time operational techniques in supplying their stores compared with the US or even French and German retailers, because of the high premium rates for retail sites. Taking inventory out of stores and other parts of the supply chain reduces costs and allows retailers to respond quickly to market changes.

Concentration

Forty years ago, retailing was a fragmented industry. The 'giants' of the time were department stores with a nineteenth century legacy of providing a range of departments for their customers. Sears and J C Penney in the US, Marks & Spencer and Harrods in the UK, Galleries Lafayette and Printemps in France, and Karstadt in Germany were the high street brands of the time. Consumers have become more mobile and their behaviour has changed, as shown in the earlier section. Retail entrepreneurs have risen to this challenge and transformed markets at home and abroad. Two of the largest retailers in the world today, Wal-Mart and Tesco, were small family companies headed by enlightened entrepreneurs, Sam Walton and Jack Cohen respectively. But this trend is mirrored in other companies, especially in the speciality retail sector.

The rise of Gap, Limited, Zara and IKEA, for example, was the result of the vision of the founder to spot a niche in the market and grow the business.

The retail marketplace has been transformed in 40 years. Instead of proximity retailing, where consumers shop at their nearest most convenient store, the emphasis is more on destination retailing, where the consumer is willing to travel further to get the best choice at lower prices. While Wal-Mart has led the way in general merchandise/food followed by 'big box' competitors such as Carrefour and Tesco, specialists or 'category killers' have changed the nature of competition in many other markets. Home Depot in the US and B&Q (Kingfisher) in the UK are market leaders in the home improvement market and have major international aspirations. Kingfisher's other major brands, Comet and Darty in Europe, are equivalent to Circuit City in the US. IKEA, Toys 'R' Us and Nevada Bob are good examples of international companies specializing in a niche sector.

Organic growth and acquisitions to spread fixed costs over larger sales volumes have led to consolidation in most developed economies.

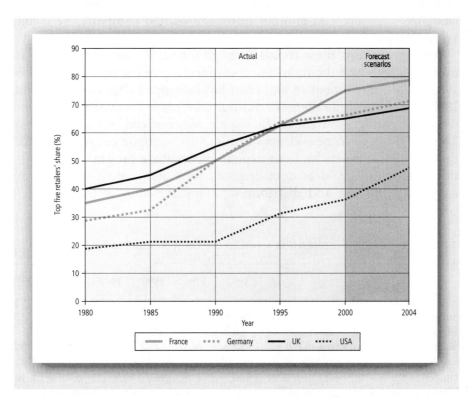

Figure 2.2 Market share of the top five FMCG retailers in France, Germany, the USA and the UK. *Source*: **Littner (2001).**

No longer can the UK be classified as 'a nation of shopkeepers' when the retail sector has been transformed from a large number of small independent retailers to large, publicly quoted corporations. The top 10 British retailers have increased their market share from around 28 per cent of total retail sales in the mid-1980s to around 42 per cent in the early 2000s. Figure 2.2 illustrates the degree of concentration of FMCG retailers in the UK compared with France, Germany and the US. Although the UK grocery market has been subjected to a Competition Commission inquiry in the late 1990s because of fears of abuse of market power, the French and German markets are also heavily concentrated among a few key players. Only the US market lags behind, but greater consolidation has occurred throughout the 1990s and is expected to continue in the next decade.

Neil Wrigley has written extensively on what he terms the 'consolidation wave' in US food retailing. He shows how the top four firms (the CR4 statistic from the *Progressive Grocer*) have increased their share from a static 23 per cent to 37 per cent from 1992 to 1999 (Table 2.6). Table 2.7 illustrates how the top six retailers have changed in this time in terms of size and scale. American Stores merged with Albertson's, Wal-Mart had entered the food market and two European companies, Ahold and Delhaize, had replaced another European-owned company, A&P, and Winn-Dixie.

Wrigley explains these trends through the regulation of the industry until the 1980s and the financial re-engineering of the sector in the late 1980s. The enforcement of anti-trust laws dropped dramatically in the 1980s, but large-scale mergers did not take place because the US food retail industry got caught up in a spate of leveraged buy-outs (LBOs). The LBOs led to increased debt burdens for companies, which forced them to divest assets and cut capital expenditure programmes. Thus, throughout the 1990s as debt burdens were reduced, investments in technology, buying and distribution, along the lines of the Wal-Mart

Table 2.6 Increasing concentration levels in the US food retail industry, 1992–99

	1992	1994	1996	1997	1998	1999[a]
Supermarket sales ($ billion)	286.8	301.0	323.2	334.5	346.1	363.3
Sales of four leading firms ($ billion)	66.9	68.9	75.0	82.8	88.8	131.7
Share of four leading firms (CR4)	23.3	22.9	23.2	24.8	25.7	36.2

[a] Supermarket sales 1999 estimated. Sales of four leading firms based on figures in Table 2.7, i.e. Wal-Mart ranked in terms of sales of food and food-related sales at its supercentres, not as a basis of total supercentre sales.
Source: Wrigley (2001).

Table 2.7 The leading US food retailers 1992 and 1999 – a changing elite

Rank	1992			1999		
	Firm	Sales ($ billion)	Market share	Firm	Sales ($ billion)	Market share[a]
1	Kroger	22.1	7.7	Kroger	45.4	12.5
2	American Stores	19.1	6.6	Albertson's	37.6	10.3
3	Safeway	15.2	5.3	Safeway	28.4	7.8
4	A&P	10.5	3.7	Ahold USA	20.3	5.6
5	Winn-Dixie	10.3	3.6	Wal-Mart[b]	19.8	5.5
6	Albertson's	10.2	3.5	Delhaize America	14.4	4.0

[a] Share of total US supermarket sales (see Table 2.6).
[b] Wal-Mart ranked in terms of sales of food and food-related ('supermarket type') merchandise at its supercentres, i.e. 44% of $45.1 billion Wal-Mart supercentre sales in 1999.
Source: Wrigley (2001).

operation, made these companies more efficient and hungry for growth to achieve further scale economies.

Locational shift

When we take a leisure trip to any of the Disneyland theme parks, the main street features prominently as one of the key attractions. It is therefore somewhat ironic that the suburbanization of the US way of life and the resultant mushrooming of out-of-town shopping malls has led to the decline of traditional main streets. The concept of the modern shopping mall can be traced to the Austrian architect, Victor Gruen. Gruen fled the homeland of Hitler and began to develop blueprints of his utopian mall. His idea of an out-of-town mall was that it was to be the civic, social and cultural heart of the community, incorporating apartment housing and offices in addition to shopping provision. Although his 'ideal' mall never truly materialized, his concept of an all-year-round shopping environment quickly took root. The Southdale mall in Minneapolis was built in 1956 and became the prototype for thousands of others throughout America. Gruen reckoned that in the Mid-West you only had about 25 good shopping days a year. The development of the enclosed shopping mall with air conditioning and a constant temperature of 20°C changed all of that. It is perhaps no coincidence that two of the most popular malls in North America are in areas with extreme climates, namely the West Edmonton Mall in Alberta, Canada, and the Mall of America in Minneapolis/St Paul.

The classic mall attracted two key department stores as anchor tenants with speciality stores linking them. For the next 30–40 years, geographers and realtors sought prime sites for new mall development. In the days before sophisticated geographical information systems (GIS), mapping of areas of population growth and interstate intersections offered the best sites for development as America became an automobile-orientated society. By the 1970s and 1980s, locational analysts began to use spatial interaction models to determine the success of one mall in relation to another and to glean a picture of saturation compared to undercapacity in particular parts of the US.

By the 1990s the out-of-town shopping mall had become a mature retail format in the US and Canada. The rather monotonous formulaic structure may have been fine for consumers in the 1960s and 1970s, but not for the more demanding consumer of the last two decades. This enclosed environment was also a controlled environment with its closed-circuit TV and security guards. Whilst policing existed within the malls, invariably crime increased in the large parking lots outside.

The urban landscape began to be transformed by other smaller but 'themed' shopping centres or free-standing/clusters of 'big box' formats. Already by the 1970s, many downtown areas of cities, especially those with historical landmarks, began to develop speciality centres based on restaurants and leisure attractions. The Californian coast from San Francisco to San Diego has numerous examples of old warehouses, canneries and piers which have been redeveloped using the waterfront as a key feature in urban regeneration. Former fashionable areas which declined with the growth of the traditional mall in the 1980s have been gentrified using their natural setting. Pasadena in Southern California is an example of this type of development.

The growth in popularity in the US of warehouse clubs, factory outlet centres, supercentres and category killers added to the pressure for new urban development. In several instances failed shopping malls were redeveloped for these new formats. This is not to suggest that the traditional mall is in terminal decline. It is facing competition from other out-of-town developments. The top 10 US retailers still include Sears Roebuck and J C Penney, the bastions of the mall, but others are Home Depot (category killer), Costco and Wal-Mart (warehouse clubs), K-Mart/Target/Wal-Mart (supercentres).

The development of the shopping mall and various hybrids of the US prototype are evident in most countries of the world. In Europe, the shopping mall was not planned on such a *laissez-faire*, automobile-dominated manner. The preservation, and in many cases the rebuilding, of city centres in the post-war period was the main priority of governments. The eventual development of sizeable in-town malls, recreating the controlled environments of the US malls, took time because of difficulties in assembling land parcels with multiple ownership. Unlike the US, development was focused towards city centres. In the UK, many schemes were small scale in most towns and cities, as the high street continued to maintain its pre-war dominance of shopping activity. The enclosed mall, when it was a large development, as in Eldon Square in Newcastle or the Arndale Centre in Manchester, did result in urban decay in city centre streets where major retailers vacated premises to move into new malls. Also, some of these developments, the Arndale for example, were heavily criticized for their lack of architectural quality.

It was not until the mid-1980s that the UK began to plan for US-style out-of-town shopping malls. The catalyst for such developments was Marks & Spencer (M&S), then the anchor store of many in-town shopping schemes. M&S announced in 1985 that it was pursuing a dual location strategy whereby it would invest in out of town developments in addition to traditional high street areas. Initially there were plans for between 35 and 50 schemes throughout the country, but the stock market crash of 1987, prolonged recession and changes in planning policy worked against any new out-of-town developments, reducing the number to a handful of large schemes. For example, the Bluewater scheme in Kent is the largest in Europe, accounts for 3 per cent of Britain's retail expenditure and is one the largest employers in the county (8000 employees).

Although government policy is the subject of the next major section, it is worth noting that the development of these large shopping malls and other out-of-town developments have become an element of the government's policy on social exclusion and urban regeneration. Before this issue was high on the political agenda, the early schemes were also geared to a policy of regeneration. The Metro Centre in Newcastle was an enlarged retail park which had been built on former colliery wasteland and Meadowhall near Sheffield was the site of former steelworks. More recent developments, such as Braehead in Scotland, have been planned through partnerships between the developer and urban regeneration agencies. The Braehead complex is a massive (285 acres) mixed use development encompassing retailing, leisure, housing and public parkland on the site of a former shipbuilding area on the River Clyde within the Glasgow–Paisley conurbation. Although there was considerable opposition to the scheme when it was first proposed, Braehead is now promoted as a growth area within the conurbation and the development of the site represented a major opportunity for employment generation in nearby social inclusion partnership areas.

Waves of retail decentralization

Out-of-town shopping centres have been classified as the third wave of retail decentralization. Schiller, writing in 1986, viewed M&S's commitment to out-of-town investment as the 'coming of the third wave'. As we have seen, this wave has broken into a small number of large-scale developments. The two earlier waves of decentralization had a much greater impact upon the urban landscape. The superstore, pioneered by ASDA in the late 1960s, became the predominant food trading format in the UK for the major multiple retailers by the 1980s. Unlike in France, where the hypermarket (over 50 000 sq. ft) was the main large store format, the superstore (25–50 000 sq. ft) was the preferred model in the UK. Initially there was considerable opposition to these large-scale formats and protracted planning enquiries were a feature of the 1970s. At this time ASDA traded from sites where they could obtain planning permission, often disused mills in the textile regions of Yorkshire.

The acceptance of the superstore format by consumers, retailers and, somewhat reluctantly, planners saw the closure of small, in-town, food stores and the construction of purpose-built superstores, invariably as anchor tenants in district centres. The fight for market share led to the so-called 'store wars' in the late 1980s/early 1990s as retailers scrambled for available sites. Throughout the 1970s and 1980s, discussion on saturation levels always featured prominently in the trade press. Figures of 600, 700 and 800 were mooted and then passed. By the early/mid-1990s the position began to change. Some retailers, including ASDA, became financially crippled because of their expansion plans, asset values for store properties fell and fewer planning appeals at public inquiries were accepted for superstore development. The rate of growth has slowed in the 1990s/early twenty-first century. Nevertheless, there are still around 1200 superstores in operation and the key players are actively developing new sites, although the focus has changed. Tesco and Sainsbury have moved back into town centres with their Metro and Local formats, whilst at the same time, along with their main competitors, Safeway and ASDA, they are developing larger hypermarket formats to increase sales and profit margins from non-food lines.

The second wave of retail decentralization began in the late 1970s and quickly gained acceptance as an established trading format. Much of this can be attributed to the success of superstores. Just as consumers preferred the 'one-stop' shop for their bulky weekly groceries, they did not want to carry heavy DIY materials through town centre streets to car parks or bus stations. The forerunner to retail parks was the retail discount warehouse. Here the early pioneers of out-of-town non-food retailing traded from an assortment of makeshift, converted properties.

Thus, just as ASDA was the pioneer for superstores, MFI championed the case for out-of-town furniture retailing, B&Q for DIY and Comet for electrical goods. By the 1980s, retail parks mushroomed up on the ring roads of most towns as planners acknowledged that industrial sites could not attract manufacturing jobs compared to those retail opportunities. By the mid-1990s, the pace of growth had slowed down and the composition of tenants in retail parks was changing. The original tenant mix was strongly based on the DIY, electrical, furniture and carpet warehouse format. New entrants appeared that were more associated with high street retailing. Clothing and sports retailers (JJB Sports) and even that bastion of in-town retailing, Boots the Chemist, are represented. This trading up of the original format make retail parks an attraction to consumers for comparison retailing to the extent that they could be classified as third wave decentralization.

The conversion of a retail park to the Metro Centre illustrates the blurring of categories. This has also occurred with Fernie's fourth wave of decentralization. He argues that a new wave of retail decentralization began in the 1990s in the UK based on a more upmarket, but value for money, retail proposition. The importation of two US formats to the UK – warehouse clubs and factory outlet centres (see Box 2.1) – were different from the third wave and coincided with the advent of other discounting formats in the UK in both food (hard discounters) and non-food (Matalan, New Look, Peacocks).

Box 2.1   Factory outlet centres in Europe

Factory outlet centres (FOCs) were one of the fastest growing formats in US retailing in the 1980s. They were developed initially as a profitable means of disposing of excess stock by manufacturers. The original formats were more like factory shops, but by the late 1970s/early 1980s purpose-built outlet malls were being constructed and managed in a similar way to conventional shopping centres.

By the mid-1990s, FOCs accounted for around 2 per cent of all US retail sales but the format was maturing, with around 350 outlet centres with an average size of 14 000 square metres. It was around this time that US developers sought growth opportunities in new geographical markets. Europe was a logical choice for market entry, as the main country markets of the UK, France and Italy had a tradition of factory shops.

The UK, however, was the initial target area for US developers, notably McArthur Glen, Value Retail, Prime and RAM Eurocenters. In 1992 and 1993, two small indigenous schemes had been developed at Hornsea and Street by companies which had gleaned some experience of US operations. By 2001, the UK accounted for one-half of all schemes in Europe and over 60 per cent of outlet floorspace. It had 34 schemes open with 18 in the pipeline but, like the US a decade earlier, saturation in the market was being reached.

The UK development of FOCs can be viewed in three distinct stages: 1993–1996, 1997–1999 and 2000 to the present. In the first phase, there were ambitious plans to build over 30 US-style FOCs within 3–4 years. Unfortunately for developers, these proposals came at a time when the government was hardening its stance towards out-of-town retailing and planning permission was often refused or deferred. A notable landmark was the Secretary of State's decision to reject RAM Eurocenter's proposal for Tewkesbury after a 2-year deliberation (despite local council support). This resulted in a scaling down of some developments and the withdrawal from the UK market by some US developers.

The 1997–1999 phase witnessed a gradual acceptance of the format. Developers changed their strategies and looked for sites which either already had retail use designation for planning purposes or sought brownfield regeneration areas. The acceptance of the format was reflected in the attraction of institutional investors to schemes, as some companies such as BAA/McArthur Glen sold equity stakes in existing schemes to fuel further expansion or initial developers sold out to property companies (C&J Clark to MEPC).

The most recent phase from 2000 to the present has led to the redevelopment or extension of some of the earlier sites. To differentiate from other FOCs and competing retail formats, new developments have had innovative designs such as Ashford in Kent or stressed leisure-related activities (Gunwharf at Portsmouth, Manchester). This will be necessary as overcapacity is reached in certain regions, such as Scotland and the North-West of England.

In theory, other European markets should be receptive to FOCs because of their culture of factory shops and, in the case of France and Germany, a strong price-led retail environment. Developments have been slow to materialize, however, because of extensive lobbying by interest groups resistant to change in the retail structure. This has not deterred developers from moving into Europe having gained experience in the UK. BAA/McArthur Glen, Value Retail, Freeport Leisure, Morrison Outlets, in addition to Outlet Centres International and Prime Retail, plan to open up to 75 factory outlet centres by 2007.

Although France has most of the FOCs outside of the UK, most sites are discount retail Usine Centres. BAA/McArthur Glen opened an FOC in Troyes in 1996 after years of protracted negotiations with the Local Chamber of Commerce because other Usines are located in the city. Most developers have focused their attention on specific markets, notably:

- upmarket areas close to capital cities or cosmopolitan cities – for example, Paris, Berlin, Vienna, Madrid, Barcelona, Munich, Florence;
- near large catchment areas, often on cross-border routes – for example, Mendrisio, Roermond, Zweibrucken, Maasmechelen (the latter two are brownfield sites).

Although FOCs are only at the early growth stage in these markets, it is likely that their success will attract stakeholders into this business, i.e. customers, retailers, developers and institutional investors. This will be most marked in Northern Europe, where many sites under development will compete for cross-border customers.

Warehouse clubs were originally envisaged to be represented throughout the country with 50–100 sites being developed but by 2001, Costco, the only operator, had 10 sites open after 8 years of experience in the UK market. Planning problems can account for some of the slow growth but the UK consumer, unlike its US counterpart, neither has the physical space to stock bulk purchases nor has the appetite for shopping in limited-line, discount sheds.

Factory outlet centres have fared much better and by 2001 had become a mature retail format with operators looking to the rest of Europe for expansion. It can be argued that the nature of UK developments differs from the original US model as developers have had to comply with changes in government policy (see Box 2.1). As with earlier waves, locational 'blurring' exists. The Galleria, a failed off-centre shopping mall, was successfully converted to a factory outlet centre and BAA/McArthur Glen's site at Livingston in Scotland is adjacent to a retail park *and* a superstore operator!

The role of government

The regulation of retail activity has shaped the structure of retailing in many country markets. Whilst most retailers have had to conform to national legislation with regard to 'operational' legislation, such as health and safety at work, hours of opening and employment laws, the internationalization of retailing and the advent of the Internet has led to the establishment of legal frameworks *across* national boundaries. This is particularly relevant to the EU, where Directives emanating from Brussels are implemented by national governments (see Box 2.2). Of course, the most significant change to European retail business is the changeover to the Euro for 11 member states in 2002. This will lead to short-term costs for retailers as they change prices in their stores, modify their IT support systems and train staff to cope with the change. The benefits are more long term in nature. A single currency will promote freer movement of goods and make it easier to source from foreign markets. Furthermore, price transparency will become much clearer and the so-called 'rip-off Britain' claims will be put to the test once exchange rate fluctuations are removed from the equation. In order to avoid excessive detail on all aspects of public policy, the focus of this section will be on competition policy and retail planning.

Box 2.2   EU legislation relevant to retailers

Directive on the sale of consumer goods and associated guarantees (1999)
The aim of this directive is to establish minimum rules of protection around which member states can adopt or maintain more stringent provisions. Consumers can now seek redress for the sale of a defective product within 2 years of delivery and receive a price reduction or their money back within 1 year.

Directive 97/55/EC amending Directive 84/45/EEC concerning misleading and comparative advertising
This amendment now allows for comparative advertising as long as the advertising is objective, it is not misleading, it does not discredit a competitor's trade mark/name and it compares goods/services meeting the same needs or intended for the same purpose.

Directive 96/6 on consumer protection in the indication of prices of products offered to consumers 1998
This is better known as the unit pricing directive in that it stipulates that the selling price of a product should be indicated as a price per unit to facilitate comparison of prices and clarify consumer information.

Directive 97/7 on the protection of consumers in respect of distance contracts
This directive aims to protect consumers from aggressive selling techniques by non face-to-face methods, or by mail order or electronic retailing. It allows consumers the right to withdraw from a contract for up to 7 days without penalty

It is interesting to note that a draft directive is proposed to establish a legal framework for the development of electronic commerce.

Competition policy

We will first of all look at anti-trust legislation in the US, because policy here has had some bearing on governments elsewhere on how they have tried to control companies which exhibit anti-competitive behaviour. Table 2.8 provides a summary of the key laws which have been enacted in the US. The three main Acts which provided the basis for subsequent modifications to anti-trust legislation were the Sherman Act of 1890, the Clayton Act of 1914 and the Federal Trade Commission (FTC) Act of 1914. The Sherman Act prohibited contracts and conspiracies in restraining trade and outlawed monopolies. The Clayton Act reinforced this legislation by further prohibiting price competition that lessened competition and forbade tying clauses on exclusive dealing arrangements which would impede competition. In the same year it was deemed appropriate that an organization should be created to oversee the implementation of this legislation. The Federal Trade Commission (FTC) was created from the Act of the same name and was charged with stamping out 'unfair methods of competition'. This 'catch-all prohibition' was invariably left to the courts to decide and the history of anti-trust legislation is inevitably bound to the interpretation of the law according to the political administration of the time. As a rule of thumb, Republican administrations have a tendency to favour business, Democratic-majority administrations have championed consumer interests.

Table 2.8 Anti-trust legislation in the US

Year enacted	Legislative act	Practices which impact on the retail sector
1890	Sherman Act	Resale price maintenance, illegal vertical integration and mergers, exclusive dealings, refusals to deal, resale restrictions.
1914	Clayton Act	Tying contracts, exclusive dealings arrangements, dual distribution.
1914	Federal Trade Commission	Price discrimination, dual distribution.
1936	Robinson–Patman	Price discrimination, promotional allowances.
1950	Celler–Kefauver	Horizontal mergers, vertical mergers.
1975	Consumer Goods Pricing Law	Resale price maintenance.

Regardless of the political dimension, most of the ensuing legislation tended to favour the small trader at the expense of the corporate giants. The landmark Robinson–Patman Act in 1936 made it unlawful for a company to knowingly induce or receive a discriminating price. This meant that sellers must charge the same prices to all buyers for 'goods of like quality'. There were exceptions where price discrimination was allowed, most notably where there were differences in the cost of manufacture, sale or delivery resulting from different quantities sold. Hence, 'quality discounts' were allowed for bulk purchases. This Act also ensured that powerful buyers would not extract special promotional allowances from weaker suppliers.

Of more significance to our discussion on the history of US food retailing was the Celler–Kefauver Act of 1950, which responded to an FTC report which expressed concern at a spate of merger activity in 1948. Not only did this Act reinforce anti-competitive activity as a result of horizontal mergers, but it brought into play mergers at inter-channel level, i.e. vertically integrated mergers. The final piece of legislation shown in Table 2.8, the Consumer Goods Pricing Law, brought resale price maintenance (RPM) under federal anti-trust legislation and closed a loophole which had allowed manufacturers vertical pricing arrangements with retailers in some states. RPM primarily sets a minimum price at which goods can be sold to prevent retailers from using manufacturers' products as 'loss leaders' to attract customers into the store but undermine the suppliers' reputation for quality.

In the 'Retail response' section, it was shown that consolidation in the US food retailing industry was slow until the 1990s because of the regulatory environment and the debt incurred by supermarket groups in the late 1980s/early 1990s. If we examine this more closely it can be argued that the anti-trust legislation inhibited the growth of large supermarket groups from the 1930s until the 1980s. Indeed, Wrigley notes that, by the early 1980s, the food retail industry was less consolidated than 50 years earlier, when A&P controlled 12 per cent of the entire US market. The Robinson–Patman and Celler–Kefauver Acts were very successful at protecting the small trader and inhibiting the growth of companies such as A&P by merger activity. The net result was that the US had become structured into a series of regionally focused chains. In 1989, the Chairman and Chief Executive of A&P contrasted the US situation with that of the UK: 'in the post-war years . . . the US marketplace, because of Robinson–Patman, moved to a regional structure and the old large chains lost out . . . (but) the UK without this disadvantage, moved to the consolidation route with the advantages of purchasing leverage driving the success of a few national chains' (Wood, 1989, p. 15).

From the early 1980s, for over a decade, the Reagan/Bush administrations began to loosen the regulatory net, allowing mergers to take place which may have been stopped in the 1960s and 1970s. The approach to horizontal mergers had been a 'fix-it-first' approach whereby predators attempting to appease the FTC agreed to divest themselves of some acquired stores where horizontal market overlaps occurred at local levels. During the 1990s, however, there was pressure from food manufacturers and smaller retailer chains for the FTC to tighten its regulatory stance. Criticisms were levelled at the divestment process in that the acquiring company was allowed to 'cherry pick' the stores to be disposed of. This meant that weaker stores were sold to weaker competitors, allowing the predator to win back market share and increase consolidation of market power.

By late 1999/early 2000, the FTC took a tougher enforcement stance, especially on the divestment of acquired stores. The notable case was the proposed acquisition by the Dutch group, Ahold, of the New Jersey Pathmark chain. Although Ahold was willing to divest a considerable number of its stores in the New York/New Jersey region, the FTC opposed the deal, which subsequently collapsed.

By early 2001 the US had a new administration when Bush replaced Clinton in the White House. So will the regulatory environment change again? The early signs are that the revival of anti-trust enforcement towards the end of the Clinton era will be replaced by a more lax enforcement policy as FTC judges reflect the pro-business approach of the Bush administration.

In Europe, competition policy is normally dictated at national government level unless an acquisition *across* national boundaries leads to the predator achieving a market share which would be deemed uncompetitive. In 1999, the German supermarket group, Rewe, notified the EU Commission that it intended to acquire the 343 outlets of the Julius Meinl chain in Austria. As Rewe was already represented in the Austrian market through its Billa subsidiary, the merger would give the combined group 37 per cent of the Austrian food retail market. In order to appease the Commission's objection to the bid, Rewe followed the US 'fix-it-first' policy and agreed to acquire only 162 stores, 45 of which were converted into drugstores.

In the UK, much of the focus on competition policy has been on price competition and the potential abuse of market power by large grocery retailers. It can be argued that the abolition of resale price maintenance (RPM) in 1965 was the catalyst to greater concentration in British retailing. Until then, retailers were obligated to sell products at suppliers' recommended retail prices. The 1965 legislation allowed retailers to complete on price for all products except books and pharmaceuticals, which were allowed RPM until the late 1990s. It was pressure from the large supermarkets in the 1990s to give customers competitive prices, especially on over-the-counter drugs, which led to the removal of legal support for RPM in these last two product categories.

The growing power of retailers, especially the grocery multiples, has been a recurrent feature of competition policy during the last two decades. In the first half of the 1980s, food retailers came under the scrutiny of the Office of Fair Trading (OFT) through two reports, Discount to Retailers (Monopolies and Mergers Commission) and Competition and Retailing (OFT). The latter report, published in 1985, assessed the nature of competition and the degree of profitability of food retailing from 1975 to 1983, whereas the Monopolies and Mergers Commission report in 1981 assessed whether volume discounts to large retailers were being passed on to grocery shoppers. In both cases the growing power of the multiple retailer was not deemed to be against the public interest.

In the mid- to late 1990s, there was a further upsurge of discussion on retail power and competition. A series of research reports were published by the OFT from 1996 to 1998, the new Blair government argued that the British consumer was being 'ripped off' by retailers and it initiated an investigation into the competitive behaviour of the largest supermarket groups by the Competition Commission (published in 2001). After a lengthy review and a delay in publication (did the government not like the findings?), the Commission did *not* find evidence of anti-competitive behaviour or that the British consumer was being 'ripped off'. Indeed, it argued that the higher British prices was partly related to higher costs, but mainly because of the high pound and exchange rate fluctuations.

Retail planning policies

It is interesting to note in a comparison of UK and US competition policies that the UK government had not gone down the route of insisting that the predator divest of stores in areas where local monopolies can occur as a result of an acquisition. By contrast, it is much easier in the US to receive planning approval for new store development. The rise of the 'big box' retail formats in the US, and to some extent Canada, can be attributed to the availability of land and the need to accommodate a car-orientated society. In its early decades of expansion, Wal-Mart was welcomed to many small towns in middle America as a sign of modernity and growth for the community. These communities even offered tax incentives to build! In the last 15 years opposition to Wal-Mart has grown as evidence showed that small traditional retailers closed down unable to compete with the price discount format. Ultimately this has slowed down the process of acquiring and developing sites in North America, but the developers have sufficient sites to fulfil their development plans.

This is not the same in Europe, as Wal-Mart and other US retail chains are discovering when they plan expansion outside of their domestic market. Most planning legislation has been geared to protect traditional town centres and small-scale retailers from excessive out-of-town shopping developments. The international growth of multinational retailers such as Carrefour, Ahold and Delhaize can be attributed to restrictive planning regulations in their home market. For example, the Loi Royer was introduced in France in 1973 after extensive lobbying by independent retailers who feared the growth of hypermarket development in the 1960s. In 1996, the Rafferin Law introduced further restrictions whereby developers have to apply for permits to open new or extended units over 300 square metres.

The German market is also highly regulated and it is very difficult to receive planning permission for stores over 1500 square metres in out-of-town sites. Restrictions also apply to type of goods sold. For example, textiles and shoes can only be sold in town centres, and this explains objections by retailers selling these goods to the development of factory outlet centres in off-centre locations.

In markets which have only experienced large-scale format developments in the last decade (mainly because of the expansion of the large European retailers into their countries), policies have been enacted to restrict the size and scale of new development. For example, Portugal's planning laws were tightened in 1997 for new store development and retailers with existing store space require authorization over a 15 000 metres threshold. In Spain, planning permission for stores over 2500 square metres has required regional government approval since 1996. In Ireland, the entry of Tesco through its acquisition of Power Super-markets and the proposed entry of Costco initiated extensive lobbying of the government by symbol groups and independents to review planning policy. In June 1998, the Irish government introduced a Policy Directive which effectively halted the development of formats over 3000 square metres.

Not all countries have tightened their policies on this issue. The Dutch have relaxed their stance on out-of-town development, including the approval of two factory outlet centres. The Italian government introduced the Bersani Law in 1999, which simplified the complex, multilayered system of approvals required, in addition to specific authorizations for product types sold. The categories are now food and non-food, and clearer rules have been initiated with regard to planning approvals in relation to size of store and size of town. For example, to open a small outlet (150 square metres) in towns of less than 10 000 people, the local authority gives approval; for large outlets (over 2500 square metres) in towns of over 10 000 population, permission must be sought from a committee representing the city, province and the district.

We now turn in more detail to British retail planning policy, primarily because it was seen to be more *laissez-faire* than policies in other parts of Europe, thereby attracting US companies to the UK to develop warehouse clubs, factory outlet centres and other large-scale formats. An outline of retail planning policy in the UK is given in Box 2.3. In essence, the first 20 years of planning policy was geared to maintaining the existing shopping centre hierarchy with a presumption *against* any type of development which was not zoned for retail use, i.e. in-town centres or district centres. Since 1977 the government has used a range of policy initiatives which have attempted to strike a balance between the needs of consumers, retailers, developers and local authorities. In the 13 years of the Thatcher administration (1979–1992), there was a considerable relaxation of planning controls. Advice to local authorities through Development Control Policy Notes (DCPNs) ensured that first and second wave operators could develop off-centre sites for food and non-food superstores.

Box 2.3   Retail planning policy in the UK

The basis for modern British retail planning dates back to the 1948 Town and Country Planning Act, when planning authorities had to produce plans to guide developers towards preferred locations for particular land uses. Regional authorities would provide broad structure plans and lower-tier authorities developed local plans for their areas.

When the legislation was introduced, Britain was embarking upon a redevelopment of cities after the war. Local authorities were often the main instigators of these developments as they invariably owned much of the land in town centres. The focus of retail investment was therefore in these centres and in district centres in suburbia.

The so-called retail hierarchy was established at this time in that the land use category for retailing was designated in central areas and any development outside these zones would be deemed to be outside the local plan. It was the development of superstores in the late 1960s and early 1970s which challenged the status quo. Several high-profile public inquiries took place at this time as developers argued that bulk grocery shopping was better suited to edge-of-town sites and that town centres would not lose the large amounts of trade predicted from such developments.

By 1977, the government acknowledged that some developments were better suited to edge-of-town sites because of their space requirements. This was embodied in advice to local authorities through Development Control Policy Notes (DCPNs). DCPN13 opened the door for the rapid expansion of the 'second wave of decentralization', the development of retail parks throughout the 1980s. Although most shopping centre developments continued to be built in conventional downtown sites, the coming of the 'third wave' of decentralization in the late 1980s led to the government amending DCPN13.

By 1988, the government introduced Planning Policy Guidelines (PPGs). The relevant guidelines for retailers were PPG6 and PPG13. PPG6 sought to maintain a balance between the vitality of town centres and these new retail formats located in edge- or out-of-town sites. By 1996, PPG6 was substantially revised and amended to tighten the tests of acceptability for new out-of-town proposals. A sequential test was introduced whereby developers had to show that no sites were available in town centre locations for their form of development. It was in 1994 with PPG13 that the sequential test was first mooted in relation to the accessibility of sites by all forms of transport.

The change to a Labour administration has not led to a change in direction of policy. Since 1997 it is clear that a developer cannot expect to receive planning permission just because the proposed development is too large to be built in a town centre site. The assumption is that an element of 'downsizing' may be necessary. Furthermore, developers wishing to expand on existing sites will also have to undergo the sequential test.

It was the development of third wave decentralization which prompted a revision of government policy through Planning Policy Guidelines (notably PPG6 and PPG13) introduced in 1988. PPG6 and its subsequent revisions aimed at giving advice on achieving a balance between the vitality of town centres and new development; PPG13 sought to integrate transport and land use planning and, in the case of retailing, tried to ensure that new retail developments would be reached by public transport.

Until the early 1990s, retailers had limited opposition to their plans and market share could be achieved through the so-called 'store wars'. Retailers would appease local authorities with sizeable donations to community projects to secure planning permission (the term for this was 'planning gain'). If a local authority rejected the application, the retailer appealed and had an 80 per cent chance of success at the subsequent public inquiry.

By the mid-1990s, policy was changing. PPG13 and PPG6 were revised in 1994 and 1996 respectively, and government ministers began to take a harder line towards new out-of-town developments, especially as an all-party House of Commons Select Committee in 1994 recommended that the 'tests of acceptability' in the PPGs should be enforced more rigorously.

The main thrust of the new policy was the sequential test whereby a developer had to show that a proposed new out-of-town development could not be located in nearby town centres or district centres. Under the Secretary of State of the time, John Gummer, a strict interpretation of the planning guidelines was introduced, culminating in the rejection of a factory outlet centre at Tewkesbury which had received strong local authority support.

This shift in stance continued with the election of a Labour government in 1997. The sequential test was extended to include extensions of existing sites and this firming of planning controls was reflected in the fall in success rates of those retailers taking a rejection of planning permission to appeal (20 per cent compared with 80 per cent a decade earlier).

'Social exclusion' was an important initiative of the new Blair government and Policy Action Teams (PATs) were established to formulate policy in this area. PAT13 reported on ways at improving access to shopping and financial services through eliminating 'food deserts' and facilitating urban regeneration in areas ravished by blight and disinvestment. Retailers seeking new opportunities because it was going to be difficult to secure planning permission in their preferred sites began to explore the possibility of developing in-town sites in 'brownfield' areas. It was shown earlier how factory outlet centre developers had reassessed their locational policies and began to develop sites in existing centres, many of which were in need of regeneration. Food retailers have also incorporated social inclusion initiatives as part of their strategy for receiving planning permission in areas with social inclusion partnerships. The most quoted case is the development of a Tesco Extra store at Seacroft, Leeds in 2000. Seacroft is one of the largest housing estates in Europe and its district centre, built by the local authority in the 1960s, was largely derelict. Tesco has redeveloped the whole site, trained and recruited the long-term unemployed in the area for its store, and given lower prices, more choice and a better diet for local residents. Tesco is planning seven more stores of this type using a similar regeneration partnership to that in Leeds.

It is worth noting that large store development of this type is in conflict with PPG6, which advises local authorities *not* to release urban land for retail development if the land had potential for other employment opportunities. There are other inconsistencies in government policy. We have already shown that the government is keen to promote competition by investigating allegations of abuse of market power. But how can retailers offer low prices in suboptimal sites. Large store formats benefit from scale economies, within the store and through supply chain efficiencies, which are passed on to customers. Companies which built large store formats prior to the tightening of planning controls have a competitive advantage over late entrants who either cannot get sites or have to settle for a poorer location. This occurred in a haphazard way in the 1970s and 1980s when local authorities seemed to be the determinants of competition policy rather than the retailers themselves. History is now repeating itself in that pre-1997/98 operators have 'open A1' planning consent, which allows them to introduce any retail items in a store conversion. This approach is being adopted by ASDA in the introduction of supercentres and by Big W in the conversion of old B&Q stores.

Another area of dispute is the government's sustainability policies. Whilst PPG13 encouraged the development of sites with access to all forms of transport, large store formats can have positive environmental benefits if developed on 'brownfield' sites. Most developers of these formats have enlightened sustainability policies and such formats are arguably better for the environment than town centre sites, which are difficult to access by customers and distributors of store stock.

Summary

The last section on retail planning policy illustrates the complexities of managing and regulating the retail environment. Consumers are more demanding, affluent and mobile than ever before, *but* a sizeable segment of the population is poor and socially excluded from a range of services, including retailing.

Retailers have to respond to consumers' needs by providing a retail offer through appropriate formats. For many 'big box' retailers and category killer specialists, this means large store formats in out-of-town sites. In much of Europe, such developments are viewed by many governments as a threat to the viability of existing town centres and planning regulations have been developed accordingly. The problem here is that the lobbying by retailers and local authorities is geared to maintaining the rigid status quo hierarchy of shopping centre provision. Is this in the public interest or is it a form of protectionism of existing retail structures? The creation of regeneration partnerships to benefit areas deprived of retail investment is a positive step to address the issue of 'food deserts' and other accusations that large format developments cater for the wealthier, more mobile segments of the population. Clearly, to achieve maximum operating efficiencies, these retailers need large sites, which are unlikely to be available in town centres. Policy makers must therefore ensure that restrictive policies on large format development does not impede retail competition, which will lead to higher prices and adverse affects on economies.

Review questions

1 Discuss the main consumer trends in the 2000s and the impact such trends will have on future retail provision.
2 Outline the four waves of retail decentralization in the UK and discuss the role of planning policy in shaping these developments.
3 Compare and contrast competition policy in the US with that of the UK in the context of the retail supply chain.
4 Discuss the role of planning policy in shaping retail development in different geographical markets.
5 To what extent do you agree that the UK government's policy towards the retail sector has been inconsistent and contradictory in its formulation and implementation?

References and further reading

Broadbridge, A. (2001). *Distributive Trade Profile, 1999–2000: A Statistical Digest*. Institute for Retail Studies, University of Stirling.

Competition Commission (2001). *Supermarkets: A Report on the Supply of Groceries from Multiple Stores in the United Kingdom*, three volumes. The Stationery Office, Norwich.

Dawson, J. A. (2001). Viewpoint: retailer power, manufacturer power, competition and some questions of economic analysis. *International Journal of Retail and Distribution Management*, **29**(1), 5–9.

Fernie, J. (1995). The coming of the fourth wave: new forms of retail out of town development. *International Journal of Retail and Distribution Management*, **23**(1), 4–11.

Fernie, J. (1997). Retail change and retail logistics in the United Kingdom: past trends and future prospects. *Service Industries Journal*, **17**(3), 383–96.

Fernie, J. (1998a). The breaking of the fourth wave: recent out of town retail developments in Britain. *The International Review of Retail, Distribution and Consumer Research*, **8**(3), 303–17.

Fernie, J. (ed.) (1998b). *The Future for UK Retailing*. FT Retail and Consumer, London.

Fernie, S. (1996). The future for factory outlet centres in the UK: the impact of changes in planning policy guidelines on the growth of a new retail format. *International Journal of Retail and Distribution Management*, **24**(6), 11–21.

Field, C. (1998). The new consumer. In *The Future for UK Retailing* (Fernie, J., ed.), Chapter 1. FT Retail and Consumer, London.

Guy, C. (2001). Urban regeneration and very large store development in the UK: a new policy agenda. Paper presented at the 11th International Conference on Research in the Distributive Trades, Tilburg, The Netherlands, A42.

Guy, C. and Bennison, D. (2001). *Retail Planning Policy in the UK: The Implications for Superstore Development and Retail Competition*. British Council for Out of Town Retail, London.

Johnson, M. (2001). The future of bricks and mortar. Presentation at the ECR Europe Conference, Glasgow, May.

Littner, A. (2001). Losing share of wallet. Presentation at the ECR Europe Conference, Glasgow, May.

Maclure, C. (1999). *The Outlook for West European Retailing*. FT Retail and Consumer, London.

Oxford Economic Forecasting (1998). The economy. In Fernie, J. (ed.) op cit., Chapter 1.

Schiller, R. (1986). Retail decentralisation: the coming of the third wave. *The Planner*, **72**(7), 13–15.

Webb, B. (1998). New marketing. In *The Future for UK Retailing* (Fernie, J., ed.), Chapter 5. FT Retail and Consumer, London.

Wood, J. (1989). The world state in retailing. *Retail and Distribution Management*, **17**(6), 14–16.

Wrigley, N. (2001). The consolidation wave in US food retailing: a European perspective. *Agribusiness*, **17**, 489–513.

3

Theories of retail change

Introduction

A number of explanations have been made about how retail organizations grow, develop, expand and succeed. Theories of retail change make sense of what has happened to retail organizations in the past, and more importantly, help retailers to foresee future scenarios for their business, and those of their competitors.

In this chapter the main theories of retail change are presented, explained and applied to current retail organizations.

There are three main categories of theory:

- Cyclical theories.
- Environmental theories.
- Conflict theory.

Cyclical theories

Cyclical theories are those which trace common patterns in retail development over time and include the earliest theories of retail change. There are three primary cyclical theories:

1 Wheel of retailing.
2 Retail life cycle.
3 Retail accordion.

The wheel of retailing

This early hypothesis (McNair, 1958) attempted to explain the evolution of retail institutions as a wheel-like progression of three phases, as illustrated in Figure 3.1.

According to this theory, retail organizations enter the market with a low-cost, low-price, low-service format, using opportunistic buying and basic premises to undercut established competitors and establish themselves in the market. For those which succeed, there is a tendency over time to add product lines, upgrade stores and add services, which will tend to increase price levels for the merchandise. In stage 3, retail organizations tend to operate at the high end of the market, offering quality merchandise and service at price levels which alienate their original customers, and increase vulnerability to innovative new market entrants.

In stage 1, an entrepreneurial, opportunistic management style can lead to success, whether the organization be completely new to the market, or a new format brought on-stream by an existing organization. As the organization/format grows, management strength is needed in

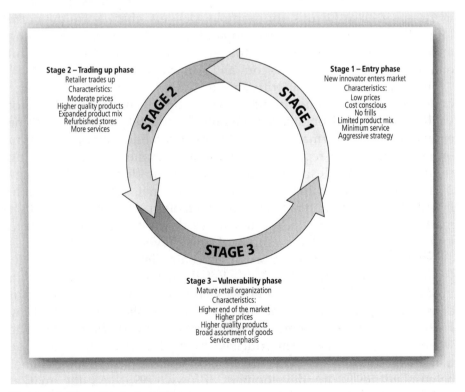

Figure 3.1 The wheel of retailing.

terms of leadership and organization of the growing number of staff and units. Even organizations as resolutely embedded in stage one as value retailers Lidl and IKEA have found it difficult to resist widening their merchandise range or adding services such as delivery.

According to Verdict (2002), 'scale will be a much stronger influence over the fate of retail companies', and opportunities for physical expansion are now limited in many areas due to market saturation and planning policy, so retail companies will have no alternative but to seek alternative growth strategies, such as merger and acquisition, or use of non-store-based retailing. IKEA, for example, has experienced problems in UK expansion. Although 20 new stores in 10 years were planned, site development has been restricted (the Glasgow site took 6 years to open), and the organization has had to resort to extending its existing stores to accommodate demand (David, 2002). Organic growth, merger and acquisition all tend to dilute the entrepreneurial style of management, and to make inevitable the characteristics evident in stages 2 and 3 of the wheel of retailing.

Without doubt, many retail organizations have developed in line with the wheel theory, for example department stores and variety stores such as C&A and Marks & Spencer. Internet retailing also seems to be moving the same way. Discount pricing has given way to parity pricing in groups such as Dixons, for example. Delivery charges are the norm rather than the exception. Expansion of the merchandise range, adding to services and upgrading of virtual stores, has occurred in successful online retailers such as Tesco.com and Amazon.com.

There have been many criticisms of the wheel theory. One major criticism is that it cannot be universally applied and is therefore not valid. Not all retail organizations enter the market at stage 1 – some enter as upmarket formats. Other retailers streamline their operations in order to retain their reputations for value for money while upgrading shops and services. Tesco, for example, has not traded up beyond stage 2. A second criticism is that the theory does not appear to apply to internationalization of retail formats, which often enter new, less mature markets as upmarket retailers and move downscale as they adapt to local environments. An example of this 'reversed wheel' effect is evident in the progress of factory outlet centre development in the UK. Upmarket developers such as Value Retail entered the UK market as an upscale innovative format offering value branded merchandise, but domestic applications of the format such as those developed by Freeport were smaller, more downmarket versions (Fernie, 1996). The wheel theory has also been criticized by post-modernists who argue that time is linear rather than cyclical and therefore past patterns cannot be applied to future development (Brown, 1995). As the market environment is now too fragmented to apply concepts from 40 years ago, it is likely that new retail formats will be developed through the innovative combination of past, disparate retail practices.

The main utility of the theory is that it enables retailers to recognize their tendency to alter the characteristics of the format which has brought them success, and to be aware of organizational vulnerability in stage 3. Retail organizations operating at the higher end of the market, offering quality, service and higher prices, are vulnerable to innovation. Matalan and TK Maxx, entering the 'high street' fashion market in the 1990s, for example, shifted customer expectations for value/price in the fashion market. This upset the status quo in high street fashion retailing, which led to rationalization of high street stores by leading fashion retail group Arcadia and contributed to the withdrawal of C&A from UK retailing.

Retail life cycle

This second cyclical theory of retailing, in common with demographic and product life cycle theories, assumes that all retail organizations have a finite lifespan, during which they go through four phases of development:

- Innovation.
- Growth.
- Maturity.
- Decline.

The theory assumes that retail organizations and retail formats will move through all four phases. The time dwelt within each phase will, however, vary widely, as will the total lifespan of the organization or format. Jenners, for example, is still going strong over 100 years after its launch, while the lifespan of many retailers is much shorter and many new retailers enter and exit the market rapidly.

A new retail format will spend a short time, only a few years, in the innovation stage of the life cycle. Non-successful innovators will not enter the next phase, while successful innovators can take advantage of a lack of direct competitors to grow sales rapidly and develop retail unit numbers, entering the growth phase. Profits during this phase are low or non-existent due to investment in creation, infrastructure, expansion and promotion of the format. For example, Tesco.com planned for loss during its first few years of existence, investing in a national infrastructure for the online format.

During format growth the number of units is expanded rapidly, often with strong centralized planning and control. Both sales and profitability growth should follow. Investment levels will remain high, both due to the high cost of expansion, and due to the cost of developing a prime market position because during this phase, the number of competitors will also grow. The retail majors, often innovators in their own right, are also quick to exploit successful ideas. For example, when the hard discount box stores began to expand rapidly in the UK during the 1980s, the grocery retail majors successfully introduced basic retailer brands at discount prices along-side their normal merchandise. The growth phase normally lasts for several years before the format is established, or mature.

Maturity, on the other hand, will last indefinitely as long as the retailer is customer and competition orientated. A mature retail format will have many direct competitors and the rate of sales growth slows together with the level of profitability. In public limited companies, the delivery of continued growth to shareholders will drive growth of the format in untapped markets, through organic expansion, or through acquisition and merger activity, or the development of new, innovative activities. The maturity of some of the UK grocery majors has driven expansion in areas of the UK with development potential such as Scotland and Ireland, and in international markets, as well as investment in town centre and forecourt formats.

The decline phase, when sales growth becomes negative and profitability is very low, can also last indefinitely. The declining format will have fewer direct competitors and more indirect competitors in the growth and maturity phases of the life cycle. Organizations with declining formats require active search and investment in format innovation or acquisition/merger with organizations delivering for-mats in the innovation, growth or maturity phases of the cycle.

Life cycle theory has been criticized because of the difficulty in defining the exact time when the organization, or format, moves from one stage to another. To be truly useful, a retailer would want to know exactly when the growth or maturity phase has ended, so that marketing objectives and strategies could be adjusted accordingly. However, in practice, it is not too difficult for a retailer with understanding of life cycle theory to judge movement from one phase to the next in time to make innovations and format alterations. Figure 3.2 estimates the life cycle phases for selected UK retailers in 2002.

It is commonly agreed, however, that the time spent within each stage of the life cycle is becoming shorter. New retail formats are launched more frequently and grow to maturity much more rapidly than in the middle of the twentieth century. Department stores as a format grew to maturity over decades, while the factory outlet centre format grew to maturity over a period of years.

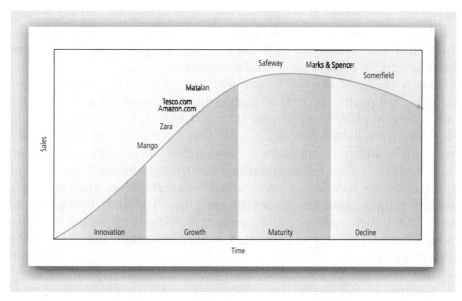

Figure 3.2 Estimated life cycle stages for selected retailers in the UK.

Retail accordion

The third cyclical theory is the retail accordion, which relates retail development over time to merchandise range. This theory (Hower, 1943) noted that there was a tendency for retail organizations to move alternately towards specialization and diversification over time. This US-based theory is rooted in its historical pattern of retail development. The earliest stores were general stores delivering a wide merchandise range, with narrow depth of category to small, dispersed communities. As urban areas grew, they could support speciality retailers with limited product assortment but depth of category, such as shoe stores, drugstores and clothing stores. The next expansion of the accordion brought the development of department stores offering a wide merchandise range and depth of category. The latest contraction of the accordion during the 1980s and 1990s brought more concentration of merchandise range in niche retailers such as Tie Rack and category killers such as Toys 'R' Us.

It is debatable whether this theory can be applied to future development of the retail industry. Certainly, the growth of scrambled merchandising among dominant grocery retailers, particularly in hypermarkets, is developing simultaneously with restricted line formats delivered to drivers, city centre workers or home workers. Nevertheless, it is evident at organizational level, in, for example, the expansion and retraction of store formats in Next and Arcadia during the 1980s and 1990s. It is also possible that the growth of formats in organizations such as Toys 'R' Us, which expanded into Babies 'R' Us, Kids 'R' Us, Imaginarium and Toysrus.com, may at some future point be followed by organizational rationalization.

Hart's (1999) study on assortment strategies in food and mixed retailing supported accordion theory, but concluded that this theory was more applicable to trends in merchandise assortments than to development of store formats. Noting that the number of lines in itself was not a sufficient measure of assortment width, she felt that an additional dimension is required to measure assortment 'coherence' or the real degree to which merchandises was scrambled. She concluded that if ranges were more clearly categorized within the width of assortment, then a more realistic picture would emerge of the extent to which product ranges were related to the core retail offer. Her study also found:

- Assortment and market diversification decisions are rarely supported by market research; some companies reverse these decisions after incurring high development costs.
- Inconsistent assortment additions can have an effect on the retailer's image.
- There is no clear dominance of generalist or specialist retailers.
- Food retailers, in adding new merchandise lines with service requirements unrelated to existing lines, followed a more risky strategy than mixed retailers, which tended to concentrate on their core business.
- These strategies are not based on customer requirements.

Where the retail accordion theory is useful is that historical patterns of retail development indicate that there is a distinct tendency for both small and large retailers to add new and unrelated lines, eventually blurring the focus of the organization to the level where specialization, or contraction, will inevitably occur. Indeed, the recent growth of home shopping formats and city centre limited-line grocery and convenience formats may well indicate that specialization is beginning to occur in the food sector as a result of environmental forces and consumer desire.

In order to minimize the cost of faulty developments, retailers should be careful regarding:

- The extent to which new, unrelated merchandise lines are added.
- The relationship between new merchandise lines and the core offering in terms of the benefits they offer customers, and the synergy offered in terms of service requirements.

- Supporting merchandise diversification and specialization strategies with market research focusing on the requirements of their core customers and potential customers.
- The effects which diversification or specialization strategies will have on corporate image.

Environmental theories

Environmental theories are concerned with the interplay between the external environment and organizational environment. The various influences of the external environment – political, legal, socio-cultural and demographic, economic and technological – on retailers change over time. Conditions can change slowly or rapidly, and only those organizations which can adapt to change and take advantage of the opportunities offered by the environment will grow, develop and thrive.

A range of examples supports environmental theories. Department stores would not have existed but for developing urban spaces, nor would out-of-town shopping centres but for the development of the road network, suburbanization and growth of car ownership. An organization's movement through innovation and growth to maturity depends upon successful response to changing environmental conditions.

There are two dominant environmental theories of retail change:

1 Evolution theory.
2 Institutional theory.

Evolution theory

The theory of retail evolution is, naturally, linked to the theory of evolution observed by Charles Darwin in the nineteenth century, the process of natural selection in which the survival of organisms is based on their ability to adapt to changing conditions. In retailing, organizations which successfully adapt to changes in the external environment are those most likely to thrive.

Davies (1998) discusses evolution theory in the context of environmental 'design spaces' which offer opportunities and threats for the retail organizations operating within them. The viability or otherwise of the 'design space' is related to:

- the size and distribution of the population;
- the need structure for goods, which is related to demographic variables such as family size and income;

- regional income and income distribution;
- technology;
- government regulation;
- social visibility of the design space.

According to this 'ecological' theory, changes in the environment will cause retail change, and therefore the structure of retailing at any point in time is the result of all previous retail management decisions, together with the political, social, economic and technological environment within which retailers operate.

One of the problems with this refinement of evolution theory is that it does not allow for the effects of retail organizations on the environment in which they operate and these are many. For example:

- Planning gain – for instance, in order to secure a site a retailer may develop roads or leisure facilities which will bring with them housing development, which will have effects on the economy.
- Lobbying – most of the largest retail groups have close political connections, which can have effects on locational policy.
- 24-hour opening – expansion of opening hours has brought with it a rapid move to the 24/7 society; it has increased the propensity for part-time flexible working and has had a role in raising the proportion of women in the UK workforce to over 50 per cent; this in turn has affected marriage and divorce statistics, and, it could be argued, the rise of single parent families.
- Online retailing – the growth of e-tail has contributed to the uptake of computers in the home, improving the technological skills of the workforce.

Ultra-Darwinism is a form of evolution theory which relates development not to survival of the fittest, but of the fittest's genetic material. In socio-cultural evolution, the equivalent of the gene has been called the 'meme', an idea, saying or ritual which propagates itself through a society in much the same way as the spread of a computer virus. Thus, technologies could be considered 'memes' carried by organizations and replicated at different levels within an organization and beyond the organization. For example, the first-in, first-out practice in merchandising can be replicated in staff or management promotion practices as 'buggins turn' or at the organizational level in terms of early retirement. Another example might be where customer service through stock availability is replicated in staffing practices through flexible hours contracts, in organizational practices such as 24-hour opening, and beyond retail into road development and maintenance to maintain access to stores.

According to Davies there is a distinction between the development of firms and formats, the former evolving relatively slowly with the environment, the latter adapting more dynamically to meet the needs of local environments. Therefore, a retail organization can run a variety of successful formats which may or may not carry the 'memes' of the parent organization. He also argues that, when change is slow and predictable, firms and formats have a better chance of survival; conversely, when change is rapid and unpredictable, greater opportunism exists and the number and variety of formats and firms will change.

According to Hannan and Freeman (1989), within any design space there are two types of firms and strategies: R-strategies occur when the environment is rapidly changing and discontinuous, throwing up opportunities that are seized and developed by opportunist organizations, and resulting in the proliferation of new formats. These organizations could be said to be charting the new, emerging design space. As the pace of change slows again organizations select the best of the new formats with which to occupy the new design space and the second type of strategy dominates. These K-strategies occur when the environment is relatively stable. Larger, dominant organizations converge on the successful formats, applying them with the efficiencies of scale and power on a wide scale.

Hence, the current position in e-tailing, in which the evolving virtual design space was charted by innovative dot.com organizations, which then failed or were absorbed by 'clicks and mortar' retail organizations, could have been forecast. Indeed, it should be expected that these K-strategy organizations and surviving R-strategy organizations such as Amazon.com should be well placed to take advantage of the refinement of Internet and digital TV technology in the future.

A range of strategies have been used by successful firms to ensure survival (Brockway et al., 1988):

- *Experimentation*. This is widely used by successful retailers, who will test out unrelated merchandise or new systems in one or a few stores before rolling out successful innovations. Examples include Safeway selling TVs and rugs, and testing then rolling out its self-scanning operation.
- *Joint retailing*. Two normally separate organizations combine to create a synergistic offer to their customers. A good example is the joint offering of Burger King, Little Chef and Travelodge – offering accommodation and a selection of fast food or full meals to travellers.
- *Physical premises mutation*. The retailer changes its usual location or combines innovative activities under one roof. An example of both is

the move out of town by the Co-op Travel Group, which, in a purpose-built unit five times the normal size of its normal outlets, combined travel agency with an Internet area, café and children's play area (Parker, 2002).

- *Copycatting*. Exploiting innovative systems or formats which have been developed by other organizations. Examples include provision for cleaning, photographic, pharmaceutical and financial services within grocery retail units.
- *Vertical integration*. Retailers take over other distribution channel functions such as manufacturing or wholesaling in order to gain organizational power over supply of goods. This also operates in the opposite direction, with manufacturers entering the retail market to gain higher margins.
- *Horizontal integration*. Retailers acquire control of other retail organizations in order to boost market share, gain market innovation or management/operational expertise. An example is Talk 4 All buying 30 stores from failing mobile phone retailer The Wap to build strength and share in the maturing mobile phone retail market.
- *Micro-merchandising*. Retailers involved in micro-merchandising make use of market segmentation techniques to focus on meeting the needs of a demographic or lifestyle group through creation of a suitable retail format. Girl Heaven and Claire's Accessories are two UK examples, targeting the 'Tweenie' market of 7- to 12-year-olds with 'girly' toys, make up, clothes and accessories.

Box 3.1 Retailer profile – Casino

The use of innovation, horizontal and vertical integration contributes to the successful growth of Casino.

The well-known, long-established French retailer Casino has used innovation, vertical and horizontal integration to grow, develop, internationalize and finally to compete in the global retail marketplace. The original shop was set up in a former casino – hence the name. One of the first European grocery retailers to introduce self-service into its stores, early expansion took place through horizontal integration – concentrating on neighbourhood stores. Casino also developed manufacturing subsidiaries, which contributed to the growth of its own brand business. In 1999, it operated both a wine bottling business and a meat processing business. Casino was also an early entrant into the hypermarket format in the 1970s and is one of France's major retailers, with 10 per cent of the market.

The organization is itself majority owned by Rallye Group, which owns the Athlete's Foot chain of footwear outlets in addition to having interests in a variety of other organizations. Casino operates a variety of food retail formats and fascias: Geant hypermarkets, Casino supermarkets, Petit Casino superettes, Franprix and LeaderPrice supermarkets, and Spar, Vival and Coccinelle neighbourhood stores.

The group developed through the 1980s, mainly through acquisition, and during the 1990s it has continued this successful method of expansion abroad. For example, its presence in Latin America and Asia has been developed primarily through acquiring stakes in local retail groups. Although its domestic business dominated sales, in 2002 the group operated stores, or had acquired stakes in retail businesses, in:

- the USA (United Grocers cash and carry);
- Poland (Polska and Leader Price);
- Argentina (Libertad and Leader Price);
- Uruguay (Disco and Devoto);
- Colombia (Exito);
- Venezuela (Cativen);
- Brazil (Pao de Acucar);
- Thailand (Big C);
- Philippines (Uniwide Holdings);
- Taiwan (Far Eastern Geant).

By 1999, Casino's sales already accounted for 20 per cent of its business, half from the US cash and carry operation. In 2002, the group was continuing its global expansion plans through acquisition, particularly in the Philippines and Korea, and was also considering expansion in the Middle East.

In Europe, Casino operates company-owned stores, but also has a large number of franchised outlets in its Petit Casino, Spar, Vival and Coccinelle fascias. The group acquired Franprix in 1997, which brought in a mix of franchised and own-operated outlets in Franprix (supermarkets) and LeaderPrice (discounters) formats. In 2000, it acquired SLDC, the holding group for Auchan's convenience store network, and acquired a 50 per cent share in Monoprix. The group also owns a chain of restaurants called Cafeterias Casino.

Innovation was the foundation for Casino's early growth – successfully importing the idea of self-service from the US in 1948 and opening its first hypermarket in 1970. Since then, Casino has used both horizontal integration to grow its retail business successfully, acquiring a variety of formats across the grocery sector from convenience store to hypermarket. The group has also vertically integrated into manufacturing and cash and carry operations. In 2002, the group was the fourth largest in the

French grocery market, with 10.6 per cent market share, and was considering strengthening its position through takeover. In 2002, however, the Casino group itself remained vulnerable to takeover by global retail groups, the Dutch Ahold and US Wal-Mart.

Sources: Young (2002), Retail Intelligence (1999), www.groupe-casino.fr (2002).

Institutional theory

Institutional theory recognizes that the organization is an organic part of its environment and that there is a degree of interdependency between them (Arnold et al., 2001).

According to this theory, the decisions and actions of a retail organization reflect the economic and cultural norms of the environment in which it exists. These norms exist at task and institutional levels.

At task level, the organization responds to its environment through actions aimed at retail performance – from a customer perspective, these are linked to retail performance-related decisions on, for example, merchandise assortment, pricing strategy, inventory and location.

At institutional level, the retailer's actions are constrained or framed according to cultural and moral norms which will influence both the internal culture of the organization and its perceived role in the society in which it exists. For example, customers may expect it to employ and promote local talent, be active in the community, and sell local products along with those which are sourced nationally or internationally.

The performance actions which retailers take can adhere to norms in an objective manner – for example, selling goods will be of consistent high quality. However, they can also take a symbolic form – for example, Sainsbury's 'The Best' range, or Safeway's 'Finest' range.

Likewise, symbolic institutional actions can reflect the organization's adherence to the norms of its socio-cultural environment – for example, Iceland's well-promoted purge of suppliers of goods with genetically modified ingredients in the 1990s, which responded to the upsurge of European concern regarding genetically modified foods, can be contrasted against the objective actions of organizations which source products which are deemed by various regulatory authorities to be safe or healthy to eat.

When a retailer's actions reflect the norms of its environment (termed isomorphism), this legitimizes the organization (and its institutional and performance actions) in the minds of the various institutional stakeholders (customers, shareholders, staff, suppliers). The institutional/environmental interaction is illustrated in Figure 3.3.

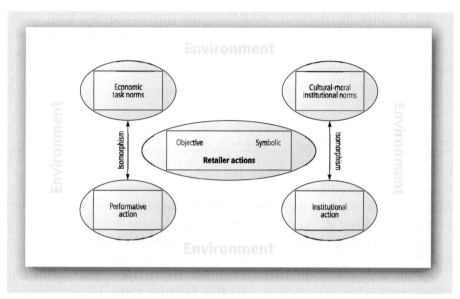

Economic Task Norms: the economic environment in which the organization operates and within which it frames its performance objectives and actions.

Cultural-moral Institutional Norms: the organization's stakeholders create an institutional environment with cultural and moral requirements which reflect the norms of social conduct in the external socio-cultural environment.

Performative Action: performance levels and actions taken by the organization, e.g. pricing strategy, merchandising decisions.

Institutional Action: non-performance actions taken by the organization, e.g. community involvement, environmental policies.

Symbolic Actions: use of symbols such as slogans, signs and promotional literature which relate the organization's actions to its social and economic environment.

Objective Actions: actions taken to compete successfully within the economic task environment.

Figure 3.3 Institutional/environmental interaction. *Source*: **adapted from Arnold et al. (2001).**

For example, the political climate of the 1980s and 1990s created destabilized unionism and high unemployment. This brought about the flexible labour market conditions which would bring the United Kingdom inward investment and allow organizations in the country to become more competitive, productive, profitable and adaptable. A retailer which exploits the labour market conditions by offering staff flexi-hours contracts, binding them to the organization for a variable number of hours each week, is therefore seen to be acting in an acceptable fashion, particularly in a sector which promotes efficiency as a means of keeping prices reasonable.

Socio-cultural norms are vague, variable over time and difficult to monitor. It is easy for a retailer's institutional actions to exceed what is acceptable. For example, in 2002, Sainsbury's acted in a manner regarded as 'mean' by many stakeholders when it fired managers in a morally dubious manner. This reflected the organization's 'meanness' in allowing store staff to work 6 hours with only a 10-minute break, 7 hours with a 20-minute break and 8 hours with a 30-minute break. This compared poorly with the other grocery majors, which already were regarded as 'exploitative' by many staff, and contrasted with their transmitted image of quality and customer care. There is a limit to the number of objective actions that a retail organization can take in the interests of successful competitiveness – but which transgress social norms of institutional conduct – without affecting perceived service quality and tarnishing corporate image.

Conflict theory

Conflict theory addresses what happens when a new innovation or format challenges the status quo in a retail sector. As retail organizations adapt to each other in the competitive marketplace, new and different forms of retailing develop. This continual shift in operating forms is derived from a dialectic process which consists of action–reaction–synthesis.

As an innovator successfully enters the market through some competitive advantage (action), existing organizations will take actions designed to minimize that competitive advantage (reaction), which eventually lead to a modification of their operating methods. Meanwhile, the innovating organization will also adapt as it becomes established in the market (trading up according to wheel theory). The continual adaptation will bring the two differing types of trading closer and closer together until they are virtually indistinguishable (synthesis) (Maronick and Walker, 1974). The retail organizations which evolve deploy organizational elements (carry the memes according to ultra-Darwinist theory) of both innovative and established formats.

There are a number of examples which illustrate this theory in action. The latest is perhaps Internet retailing, in which many retailers faced the challenge of manufacturer/wholesaler-led dot.coms bypassing retail outlets, selling merchandise direct to customers at discount prices. In order to offer an effective service on a large scale, investment was required in warehouse, transport and customer service facilities in addition to an enormous marketing spend, which in most cases undermined their business viability. Meanwhile, major retail groups added web-based retailing to their existing formats and exploited their established brand names to embed their e-tail offering with existing and new customers. At the same time, they made use of their logistics network to find solutions to delivery and returns problems. The e-tail format of Amazon.com, one of the earliest purely online retailers, is virtually indistinguishable from that of Dixons, a bricks and mortar retailer successfully trading online. A second example is forecourt retailing, which is a successful merger of petrol stations with convenience stores, which was partly fuelled by pressure for 24-hour retailing. A third example is the merging of retail and leisure parks.

According to conflict theory there are four stages of response to a retail innovation:

1 Shock.
2 Defensive retreat.
3 Acknowledgement.
4 Adaptation.

Initially, retailers are hostile to the threat to their established role within the industry and distribution channel. Firm size, re-seller solidarity, organizational rigidity and channel politics can all promote hostility towards the 'interloper'. In phase 2, established retail organizations will ignore or play down the possible effects of the innovation. As the threat of the innovation becomes more sustained and severe, there may be movement to block the progress of the innovation in phase 3, which, if unsuccessful, will give way to the final phase.

In a study on the impact of warehouse membership clubs (WMCs) in the US, Sampson and Tigert (1994) claimed that supermarkets are the primary targets of WMCs, with 43 per cent of customer supermarket spend transferred from the former to the latter. Nevertheless, it was only in the maturity stage of the WMC life cycle that food retailers acknowledged the threat to their viability and took defensive action through the reactive or proactive strategies outlined in Box 3.2.

Box 3.2 Response strategies of food retailers to the growth of warehouse membership clubs

1 Small section of warehouse club pack sizes at WMC prices put into stores.
2 'Power alley' with a larger number of stock-keeping units (SKUs) in club pack size at WMC prices.
3 Store-within-store warehouse club section, upwards of 200 SKUs at WMC prices.
4 Food-only warehouse club of 40 000 operating without a membership fee.
5 Food- and drug-only warehouse clubs built in recycled supermarkets.
6 Petitioning against zoning applications by WMCs.
7 Petitioning against differing regulations on pricing on SKUs to create level playing field between WMCs and supermarket chains.

Source: adapted from Sampson and Tigert (1994).

Sampson and Tigert concluded that the proactive strategies aimed at synthesis were those which offered the established food retailers the greatest chance of success – food-only, or food- and drug-only WMCs.

In terms of retailer response to the dot.com threat, it is interesting to note that those retailers which confronted the threat and adapted the earliest are among the most successful at gaining market share. Tesco's online market share advantage over Sainsbury's is six times greater than in stores and Argos' online share three times greater than Woolworths. In addition to establishing market leadership, embracing change and investment in e-tailing has brought benefits in terms of the technical experience to refine online shopping, plus the ability to tap into and exploit the online movements of the growing number of technically-proficient potential customers.

Combined theory

Having established that the development of a new retail format followed the principles established by the wheel, life cycle and conflict

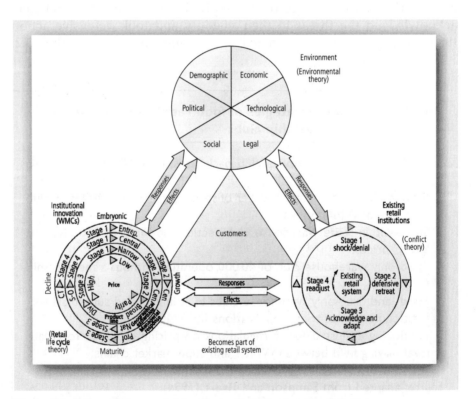

Figure 3.4 A descriptive model for the evolution of new retail forms.

theories, the links among these various theories as they drive retail change were also explored by Sampson and Tigert, who came up with a descriptive model for the evolution of new retail forms (Figure 3.4).

Environment theory – environmental conditions enable the creation and development of the innovation. Political and economic conditions created negative growth in income for the majority of Americans during the 1980s, which, together with a car-based social environment, created conditions favourable for the growth of value retail formats such as factory outlet centres and WMCs. Internet use soared in the late 1990s, creating a technological and social environment, which was successfully exploited by some retailers as a viable format and by many retailers to streamline their logistical efforts in a bid to drive down costs and increase competitiveness.

Cyclical theory – there are four main indicators retailers can use in establishing the life cycle stage of their organization (or format). These are:

- Price.
- Product range.
- Geographical expansion.
- Management style.

In the figure, these are portrayed as rings because each has its own separate stages, which may 'revolve' at varying rates according to external environmental forces. In the innermost ring, price varies from low to high, with higher prices generally associated with later stages in the life cycle. In formats reliant on price for their competitive advantage it is essential that low price levels are guarded from adverse environmental impacts, and this is the case with WMCs and factory outlet centres. However, the price advantage in online retailing is less important. Customers pay for the convenience of home delivery and, in organizations operating several formats, price parity with bricks and mortar stores is regarded as advisable, partly due to the comparability of costs, but also due to the high cost of returns.

The second innermost ring is that of product range – as retail formats mature the trend is from narrow to broad and then to diversified product ranges. In WMCs this has been the case, as it has in factory outlet centres in the UK and in online retailing.

However, according to retail accordion theory there should come a point when a move towards specialization will occur, as a defensive measure against decline or an innovator. An example of the former is illustrated in specialized factory outlet centres and of the latter in the food-only WMCs which have been set up by food retailers in the US.

The second outermost ring represents geographical expansion. Retailers tend to expand outwards from their base location as they grow and mature, firstly into adjoining markets, then nationally and internationally. The last phase of expansion fends off decline as the national market is saturated, as has happened with both WMCs and factory outlet centres. It seems likely that online retailing will progress in a similar fashion as it matures.

The outermost ring represents the most effective management style in each of the four life cycle phases: entrepreneurial in the innovation phase, centralized during growth, professional during maturity and caretaker during decline. Some retail organizations recognize this and selected entrepreneurial managers take care of new start-ups.

A maturing retailer will become part of the established retail system as existing retail institutions acknowledge and adapt to accommodate them (conflict theory). Sampson and Tigert cite Source Club as an example of a new type of warehouse club with low membership fees, retail focus and supermarket-like atmosphere. McArthur Glen's factory outlet centre in Livingston, Scotland is indistinguishable from a conventional covered shopping centre in size, atmosphere and location (in the town centre), and even its prices are matched by offsite competitors such as Matalan and TK Maxx. Many retailers have absorbed online facilities into their bricks and mortar stores, which shows a similar development in online retailing.

At the centre of Figure 3.4, customer needs, wants and desires drive all three parts of the model – because for a retail organization to succeed to the level of being absorbed into the existing retail system, it must operate in a manner which is acceptable and attractive to its customers.

Summary

Theories of retail change have been developed by studying past and current patterns of retail development, at format, organization and industry levels. There are three main categories of theory discussed in this chapter:

1 Cyclical theories.
2 Environmental theories.
3 Conflict theory.

A combined theory has also been presented which links the three theory categories.

The cyclical theories include the wheel of retailing, retail life cycle and retail accordion, all based on the thinking that there is a cyclical pattern in the evolution of retail institutions from which future business scenarios can be built.

Two main environmental theories have been outlined – evolution theory and institutional theory – both based on the effects of the external, uncontrollable environment on the retail industry and the organizations operating within it. Where evolution theory suggests that successful organizations adapt to survive and succeed in the changing environment, both the ultra-Darwinists and the institutionalists propose that organizations go beyond tactical adaptation to absorb into their fabric, design and organizational culture the 'technologies' and socio-cultural influences of the external environment.

Conflict theory is explained as a series of phases which existing retail organizations pass through when challenged by a retail innovation. After the initial shock, organizations engage in defensive retreat, which may involve an industry initiative to prevent the success of the innovator, then they pass through a phase of acknowledgement that the innovation is going to succeed, during which they engage various adaptation strategies. Meanwhile, the innovator is also adapting to survive and grow until a degree of syntheses exists.

Finally, a combined theory has been described, which integrates the various branches of retail theory. The main utility of theory is to predict outcomes, and research has indicated contradictory results for all the various theories presented. However, they remain useful tools for retailers to build alternative visions for the future of their organizations and their place within the changing retail industry.

Review questions

1 Apply the three main cyclical retail theories to the current status of a fashion retailer. According to each theory, explain the likely future development of the organization.
2 Ultra-Darwinism is a form of evolution theory which relates development not to survival of the fittest, but of the fittest's genetic material. Describe what is meant by the term 'meme' and give an example of a 'meme' which has been replicated in retailing.
3 Explain what is meant by the terms 'symbolic' and 'objective' retailer actions. Give an example of a symbolic action taken by a well-known retail organization and explain how it relates to the socio-cultural environment.

4 Give an example of conflict theory in action in today's retail market and show how you think the situation will develop, according to the theory.
5 The combined theory attempts to relate cyclical, environmental and conflict theories. Apply combined theory to one retail sector and draw conclusions regarding the utility of this theory.

References

Arnold, S. J., Kozinets, R. V. and Handelman, J. M. (2001). Hometown ideology and retailer legitimation: the institutional semiotics of Wal-Mart flyers. *Journal of Retailing*, **77**(2), Summer, 243–71.

Brockway, G., Gary, R. and Niffenegger, P. (1988). Retailing evolution in the 1980s: survival through adaptive behaviour. *Journal of Midwest Marketing*, **3**(2).

Brown, S. (1995). Postmodernism, the wheel of retailing and will to power. *The International Review of Retail, Distribution and Consumer Research*, **5**(3), 387–414.

David, R. (2002). IKEA in £50m store expansion to offset planning frustration. *Retail Week*, 11 January.

Davies, K. (1998). Applying evolutionary models to the retail sector. *The International Review of Retail, Distribution and Consumer Research*, **8**(2), 165–82.

Fernie, S. (1996). The future for factory outlet centres in the UK: the impact of changes in planning policy guidance on the growth of a new retail format. *International Journal of Retail and Distribution Management*, **24**(6), 11–21.

Hannan, M. T. and Freeman, J. (1989). *Organisational Ecology*. Harvard University Press, London.

Hart, C. (1999). The retail accordion and assortment strategies: an exploratory study. *The International Review of Retail, Distribution and Consumer Research*, **9**(2), 111–26.

Hower, R (1943). History of Macy's of New York 1858–1919. In *Retail Marketing* (Lush, R. F., Dunne, P. and Gebhardt, R., eds), revised 1993 edn, pp. 113–14. South Western Publishing, Cincinnati, OH.

http://www.groupe-casino.fr (2002).

Maronick, T. J. and Walker, B. J. (1974). The dialectic evolution of retailing. In *Proceedings: Southern Marketing Association* (Greenberg, B., ed.), p. 147. Georgia State University.

McNair, M. P. (1958). Significant trends and developments in the postwar period. In *Competitive Distribution in a Free High-Level Economy and Its Implications for the University* (Smith, A. B., ed.). University of Pittsburgh Press, Pittsburgh, PA.

Parker, G. (2002). Travel firms seek to increase portfolios. *Retail Week*, 18 January, p. 3.

Retail Intelligence (1999). Profile of Casino (Rallye).

Sampson, S. D. and Tigert, D. J. (1994). The impact of warehouse membership clubs: the wheel of retailing turns one more time. *International Review of Retail, Distribution and Consumer Research*, **4**(1), 33–59.

Verdict (2002). Verdict forecasts UK retailing to 2004. http://www.verdict.co.uk/fcpr.htm, 11 January.

Young, J. (2002). Playing to win at Casino. *Retail Week*, 18 January, p. 16.

4

Retail strategy

Introduction

Retail strategy is about corporate survival and prosperity in a changing retail environment. It is about environmental analysis; identification of those factors critical to success; recognition and building of corporate competences; developing, maintaining and communicating strategic direction – to staff, to customers, to competitors.

The organization's mission encapsulates its direction and its values in the changing marketplace, which are then developed into corporate objectives. Environmental audit and analysis will highlight the main opportunities and threats to the retailer, while resource audit and analyses will develop understanding of its strategic capability. Strategic choice involves the consideration of strategic options and their evaluation in relation to organizational capability.

This chapter outlines the strategic planning process, defines mission and corporate objectives, and explains environmental, competitive and resource audits. The scope of strategic choice for retailers incorporates generic strategies, expansion strategies and methods of evaluating strategies.

Location strategy, which is one of the most important facets of retail strategy because of the degree of investment in location decisions, is covered in a section which explains methods of catchment definition, analysis and comparison to allow informed decisions to be made regarding location choice.

The strategic planning process

The strategic planning process encompasses three main steps. Firstly, the external, competitive and organizational environment are audited and analysed. Secondly, strategic options are explored and evaluated, before a strategy or strategies are selected. Thirdly, strategy is implemented through setting up action plans and allocating human, financial and material resources to meet objectives.

Corporate strategy and objectives

Despite the changing environment, successful retail organizations tend to have a clear direction, or mission, which is really a rationale for the existence and progress of the company. Often, organizations verbalize this mission in a mission statement. However, even if they don't, the mission or direction creates the focus for corporate strategy, and the setting of corporate objectives. The mission should encapsulate the core competences and critical success factors for the organization – that is, the company strengths and the areas in which the company has to succeed to thrive – as well as try to inform internal and external customers about what their role is in delivering success (Piercy, 2001). Box 4.1 shows the mission and corporate values of ASDA and the John Lewis Partnership.

Box 4.1   Company mission statements and corporate values

ASDA (2002)

Mission
'To be Britain's best value fresh food and clothing superstore, by satisfying the weekly shopping needs of ordinary working people and their families who demand value.'

Values
We are all colleagues; we are one team; we each need to improve the business every day in every way.

- Think about your work and put forward your ideas for improvement.
- Question or challenge if you don't agree.
- Learn from your mistakes and successes. Share your learning with your colleagues.
- Give people honest feedback so that they can improve.
- Ask yourself 'if this was my business, what would I do?'
- Praise good ideas and encourage others to put ideas forward.
- Give feedback to Colleague Circle members so that we can improve our working environment.

What we sell is better value

- Be aware of current promotions and offers so that you can tell customers.
- Only offer quality products to the customer; remove any poor quality products from display.
- Have a passion for product knowledge and keeping it up to date.
- Handle products with care.
- Help customers understand our Rollback policy and ensure all price communication is clear and accurate.
- Talk about our value message to customers.
- Feedback all customer comments to someone who can take action.

Selling is our universal responsibility

- Love selling and actively gets involved in company sales initiatives.
- Deal with availability issues as a priority.
- Know your products; explain features, give advice, offer alternatives or complementary products to customers where possible.
- Run a store and drive sales.
- Know your internal customers and how you can help them.
- Encourage customers to sample products being demonstrated.

Through selling we make our service legendary

- Meet and greet customers with a smile.
- Always take customers to a product rather than pointing.
- Offer assistance to customers if you see them struggling.
- Recognize and help customers with special needs.
- Always strive to deliver what the customers wants. Remember that the customer is always right.
- Take ownership for a customer's problem and ensure it is resolved.
- Make a special effort to ensure children enjoy their shopping trip.

We hate waste of any kind

- Shout out about things you notice that waste time, energy or money.
- Look after our resources.
- Car share where possible.
- Use stationery sparingly (e.g. if you have to photocopy always use double sided).
- Recycle where possible.
- Switch off lights, keep freezer/chiller doors shut and don't fill above the load lines.
- Keep phone calls short.
- Rotate stock correctly and follow all waste management procedures.
- Would you spend it? Think of ASDA's money as your own.

John Lewis Partnership (2001)

Mission and values

'*We have a constitution – a framework of rules that defines how we run our business.*'

Purpose: The partnership's ultimate purpose is the happiness of all its members, through their worthwhile and satisfying employment in a successful business. Because the Partnership is owned in trust for its members, they share the responsibilities of ownership as well as its rewards – profit, knowledge and power.

Power: Power in the Partnership is shared between three governing authorities, the Central Council, the Central Board and the Chairman.

Profit: The Partnership aims to make sufficient profit from its trading operations to sustain its commercial vitality, to finance its continued development and to distribute a share of those profits each year to its members, and enable it to undertake other activities consistent with its ultimate purpose.

Members: The Partnership aims to employ people of ability and integrity who are committed to working together and to supporting its principles. Relationships are based on mutual respect and courtesy, with as much equality between its members as differences of responsibility permit. The Partnership aims to recognize their individual contributions and reward them fairly.

Customers: The Partnership aims to deal honestly with its customers and secure their loyalty and trust by providing outstanding choice, value and service.

Business Relationships: The Partnership aims to conduct all its business relationships with integrity and courtesy and scrupulously to honour every business agreement.

The Community: The Partnership aims to obey the spirit as well as the letter of the law and to contribute to the well being of the communities where it operates.

Sources: adapted from http://www.asda.co.uk/asda_corp/scripts, 9 August 2002; http://www.john-lewis-partnership.co.uk, 1 November 2001.

The organization's mission and strategy is normally set out in a series of corporate objectives, which are explicit time-related goals against which to assess organizational progress and achievements. They often incorporate marketing objectives, for example setting a percentage of market share, or a level of sales as a corporate target. However, particularly in large organizations, the corporate objectives are sometimes more general targets (see Box 4.2). Corporate objectives form the basis for planning and setting objectives for other operational areas such as logistics, marketing and human resource management.

Box 4.2   J Sainsbury plc – Objectives

To provide shareholders with good financial returns by focusing on customers' needs, adding value through our expertise and innovation, and investing for future growth.

To provide unrivalled value to our customers in the quality of the goods we sell, in the competitiveness of our prices and in the range of choice we offer.

To achieve efficiency of operation, convenience and customer services in our stores, thereby creating as attractive and friendly a shopping environment as possible.

To provide a working environment where there is a concern for the welfare of each member of staff, where all have opportunities to develop their abilities and where each is well rewarded for their contribution to the success of the business.

To fulfil our responsibilities by acting with integrity, maintaining high environmental standards, and contributing to the quality of life in the community.

Source: http://www.j-sainsbury.co.uk/aboutusmain.htm, 15 September 2000.

Environmental analysis

Environmental scanning will highlight major external influences which create the climate of opportunity for the organization (many of which are considered in Chapter 2). Commonly known as the PEST, STEP or SPELT factors (Political, Economic, Social, Legal and Technological), the main sectors of the environment are:

- Demographic and socio-cultural developments
  Examples: population structure and change; income distribution; lifestyle changes; communication methods; work and leisure trends; consumerism; environmentalism; attitudes to globalization.
- Government policy, regulatory agencies, pressure groups (at transnational, national, regional and local levels)
  Examples: stability of home and market governments; policies on taxation; transport; environment; planning; construction; agriculture, horticulture, fisheries and food; training and education; consumer associations and environmental groups.
- Legal framework – European and UK laws and regulations
  Examples: legislation on health and safety; packaging and waste; disability discrimination; data protection; e-commerce (see Box 4.3) ; equal opportunities; monopolies; environmental protection.
- Economic environment, capital and labour markets
  Examples: taxation and interest rates; pension values; spending and saving patterns; employment levels; stage of business cycle (recession, recovery, prosperity); Gross National Product (GNP) trends, inflation, disposable income.
- Technological environment
  Examples: government spending on research; focus of technological effort; speed of technology transfer; rates of obsolescence; biotechnology, robotics; information technology.

Although it is important to identify and focus on those elements of the external environment which most closely affect the workings and operational direction of the organization, a broad knowledge of PEST trends and developments is essential for retail organizations because they operate in fast-paced, highly competitive environments, and many problems and opportunities are created by trends in the wider environment.

The key environmental influences on the organization should be listed in a simple PEST analysis. More extensive PEST analysis can be used to assess the variable potential impacts of the key influences, or to gauge the extent of the impact of the key influences on the main competing organizations in a sector (Johnson and Scholes, 1999).

Some analysts would also consider the competitive market and the organizational environment at this stage. Others would propose structural analysis of the competitive environment as a sequential stage to environmental analysis.

Box 4.3   UK E-Commerce Regulations (2002) – information required on all websites (implementing the EU e-commerce directive as UK law)

Name of service provider

Address of service provider

Contact details

E-mail address

VAT registration number

Details of trade association membership; registration number

Details of supervisory authority if relevant

Prices referred to on-site must state whether inclusive of tax and delivery costs

Where company belongs to a regulated profession, details of professional body, professional title; EU member state where granted, reference and access (e.g. by link) to applicable professional rules

Source: Davies (2002).

The 'five forces' approach to analysing the structure of competitive environment was advocated by Michael Porter (1980), and although dated, it forms a useful tool in assessing the competitive situation at a local, national or transnational level. According to this approach, the five forces which form the theatre of competition are:

1 Threat of entrants.
2 Bargaining power of suppliers.
3 Bargaining power of buyers.
4 Threat of substitutes.
5 Competitive rivalry.

Threat of entrants. This depends on the barriers to entry such as economies of scale, capital needed to enter the market, likely retaliation of existing competitors and access to distribution channels. In retailing the barriers to entry are low. It is relatively cheap and easy to set up a retail store on a small scale. One of the reasons it can be difficult to get comprehensive data on the extent of retail activity on a regional basis is because so many small retailers start and fail on an annual basis. It is also relatively feasible for a retail major to enter a local market and undercut local retailers through price competition enabled through cost advantages achievable through dominance in distribution channels. At transnational level, large-scale entry can be achieved through commercial, financial and political influence.

Bargaining power of suppliers. Supplier power is likely to be high when there is a concentration of large suppliers with strong established brands. A high cost of switching from one supplier to another increases power, as does technological 'tie-in'. Supplier power is also linked to the likelihood of forward integration in the marketing channel. The growth of retailer power over the last few decades has weakened the bargaining power of suppliers, as has the growth of globalization, where manufactured goods are sourced from cheap overseas suppliers. However, the growth of technological supplier–retailer links increased bargaining power, as does the potential for larger scale forward integration offered by factory warehouses, outlet centres and e-tailing.

Bargaining power of buyers. Buyer power is clearly likely to be high when there is a concentration of buyers and volume of purchases is high, and this is especially the case where the goods being bought are difficult to differentiate in the eyes of the end customer. Bargaining power is also increased by the potential for buyers to integrate backwards in the distribution channel. Bargaining power is high among major retail organizations due to their large size and concentration in number; backward integration is also a feature of large-scale retailing and the growth of own-branding (and especially premium branding) also contributes to buyer power. In retailing it is also possible to conceive of 'the consumer' as buyer, and retailers who refer to the 'customer as dictator' are perhaps referring to the collective influence of customer bargaining power on the retail industry.

Threat of subsititutes. This means substitution of organization, product or process. There have been a number of threats to the equilibrium of the retail market – the arrival of hard discounters threatened the grocery majors during the 1980s; the growth of retail parks threatens established town centre retailers; the dot.com boom threatened store-based retailing. Substitution also exists in the form of competition for customer spend. For retailers, the growing proportion of disposable income spent on leisure, travel and mortgages can pose a threat of substitute.

Competitive rivalry. This increases where barriers to entry are low, supplier or buyer power is high and there is a high threat of substitutes. Other features of enhanced competitive rivalry which are evident in the retail market include:

- equality of size among the dominant organizations as each will push for market share;

- market in slow growth will further fuel rivalry;
- conditions in which weaker organizations will be absorbed (through merger, acquisition, alliance) by larger ones to increase share;
- high market exit costs through established property portfolios and long leases.

Five forces analysis can establish the balance of the competitive market and form a foundation for future strategy. Is it possible to reduce the threat of substitute by diversification, for example? Can barriers to entry be raised? What are the strengths and weaknesses of rival companies in relation to the key forces? Establishing the underlying forces – for example, government policy towards foreign retailers establishing networks in the UK, technological and social forces creating new patterns of buying – can indicate potential variation of the nature and balance of the five forces.

Market analyses such as the product–market expansion grid, market positioning and growth–share matrix (see Chapter 5) help to relate the organization's position and potential to market opportunities, in order to achieve competitive advantage.

Resource audit and analyses

Environmental audit and analysis will highlight potential external opportunities and threats to the organization. The exploitation of environmental opportunity requires:

1 Recognition that an opportunity exists.
2 Assessment of whether the opportunity is viable.

The former requires management experience, creativity and acumen, in addition to organizational capability in environmental scanning and analysis and organizational communication systems which facilitate the vertical flow of market and consumer information. The latter requires assessment of the opportunity against organizational capability. Corporate audit is the objective assessment of the organization's financial, material and human resource capability, and should also take into consideration intangibles such as corporate image, goodwill, brand name, strength of supply network and contact network.

The financial resource audit may include:

- Sources of capital and credit.
- Control of debtors and creditors.
- Cash management.

- Relationship with key financial contacts.
- Investments.

The physical resource audit may include:

- Property portfolio – size/age/location/state of repair.
- Equipment – amount/capability/location/age/durability.
- Physical resource outsourcement organizations and relationships.

The human resource audit may include:

- Organizational structure.
- Numbers and deployment of staff.
- Contracts/job descriptions/flexibility.
- Staff skills and capabilities.
- Human resource recruitment agency and relationships.

A comprehensive, objective audit should highlight where the organization's core competences lie – that is, those strengths which give it a competitive edge. This allows a more rational judgement of its potential to exploit opportunities.

Organizations do not operate in isolation, and there are a variety of supplementary theories and analyses which give further insight into resource capability in the retail context, four of which are value chain analysis, resource-based theory, network theory and, most widely known, SWOT analysis. Value chain analysis (see Chapter 7) focuses on achievement of competitive advantage through organizational competences, and helps to show where the organization can add value and create cost savings in business and supply chain processes.

Resource-based theory of the firm focuses on the various resources, capabilities and core competences within organizations, which will allow it to compete effectively (Cox, 1996). Dynamic capabilities are created over time and may depend on the organization's past use of resources (Barney, 1991). Sustainable competitive advantage depends on the ability and creativity of the organization in acquisition, combination and deployment of resources to yield productivity or value advantages. The resources which are a source of sustainable value are those which are difficult to copy because they lie within organizational activities and routines which represent core competences. Competitive advantage is dependent upon the ownership or acquisition of superior rent-earning, unique resources and relationships. The outsourcing of functions can be seen, therefore, as a means of accessing the resource base (and hence core competences) of other organizations to create sustainable value. A company with specific core skills in logistics should contract internally for the use of these skills, but complementary skills such as merchandising or human resource management might be better contracted out on a partnership basis, securing access to the resource base of partnership organizations. Unrelated skills such as car park maintenance would be outsourced on an 'arm's length' basis.

The network perspective assumes that organizations depend on resources controlled by other firms. Access to these resources is gained by interactions with these firms, forming value chain partnerships and networks.

Network theory focuses on creating partnerships based on trust, cross-functional teamwork and inter-organizational co-operation (Ford, 1997). Rather than one organization gaining competitive advantage over another, it is more a case of one network competing against another (Christopher, 1997). Again, non-core organizational activities are outsourced but efficiencies and the effectiveness of the network are regarded as essential for organizational success.

SWOT (Strengths, Weaknesses, Opportunities and Threats) analysis is a widely used means of rationalizing and prioritizing the outcomes of environmental analysis and the resource audit. Firstly, the main strengths and weaknesses of the organization, highlighted through the resource audit, are listed. Then the main opportunities and threats for the organization, revealed by analysis of the external and competitive environment, are summarized (see Box 4.4).

The SWOT analysis can be further refined by matching core competences to the key environmental trends and weighting according to the potential level of effect – positive or negative – on the organization. Even after refinement, the SWOT analysis remains a subjective tool; nevertheless, it remains a well-used aid to strategy which is also used at a functional level. For example, a SWOT analysis is frequently carried out as part of the marketing planning process.

Strategic choice

Generic strategies

Traditionally, retailers have three main strategic choices (Michael Porter in Johnson and Scholes, 1999). Firstly, they can focus on cost, driving down organizational costs through streamlining their operations, logistics and other functions. This cost efficiency can be used either to create sufficient margin to provide quality products and services, or to drive down prices and create volume throughput. This cost focus has

---

Box 4.4   Sample SWOT analysis

Strengths

- Low turnover of permanent staff.
- Located near motorway junction.
- Three million people within 1 hour drive time.
- Growth in sales over the last 3 years.
- Brand image.
- Creative organization.

Weaknesses

- Low sales November–March.
- Decline in profitability.
- Growing crime figures.
- Training of temporary staff.
- Joint marketing.
- Increased turnover in managers.

Opportunities

- Growth of population within 1 hour drive time.
- Increase in market share.
- Increase profitability.
- Non-store retailing.
- Expansion into entertainment, leisure, takeaway.

Threats

- Expansion of retail/entertainment park nearby.
- Legislation on e-commerce, packaging and waste, disability discrimination.
- Recession forecast.
- Takeover by global retail group.

---

created success for a great many retailers, including the UK's Tesco, Germany's Aldi and the USA's Wal-Mart.

Secondly, retailers can differentiate their offer, creating value for their customers in the retailer brand itself. Here the organization's efforts are concentrated on achieving an offer which is different from those of other retailers, thereby attracting customers who are willing to pay a premium price for added value.

Many retail organizations have benefited from this strategy, among them fashion retailers Next and French Connection (see retailer profile below), department stores such as Harrods and Harvey Nichols, and food retailers such as Fortnum & Mason.

Thirdly, retailers can focus on a highly targeted market segment, directing organizational efforts to filling the needs of a known and predetermined group of customers, using either a low cost base or differentiation depending on the segment. Smaller retailers with limited resources can develop using this strategy, and during the 1990s larger retailers have used 'focus' as a means of developing successful targeted versions of their 'mother' retail format – for example, Tesco Express and Tesco.com.

A fourth option, which is currently pursued by some large retail groups, is to pursue simultaneously all three strategies under the guise of differing retailer brands. This is facilitated by the growth in multichannelling (see Chapter 7), in highly detailed customer and segment information, and in ways to shop – including by foot, online, mail order, TV and mobile phone. However, there is a risk that cost focus in one subsidiary of the business will compromise the differentiated quality brand of another subsidiary.

Piercy (2001) claimed that *revolutionary* strategy is about *breaking free*. This means that organizational strategists should free themselves from management tools and tactics such as TQM, business re-engineering and efficient consumer response, because these focus on operations – no substitute for leadership and visionary strategic direction. It means that strategy is about breaking free of industry 'rules' and 'dogma', because customers don't know the 'rules' anyway. The term 'breaking free' really means that strategists:

- should embrace rather than fear change;
- should not be confined by current operational issues;
- should be careful not to be over-influenced by trendy management tools and theories;
- should not be over-reliant on performance indicators – which reflect only past performance;
- need to understand the core competences of the organization;
- have to think laterally to apply these core competences to add value to the business and build differentiation from the competition.

It is important here to distinguish between corporate strategy and marketing strategy. The former relates to the direction taken by the organization and the latter relates this to the market situation. However, in many market-orientated commercial organizations such as retailers there is a strong correlation between the two, and then corporate strategy may incorporate strategic marketing elements such as format development, market entry, market penetration and diversification of market activities (see Chapter 5).

Expansion strategies

There are a variety of strategies which can be employed to grow the retail business. The product–market expansion grid relates growth opportunities to the organization's present and potential products and markets. It is outlined and discussed further in Chapter 5. McGoldrick (2002) summarizes the major growth vectors for retail organizations under the headings:

- Existing proposition.
- New products/services.
- New segments.
- Geographical development.
- New channels.
- New formats.

Each direction of growth offers scope for expansion on a continuum from the existing operational platform through related activity to a new operational platform (see Figure 4.1). Expansion of a nature related to the core retail offer (which houses the core competences of the organization) is less risky than expansion into an operational platform which is new to the organization.

Expansion of core operational platform is where the existing proposition grows market share through organic growth, that is, through investment in growing the current business; or by acquiring share through acquisition, merger or other methods of expansion, bringing the new business into line with the core business. Non-organic growth is likely to require adaptations to the core business, which inter-relate with other growth vectors such as format modification and channel development, in order to integrate diverse operational platforms successfully.

New segment development involves developing, profiling and targeting new consumer and organizational segments. A fashion retailer could, for example, extend into childrenswear and menswear. A more radical strategy would entail moving into unrelated segments such as uniforms or workwear.

New products/services development has been the focus of much recent retail strategy, as new merchandise and an extended service

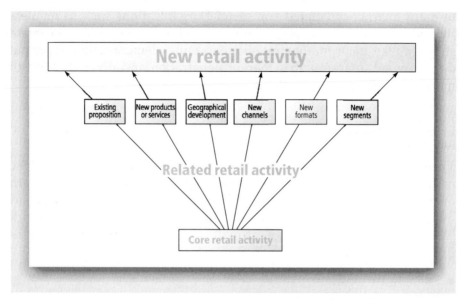

Figure 4.1 Growth vectors.

offering exploits the potential of current markets. Simple examples include extended opening of grocery stores and addition of food or beverages in non-food retailers such as bookshops and travel agents.

Format modification and development is a further focus of retail strategy in which styles of retailing are tailored to the needs of customer segments. Examples include off-price stores and factory outlet units offering excess or experimental stock at value prices.

Channel strengths can be exploited in the development of new retail activity – Tesco, for example, made use of its national store network to rapidly roll out its e-tail format, then used its online platform to develop its range of producer–customer and wholesaler–customer distributed goods.

Geographical development involves growth of market share through movement into adjacent areas and regions, and more radically, into international or global expansion.

There are many links among the various growth vectors. Segment development will normally require development of new products and services; channel and segment development may be inter-related, as may format, segment and product/service development.

Evaluating strategies

Strategic alternatives need to be assessed for their strategic fit with the current organizational operations. Does the strategy exploit organizational strengths and extend use of core competences? Does it compensate for organizational weaknesses or add to existing competences? Does it fit with the organization's mission? Some of the analytical tools outlined in other chapters of this book can also be used. For example, portfolio analysis (see Chapter 5) can be used to show where a new format fits with the current portfolio of formats. Life cycle analysis (see Chapter 5) can be used to indicate whether a strategy is liable to extend or renew the life cycle of a format or product group. Value chain analysis (see Chapter 7) can be used to assess where a strategy adds to the value system.

The feasibility of implementing various potential strategies can be assessed and compared to facilitate choice. This can be done by estimating relative costs of implementation and deciding such factors as whether and how the organization is capable of funding the strategy, whether it can be implemented by the existing organization and the extent of structural change that will be needed. The acceptability of implementing the various potential strategies can also be compared in terms of stakeholder expectations, profitability, and financial, corporate and environmental risk.

Location strategy

Retailing is about delivering to the customer the right products or services in the right quantities, at the right time, in the right place. Retail location, therefore, is fundamental to the success of the business.

Retail location is important to customers, who take the location of the store into consideration when making the decision of where to buy. For frequently bought goods such as groceries, customers tend to choose the closest shop (to home or work); whereas for shopping goods such as clothes, or speciality goods, customers are influenced by a variety of factors such as distance to travel, cumulative attractiveness of the town or shopping centre in terms of the total retail and entertainment offer, access, availability and cost of car parking and other ancillary facilities.

The investment made in building, leasing and shopfitting a retail unit, and the length of time retailers are tied into a lease – in some cases 10 or more years – means that changing location is difficult, time-consuming and expensive. The research and comparison of catchments, trading areas and site specifics can aid the identification of sites with current and future trading potential, through which a retailer can develop a sustainable advantage over competitors.

Location is an essential strand of corporate strategy which has to be considered in an integrated manner when expanding a retail business.

Location and methods of expansion

The three main methods of expansion are:

- Organic growth.
- Mergers/acquisitions.
- Strategic alliance.

Organic growth is investment channelled from the financial capability of the current organization into development of organizational capability – for example, to fund the development and roll-out of formats, horizontal or vertical integration and international growth. Growth tends to be slow or steady, and the organization retains autonomy, decision-making control and benefits from development of new areas of competence, while avoiding the difficulties of integrating differing organizational cultures and management systems which are experienced by organizations growing through acquisition or merger. However, rapid organic growth is possible where there is access to capital, by, for example, raising money through issuing extra shares rights to investors (Guy, 1994).

From a locational perspective, there are two major types of organic growth. Local and regional expansion from a single outlet, termed contagious diffusion, describes the early growth experience of long-established retailers which were geographically confined by transportation and distribution networks. It is the expansion method chosen by many small retail businesses, but has also been used by dominant retailers such as Wal-Mart (Birkin et al., 2002). The second type, hierarchical diffusion, is the growth route for many established retail organizations which open outlets in major cities and towns. J Sainsbury's entry into Scotland is an example. Stores were opened in rapid succession in Glasgow, Edinburgh, Aberdeen and Dundee – Scotland's four largest cities. Smaller stores were opened in regional town centres, and 'local' stores built to serve less populous communities as J Sainsbury's progressed its expansion. Both strategies can be deployed simultaneously by rolling out operations in selected large urban centres and expanding outwards by contagious diffusion.

Merger and acquisition offers a route to growth in market share and market dominance in addition to rapid entry of new product and market areas. A merger is where two retail organizations come together to form a combined operation, whereas acquisition describes the action of one retailer buying more than a 50 per cent share of another. Both methods have been widely used by retailers competing in the international retail market, such as Tesco, Ahold and Casino, which benefit from the acquisition, across diverse markets, of sources of established expertise, knowledge, property portfolio, contact and supply networks in addition to the customer base.

Tesco's expansion into Scotland, in competition with J Sainsbury's, was accelerated through acquisition of Wm Low & Co, a regionally dominant grocery multiple, and established the organization as a main player in the Scottish market both physically and in the minds of the Scottish consumer. Stricter planning policy came into force at about the same time, which also made organic growth through new-build operations more expensive and time-consuming. Wal-Mart used this method of international expansion when it acquired the chain of ASDA superstores to secure entry to the UK market. While access to a wide geographical coverage in the UK 'fit' Wal-Mart's ambitions for global expansion, the property portfolio offered the potential for expansion of existing superstores to ASDA–Wal-Mart supercentres. The ASDA mix of successful clothing and non-food merchandise categories with groceries also resembled that of the parent company. In addition, it could be argued that there was also a psychological 'fit', because ASDA was one of the superstore pioneers in the UK, with a long-established and popular reputation among its customers for good value at low prices; indeed, its 'every day low pricing' strategy also matched that of the parent company.

One of the main problems with acquisition is the merging of organizational cultures and styles of management, and this is exacerbated by the prospect of rationalization of activities and closure of outlets, which creates job uncertainty. Where organizations merge voluntarily the potential for organizational conflict is reduced due to the focus on synergistic benefits of the merger. However, rationalization is a common feature post merger and acquisition, particularly where the organization is left with two or more competing stores, which affects potential profitability. In the case of Wal-Mart, where the parent company has a reputation as a 'category killer' which has opened seven ASDA–Wal-Mart supercentres between 2000 and 2002, rationalization remains a possible future scenario. Future merger or acquisition between grocery majors in the UK is likely to bring a level of monopoly which would force rationalization through the actions of the Competition Commission.

Strategic alliances, where two or more organizations come together to complete a project, to wield combined power or to gain synergy from the combination of diverse organizational competences and assets, are a growing feature of retailing, aided by implementation of principles of relationship marketing and facilitated by enhanced communication capability. There are three main types of strategic alliance:

1 *Loose relationships* – collaborative networks and alliances to exploit a market opportunity or to combat a market threat. Examples are buying groups such as the WorldWide Retail Exchange (WWRE) and

GlobalNetXchange (GNX). The WWRE acts as an independent organization operating on behalf of a large number of major retail members, such as Kingfisher and Tesco, with the aim of improving cost efficiency (McGoldrick, 2002). GlobalNetXchange, a similar operation, operates on behalf of another group of large retail organizations, including J Sainsbury and Carrefour.

2 *Contractual relationships* – subcontracting of licences and franchises. The former is where the right to produce or distribute a product is granted for a fee; the latter involves a contract to a franchisee to produce, distribute or sell merchandise or services, while the franchisor maintains and markets the brand. In-store franchising (or concessions) is where a retail or service organization leases floorspace within an existing store format such as a superstore or department store.

There are four main types of franchise (Stern and Stanworth, 1988):

(a) Manufacturer–dealer. In this relationship the manufacturer is the franchisor and the dealer sells to the consumer. Cars and petrol manufacturers have traditionally used this method of distribution.

(b) Manufacturer–wholesaler. The manufacturer is the franchisor while the wholesaler acts as franchisee, selling to retailers. Examples are cola and beer manufacturers.

(c) Wholesaler–retailer. Voluntary chains such as Mace and Spar are examples. The parent organization offers marketing, distribution and merchandising support.

(d) Business format. The parent company allows the franchisee to sell its products or services, and provides an established format together with help and support in setting up business.

Franchising allows rapid expansion through the utilization of the financial and human resources of franchisees, although there is some loss of control, together with concomitant reduction in costs, of implementing standards and procedures.

3 *Formalized ownership/relationships* – joint ventures and consortia where two or more organizations set up a jointly owned organization, to facilitate expansion or exploit a market opportunity. In many cases this may be the only feasible method of entering an international market, for example Wal-Mart's initial entry into Mexico and Japan, and McArthur Glen's entry into the UK with factory outlet centres. In Wal-Mart's case the 1991 expansion in partnership with Mexican retailer Cifra was followed 6 years later by acquisition. The Cifra name was replaced by Wal-Mart de Mexico.

A joint venture also minimizes risk when diversifying into new product markets, for example when J Sainsbury moved into the DIY market with GB Inno and the clothing market with Bhs, to develop Homebase and Savacentre respectively.

Catchment definition and site selection

The catchment is the area from which a town centre, a shopping centre or a store draws its customers. Typically, the higher the cumulative attraction of the centre, the further customers will travel to shop there. Cumulative attraction comprises the number, variety and quality of shopping provision plus, increasingly, alternative opportunities to spend or do business – including leisure, sporting, entertainment and hospitality venues. Ancillary facilities also make a town or shopping centre attractive to shoppers. Particularly important are access, availability and cost of car parking, and toilet facilities. However, pedestrianization (in the case of a covered shopping centre, type/quality of flooring and décor); associated street furniture and signage; lighting; cleanliness and provision for waste; security; greenery and events add to overall attraction.

Edge/out-of-town retail developments such as regional shopping centres, retail parks, transport retail outlets and factory outlet centres attract custom from multiple catchments, defining catchment in terms of drive time, drive by or customer flow, rather than spatially. For example, a retail park located close to a busy motorway will have access to tens of millions of potential customers per year; an alternative location would be where there are millions of potential customers available in a number of city centres within 1 or 2 hours drive time.

The catchment of e-tailers, potentially unlimited, is being defined in a variety of ways, for example by the number of 'click-throughs' on the website, or through the weblinks and portals with which they are associated. In addition, customer access to and usage of e-tail sites is currently confined by a variety of factors. These include physical delivery limitations, for example delivery to cities or urban areas only (see also Chapter 7), currency limitations (e.g. payments made in dollars only, or purely by credit card) and language limitations (websites accessible for users of only one language).

There are a variety of methods which have been developed to aid catchment definition and location decision making, and given the importance of the location decision in terms of success or failure of the business, most retailers use more than one method.

One of the easiest ways to define a catchment is to ask potential customers where they have travelled from and plot the results on a map. Known as customer spot mapping, this widely used method requires a representative sample of all customers (over time) in order to accurately estimate the catchment area.

There are a number of traditional methods of defining a catchment which make use of secondary data. Among the earliest is the law of retail gravitation, developed by William Reilly (1931). Reilly's law relates catchment of a potential retail site to the population size of competing centres and the distance between them. Converse built on Reilly's work to develop his Breaking Point model. The break point between two competing centres – that is, the point at which a person residing in an intermediate community would be likely to travel to one centre rather than the other – could be calculated as follows:

$$\text{Break point (miles from town A)} = \frac{\text{Distance between towns A and B (miles)}}{1 + \sqrt{\dfrac{\text{Population town B}}{\text{Population town A}}}}$$

A crude but simple method of estimating catchment size is by drawing the sphere of influence of the town and totalling the population of all the settlements which lie within it. In the example above, this can be done by drawing a circle, the radius of which lies between the centre of the town and the break point. A more accurate measure of the catchment would require similar calculations to be made between all competing settlements.

A more up-to-date gravity model is that of David Huff (1964), which determines the probability that a customer living in a particular area will shop at a particular store or shopping centre. According to Huff, this probability is related to the relative sizes of competing shopping centres, travel time to the centre and the type of merchandise being sought. The formula is:

$$\text{Probability}_{ij} = \frac{S_j/T_{ij}^b}{\sum\limits_{J=1}^{n} S_j/T_{ij}^b}$$

where:

Probability_{ij} = probability of a customer at a given point of origin i travelling to a shopping centre j

S_j = size of shopping centre j

T_{ij} = travel time or distance from customer point of origin to shopping centre

b = exponent to T_{ij} which reflects effect of travel time on different kinds of shopping trips.

The value of b is related to the type of merchandise and, because travel time is more important for convenience goods than shopping goods, is higher for shopping centres with a high proportion of convenience goods in their merchandise mix. The value of *b* is found through surveys of shopping patterns or from experience (Levy and Weitz, 1995).

Once catchments have been defined, they can be profiled to gauge relative attractiveness by analysing data on population size, structure and expenditure, road and public transport network, car ownership, rent, rates and development costs. This data can be collected from websites (such as www.open.gov.uk, www.dti.gov.uk, www.statistic. gov.uk and www.brc.org.uk) or from the wealth of statistical and other data held within city public library reference rooms.

More recently, the availability and refinement of complex data has led to the development of the wide range of methods which are currently used to find the best location for stores. Table 4.1 outlines the main methods used in determining retail location decisions today. In a study on the techniques employed by major retailers in the UK in 1998

Box 4.5   The Retail Saturation Index

The Retail Saturation Index (RSI) is a basic method of comparing the potential return within different urban locations. It is a means of calculating the potential sales per square foot of retail space for a retailer wanting to open a shop in a town, or within a catchment area. The population of the town or catchment area is multiplied by the annual expenditure on the category of goods the retailer wants to sell. This is divided by the total square footage of selling space for the category of goods in the town or catchment.

For example, the RSI for a retailer interested in selling widgets in Anytown can be calculated as follows:

Population of Anytown = 46 314
Annual per capita expenditure on widgets = £160.68
Retail floorspace for widgets in Anytown = 14 700 sq. ft

$$RSI = \frac{46\,314 \times £506.24}{14\,700} = £1595$$

The higher the RSI, the higher the likelihood of the retailer succeeding in the new location. There are, however, a number of drawbacks to the method, including the assumption that increased floorspace will decrease sales potential when it can increase the cumulative attraction of the town.

Table 4.1 Decision-making techniques for retail location

Technique	Description
Experience/subjective	Experienced retailer judges location potential through experience and 'gut feeling'.
Checklist	Retailer compiles a simple or complex checklist of important factors under headings such as Access, Population, Competition, Existing Specification, and Costs. Information compiled is used to compare the potential of sites.
Analogues	Potential of new stores/sites is estimated through comparison with existing and similar stores/sites.
Cluster/factor analysis	Location analyst makes use of statistical techniques to interpret complex data (e.g. catchment characteristics, turnovers, floorspace) in order to create a model which can be used as a benchmarking tool for future development
Gravity modelling	Gravity modelling is computer and data intensive – such models quantify the relationship between consumer movement and attractiveness of retail centres. Performance is forecast based on analysis of size and image of store, distance, population distribution and density.
Neural networks	Computer and data intensive, neural networks can be loaded with information on existing stores to analyse success factors which can then be applied to forecast the likely success of new sites.

Source: adapted from Hernandez and Bennison (2000).

(Hernandez and Bennison, 2000), it was found that most used experience, supported by one or more other techniques. Two-thirds made use of checklists and two-fifths made use of the more complex analytical techniques – analogues, cluster and factor analysis and gravity models. The most advanced, data-driven, knowledge-based techniques were used by a low percentage of retailers.

Further, it was found that the number of techniques used was related to the number of outlets operated by retailers, with most retailers operating less than 250 outlets reliant on three or less location techniques, while most retailers operating more than 750 outlets made use of up to six techniques. Usage of a variety of techniques was highest in the grocery, variety, public house and finance sectors of retailing.

Checklists are an easy way to compare store sites and they are used by most retailers to supplement intuition. They are used to collect and compare data on population size and profile; to assess town/site accessibility issues such as car parking, site visibility and public transport; to weigh up the amount of direct/indirect competition and cumulative attraction; to assess unit or site issues such as size of selling area, RSI, potential for expansion and costs.

Analogue models involve forecasting potential sales for a potential store through reference to trading data for an existing store in the retail organization's portfolio, which is similar in terms of size, trading area and location (Birkin et al., 2002). Alternatively, the retailer can define the key trading and locational criteria which underpin the performance of their leading store and attempt to replicate these in other areas.

Birkin et al. (2002) are strong advocates of the use of the gravity model, in its simple, aggregate form shown below:

$$S_{ij} = A_i \times O_i \times W_j \times f(c_{ij})$$

where:

S_{ij} = flow of people/money from residential area to shopping centre
O_i = measure of demand in area i
W_j = measure of attractiveness of centre
c_{ij} = measure of cost of travel, or distance between i and j
A_i = balancing factor related to the competition, which ensures all demand is allocated to centres in the region, using the following formula:

$$A_i = \frac{1}{\Sigma_j W_j \times f(c_{ij})}$$

This assumes that flows of expenditure between origin and destination are proportional to the relative attractiveness of destination in comparison with all other destinations, *and* that the flows will be proportional to relative accessibility of destination in comparison with all competing destinations.

Due to the complexity of data sources, Birkin et al. prefer the term spatial interaction model. They feel that retail analysts could customize the spatial interaction models available in some geographical information systems packages to take account of the complexity of retail markets and by doing so could forecast expenditure flows and revenue totals of a given location to a very accurate level.

Types of location

There are a number of locational classifications in simultaneous use by various agencies. The Institute of Grocery Distribution, for example, classifies location opportunities as:

- Purpose-built shopping centre.
- Traditional 'high street'.
- Local or neighbourhood centre.
- Edge of town (free-standing).

This classification at least identifies that location within town centres offers the choice of purpose-built and traditional high street locations, but it does not identify the similar choice at suburban and edge-of-town level, and out-of-town locations are not included.

Retail location opportunities are much more complex and a more mature classification of location opportunities was devised in 1994 by Clifford Guy (Table 4.2).

Table 4.2 Location choices for retailers

Location	Traditional retail status		
	Non-retail	**Unplanned retail**	**Planned retail**
Town/city centre	Ancillary uses	Traditional 'high street'	Infill or shopping mall
Inner suburban	Brownfield site	Retail ribbon	Infill or district centre
Outer suburban	Industrial estate	N/a	Free-standing or district centre
Edge/out of town	Greenfield site	N/a	Free-standing or district centre or shopping mall

Source: adapted from Guy (1994).

This classification has the advantage of relating location opportunities within non-retail, unplanned and planned retail use to spatial location, and serves as a reminder that retailers can consider less usual options in their quest for expansion. However, it neglects one viable option used by many retailers – in-store franchising (concessions). Table 4.3 details simple location strategy options for new build and property acquisition or rental.

New retail development is increasingly being directed towards the brownfield sites of former industrial premises and former industrial estates in outer suburban or edge-of-town locations.

Table 4.3 Location options for retailers

New-build options	Property acquisition or rental options
Greenfield	In store
Brownfield	In town
In town	In-town shopping centre
Suburban	Suburban shopping centre
District	District or neighbourhood shopping centre
Edge of town	Edge-of-town shopping centre
Out of town	Out-of-town shopping centre
	Retail park
	Factory outlet centre
	Regional centre

In- and out-of-town location

In-town location tends to suit retailers of shopping goods – those goods for which customers like to compare information on quality, styles and prices before buying. Locating within, or close to, other retailers with a similar or complementary merchandise range can be beneficial to new and existing retailers, as it increases the total attraction of the area. Similarly, locating near to a magnet store (a main destination retailer) with the same target market can bring rewards. Chocolate retailer, Thorntons, for example, successfully located many stores next to Marks & Spencer's outlets.

There are many environmental factors underpinning the growth of out-of-town retailing, which are discussed in Chapter 2. The growth in the suburbanization of towns and cities has caused people to move from walking to driving as a means of transport. UK car ownership levels have doubled in 25 years, and the road network linking towns and cities has also expanded to link the main population centres by dual carriageways and motorways. This enhanced mobility has led to a growing proportion of the population working and shopping in centres distant from their home. People are also more promiscuous in their shopping habits – where there are two or more superstores in one area, people will happily shop in one store one week and another the next, taking advantage of promotional offers. In addition to convenience, out-of-town shops attract due to easy access and free car parking, which is also a plus for suppliers and retail staff. Retailers also benefit from the lower cost of development and location in out-of-town sites.

Planning policy in the mid-1990s tightened guidance on out-of-town retail location to protect the vitality and viability of town centres, and to ensure the population of a wide range of shopping opportunities within an innovative and competitive retail industry (Fernie, 1996). More specifically, development within existing centres was encouraged, particularly those which were accessible on foot, while siting of comparison goods shopping was discouraged outside existing centres and along road corridors. Although edge- and out-of-town developments continued to be built, particularly on sites with existing planning permission, the policy has led to a distinct revival of many town centres, particularly regarding grocery provision.

Summary

Retail strategy is about corporate survival and prosperity in a changing retail environment. The strategic direction of most large retail organizations is usually encapsulated in a mission statement. Corporate objectives expand this into a series of explicit time-related goals against which organizational progress and achievements can be measured. These form the basis for setting objectives and planning in other operational areas such as marketing and human resource management.

Scanning the politico-legal, social, economic and technological environment will throw up a variety of opportunities and threats for retail managers to consider when developing organizational strategy. The key influences on the organization can be summarized in a PEST analysis, which can form the basis for strategic decision making.

The competitive environment can be analysed using the five forces approach, which considers the position of the retailer in relation to the threat of entrants to the market, the relative bargaining power of market suppliers and buyers, threat of substitutes to format or organization, and the degree of competitive market rivalry. Market analyses such as the product–market expansion grid, market positioning and growth–share matrix also help to assess and summarize the position of the retailer in the competitive market.

The resource audit is an objective assessment of organizational capability which will highlight where its core competences (those key strengths which have the potential to give a competitive edge) lie and will allow a rational judgement of its potential to exploit opportunities. As retailers operate increasingly in interdependent relationships with other retailers and organizations up and down the supply chain, it is also useful to apply to the results of the resource audit further analyses and theories such as value chain analysis, resource-based theory of the firm and network theory. The most common analysis applied is SWOT analysis, which identifies the main strengths, weaknesses, opportunities and threats for the organization.

Traditionally, retailers were confronted by three main choices of strategic direction, cost, differentiation or focus. However, all three are pursued by some large and complex retail organizations in the guise of various formats, and some theorists propose that the use of lateral thinking in applying core competences to add business value and build differentiation is the key to revolutionary strategy.

A variety of expansion strategies are highlighted through application of the product–market expansion grid to assess the organization's current and future products and markets. Following a more complex series of growth vectors derived from the product–market expansion grid, expansion strategy can take a series of directions related to the existing proposition, new products/services, new segments, geographical development, new channels and new formats. In each direction there is a continuum of potential development from closely related activity to new activity, with the risk increasing the further the strategy from the existing operational platform. Main methods of expansion include organic growth, merger and acquisition, and strategic alliances. The latter includes a range of alliances from loose networks and partnerships through to contractual arrangements such as franchises and, indeed, merger.

The strategies which are most likely to succeed are those which fit most closely with the current organizational direction and capabilities. Strategies can be evaluated and compared on a range of dimensions, the main three being suitability, feasibility and acceptability.

Location strategy forms a major strand of corporate retail strategy which is crucial due to the importance of location in customer choice, the level of investment in buying, leasing or building retail units, and the financial consequences of poor location decisions.

Catchments can be defined using a variety of methods, including subjective/intuitive judgement and customer spot mapping. Two simple methods using secondary data are based on Reilly's law and Huff's model. Catchments can be profiled and compared in a variety of ways to aid selection. Some, such as checklists and Retail Saturation Index, are methods which are simplistic and make use of locally or regionally available secondary data sources. Others, such as cluster/ factor analysis and gravity modelling, make use of computer programs to analyse and interpret multiple data sources from inside and outside the organization and to predict the likely success of new sites. Most retailers rely on more than one technique, but the more complex analytical techniques are used by a relatively small percentage of larger retail organizations.

Although there is a variation in the way location options are described, retailers are faced with a basic choice of locating within an existing retail format (whether it be in place or new-build), within a shopping centre, in a traditional high street, in a suburban or district centre, or locating on the edge of town or out of town.

Out-of-town location brings benefits to retailer and customer in terms of parking, car and delivery access, bulk buying and low costs, although planning permission is more difficult to obtain. In-town location gives better pedestrian access, access by a variety of means, more options for comparison shopping, and a greater variety of complementary service and entertainment facilities.

Review questions

1 Analyse and evaluate the mission statements of three leading retail organizations. What do they tell us about the strategic direction and the values of these organizations?
2 How does five forces analysis help to define the competitive environment of retail organizations?
3 Read through the material on the corporate web pages of one of the UK grocery majors (http://www.j-sainsbury.co.uk; http://www.asda.co.uk; http://www.tesco.com). Outline the organization's main strengths, weaknesses, opportunities and threats.
4 What is meant by the term 'growth vectors'? For a retailer of your choice, explain how it has expanded along at least two growth vectors.
5 Select and investigate the growth history of a major retail organization (many large retail organizations provide timelines or histories on their corporate web pages). What methods has the retailer used to expand its business?

References

Barney, J. (1991). Firm resources and sustained competitive advantage. *Journal of Management*, **11**, 99–120.

Birkin, M., Clarke, G. and Clarke, M. (2002). *Retail Geography and Intelligent Network Planning*. John Wiley, Chichester.

Christopher, M. (1997). *Marketing Logistics*. Butterworth-Heinemann, Oxford.

Converse, P. D. (1949). New Laws of Retail Gravitation. *Journal of Marketing*, **14**, 379–84.

Cox, A. (1996). Relationship competence and strategic procurement management. Towards an entrepreneurial and contractual theory of the firm. *European Journal of Purchasing and Supply Management*, **2**(1), 57–70.

Davies, G. (2002). E-selling by rules. *Retail Week*, 30 August 2002.

Fernie, S. (1996). The future for factory outlet centres in the UK: the impact of changes in planning policy guidance on the growth of a new retail format. *International Journal of Retail and Distribution Management*, **24**(6), 11–21.

Ford, D. (ed.) (1997). *Understanding Business Markets*. Academic Press, London.

Guy, C. (1994). *The Retail Development Process: Location, Property and Planning*. Routledge, London.

Hernandez, T. and Bennison, D. (2000). The art and science of retail location decisions. *International Journal of Retail Distribution Management*, **28**(8), 357–67.

http://www.asda.co.uk.

http://www.john-lewis-partnership.co.uk.

http://www.j-sainsbury.co.uk.

http://www.walmartstores.com.

Huff, D. L. (1964). Defining and estimating a trade area. *Journal of Marketing*, **28**, 34–8.

Johnson, G. and Scholes, K. (1999). *Exploring Corporate Strategy*. Prentice-Hall, Hemel Hempstead.

Levy, M. and Weitz, B. A. (1995). *Retailing Management*. Richard D. Irwin, USA.

McGoldrick, P. (2002). *Retail Marketing*. McGraw-Hill Education, Maidenhead.

Piercy, N. (2001). *Market-Led Strategic Change*, 3rd edn. Butterworth-Heinemann, Oxford.

Porter, M. (1980). *Competitive Strategy: Techniques for Analyzing Industries and Competitors*. Free Press, New York.

Reilly, W. J. (1931). *The Laws of Retail Gravitation*. Knickerbocker Press, New York.

Stern, P. and Stanworth, J. (1988). The development of franchising in Britain. *The NatWest Bank Review*, May, 38–48.

Part 2

Managing the Retail Supply Chain

5

The development of retail marketing

Introduction

Marketers have long recognized the place of retailers in the process of developing, distributing and selling goods and services which meet or exceed customer requirements. However, it is relatively recently that most retailers have realized:

- the value of marketing in maintaining a successful retail business in a rapidly changing market;
- their own key role in driving recent developments in the marketing of goods and services.

Traditionally, retailers have focused their efforts on the buying and merchandising of goods. However, understanding the concepts and tools of marketing is now vital to developing and maintaining a successful retail business. Major food retailers developed category management in the 1990s as they finally understood that customers buy goods in groups according to their needs satisfaction – a fact that was perceived with clarity by marketing theorists for decades. The value of building lasting supplier relationships is slowly being recognized and used to drive down distribution costs. The importance of understanding customers' changing needs – thinking beyond the store – is slowly being understood and is driving e-tail developments.

Even Marks & Spencer, the sleeping giant of British retailing, finally had to recognize the importance of their customers and marketing when their profits slumped in 1999, after a rapid series of moves which left loyal customers bewildered and disillusioned marketing experts questioning their strategy.

- They cancelled their long-standing supplier of clothes – causing thousands of redundancies – to reduce costs, ignoring the potential impact of negative publicity on their loyal customers for the cost gains from cheaper imports.
- They misunderstood the importance of the value/price relationship which had created customer loyalty and business success over decades. By allowing quality to slip, they broke their 'pact' with their traditional customers.
- They failed to recognize the demographics which would naturally increase their natural clientele in the next 20 years.
- They focused on fashion to compete in the crowded high street cheap-fashion scene – indicating an ignorance both of their customers' needs and of the changing fashion market.

Marks & Spencer's management were reacting to poor financial performance in the way of traditional retailers – tweaking the buying and merchandising of their goods. Many decisions were made to improve short-term financial performance and it was clear that Marks & Spencer misunderstood that the reasons for the fall in profits included plummeting levels of quality and disaffected customers, together with old-fashioned ideas regarding use of credit cards and advertising. The rise of fashion brands and off-centre value retailers, to which Marks & Spencer attributed many of their problems, tends to attract a younger and more fashion-brand-conscious clientele rather than hard-core Marks & Spencer shoppers. In the year 2000, this retailer finally appointed a Marketing Director.

The recognition of their key role in driving product and service development and delivery has led retailers to focus on streamlining the links and processes of the supply chain to achieve cost savings and improve competitive advantage. By 'owning' the final stage in the distribution channel, retailers can monitor buying trends and feed information down the channel to drive product generation from suppliers. The power retailers hold in the channel of distribution has grown with the application of IT systems which speed up distribution capability, and retailers have used this power to generate and grow strong national, international or global retail brands.

Retailers have come a long way from buying goods and 'setting out their stall' in terms of merchandising. There has been an evolution from this macro-marketing approach to micro-marketing – focusing on precisely defined market segments. This focus is further developing, supported by IT and database marketing, into the movement of mass customization – that is, creating the potential for selling unique product/service bundles to each customer. The fashion retailer of the future will know my shape, size and colouring, will show me how I will look in their garments and will customize them for me. They will suggest a range of accessories from their knowledge of my lifestyle and preferences. They will deliver them to my door and they will offer a wide range of associated services.

What is retail marketing?

One of the best definitions of marketing is:

> Marketing consists of individual and organizational activities that facilitate and expedite satisfying exchange relationships in a dynamic environment through the creation, distribution, promotion and pricing of goods, services and ideas.
>
> (Dibb et al., 2001)

Retail marketing is really the application of marketing concepts, theories and actions within the context of retail organizations. As such, the above definition explains that marketing consists of activities undertaken by individuals and managers which make exchange relationships easier and faster. This indicates that marketing, although a management process, is not just the role of managers, or the marketing department, but of the workforce, particularly those whose role is customer related. Therefore, 'internal' as well as 'external' marketing is important. For example, staff need to know the message and timing of advertisements in order to prepare themselves to respond to customer demands.

The term 'exchange relationships' recognizes that there can be a non-monetary element in the exchange transaction – for example, coupons or incentives for customers to introduce a friend to the company. The term also intimates that exchanges are made with non-end customers such as internal departments and external partners or suppliers. Certainly, this is a feature of successful retailers, in which close liaison is maintained both among stores, call centres and warehouses, and between retailers and their suppliers, in ensuring efficient consumer response (ECR).

The definition also recognizes that organizations, and marketing, exist in a dynamic, rapidly changing environment. In order to facilitate satisfying exchanges, marketing requires the creation, distribution, promotion and pricing of goods, all activities in which retail organizations are primarily engaged, and of services and ideas. Retailers are service organizations: they provide service to their customers in bringing together a collection and inventory of goods to buy, but also offer numerous services in adding value to the goods – for example, through bag packing or parcel wrapping, offering guarantees and credit, and so on.

Marketing, therefore:

- is a whole-business orientation;
- is customer-led;
- requires internal plus external customer fulfilment;
- is management-facilitated;
- requires integration of marketing effort;
- achieves organizational objectives – one of which is profit;
- rapidly responds in a changing environment.

There has been a recent rise in importance of marketing in retail organizations because of: increased competition with the advent of discounters, and globalizing retail formats; the advent of ECR initiatives in which organizations across the supply chain need to work together to satisfy the customer at lowest cost; improvements in technology, especially database/web marketing; the rise of the store brand to challenge manufacturers' brands in the marketplace (Collins, 1992).

Marketing environment

Organizations exist within a changing environment which influences their success or failure. These environmental influences include:

- Politics and law.
- Socio-demographics.
- Economics.
- Technology.
- Competitive environment.
- Organizational background.

Government policies and agencies clearly direct and implement the laws of the country, and retailers need to understand the direction of government policy in terms of various legal areas – for example, planning, employment law, health and safety, consumer law, and so on. An understanding of policy direction can give an organization the edge in adapting its own objectives. For example, some of the grocery majors, swiftly understanding the impact on their future store portfolio of changing government policy towards out-of-town retail developments in the late 1990s, moved to develop successful, alternative, targeted downtown supermarkets.

The economic environment influences the wealth, spending power and willingness of consumers to buy goods and services. In an era of prosperity, with low levels of unemployment, people may want to buy quality goods and services, whereas in recession, with high unemployment and uncertainty, people will focus on basics and value for money. In addition, international economic trends increasingly affect the success or failure of organizations, both because of interlinked financial and product markets and because large retail groups are vying for European and global dominance.

The social and demographic environment influences patterns of expenditure on goods and services. Social trends such as improved mobility and growth of international travel influences what and where customers will buy. Demographic trends influence both the types of goods and services bought (and the ratio between goods and services bought), and the workforce available for retailers to employ. For example, the ageing population has brought about a focus on services rather than products, and has brought about speculation on the

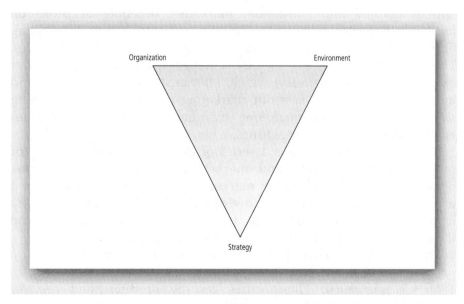

Figure 5.1 Organization, environment and strategy in equilibrium. *Source*: Collins (1992).

outlawing of ageism and raising of the retirement age, and in addition about the raising of barriers to immigration.

The technological environment has allowed the development of just-in-time systems, and wider application of home shopping, and has immensely shortened the time and cost of developing and bringing new products to market. It has necessitated managers to formulate objectives, strategies and tactics much more quickly – to think in 'Internet time', whether the organization is intent on innovation or copycatting successful innovations.

These influences shape the environment of organizations, but organizations have very little reciprocal influence. The triangle in Figure 5.1 represents an equilibrium between the organization, its strategy and the environment. When the environment changes, either the organization or its strategy – and probably both – need to change. When the environment is continually changing, therefore, the organization and its strategy will tend either to adjust incrementally to keep in balance, or eventually a crisis will occur, and the organization and its strategy will require major, transformational, change.

Marketing strategy and objectives

The corporate strategy and objectives form a strategic framework for marketing in an organization. The role of marketing as a departmental or integrative function is decided at corporate level. In an organization with a defined and substantial marketing function, decisions on marketing strategy and more specific and measurable, timed marketing objectives will be developed to support and meet corporate objectives. These will be formulated as part of a periodic marketing plan (for example, annual or 5-yearly) which, after analysis of the external and internal environments, sets out marketing objectives and marketing strategies, defines the marketing mix and tactics, and establishes evaluation and control procedures.

Marketing strategy entails a series of decisions about products (or product/service bundles) and markets which will exploit market opportunities. Although many market opportunities are spotted and exploited through market knowledge, networking and business instinct, there is a simple though useful aid to decision making called the product–market expansion grid (see Figure 5.2).

This grid categorizes opportunities under four headings:

1 *Market penetration.* This focuses on the products and services currently offered by the organization; opportunities are sought which will increase the organization's share of the market. There are a

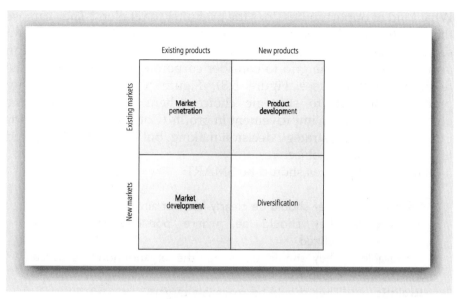

Figure 5.2 Product–market expansion grid. *Source*: **after Ansoff (1957).**

variety of ways in which this can be done, depending on the nature of the organization's business activities. It can be done by increasing the amount and scope of promotional activities – through advertising or sales promotions, for example. A change of pricing strategy can also increase penetration, as can making products more widely available within the current distribution network.

2 *Product development.* Here the focus is on changing the products and services offered by the organization, through increasing the range or through product/service modification or extension. Marketers can build brand recognition and use the brand to launch new products/ services, or to extend the product line through new additions. They can make current products more 'buyable' through the design of new or additional features.

3 *Market development.* This focuses the efforts of marketers on developing, profiling and meeting the needs of new segments of the market. This can be done by extending the range of the market into new areas, regions or countries, or by promoting products/services to a new category of users.

4 *Diversification.* Opportunities can be sought which are very different from those traditionally exploited by the organization, through buying a new business, or using the strength of the organization's brand to launch new products or services which meet the needs of a new market area. Normally, opportunities for diversification exploit the core competences of the organization and will be confined by its resource capabilities.

What kind of opportunities does the grid offer to retailers? They can use the grid to consider market opportunities for extending product and service range and markets as explained in points 1–4 above. They can also, however, use the grid to consider corporate opportunities for the retail organization (see Figure 5.3). Figure 5.4 illustrates another practical approach to strategic choice where the main corporate objective is long-term improvement in profits (Collins, 1992). Both grids can help marketing strategy decision making, but also constitute an aid to setting marketing objectives.

Marketing objectives should be SMART:

Specific	They should be clearly laid out aims.
Measureable	They should be, where possible, quantitatively defined.
Achievable	They should be within the organization's resource capability.
Realistic	They should be reachable targets.
Timed	At the end of the time-period you should be able to tell whether or not the objectives have been achieved.

Where the marketing strategy is focused on increasing volume of goods delivered through market penetration, an example of a marketing objective might be:

Increase market share by 10 per cent within the next 6 months.

At the end of 6 months the original and new market share can be compared, and the success of marketing activities in achieving the objective can be assessed.

Where marketing strategy focuses on market development, an example of a marketing objective might be:

Open five units in major UK factory outlet centres by the end of June.

Again, this is a clearly defined objective towards which marketing activities can be directed.

Market segmentation

A market is a set of actual and potential buyers of a product. Market segmentation involves:

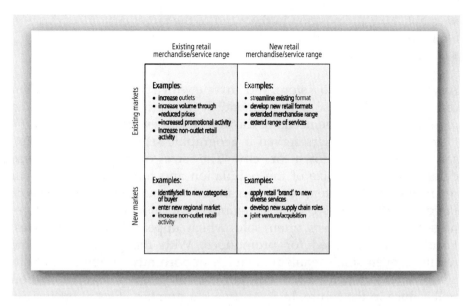

Figure 5.3 Examples of marketing strategy opportunities for retailers.

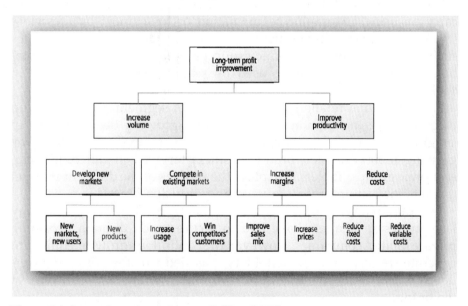

Figure 5.4 Strategic options. *Source*: **Collins (1992).**

- determining which segment or segments of the market that the organization can serve profitably;
- profiling the customers – building an understanding of their values and buying habits, and finding out where they are;
- positioning the organization's offer against competitors in the marketplace;

- establishing the position in the mind of the target customers through building brand identity;
- deciding on a coverage strategy.

Anyone can come into a store, and anyone with a computer and modem can enter a website, so why segment? Segmentation helps to build the retail offer around the needs of the key customer group or groups.

Traditionally, retailers served a geographic segment of the market, serving a village, town or city. The size of the segment was determined by the size of the population and hinterland. Traditional retail organizations tend to be organized around the regions served. Prices are often set according to regional or local levels of competitiveness and products are often sold which appeal to regional tastes. Local media are used for promotions. With the growth of online retailing, even small retailers have the opportunity to operate nationally or internationally, and the importance of geographic segmentation will reduce in the future. In St Andrews, a number of retail businesses sell golf merchandise to visiting golfers and tourists. Now they can sell to golfers worldwide. These retailers have to decide whether to carry on using geographic segmentation or to segment by lifestyle – travellers, golfers, Internet users – and/or by demographic variables such as income, socio-economic group or age. Examples of segmentation variables which can be used by retail marketers are shown in Table 5.1.

Fashion design retailers have made use of segmentation to develop their markets. In addition to entering and growing their presence in geographical markets, they developed their product markets by growing their 'diffusion brand' business targeted at different socio-economic groups. Table 5.2 displays the profiles of the different product markets for couture, ready-to-wear and diffusion brands.

In order to develop the profitable markets for diffusion brands, many fashion design retailers have had to secure funds through becoming private limited companies. However, the continuous growth required to generate returns for shareholders has led to the risk of over-development of these markets, in turn undermining the exclusivity of the brand.

Tesco is an example of a large retail organization which has successfully changed from using geographic segmentation to behaviour segmentation, building successful formats around the way people buy (convenience shop, work shop, one-stop shop, e-shop, etc.). Everyone shops for groceries, so that demographic segmentation would have been inadvisable. Behaviour segmentation in this case recognizes the growing trend for individuals to shop in different ways at different times. The same person on one occasion may want to grab a sandwich

Table 5.1 Examples of market segmentation variables

Demographic segmentation

● Age	18–24, 25–35, 35–50, 50+, etc.
● Sex	Male, female
● Family life cycle	Young single, young married no children, married young children, married older children, etc.
● Occupation	Unemployed, student, craftsman, retired, etc.
● Education	No qualifications, college graduate, university graduate, etc.
● Religion	Protestant, Jewish, Muslim, etc.
● Nationality	English, Scottish, Welsh, etc.
● Income	<£10 000, £10–20 000, £20–30 000, etc.

Geographic segmentation
● Country	GB, France, The Netherlands, etc.
● Region	South-East, South-West, North, etc.
● City size	Under 5000, 5–20 000, 20–50 000, 50–100 000, etc.
● Population density	Rural, semi-rural, suburban, urban
● Continent	North America, South America, Europe, Asia, etc.
● Climate	Hot dry, hot wet, temperate, desert, etc.

Psychographic segmentation
● Socio-economic group	1, 2, 3, 4, etc.
● Social class	Unemployed, working class, middle class, etc.
● Activities	Golfers, swimmers, theatre-goers, travellers, etc.
● Personality	Conservative, gregarious, competitive, etc.
● Lifestyle	Belongers, achievers, aspirers, etc.

Behaviour segmentation
● User status	Non-user, occasional user, frequent user, etc.
● Usage rate	Light user, medium user, etc.
● Purchase occasion	Occasional, regular, special occasion, etc.
● Buyer readiness stage	Unaware, aware, interested, desire to buy, etc.
● Benefits sought	Economy, quality, service, speed, etc.

---

and a ready meal for dinner from a town centre shop, and on another occasion may want to enjoy a leisurely monthly superstore shop. This eventually, and logically, resulted in organizational change, with groups of stores not managed regionally, but by format.

Profiling – understanding customer values

Finding out about the size and make-up of the segment and building up a profile of customers within it is the key to successful positioning and

Table 5.2 Product markets for couture, ready-to-wear and diffusion brands

Collection	Description	Examples
Couture	Targeted towards world's richest women Garments hand-made/made to measure Collection no more than 100 pieces Evening gowns cost upwards of £8000 Designer responsible for design Rarely profitable	Georgio Armani Couture Donna Karan Couture Kenzo Couture

Ready-to-wear	Targeted towards men/women in wealthy
	    social groups
	Garments sold off-the-peg
	Premium prices
	Marketed under a distinct brand name
	Designer shares design responsibility with
	    design team
	Net margins 25–50%
		Giorgio Armani –
		Le Collezione
		Donna Karan
		Kenzo

Diffusion	Targeted at middle retail market (e.g. B–C2)
	Marketed under a distinct brand name
	Mid-high prices
	Designer has minimal, often no
	    involvement in design
	Net margins are high, typically between
	    60% and 85%
		Emporio Armani
		DKNY
		Kenzo Jeans/Jungle

Source: after Moore et al. (2000).

branding. A variety of information on markets and customers can be found using secondary research, making use of reference materials, government and commercial statistical sources. Mintel Retail Intelligence, the Institute of Grocery Distribution (IGD), the Oxford Institute of Retail Management and the *Financial Times* all publish periodic market reports which retailers find useful. For example, the IGD publishes key account profiles of the leading grocery retailers in the UK.

Widely used secondary reference materials include:

- Social Trends.
- Economic Trends.
- Census of Population.
- Production Statistics.
- Business Monitor.
- Census of Distribution.
- Family Spending.
- Labour Market Trends.

A deeper understanding of customer needs and wants can be developed through primary research. For example, US retailer Eddie Bauer undertook research which identified four dimensions of customer relationship – spending level, channel preference, spending pattern and product preferences.

From the representative survey sample of 615 cases, four customer groups were identified and labelled as follows:

1 Too busy to shop – 22 per cent of sample, 28 per cent of revenue.
2 Professional shoppers – 16 per cent of sample, 24 per cent of revenue.
3 Stylish wannabe – 30 per cent of sample, 17 per cent of revenue.
4 Recreational shoppers – 32 per cent of sample, 31 per cent of revenue.

The customer group labelled 'too busy to shop' had little leisure time, did not like to shop and spent little time in comparison shopping. They were not particularly brand conscious or fashion orientated, but had a practical approach to clothing, looking for classics, comfort and an extended size range.

The 'professional shoppers' were both fashion and brand conscious, looking for the latest styles. These comparison shoppers looked for deals at department and speciality stores, and had enough confidence to mix and match outfits.

'Stylish wannabes' were not brand conscious, but shopped where clothes were stylish and trendy, although they were not particularly store-loyal. They liked help from salespeople to make decisions.

The fashion- and brand-orientated 'recreational shoppers' enjoyed shopping for trendy clothes, were less quality orientated and, being price conscious, shopped at discount stores.

Positioning

Positioning is about understanding and establishing the position of your retail brand in comparison to the relative positions of your competing retailers in the minds of your target customers, in terms of key dimensions such as price and quality (see Figure 5.5).

Which are the dimensions in which to establish a position? Examples include quality, value for money, value added, width of product range, reputation, convenience, level of service and level of credit. However, a comprehensive profile of the selected market segment (or segments) should include information on the criteria which govern target customers' choice of products within the proposed merchandise range.

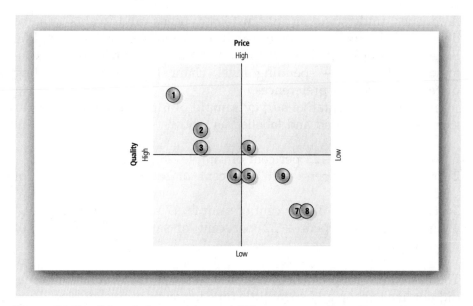

Figure 5.5 Possible relative positions of UK grocery retailers. *Key*: 1, Fortnum & Mason. 2, Marks & Spencer. 3, Sainsbury. 4, Tesco. 5, ASDA. 6, Safeway. 7, Aldi. 8, Lidl. 9, Somerfield.

Mapping the major grocers against the double demographic criteria of social class and age of housewife indicates reasonably clear demographic positioning (see Figure 5.6). Somerfield shoppers were distinctly older, and primarily from the lower socio-economic groups, than customers of Waitrose, Safeway and Sainsbury's, which left this retail organization vulnerable to competition from the hard discounters.

In the FCUK retail profile in Box 5.1, French Connection claimed that, rather than repositioning, the intention was to reframe the FC brand to add 'attitude' to what French Connection already stood for. In fact, it is possible to argue that what French Connection did was to change the criteria in which they were positioning the brand from price/quality to price/brand attitude. By doing so, this brand became clustered with more aggressive, design-led fashion brands in the minds of fashion shoppers, instead of being clustered with the more passive, mainstream fashion brands such as Gap, Next and Principles.

Understanding the relative positions of competing retailers helps a retail organization to decide its desired position, to establish it in the minds of its target customer group through branding and promotion, and to defend or redefine it as markets change.

Positioning helps to establish the organization's unique selling proposition (USP) – that is, what it is that makes it different from other

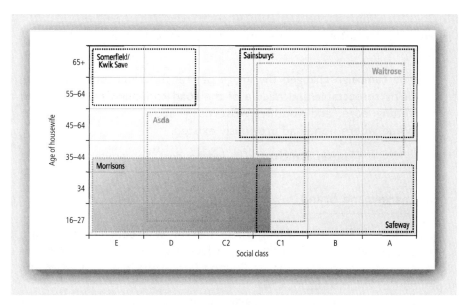

Figure 5.6 Competitive demographic overlap. *Source*: **created using base data from Taylor Nelson Sofres Superpanel, 8 March 1998.**

retailers, and which will bring in the customers. In the case of French Connection, the 'in-yer-face' slogan, which in the minds of customers was applied to the attitude of the merchandise, became the USP.

Positioning in a physical sense is also a useful tool for retailers (see also section on 'Place'). For comparison goods – merchandise for which customers visit several retailers to compare quality, prices, styles – location close to an established retail brand with a similar or complementary range of merchandise can bring customers of the right demographic or buying behaviour profiles. Thorntons established itself as a high street confectionery retailer by establishing small units close to M&S outlets to attract volume ABC1 shoppers. Space NK locates close to Whistles to attract the high-spending fashion brand shoppers. In Edinburgh, French Connection opened on George Street, distancing itself physically from the high street fashion brands located on Princes Street, instead positioning itself with the design-led fashion brand retailers located on the street which ends at Harvey Nichols new department store.

In the electronic shopping sphere, positioning via links and web-rings is a trend which is likely to continue. For example, e-tailers of investment-related goods, such as art and photography (eyestorm.com), business travel (travelstore.com), fine wines (Virginwines.com) and upmarket foods (lobster.co.uk), make offers to the moneyed investors on the interactive investors members database.

Box 5.1   Retailer profile – French Connection UK

> The campaign changed the image of French Connection from being respectable and middle of the road to being dangerous, cutting edge, and youthful. Advertising above has created a brand where none had previously existed.
>
> (Tamsin Blanchard, *The Independent*, September 1999)

The market and brand

In the late 1980s, the fashion retail market was concentrated, with ownership and power dominated by a few large but unexciting fashion brands. Marks & Spencer and the Burton Group together had nearly 40 per cent of the market.

The recession of the late 1980s produced customers who were cautious both in their spending and in their choice of merchandise. The focus was on value for money and choice. Retailers developed their ranges on similar lines and there was little or no product or brand differentiation.

At the same time, there was an unprecedented increase in competition within the fashion retail market, with the expansion of fashion retailers such as Jigsaw, Hobbs, Karen Millen, Kookai and Morgan.

After the recession, during the period from 1992 to 1997, the UK fashion market was characterized by a low increase in spending. Over the 5 years, expenditure increased only from £10.5 billion to £13.5 billion.

The position of French Connection in fashion retailing

During the recession, French Connection's profits slumped by 35 per cent. Management response was to concentrate on new product development and to differentiate the stores and the brand. Merchandise ranges were broadened and stores redesigned with white walls, oak floors and simple merchandising to attract customers with the 'allure of sophistication'.

The refurbishment and range development undertaken in 1996 unfortunately did not have a significant consumer impact. Sales were static and profits in decline. As a brand, French Connection did not rate with potential customers – it had dropped off their shopping list.

The decision was made to build a distinct 'must have' brand – to give customers a reason for shopping at French Connection which went beyond mere clothes shopping.

Fashion retailer advertising

At the time, UK advertising campaigns in the sector were very similar, making it difficult for customers to differentiate between the ethos of the various brands – there was a lack of core brand identity. Advertising focus was on the products – but due to lack of product differentiation to consumers, advertisements appeared almost interchangeable. There was no attempt to engage the customers emotionally, to build emotional ties with the brand itself, rather than the merchandise.

FC strategy

Instead of conventional marketing strategy in which fashion advertising features and sells the clothes, not the brand, the French Connection strategy favoured 'disruption' – a focus on the brand and what the brand stands for, rather than the merchandise. It was felt that in the competitive fashion retail market, brand image had to transcend the product.

Advertising objectives

The advertising objectives were threefold. In the short term, the objective was to increase store footfall, increase awareness and interest in visiting the stores, and increase sales. In the longer term, the objective was to encourage customer reassessment of the brand – to build an FC attitude. At the same time, it was the intention to attract media attention and support in order to maximize the impact on the consumers of a limited budget.

The FC shopper profile

The profile of the target FC shopper was:

● mid-20s to late 30s;
● fashionable – not fashion victim;
● prepared to pay extra for design and differentiation;
● image literate;
● 40 per cent male (but males had low brand recognition level);
● campaign not to alienate older customers.

Positioning the brand

Rather than repositioning, the intention was to reframe the FC brand, to add 'attitude' to what French Connection already stood for. The campaign had to communicate the following values to FC customers:

● unpredictability;
● humour;

- *not* anti-establishment;
- daring;
- independent;
- not told how to wear the ranges.

The focus of the advertising campaign was on the brand *not* the product. The campaign had to contrast or stand out from other fashion advertising, and part of the purpose of the campaign was to generate controversy and intense media coverage and discussion.

The advertising campaign

The campaign slogan, aimed to be provocative and to generate customer and media attention and interest – was 'FCUK fashion'. There was no French Connection logo. The intention was to create a hidden language, a sense of being 'in the know' among customers of French Connection.

Media selection had to reach the target customer group, but had to be unexpected and break conventions. The style press was used as the backbone of the campaign in order to attract the key fashion opinion-formers, and to move this high street fashion brand into designer domain. Outdoor posters were selected as an unconventional medium for fashion advertisements. The outdoor poster content was integrated with the press advertisements in order to reinforce the impact of the new image. Each poster site was chosen for visibility, with positioning on the main route to shopping centres. Forty per cent of the budget was spent on only five London City sites. These included the largest ever site in Europe (240 ft long) at Vauxhall Cross, and the largest Underground poster (140 ft long).

The use of FCUK, predictably, brought complaints from some members of the public to the Advertising Standards Authority (ASA), and French Connection had to withdraw their original slogan, and had to use the initials in a context in which they could not be misinterpreted. The second stage of the campaign, including the new slogans 'FCUK advertising' and 'FCUK fashion', was developed with a 3-month press, poster and cinema campaign. The ASA insisted upon French Connection UK on adverts. Although there were 26 complaints about the new campaign, it had ASA approval.

By spring 1998, customers had become accustomed to the FCUK slogan and were comfortable within the meaning. The next stage was to take FCUK to the limit with word association:

    ... french connection me
    ... french connection someone
    ... french connection yourself
    ... what the french connnection

The campaign included customers as advertisers. The campaign T-shirts proved popular with customers, offered substantial brand coverage and brought in significant revenue. In one year, sales of T-shirts were:

FCUK fashion	70 000
FCUK advertising	40 000
French connection me	50 000
French connection someone	30 000
French connection yourself	30 000
What the french connection	40 000

The income from T-shirt sales was £5.2 million – £3 million profit, which covered the £1.6 million cost of the advertising campaign.

The impact of the advertising campaign

The campaign had a spectacular impact on sales. After removing the effect of store openings and allowing for inflation, sales increased by £2.6 million within the first 7 months of the campaign. Sales in the 6 months prior to the campaign had been down £125 000. For the year 1997/1998, when average UK growth was 3 per cent for the sector, French Connection sales increased 17 per cent. For the period April 1997 to May 1998, the company identified sales increases between £6 and £8 million. Both share price and earnings per share rose substantially.

The public relations effect of the campaign was extensive. Forty features appeared in the national press and magazines with a media value of £441 688.

The relationship between French Connection and the opinion-formers of the style press improved, with good coverage and commendation for the advertising campaign.

In terms of building the brand, the success of the advertising campaign was undeniable. Among consumers, French Connection achieved the highest levels of brand awareness and respect among high street fashion retailers. The perceptions of customers were altered, with FCUK seen as a real brand, and new awareness and interest stimulated among men. The brand affinity is underlined by the sale of 260 000 basic T-shirts at a premium price, in a one-year period.

There were further positive results of the campaign. Staff morale improved due to the success of the campaign and the 'talk factor' generated by it. The calibre of applicants for employment improved. In the broader context, there was an increase in the number of wholesale customers and demand for the brand gave access to the best retailers. The success in building loyalty to the brand beyond the merchandise allowed line extension into make-up and accessories.

Retail branding

If positioning is made easier through identifying target customers' perception of the retail offering relative to competing offerings on the desired dimensions, branding is the way to establish the position in the minds of customers. Successful branding, based on a consistent offering at the desired position within those dimensions, will build retail success.

A brand is a *'name, term, sign, symbol or design or a combination . . . intended to identify the goods or services of one seller or group of sellers and to differentiate them from those of competitors'* (Gilbert, 1999).

But branding goes beyond this. Customers use brands as an extension of their identity, to communicate their lifestyle, personality and attitude to others. They *'select the brand or brands which fits the image with which they wish to be associated'* (Piercy, 1997). This is why a strong and favourable brand identity will allow a retailer to extend the product range under the brand name. Piercy further claims that *'a brand is something that is bought by a customer'* and that *'the customer becomes the brand'*. Customer involvement with brands means that, in branding, the retailer establishes an 'expectational pact' with the target segment. Hence, a customer at Tesco will not expect to be ripped off because of brand commitment to value for money; a customer at Whistles will expect high prices and high-quality, fashionable wear; a customer at M&S will expect to buy underwear which will wear and last well. Breaking the pact will weaken or destroy the brand.

Growth and development of retailer brands

The rise of the retail brand is commensurate with the shift in balance of power between manufacturer and retailer over the last 20–30 years. Traditionally, retailers were the agents for manufacturer branded products. The suppliers of fast-moving consumer goods (FMCGs) would market their product to the consumer and consumers would buy from the retailer stocking it. As retailers moved from small family businesses to national or international companies, retailers began to move into new product development to meet the needs of an enlarged customer base, developing private brands.

Initially, private-label brands were 'generic' in nature, with a no-frills offering. Not surprisingly the launch of such brands, notably by Carrefour in France and defunct chains such as Victor Value and Shoppers' Paradise in the UK, were a response to increased price competition and the high inflation environment of the 1970s. In the grocery sector, the market began to change by the early 1980s. It will be shown later in Chapter 7 that Tesco's launch of Operation Checkout in the late 1970s gained market share, but exposed the inadequacies of its distribution system, which was supplier controlled.

There is a strong relationship between the extent of retail branding and the degree of centralization of distribution. Companies such as Marks & Spencer, J Sainsbury and Boots in the UK had established retail-controlled distribution centres from the late 1960s/early1970s. They were the market leaders in their product categories and had established a brand identity with their customers. Other retailers, especially the major grocery retailers, were quick to follow, and by the late 1980s around 32 per cent of packaged grocery sales/toiletries were private label, an increase of 8 per cent in a decade. In actual fact, market penetration was much greater than this for all grocery categories. Chilled lines in particular were almost exclusively private label. Companies such as Northern Foods and Oscar Meyer grew in response to the buoyant demand for ready meals in M&S and the supermarket chains, including Tesco, which had changed its positioning from a 'pile it high, sell it cheap' operator to one selling premium brands (manufacturer quality-level private brands).

By the 1990s, these UK retailers were beginning to challenge some of the world's most prominent manufacturer brands for shelf space. The so-called 'Cola wars' of the early 1990s were the most obvious example of this when Sainsbury, followed by others, including Virgin, introduced their own brands to challenge Coca-Cola and Pepsi in the market. Procter & Gamble and Unilever were also facing private-label brand competition to their detergents and health and beauty brands. Throughout the 1990s, retailers were spending more on promoting private-label brands than was spent by their manufacturing counterparts.

The battle of the brands has continued, prompting much debate (and lawsuits) on the extent to which look-alike private-label brands break trade mark legislation (for example, ASDA's launch of Puffin to compete with United Biscuit's Penguin). It has been argued (Davies, 1998) that it is not only the theft of the name, but also theft of identity. By looking at the values communicated by health and beauty products, Davies argues that retailers have copied the image that has been created by manufacturers in their research and development.

As consumers have become more 'brand literate' and retailers more precise in defining their market segments, store branding has become a means of positioning relatively standardized merchandise offerings in the minds of target consumers. The brand values created by retailers through private-label branding and their store brands are sufficiently strong for companies to diversify into other activities – for example, grocers into financial products, fashion retailers into perfume. Those companies, such as Tesco, with global aspirations and multichannel strategies will undoubtedly use their brand loyalty to cross-sell a range of products and services.

It should be noted also that the own label share of UK supermarkets is fairly unique compared with other markets. Fernie and Pierrel (1996) show that the French share of private label in the grocery markets is only half of that in the UK, despite the prominence of brands such as Carrefour, Auchan, LeClerc and Intermarche.

The reasons for this disparity include the nature of the retail organization (LeClerc and Intermarche are trading groups with a fragmented buying structure), the inability of French retailers to promote their stores on TV (it is illegal) and the strong emphasis on price competition (for manufacturers' brands). In the US, the level of private label is also low, but this is mainly due to the regional fragmentation of retail chains compared to the national coverage of manufacturers' brands. Wal-Mart is the exception to this, but its every day low pricing (EDLP) strategy narrows the differential between private-label and manufacturer-branded goods, thereby negating the need for consumers to trade up. The IGD in the UK has shown that in the packaged grocery/toiletries market, the own label share has levelled out at 39–40 per cent in the late 1990s. Low inflation, price competition and Wal-Mart's EDLP policy for ASDA are cited as contributory factors.

The fashion brand in many cases is the store brand with a range of brand extensions – for example, Gap, Gap for Kids. Too many extensions, however, can dilute the value of the brand, as Next found in the 1980s before returning to its core female fashion business in the 1990s. Such companies tie in suppliers to provide their private-label brands without being involved in production, unlike Benetton and Zara, which are fully integrated companies.

Marks & Spencer was always cited as the retailer without factories, but it had control over its suppliers to provide 100 per cent St Michael-branded products. This policy has been reviewed, as St Michael is a negative brand in the eyes of younger, fashion-conscious consumers. In 2001, Marks & Spencer introduced exclusive designer ranges into its stores, in addition to recruiting George Davies from ASDA in the hope that he could design a collection which could be as popular with Marks & Spencer consumers as was his successful George range in ASDA stores.

The designer labels which are increasingly popular in the high street are the diffusion brands identified in Figure 5.6. The companies which originally developed the high couture brands are becoming PLCs or are subject to takeover bids as they move into international markets. There are two potential difficulties with this branding strategy. Firstly, the diffusion brand is becoming mass market, thereby diluting its traditional values and perhaps alienating its upmarket customers. Secondly, as this fashion business grows, a web of licensing arrangements is necessary to manufacture and distribute the brand. This can lead to disputes between brand owner and licensees, and also to brands being sold through 'grey' markets to supermarket chains and other unauthorized distributors.

The relative positions of competing retail brands will change with new market entrants, so that maintaining the brand means reviewing the positioning in the market. The market for womenswear shifted fundamentally in the late 1990s with the growth of value fashion multiples Matalan and TK Maxx. The quality of low-price fashion merchandise improved, leaving a number of reasonable-quality/low-price retailers positioned precariously at the level of below average quality for average price. The effect on sales of womenswear for BhS, M&S and the Arcadia group was dramatic. To maintain volume sales, either the quality of their goods had to improve, incurring extra costs to maintain brand positions, or organizational economies made in order to lower prices, which could undermine the 'expectational pact' and weaken the brands.

This market shift took place over a number of years and could and should have been foreseen by market-aware retail managers. Then steps could have been taken to defend the positions of the brands affected. French Connection did this through repositioning and a successful marketing campaign (see Box 5.1). When similarly challenged by discounters a decade earlier, the grocery majors successfully diffused the danger to brand identity through establishing clearly identifiable value product lines within their stores. Therefore, brand identity was maintained at the same time as offering customers the alternative of cheaper, lower quality merchandise under the same roof.

In the case of Arcadia the market shift forced organizational economies through rationalization of their portfolio of brands. They disposed of weaker fascias such as Principles, disposed of hundreds of weaker stores and merged menswear with womenswear (Top Man with Top Shop, Burton Menswear with Dorothy Perkins). Retail analysts predicted that reduction of property costs and rationalization of the number of brands to the strongest three or four could move the group back into profit.

Brand extension

> More of our thinking should be directed to a share of customer than a share of market.
>
> (Piercy, 1997)

An established brand can be used to extend the retail and service offering to existing customers. Brand extensions facilitate choice for customers. The British master of brand extension is Richard Branson's Virgin group – a brand developed from a record store and applied to a variety of merchandise categories and services as diverse as investment, cola distribution and an airline. The brand has established quality levels in the minds of customers, and associations of bravado and buccaneering which the founder has fostered through carefully maintained publicity for stunts like ballooning the Atlantic and posing in a bridal dress.

The Internet has offered retailers an easy route to brand extension. Alongside their core offering they can apply their brand name to unrelated products and services. Tesco.com offers grocery shopping online with delivery in its own fleet of vans, and extended its online brand to clothing, gifts, entertainment and books through partnerships with established organizations such as Grattan and Bertrams, with merchandise delivered directly to customers via White Arrow and Parcelforce.

Care has to be taken to maintain the 'expectational pact' with customers when extending the brand. Virgin's reputation was tainted by customers' perception of poor service and high prices offered by Virgin Trains. Customers' expectations were that the level of quality associated with Virgin's stores and airline would be extended to the train service. Customers' expectations of value for money had been raised by financial products such as the Virgin Tracker Fund, which was promoted as a quality, cut-price investment. Likewise, when Marks & Spencer's customers' expectations of quality were compromised by poor fashion merchandise, it harmed not only sales of clothing, but it also undermined trust in quality of food and financial products.

Branding and customer loyalty

The main thrust of marketing in the 1990s was towards relationship building. It is well known that it costs four to five times as much to win a new customer as to retain an existing customer. Building loyalty is not just about databases and loyalty cards, but about how staff treat customers, how the retailer deals with complaints and the overall retail experience to encourage repeat business. Nevertheless, we now have a much better range of marketing tools to understand our customer than ever before. In addition to basic marketing research from the recognized consultancies and trade bodies, the use of focus groups and the data mined from EPOS data and loyalty cards allows retailers to profile their customers and respond to their needs.

This shift to database and micro-marketing comes at a cost and there is an ongoing debate about the relative costs/benefits of interacting with millions of customers (in the case of supermarket chains). Clearly, in the case of direct marketing companies and dot.com operators interaction is a built-in facet of the business, and Amazon.com provides an excellent example of how to build relationships with customers.

In the US, a proliferation of loyalty schemes have been in use for some time, but much of the evidence suggests that consumers are promiscuous rather than loyal. In the UK, loyalty cards are a more recent introduction as a customer incentive; the uptake by retailers has been patchy. The Institute of Grocery Distribution reports a high degree of loyalty for the supermarket chains (69 per cent for Safeway to 77 per cent for Tesco) in relation to the percentage of turnover from loyal customers. Tesco launched its Clubcard in 1995, to be followed by Sainsbury and Safeway. Safeway later abandoned its ABC card to focus upon promotions, and ASDA, after trialling a scheme for 5 years, abandoned it in favour of an EDLP strategy. The 'non-believers' will argue that they would rather give customers good value for money rather than points for gifts. In reality it has been the top two grocers in the UK who have stuck with their schemes, primarily because they have already invested so much in their programmes.

The cost of launching and maintaining a loyalty scheme is high. For example, Boots launched their Advantage card in 1998 for £32 million. It is also estimated that it costs around 50p per week per person to maintain a loyalty card database, in addition to the mailing costs. In a tough market there has been little evidence to date to indicate that loyalty cards have had a major impact upon performance. However, in the long run companies such as Tesco will benefit from the valuable customer data it is collecting for direct marketing opportunities. Both Tesco and Sainsbury have loyalty card schemes and Internet/direct shopping programmes. This gives these companies important data on customers, their degree of loyalty and what they purchase. As Tesco, in particular, moves into new markets the opportunities to cross-sell are extensive.

The service marketing mix

The marketing mix is the combination of elements which marketers can use to bring their service to the target customer(s) for their mutual profit. There is a range of elements to consider (see Figure 5.7).

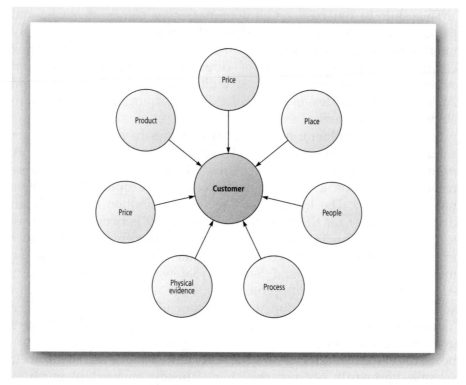

Figure 5.7 The service marketing mix.

Product

This service element can be considered on a number of levels, from the store brand or brands which make up the organization, to the merchandise mix, or the brands which make up the merchandise mix. At any level, the product consistently has to meet or exceed the needs, wants and expectations of the target customer group, or groups.

Products (and brands) go through a life cycle (see Figure 5.8), and although it can be difficult to assess accurately when the progress from one stage to the next is made, recognizing life cycle stages can help with market strategies and tactics.

Investment has to be made in developing the product, incurring costs to the firm which can be offset against the profits from successful products. During the introduction phase, the cost of product launch, publicity and advertising can mean a continued loss to the organization. During the growth phase, when sales and profits grow rapidly, marketers can concentrate on boosting sales and striving to gain a dominant share in the market sector through aggressive selling, sales promotions and continued advertising, while defending position

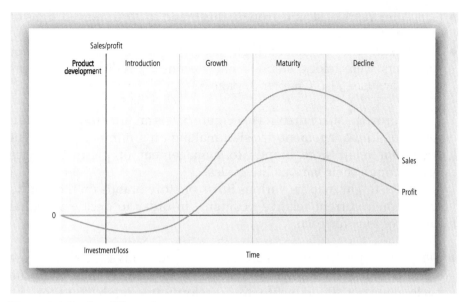

Figure 5.8 Product life cycle.

against copycat products. When growth in sales starts to decline steadily the product has entered the maturity phase. The greatest profits are during maturity, when market share and sales peak. Marketers have to continue to defend share, and to remind customers to buy through advertising and promotion, but at less intensity and less cost than during growth. When sales and profits decline steadily, or suddenly, the product has entered the decline phase, and marketers have to make the decision whether to:

- allow the product to die slowly, reducing investment to a minimum;
- terminate the product;
- redevelop and relaunch to attempt to boost it into a second growth phase.

Examples of store brands at various stages of the life cycle in 2001 were:

- *Matalan*. Still in the growth phase of the life cycle, with plans to roll out 200 more stores.
- *Next*. In the mature phase of the life cycle after strong growth followed by rationalization. A well-established high street fashion brand benefiting from problems with Marks & Spencer and closure of C&A stores.

- *Gap*. After years of strong growth, this brand in 2000 showed signs of maturity/decline as profits fell.
- *St Michael*. The dominant high street brand for decades, senior managers were taking steps to halt decline by selling off overseas operations (see also Chapter 3, page 53).

The BCG growth–share matrix (see Figure 5.9) is another tool which can be used to aid management decision making on a number of different levels, from retail store brands to management of product/service ranges through their various life cycles.

A retailer might map its various SBUs or store brands on the grid to visualize their current relative positions, in order to decide potential future directions for each.

- *Stars*: high growth, high share brands – need investment to grow share within growing market. Growth will slow as they enter life cycle maturity. Build share to transform into cash cows of the future.
- *Cash cow*: high share brands in mature low growth market – at maturity within life cycle, and profits can be used to support investment in new products/services/brands and to support star and question mark products/services/brands. Sufficient investment needed to hold share, or it may be appropriate to harvest profits.
- *Question mark*: low share of high growth market – need investment to maintain share within growing market and to boost share. Where

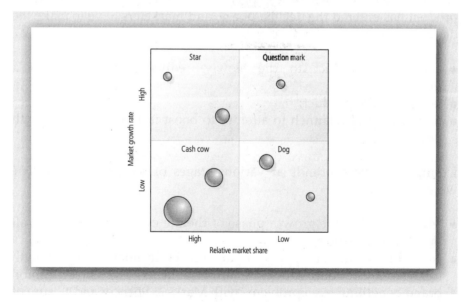

Figure 5.9 Growth–share matrix (adapted and simplified). *Source*: Kotler (1996).

there are several 'question marks', decisions are needed about which to build in terms of share and which to let go or die.

- *Dog*: low share of low growth market – in life cycle decline stage, these may generate enough profit to maintain themselves, but will not yield sufficient to support more promising products/services/ brands. Can be allowed to die, or be sold.

Price

Price is the most flexible element of the marketing mix – all other elements take time to change, but prices can be raised or reduced swiftly in response to changes in customer demand or market conditions. Price and quality are two of the most important dimensions in customer perception of the retail offer, and in customer buying decisions. Customers have an understanding of a 'just' price range for a level of quality, for a product, or for product ranges within a store brand. If the price falls below the just price, customers may suspect inferior quality. If the price rises above this range, customers will suspect they are being 'ripped off'.

Pricing strategy is therefore closely linked to product decisions, and to branding strategy. This is why price and quality are so frequently the main dimensions used for positioning in the market.

Decisions on pricing strategy can be influenced by internal and external factors (Omar, 1999).

Internal factors include:

- marketing objectives;
- marketing mix strategy;
- costs.

The marketing objectives of a retail organization will vary according to the competitiveness of the market sector and market conditions engendered by the stage in the economic life cycle. For example, in a concentrated market sector dominated by a few large and powerful organizations, competitive pricing is crucial for survival. Profit maximization can be achieved by a low-price/low-cost operation/volume sales strategy or by a high-price/high-service/cost minimization strategy.

In addition to survival and maximization of profits, there are three further common marketing objectives:

1 *Building market share*. This is seen by many retailers as the key to continued growth and success, may require competitive pricing, or 'loss-leading' in order to take share from competitors.

2 *Achievement of excellent customer service.* Investment in other elements of the service marketing mix will raise costs and at the same time customers value excellent service, so higher prices can be charged. However, it could be argued that low price itself is a service to the customer, and the savings created by streamlining logistical activities can be used to offer value for money.
3 *Building quality leadership.* Investment in quality – products, services, systems, customer service – means that higher prices can be charged.

Investment in other elements of the marketing mix generally means that there is more flexibility in pricing strategy. For example, investment in product quality and store branding, or in promotional activities, or in logistics management, can either allow a greater margin to be achieved or can be directed at increasing footfall at a lower margin. However, there does need to be integration of marketing mix decisions – for example, promoting the retail offer as 'cheap and cheerful' while retaining high prices, or vice versa, will lead to poor customer satisfaction and customer defection.

The costs incurred in maintaining the organization form the base level for pricing, and many small retailers use their costs as a basis for their pricing strategy. This is cost plus pricing, which means simply adding to costs a percentage margin for profit.

Any organization has fixed costs and variable costs. Fixed costs are those which remain fixed no matter how much is sold – for example, rent and rates, salaries. Variable costs include all those which vary according to sales – for example, materials, flexible staffing.

External factors influencing pricing strategy include:

● macro-environmental factors;
● nature of the market and competition.

Macro-environmental factors create the changing background, the framework within which retailers thrive or fail, and affect both the retailers' costs and customers' perceptions of price.

For example, the stage of the economic cycle – prosperity, recession, depression, recovery – will affect the availability and cost of staff, as well as the propensity of customers to spend. For example, in buoyant market conditions during a phase of economic prosperity, higher prices are more acceptable to customers where value for money is maintained by the retailer through merchandise quality and service provision. By contrast, during a recession, consumer willingness to spend is reduced and discounting can be used to drive profits through volume sales. However, retailers have to be careful because their positioning and branding associates the organization with a perceived fair price range on the part of the customer.

Politics can affect reliability and cost of supplies as well as determining the cost of building and operating a retail unit. The high rate of fuel tax in the UK raises the costs of distribution of goods and is passed on in higher prices as well as affecting the customers' willingness to travel to buy. Investment in technology can streamline systems and increase efficiency, lowering costs over time, but many smaller retailers with less financial clout become less competitive, fail and change the nature of the market. Social trends also affect price. For example, 50 per cent of the UK workforce are female, which makes ready meals and takeaways attractive to families. The high mark-up of these value-added items is acceptable because it reflects the worth females attach to the value of time and effort saved in the kitchen.

Price elasticity of demand is a concept which defines the consumer's reaction to price changes. If demand for a product changes more than 1 per cent with a 1 per cent change in price, demand is said to be elastic. If demand for a product changes less than 1 per cent with a 1 per cent change in price, demand is said to be inelastic.

Market conditions vary over time and according to the nature of the merchandise. Pure competition tends to exist where merchandise is cheap and plentiful, where the market is relatively easy and cheap to enter, and where there are numerous competitors. If one competitor raises the price of merchandise, customers can easily buy from another – demand is elastic and therefore prices tend to be stable. A modern example is a farmer's market. Oligopolistic competition exists in markets with very few, powerful competitors – one example is petrol distribution, another grocery distribution. In this type of market, price competition is tight – if one market competitor raises or reduces prices, the rest follow suit rapidly. The tight competitive situation means that there is a tendency for oligopolistic market competitors to reduce in number to a point where one organization dominates to the exclusion of others. This is called monopoly. In this situation there would be price inelasticity because consumers have nowhere else to shop. Because the power of the monopolizing organization would be to the detriment of both suppliers and consumers, any market situation tending towards monopoly will be investigated by the Office of Fair Trading in the UK, and the monopolizing organization broken up if necessary.

Most retailers prefer a situation in which they successfully dominate one sector of the market – referred to as a situation of monopolistic competition – where a certain degree of price inelasticity is achieved. In this situation, not only is the customer preference for the retailer's products such that a rise in price will only minimally affect demand, but also the competitive situation is such that the price changes of a competitor will not affect demand substantially.

Pricing strategies

- *High/low pricing.* Higher prices are maintained generally with vigorous discounting of selected merchandise on a rotational basis to attract bargain hunters and achieve a low-price image among customers. Safeway successfully implemented this strategy after abandoning its loyalty card scheme. The chief executive recognized that the savings from this and from reducing expenditure on customer service together could fund discounts which would drive volume sales. In doing so, they damaged the image of the Safeway brand among high-spending loyal customers, but countered this with aggressive petrol promotions for higher spenders.
- *Every day low pricing (EDLP).* EDLP protagonists use the part of their budget which would go into promoting merchandise to maintain lower prices throughout the year. This is twinned with a refund policy for customers finding lower price merchandise elsewhere. To implement EDLP successfully, costs have to be kept low through an efficient distribution system and low operating costs. ASDA successfully adopted this strategy, which matched their image as a low-price retailer and was popular with customers. The argument for EDLP is that customers become suspicious of promotions, suspecting (rightly) that the higher price they pay for some items funds the savings they make on others.
- *High price/quality service.* Higher prices are maintained and matched with quality merchandise and merchandising, customer service and loyalty schemes to retain customers and drive profits. Customers can be attracted by branded products, prestige locations or shopping convenience. Discount and premium branding of products can allow enough price flexibility to satisfy customers.

Place

In product and service marketing, the place element is about getting the goods/services to where the customer will buy. In retailing, the place element of the marketing mix is complex because of the large numbers of customers and the variety of goods and services involved. For this reason the place element is discussed in separate chapters. Not only do retail managers have to be concerned with logistics and physical distribution (see Chapter 7), they also need to understand the principles of retail location (outlined in Chapter 4) and merchandising and display (see Chapter 11).

Promotion

Promotion is about communicating with customers and is more correctly known as marketing communication. For communication to take place the sender and receiver of information both have to share understanding of the symbols, pictures and words used to transmit information, and have to make use of a mutually available medium through which the information is conveyed.

The process of communication is illustrated in Figure 5.10. The communication source, for example a group or individual who formulate an idea or concept for communication, have then to encode the idea into language, symbols, pictures or a combination of these before selecting a medium or media for transmitting the message to their target audience (selected market segment or segments). In the decoding phase of communication, the symbols, words and pictures of the transmitted message are interpreted into ideas and concepts by the receiver of the information. Feedback completes the communication process because it confirms whether the idea or concept formulated by the source has truly been received and interpreted correctly.

There is the potential for interference at every stage of the process in the form of physical or psychological barriers which prevent the desired communication from taking place. Physical barriers include physical distance, distance in time, difference in educational levels,

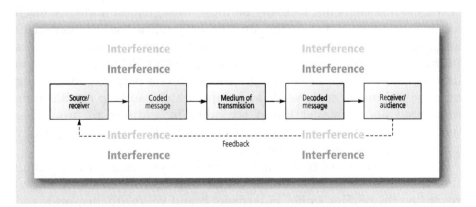

Figure 5.10 The communication process.

poor/non-access to media and sheer volume of competing information, while psychological barriers include preconceptions, emotions, perceptions and attitudes towards the sender, message or medium.

Promotion, as one element of the marketing mix, is reliant on the effective development and use of other elements – product/brand, price and place.

The promotional mix is the range of promotional elements from which a retailer can select to communicate with existing and potential customers. Traditionally, it includes personal selling, advertising, sales promotion and publicity. However, additional elements, notably sponsorship and direct marketing, which could be incorporated respectively into publicity and advertising, have grown in importance and complexity to the extent that they are considered separate promotional elements.

Promotional mix development in retailing is related to the following factors:

- Strategic objectives.
- Audience to be reached.
- Size of the market.
- The message or product to be promoted.
- Relative cost of available media.

The promotional objectives of a retailer depend upon the organization's strategic objectives. For example, a retailer intent on expansion of a successful UK format into Europe will have the promotional objective of raising awareness of and interest in the store brand in the destination country, whereas an established retailer will focus promotional effort on defending or growing its successful position against major competitors.

Retailers utilizing cost-based strategies are liable to apply cost-based criteria to mix elements, focusing on those with greatest audience reach for money spent – hence the growth of publicity which generates audience coverage without payment for media space. A variety of sales promotions are generally used to encourage spend. Retailers engaged in differentiation-based strategies can focus on comparative advertising using visual media such as TV and print, which can help establish, fix or remind about retailer brand attributes in addition to promoting merchandise. Retailers targeting a restricted market segment are ideally positioned to use direct marketing.

The effectiveness of marketing communication relies on integrating the desired message to customers (and staff and other stakeholders) regarding the retailer's offer in terms of brand value, quality, price and merchandise across all the elements of the mix.

The promotional mix elements

Personal selling is the most expensive element of the mix in relation to the audience reached, and is particularly used where merchandise is so complex or expensive that the customer needs one-to-one help in reaching the decision to buy. In self-service the sales role is more limited – to giving information and processing the customer's orders – but increasingly this role is being enhanced and staff encouraged to offer additional products and services for an additional sale. Personal selling is discussed in detail in Chapter 9.

Advertising is widely used by major retailers. Although expensive because payment for media space is required, major media such as TV and popular newspapers and magazines can reach the huge audience required at a comparatively small cost per person. The message and amount of information promoted can be varied over time, as in a 'teaser' campaign which releases more and more information to generate interest in new merchandise, or in a 'reminder' campaign in which a short clip of a previous advert is used periodically, using much less media space. Market segments can be targeted through associated media use. Advertising is particularly good for establishing awareness and interest in the retailer and merchandise.

Sales promotions include a variety of tools, including money-off coupons, competitions, two for one offers, which are primarily used to encourage customers to try or buy their merchandise, stimulating sales of promoted items. Retailers engaging in the high/low pricing strategy 'rotate' promotions, generating and maintaining the 'excitement' associated with a sale on a year round basis.

Publicity generates media coverage through the reporting of significant events and information. Events such as openings, introduction of a new merchandise line or sponsorship of a community team can generate press coverage, as can a high-profile chief executive. The message conveyed to the audience has more credibility with the audience and is often indistinguishable from news. However, media coverage is uncertain depending upon the competition for media space at the time of publication. Publicity is useful to raise awareness and interest in the organization rather than stimulating sales; however, it is sometimes linked with sales promotion in a combined retailer/media effort to raise sales.

Sponsorship is the funding of a non-related event, team or person, normally with the aim of reaching the audience through media coverage. Coverage is uncertain, however, depending on the success of the sponsored party. Kingfisher's sponsorship of Ellen MacArthur's round the world race resulted in spectacular media coverage when she unexpectedly finished second.

Direct marketing is increasingly used by retailers through mail order, website and direct mail. It allows customers to be targeted directly, at low cost, with information on which to make the buying decision or with promotional offers to generate purchase. Data-mining of loyalty card data, for example, can be used to generate a target database of individuals with needs/wants directly related to the merchandise being marketed, which improves the success rate.

People, process and physical evidence

People, process and physical evidence are three extra elements which particularly apply to service organizations. If marketing is about getting the right product at the right price in the right place at the right time and communicating this to the customer, in retailing, people, process and physical evidence are about the quality of the transaction experience.

People

Two sets of people affect the marketing effectiveness of a retail organization:

- Service personnel.
- Customers.

Service personnel are those staff in the organization who operate at the customer interface. Increasingly, in a retail context, this means all staff. In a retail organization customer satisfaction is partially generated through the product bought, and partially through the service situation – including shop cleanliness, appearance, quality, display, stock levels and maintenance, additional services, after-sales service and the process of purchase.

In addition to their sales role, whether active or processing of orders, retail staff have a role to play in in-store promotions by giving customers verbal information about sales promotions, merchandise and stock levels, and about reinforcing external promotions by reminding customers about events, new merchandise and service initiatives.

Staff represent the service quality offered by the organization and have the key role in enabling customer satisfaction. Their appearance and behaviour can serve to reinforce and supplement, or inhibit, the success of the rest of the marketing. Standardization of procedures and staff training can reduce the potential for poor service encounters, but other considerations are motivation retention and morale. The importance of retail staff is more fully addressed in Chapter 8.

Customers are the second set of people who can enhance or inhibit the marketing of retail organizations. Customers can be used in combination with other promotional elements. They can be utilized as referrals in advertising and sales promotional materials endorsing the retailer's own promotional statements. They can be used in publicity – for example, an event to celebrate a competition win. Sainsbury successfully incorporated customers into both roles by organizing a competition for schoolchildren to design a poster advertising the store opening, which resulted in an advert, free publicity and generation of community goodwill towards the new store. Customers can be used in a sales role, either through word-of-mouth advocacy of a store or its merchandise or service, or through recruitment to a more active selling role as in some mail order businesses.

The marketing effort of the organization can, on the other hand, be inhibited through customers passing on dissatisfaction or disinformation to other people.

Poor customer behaviour, overcrowding or lack of customers in a store can affect the quality of the shopping experience for other customers.

Process

Process deals with transforming resource input supplies such as bags, trolleys, baskets, merchandise and till rolls into outputs such as completed shopping and a satisfied customer.

Process can include:

- Planning and control of the process – dealing with quality, quantity, delivery and cost of merchandise and services to meet customer requirements.
- Planning operations – detailing each operation required for consistent results, such as staffing levels for merchandising, customer service and sales.
- Facilities design, layout and handling of materials – to maximize speed and efficiency of service.
- Scheduling – detailed timing of operations such as shelf-filling, serving, packing for customers.
- Inventory planning and control – making sure there is sufficient stock, staff, equipment.
- Quality control – checking and evaluation of merchandise, operations and service.

In marketing a service, the process element can be used to attract and reassure customers in addition to being an important factor in ensuring their satisfaction. Most of a retail organization's operations are both highly visible to customers and can be affected by their presence.

As retailers increasingly compete not just against other retailers for customer spend, but also against other entertainment and leisure organizations, process has risen in significance. For most people the process of shopping is becoming as important as the merchandise bought, whether it be the excitement of a sale or the calm efficiency of a well-run department store. Process is becoming more complex too – for example, web-booths in stores where customers can source merchandise unavailable on the shop floor, or male crèches with Internet access and playstations.

Process can be used as an active marketing tool in achieving customer satisfaction in a variety of ways. For example, special promotional displays of merchandise can clear shelves and allow restocking to take place, and a packing service can be scheduled at peak times to achieve volume sales. Customers can be persuaded to take on part of the process themselves, finding and scanning their own merchandise, or returning baskets and trolleys to base. IKEA happily advertises the use of its customers in keeping prices low through taking on the role of transport and assembly of merchandise.

Physical evidence

Services are essentially intangible. In retailing, while the merchandise is clearly tangible, the service offered to customers is not. Physical evidence is about how the service part of the shopping experience is tangibilized (or made physical) for customers and potential customers.

There are two types of physical evidence:

1 *Peripheral evidence*. This is evidence which is acquired by the customer as part of the service bought – the environment and atmosphere in which a service transaction takes place, but which has little or no intrinsic value in itself.

   Shoppers typically leave with at least a receipt of purchase, and normally with a bag or wrapping. Both these are used as promotional tools bearing at least the name and/or logo of the retail unit. They can also be used to symbolize the quality of the service and merchandise. Designer shops normally provide carrier bags, which both promote the store brand and its designer association through unusual colours, design or materials. These, in lending their customers fashionability by association with the store, can in themselves attract customers into the store to make a purchase. Receipts can be used in joint marketing offering customers discount offers on the back, or they can be used as a vehicle for offering coupons, points or other promotions.

Peripheral evidence allows retailers an opportunity to establish their brands in the minds of their customers after the purchase is made. Peripheral evidence in the form of loyalty cards additionally offers customers physical evidence of variable discounts offered for loyalty and the provision of extra products or services to regular customers.

2 *Essential evidence*. This is evidence which cannot be acquired by the customer, but which is important in the customer's selection of the service. Essential evidence includes external aspects of the store, such as location, parking, size, shape and quality of design of buildings, and fascia – all of which represent the quality of service to be expected and which can be used to attract customers into the store. It also includes internal aspects such as layout, quality of materials used in fixtures and fittings, lighting, signs and customer facilities.

Essential evidence physically portrays the quality of the service offered and it can be actively used in the design of targeted store formats. However, it is important that essential evidence is integrated with the rest of the marketing offer. Where essential evidence contradicts the quality of service provision, customer confusion and dissatisfaction is the likely outcome.

Sometimes retail organizations use peripheral evidence to support essential evidence – for example, free tea and coffee for waiting spouses, badges for children, collectible poster in the form of a mailshot. The St Andrews Woollen Mill gained widespread fame and custom through its 'Free Tooties for All' – a tiny nip of whisky offered to customers in the tearoom above the store. Apart from its popularity with customers, this fitted in with the tartan/sheepskin woollen mill image of the store, and gave them a memorable strap line for their advertisements.

Summary

Retail marketing is the application of marketing concepts theories and actions within the context of retail organizations. Marketing is a whole-business orientation, which is customer led, requires fulfilment of the needs of internal and external customers, and should balance the requirements of the various organizational stakeholders. This orientation needs to be management facilitated and requires integration of marketing effort across functional activities in order to respond rapidly to the dynamism of consumer markets in order to achieve profitable outcomes to sustain organizational success.

It is only relatively recently that retailers have realized the importance of marketing in the maintenance of a successful business in rapidly changing markets, and indeed understood their own role in driving the marketing process. Marketing-orientated retailers realize that customer focus should underpin corporate decision making and that the concepts and tools of marketing can be used as a secure foundation for innovation and competitive advantage.

The external environment forms the framework for organizational success, and the results of environmental scanning should inform organizational developments which exploit environmental and market opportunities. Nevertheless, clear direction and organizational values, sometimes encapsulated in a mission statement, drive the path of the organization, feeding and framing organizational objectives. Recent theorists believe that organizational objectives and strategy have been too confined by operational issues in the past (and hence, it could be argued, not truly market orientated), and that what is needed is an understanding of the organization's core competences plus the ability to think laterally in applying these to add value and create differentiation.

Organizational mission and strategy is normally developed as a series of corporate objectives, some of which may incorporate marketing terminology. Marketing objectives are generally developed as the marketing mechanism for meeting corporate objectives, and marketing strategy entails a series of decisions about products (or product/ services) and markets which will exploit market opportunities in order to meet marketing objectives. Marketing tactics or action plans specify more exactly the form marketing activities will take.

Marketing planning is the period process in which the external and internal marketing environment are reviewed and analysed to establish marketing objectives and strategy, define the marketing mix and tactics for achieving objectives, and lay down evaluation and control procedures.

Market segmentation involves finding and profiling the segment or segments of the market that the organization can serve profitably, building understanding of customer values and buying habits. Demographic, geographic, psychographic and behaviour are four main methods of segmenting markets. Segmentation also involves positioning against competitors' offers in the marketplace, and establishing the position in the mind of target customer groups through building brand identity.

Store branding has become a means of positioning relatively standardized merchandise offerings in the minds of target consumers.

The brand values created by major retailers through private-label branding and store branding have been strong enough for these organizations to diversify into other activities, such as financial products and fast food. The relative positions of competing retail brands changes with new market entrants so that in order to maintain the brand over time, periodic reviews of marketing positioning are required. Building brand loyalty is about more than building customer databases and using loyalty card incentives, it is about creating and meeting customer expectations in terms of customer care, dealing with complaints, quality of merchandise and the overall retail 'experience' for the customer. Loyalty card schemes and Internet shopping programmes give organizations important data on customers and as the retailer moves into new markets brand loyalty offers opportunities for cross-selling.

The marketing mix is the basic range of elements marketers can use in marketing a product or service. In service marketing, generally seven elements are considered:

1 Product.
2 Price.
3 Place.
4 Promotion.
5 People.
6 Process.
7 Physical evidence.

There are a range of management decisions which can be made regarding each of the elements and they provide an extremely useful framework for developing marketing tactics.

Review questions

1 Define retail marketing and explain the definition in terms of the activities of a retail organization.
2 What is the product–market expansion grid. How can it help retailers to decide marketing strategy?
3 Anyone can come into a store, and anyone with a computer and modem can enter a website, so why segment? Explain why segmentation is beneficial for retail organizations.
4 'The customer becomes the brand' (Piercy, 1997). Explain the importance of branding to fashion retailers.
5 Compare and contrast every day low pricing and high/low pricing strategies.

References

Ansoff, H. I. (1957). *Strategies for diversification*. Harvard Business Review, September/October, 113–24.

Ansoff, H. I. (1988). *New Corporate Strategy: An Analytical Approach in Business Policy for Growth and Expansion*. John Wiley, New York.

Birkin, M., Clarke, G. and Clarke, M. (2002). *Retail Geography and Intelligent Network Planning*. John Wiley, Chichester.

Collins, A. (1992). *Competitive Retail Marketing*. McGraw-Hill.

Davies (1998). Retail brands and the theft of identity. *International Journal of Retail and Distribution Management*, **26**(4), 140–6.

Dibb, S., Simpkin, L., Pride, W. M. and Ferrell, O. C. (2001). *Marketing Concepts and Strategies*. Houghton Mifflin, Boston.

Fernie, J. and Pierrel, F. R. A. (1996). Own branding in UK and French grocery markets. *Journal of Product and Brand Management*, **5**(7), 48–57.

Gilbert, D. (1999). *Retail Marketing Management*. Pearson Education, Harlow.

Johnson, G. and Scholes, K. (1999). *Exploring Corporate Strategy*. Prentice-Hall International, Hemel Hempstead.

Kotler, P. (1996). *Principles of Marketing*. Prentice-Hall International.

Kotler, P. (1997). *Marketing Management: Analysis, Planning, Implementation and Control*, 9th edn. Prentice-Hall, London.

Levy, M. and Weitz, B. A. (1995). *Retailing Management*. Richard D. Irwin, USA.

Moore, C. M., Fernie, J. and Burt, S. L. (2002). Brands without boundaries: the internationalisation of the designer retailer's brand. *European Journal of Marketing*, **34**(8), 919–37.

Omar, O. (1999). *Retail Marketing*. Pearson Education, Harlow.

Piercy, N. (1997). *Marketing-Led Strategic Change*. Harper Collins, Oxford.

6

Retail buying in the twenty-first century

> In the past two decades, the role of the buyer within retail organizations has changed remarkably. While the basic activity of buying the right product to make a profit has not changed, the context of buying the right product has changed hugely.
>
> Buying Director, UK Fashion Multiple Retailer

The role of the retail buyer

Buyers have a pivotal role within retail organizations, not least for the fact that it is their responsibility to make reality the retailer's positioning statement through their selection of appropriate products and services. Consequently, the contribution of the buyer to the success of the retailer is considerable and requires that they possess a range of skills and talents, not least of which is the ability to identify, interpret and satisfy consumer needs and wants. Various attempts have been made to locate the requisite competencies of a successful buyer, and among those that have been identified include skills of market and numerical analysis, negotiation and communication (Varley, 2001). Furthermore, and perhaps the most important of buyers' skills, is that of flair and creativity (which is arguably an intuitive competence), and which is evident as part of the process of range development and product selection.

Davidson et al. (1988) provided what has become the seminal categorization of the retail buyer's role. Their categorization recognized three primary functions.

The first is as *change agent*, where the buyer influences and alters consumer purchase behaviour by offering new products and services. Buyers who instigate new product development for own-brand ranges or who introduce new products, perhaps sourced from foreign suppliers, would typically fall into this category.

The second is as *gatekeeper*, where the buyer assumes responsibility for the flow of product from suppliers to the end consumer. Those buyers who purchase manufacturer brands and products, and who take no role in the process of developing and branding a product, assume this gatekeeper role. As such, these buyers have a relatively passive role and their companies act principally as a pipeline for product and service distribution.

The third is as *opinion-leader*, where the buyer influences consumer opinion but does not necessarily prompt a purchase from their company. As such, consumers may only use the retailer as a source for ideas and information. As an example, Heals, the upmarket London furniture retailer, has long been identified as a source of inspiration for other household goods retailers, who may provide cheaper copies of Heals' ranges, as well as for consumers, who may customize ranges purchased from other retailers in the Heals' style.

The principal buying activities

In some respects, it is impossible to provide a definitive and comprehensive account of the responsibilities of the buyer, not least for the fact that buyers' roles are as varied as the companies that employ them. For example, for an independent retailer, the buyer may be the owner of the business, as well as the manager of the retail outlet. As such, their responsibilities will be more wide-ranging than for a buyer responsible for the 'cut-flower offer' for a supermarket group.

However, despite these significant role differences, it is possible to identify a number of activities which are integral to the buying function as a whole – and these can be grouped into five categories as follows:

1 *Analysis of market opportunity.* A crucial responsibility of all buyers is the identification of profitable market opportunity for the business. This necessitates that the buyer undertakes an analysis of trends and developments in consumer buying behaviour in general, as well as in relation to the buyer's specific area of responsibility. Essential to this process is the evaluation of competitor performance, particularly in terms of their development of new products and services. From this

evaluation, the buyer must identify continuing and new market opportunities for the retailer and from this develop a merchandise plan.

2 *Creation of the merchandise plan.* Substantiated by sound market and competitor analysis, the merchandise plan details the nature and characteristics of the product range in terms of its breadth (the range of different product categories) and depth (the choice of products within a specific category). The merchandise plan must also include a forecast of future sales and profit margin within each product category. This plan is then used as the basis for determining retail price levels within the company. A sales and profit budget by week, month, quarter and year will also be included.

3 *Selecting the supply base.* Derived from the analysis of market opportunities and based upon financial forecasts, it is then the buying function's responsibility to identify appropriate sources of supply. This investigation will include the application of supplier selection criteria that will typically extend beyond merely price of supply considerations, to include issues pertinent to the supplier's record on employees' rights and the use of child labour. (This particular issue of supplier selection will be considered in greater depth later in this chapter.) Having identified an appropriate supply base, the responsibility for agreeing terms of trade with the supplier is negotiated on the retailer's behalf by the buying and merchandising team.

4 *Product development and supplier performance management.* Motivated by the desire to improve profit margins and secure customer loyalty through distribution exclusivity, many buyers, particularly those employed by the larger multiple retailers, have developed own brand ranges. This development has in many cases resulted in retail buyers assuming significant control over the supply chain, principally through their determining of product specifications. This shift in power in favour of the retailer has meant that suppliers must adhere to strict performance criteria, particularly in relation to product quality standards, and availability levels.

5 *Presentation of merchandise at point-of-sale.* In recognition of the need to ensure that merchandise is presented in sufficient quantity to meet demand and in a manner that is conducive to prompt customers to purchase the range, it is appropriate that the buying team should be involved in decisions pertinent to the presentation of merchandise at the point-of-sale. The involvement of the buying team in this area may include their directing the nature and form of product packaging, determining the mechanisms by which products will be displayed to consumers, as well as proposing the amount of space that is allocated to product categories in order that target sales volumes can be achieved.

Based upon these categorizations, it is clear that the buying activity must necessarily involve not only a number of people, but also a range of people with differing specializations. As such, the buying function, particularly within larger retail organizations, includes the following:

Buyers, who are specifically responsible for what has been described as the 'qualitative side of buying' (Varley, 2001), in that they take control of identifying the requirements of the market, in terms of products and services, and of determining which products would best satisfy customer needs. They are also typically active in identifying and selecting appropriate sources of supply.

Merchandisers are typically responsible for the management of the quantitative side of product management. They will assume financial responsibility for the buying function; they will also determine the buying budget and monitor margin performance. Along with the buyer, the merchandiser will set the retail price of a product, but it is usually they who determine any price mark-downs. In addition to their sales forecasting responsibilities, merchandisers are also responsible for the movement of stock in the business. As such, they will organize when goods will be delivered into the company and will be responsible for planning deliveries into stores.

Quality controllers are vested with the responsibility of monitoring product quality. Therefore, a sizeable part of their time is spent visiting suppliers and checking that the product specifications set by the company are followed. Furthermore, quality controllers will monitor customer product complaints and will provide technical advice to customer service departments, who, in turn, will respond to customer comments.

A number of other specialists serve to support the buying function. These include *product designers*, who (particularly for companies that market their own-brand merchandise) design product specifications in response to design briefs set by the buyer. These specifications are then used to direct manufacturers in their production.

Visual merchandisers assume the responsibility for the physical presentation of in-store product ranges. Their presentation plans are often based upon guidelines set by the buyers. These guidelines express the buyer's thinking in terms of the themes and concepts that underpinned the design and creation of the product ranges.

Space planners are responsible for the allocation of space in stores to specific product ranges. Their allocation is directed both by the buyer's sales plans as well as the sales histories of individual stores. Furthermore, the allocation of space to particular ranges may be based upon agreements made by the buyers with manufacturers who agree to pay the retailer a retainer for access to key locations within the store.

Measuring the performance of the buying function

Given the significance of buying to the realization of a retailer's success, it is vital that a company establishes criteria in order that the performance of the buying function can be monitored and assessed. There is little consideration in the literature of the methodologies used by retailers to measure the performance of the buying function. As such, the set of criteria identified below is based upon a series of interviews with buyers employed by 34 retailers that operate in a number of areas, including the grocery, fashion, department store, electrical and CTN (confectionery, tobacco and newsagents) sectors, within the UK and France.

The criteria used by retailers can be grouped into three categories as follows:

1 *Financial and resource performance measures.* The finance and resource utilization dimensions used to measure buying function performance include:
    (a) Gross and net margin performance as measured by levels achieved against budget and the previous year's margin levels.
    (b) Optimization of sales level as measured by levels achieved against budget and previous year's sales levels.
    (c) Level of market share achieved as measured by levels achieved against target level and previous year's market share level.
    (d) Minimal level of mark-downs as measured by levels achieved against targets and last year's mark-down levels.
2 *Customer satisfaction measures.*
    (a) Minimal level of out-of-stock ranges as measured by levels achieved against target.
    (b) Minimal level of customer complaints and returns as measured by levels achieved against target.
    (c) Consistent quality of goods as measured by levels of customer returns and complaints, as well as rejections and the results of company quality control checks.
3 *Innovation and market development measures.*
    (a) Development of distinct competitive advantage in terms of product ranges, price levels and quality as measured against the competition.
    (b) Level of success achieved in relation to new product development introductions as measured by previous year's performance, the terms of the development strategy and the competition.
    (c) Speed of reaction to changes in demand at the macro and micro level as measured by minimal levels of sell-outs and the profitable optimization of sales.

(d) Level of development with respect to the creation of new market segments as measured against previous year's performance levels and planned development levels.

The extent to which retailers will use all or at least some of these measures will be dependent upon their size, management structure and the characteristics of the sector within which they operate.

The defining issues in retail buying

A variety of other retailing texts provide useful insights into the various roles and responsibilities of the retail buyer, provide explanations for the increased centralization of the buying function and consider the financial dimensions of the buying process. As such, these areas will not be further considered here. Instead, three particular buying dimensions are addressed. These dimensions were identified as a result of interviews with more than 30 buyers who were employed by a variety of British, European and American retail companies. These companies operated within a variety of product sectors and ranged from single outlet organizations to those that operated in excess of 300 stores.

Based upon their own experiences, the interviewees were asked to identify those dimensions that they perceived to be important and challenging to their roles as retail buyers, both now and in the medium-term future. The three dimensions that the buyers identified were as follows:

1 Trend management strategies.
2 New supplier selection strategies.
3 Procedures for managing the development of own-brand products.

These dimensions have received only limited consideration within the academic literature. Drawing from the experiences of the buyers with respect to these particular dimensions, the remainder of this chapter will explore the three dimensions in turn.

Trend management strategies

With the increased division of labour within the buying function split between and among the various personnel identified above, the analysis of product and market trends is one task that has remained a primary responsibility of the retail buyer. Furthermore, product and market trend identification has become an increasingly more onerous responsibility for buyers in the past decade for three specific reasons.

Firstly, the rate of innovation within many product categories (but particularly the clothing, home entertainment and convenience foods sectors) is such that new product launches, as well as product refinements, extensions and relaunches, are the norm, rather than the exception. Secondly, the ever-increasing speed of consumer uptake of these product introductions has made markets dynamic and is perhaps the clearest indication not only of consumers' willingness to purchase, but also of their apparently insatiable need to have fresh, new and supposedly innovative products to buy. Thirdly, the desire to offer the most up-to-the-minute product by retailers is often motivated by the desire to achieve market differentiation. The fact that products are often indiscriminately available and/or are easy for the competition to copy means that any differentiation that is achieved through product is often short-lived and is ultimately elusive. It is this latter desire to achieve differentiation through product ranging that precipitates the cyclical and ultimately unfulfilled clamour among retail buyers to find the 'next big thing' in product terms.

Yet, while it is clear that product ranging provides only a very few retailers with market differentiation (and in these cases it is inevitably the brand and not the product itself that generates the distinction), it is a non-negotiable requirement that retail buyers anticipate and respond to the trends within their market. Furthermore, by virtue of the complex nature of the market forecasting and trend identification, it is imperative that buyers, regardless of the company or the market sector that they buy for, must develop a coherent trend management strategy. The purpose, nature and characteristics of such a trend management strategy will vary across product sectors. However, it is possible to identify the salient features of such a strategy and these are considered in terms of the analysis of three interlinked dimensions, as detailed in Figure 6.1.

Consumer trend tracking

There are three principal elements that are considered as part of the process of tracking customer trends by the retail buyer. The first involves an analysis of *macro-market consumer trends*. These trends are concerned with changes in the demographic, economic, technological and social dimensions of the market in its widest sense. While buyers are especially interested in these dimensions as they affect their specific target customer group, increasingly it is the case that buyers also cast their research attention wider to include other consumer groups. There are two reasons for this. The first is that experienced buyers recognize the convergence in behaviour between and among customer segments, and that developments within one market segment often have an

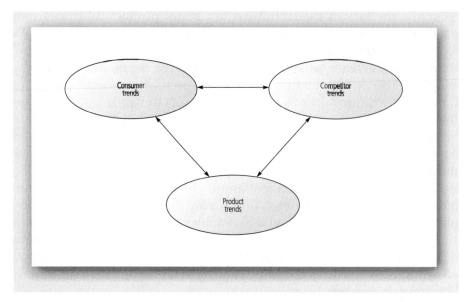

Figure 6.1 The three dimensions of a trend management strategy.

influence and bearing upon changes within other customer groups. Secondly, through having such awareness, buyers can then develop new products that capitalize upon trends just as they emerge within their target market.

The analysis of market-level consumer trends is driven not by the desire to generate a one-dimensional overview of the current and likely future status of consumers. Rather, the more expert buyers utilize general information pertaining to consumers' demography, economic status and social situation in order to provide a holistic understanding of those factors which determine the nature and characteristics of their consumption. In addition to these 'hard' facts, buyers typically overlay these with extensive, qualitative information, which provides details of trends in consumers' attitudes and behaviour patterns. By drawing together qualitative and quantitative data, buyers seek to construct a more rounded lifestyle profile of their specific customers. This lifestyle profile may take a variety of forms. A common approach is for the buyer to construct a 'lifestyle portrait' of their various customer segments. Typically presented in narrative form, the 'lifestyle portrait' presents a summation of relevant qualitative and quantitative data with the intention of identifying how these trends may explain the attitudes and behaviour of their target customer segments. Starting with an outline of their demographic characteristics, the 'lifestyle portrait' will seek to describe who delineates the attitudes, behaviours, wants and aspirations of customers. It will consider the current dimensions of the consumer's lifestyle and will also seek to predict how that lifestyle may alter in the future. The benefit of developing a 'lifestyle portrait' resides not solely in focusing the buyer's attention upon the factors that define, restrict and determine the way people consume. Instead, it also helps buyers predict which products currently, and in the future, will best match the customer's lifestyle requirements.

Buyers obtain market-level consumer trend information from a variety of sources. The market data collection strategy adopted by retailers is typically a reflection of their size and the financial resources available. The cheapest and most commonly used source of market-level consumer information is obtained from trade publications and communications direct from trade organizations. Typically drawn from aggregate sales data, trade organizations and trade journals provide invaluable insights into up-to-the-minute market sales trends and often include useful expert commentary on market developments at relatively little cost. Those retailers with modest amounts to spend on consumer trend research may supplement this information with specialist market intelligence reports in order to gather and interpret generic consumer data for the purpose of identifying current, and predicting future, trends and developments with respect to their customers. Within the UK, organizations such as Mintel and Verdict regularly publish reports that are relevant to retail buyers.

Buyers may also commission external research consultants with the task of undertaking primary research with consumers on behalf of the retailer. These studies may be longitudinal in order that the retailer can come to understand how consumers' needs and wants change over time. In other instances, the research may be an 'ad hoc' exercise that has been commissioned in order to investigate a specific of the market.

While common to only the largest and most resource-rich retailers, an additional source of market-level customer trend data comes from internal market research departments. These departments are normally charged with the responsibility of co-ordinating all market intelligence gathering, and this may involve their undertaking primary data collection and may include their overseeing the activities of commissioned research companies.

The second element which contributes to the process of tracking customer trends involves the analysis of *micro-level consumer trends*. Unlike the macro-level analysis detailed above, which considers consumer trends in a somewhat broad fashion, micro-level analysis provides much more specific intelligence. Again often drawing from trade sources, buyers will consider the consumption patterns of their target customers with respect to specific product categories with a view to their being able to create successful ranges in the future.

As well as using external consumer data, buyers (often advised by the company's merchandising function) will interrogate internal data as a means of identifying their existing customers' patterns of buying behaviour. This internal data are used to provide information across a number of dimensions. Among those areas typically considered include sales trend analysis for specific products, brands and product variants (such as size, colour or material). This analysis of sales may be even broader and include a comparison of buying trends across product categories. So, for example, a fashion buyer may compare denim category sales with casual clothing sales as a means of understanding whether jeans are in favour with their customers. Buyers will examine a number of other factors in order to generate an intimate profile of their customers' purchasing habits and these will include consideration of:

- average transaction value;
- average selling price for specific products;
- best selling products;
- worst selling products;
- linked sales (i.e. those products that are purchased at the same time);
- time and place of purchase.

With this information, buyers can extrapolate the underlying trends in their customers' purchase behaviour and assemble product ranges that match the shifts in their purchase preferences. For those retailers with customer data derived from loyalty or store credit cards, a more specific customer profile can be developed which correlates personal data with purchasing data. This enables the buyer to identify not only what is being bought from their stores, but also which customers are buying it. This type of information is invaluable for buyers since it allows them to tailor the product offer to specific customer groups and improve the acceptance rate of product ranges and the success rate of new product launches.

In addition to the information obtained from the macro- and micro-level research surveys identified above, many retailers augment these findings with qualitative studies that track the consumption behaviour of *opinion-forming consumers*. Undertaken by specialist research companies, but also in some cases by buyers themselves, these studies examine the lifestyle characteristics of people perceived to be fashion leaders, the opinion-formers who live in the influential world centres, including London, New York, Sydney, San Francisco, Tokyo, Milan and Paris. Through the application of various observation techniques, buyers record what the 'movers and shakers' are wearing and eating, how they are living and what they are buying. Based upon the assumption that the consumption characteristics of these influential groups will 'trickle down' into a wider range of social groups, the purpose of these studies is to identify emerging consumer trends and predict how these may influence other markets. With this knowledge to hand, buyers within the mass market, for example, will seek to assemble appropriate product ranges and have these available in the market exactly at the time when these trends have filtered down to reach their target customers.

This close-to-market research may focus upon the retailers' target customers themselves. The methods of data capture that are used can be highly innovative and may involve a research team spending considerable amounts of time with individual consumers in their homes in order that a better understanding of their consumption motivations, behaviour patterns and aspirations can be better understood. Furthermore, buyers also test consumer reaction to new product innovations and developments through the use of focus groups and user trials. Used primarily as a risk-reducing strategy, buyers may then modify their buying decisions on the basis of their research findings.

Drawing together from the three strands, the buying team will then seek to piece together a profile of the consumer which will identify, predict and understand their consumption needs and wants. For all retailers this is an ongoing activity, but for large retailers with a large number of people involved in the buying function, this is also a process that is formalized on a regular basis. Within the fashion sector for example, a review of consumer trends and developments occurs at least on a twice-yearly basis. The findings of these reviews often serve as an important briefing mechanism for designers prior to their development of design sketches for their fashion collections. Furthermore, these consumer trend reviews are used to direct the final selection decisions of the buyers themselves, as well as the activities of others that are involved in advertising, store format development and other areas of marketing decision making.

Competitor trend tracking

In conjunction with a clear and comprehensive understanding of the consumer, buyers must also have a competent understanding of competitor activity. By knowing what the competition is doing to entice customers, the buying team must develop adequate defensive strategies in order to secure customer loyalty. In addition, a sound understanding of the competition may enable the buyer to exploit their weaknesses, gain inspiration and ideas from their strengths, and be prepared for any new initiatives that the competition may adopt.

Like consumer trend tracking, the analysis of the competition is an ongoing activity, and is undertaken on an informal, as well as formal, basis. Typically described as a Competitor Review Report, this is a formal and systematic evaluation of the actions of the competition. Often undertaken by more junior members of the buying team, it would be expected that most reviews would consider some, if not all, of the following trading dimensions.

Product ranges

Integral to this part of the analysis is the review of the breadth and depth of the competition's product offer. Particular attention is given, where appropriate, to the mix of brands, as well as the balance between manufacturer brand and retailer own-brand products. The breadth and depth of product categories or individual products are also considered and particular attention given to those products that have been deleted or recently introduced. An assessment may also be made with respect to the type and number of lines that are exclusive to the retailer, and this will also include an evaluation of the extent to which these exclusive products provide the competition with any significant market advantage.

In some circumstances, the buyer may be interested in the suppliers that competitors use for their product ranges. This information may be easy to obtain from product labelling, while in other cases, the buyer may rely upon industry sources in order to find out which manufacturer supplied a particular product range.

In certain circumstances information concerning the origin of supply can be important from a marketing communications perspective. For example, Marks & Spencer in the UK has, since the late 1990s, sourced a sizeable proportion of its tailored clothing ranges from Italian manufacturers. This decision was primarily motivated by their buying teams' desire to exploit the positive country of origin associations that the 'Made in Italy' labelling could provide. As a result of their commitment to this sourcing strategy, other British fashion retailers have also switched to Italian suppliers in order that their products may also benefit from such positive associations.

Pricing strategy

It is unusual for retailers not to be concerned with the pricing strategy of their competition. Even within the most exclusive markets, buyers need to be aware of pricing trends in order that they are not totally adrift from market expectations. The analysis of the competitor pricing typically will consider three aspects. The first is that of the price entry point in each product range or category. The entry point is the least expensive product and this is an important consideration since it serves to define the market positioning of the company. It is common for retailers within a particular market to set common entry point prices, not least to ensure that their prices are sufficiently accessible for a sufficient number of customers. The second aspect to be considered is that of price lining. Price lining refers to the various price points that a retailer sets within a particular product range. So, for example, a wines and spirits retailer may offer champagne at five price points – such as £20, £25, £30, £35 and £50. These various price points would serve to indicate a differential to customers with respect to perhaps the quality, quantity or reputation of each of the champagne marques on sale. Consideration of the price-lining policies of the competition is useful since it provides some insight into the competition's assessment of the target market's price tolerances – in terms of how little and how much they are prepared to pay. Furthermore, it also indicates the level of price choice that customers may expect within a product range or category.

The third aspect of pricing that is typically considered relates to the extent to which competitors' prices have changed in a given period. In order to undertake this sort of an analysis, it is necessary for the retailer to record, at regular intervals, their competitors' pricing for specific products. The products that are usually monitored are those that are in high demand, which are common to the retailer and their competitors, and of which customers are likely to be price sensitive. So, for example, buyers for a food retailer may regularly track price variations on products such as dairy, household and bread products. Of particular interest to buyers are the range and number of price mark-downs undertaken by the competition. This is especially important since it provides some indication of the success of the competition's product selection and pricing strategies, as well as providing insights into consumer demand for specific products and categories.

As well as tracking the prices of specific products, buyers will also monitor changes in the overall pricing strategies of the competition. Based upon this intelligence, the buying team may then decide to alter their current pricing strategy.

Promotional strategy

In recognition of the fact that the buyer's success is dependent upon the support of a clear, relevant and distinctive promotional strategy, it is common for a review to also include consideration of the competitor's promotional activities. In general, an analysis will review the ranges of products included in the promotion, as well as the conditions of the promotion itself. Wherever possible, buyers will seek to evaluate the success, or otherwise, of product promotions by considering consumer demand for the promoted lines, the length of time in which a promotion operates and the volume of products that are left unsold.

Visual merchandising methods

Buyers constantly search for new ideas and developments in visual merchandising and display techniques. Therefore, consideration is given to the way in which competitors present merchandise in terms of store layout, and the way in which they group products and arrange product adjacency. It is also important to note innovations in terms of display shelving, lighting and store interiors. By considering the placement of products within a store, buyers are able to then identify which products are especially significant to their rival's current offer. So, for example, if a buyer notes that The Gap has placed stone-washed denim at the front of the store, alongside white tailored cotton shirts, then it is clear that these products are central to that company's current product strategy. Furthermore, by identifying which products are presented in the areas of highest visibility within a store, the buyer may also deduce that these are likely to be in high demand and may yield the highest levels of profitability.

Store windows

Store windows have often been described as the 'eye into the heart of a store' and as such these deserve careful consideration. A review of the range of goods presented in a window display may serve as a useful indicator of which products are important to the competition's current product strategy. A review may also examine the lighting, photography and display techniques that are used by the competition in order to attract and retain customers.

Customer profile review

As well as considering the various interventions that rivals adopt in order to influence consumer behaviour, it is also worthwhile for a competitor review to consider who is actually shopping with the competition at any given time. As such, a record may be made of the number of customers, their age and any other distinguishing characteristics. Of the latter, some buyers will record, where possible, the bags that competitor's customers are carrying, the types of cars that are in the car park, and the sorts of products that they are buying. It is not uncommon for determined buyers to strike up conversations with a rival's customers in order to obtain some insights as to why they chose to shop with that retailer in the first place.

Typically, buyers will focus their competitor analysis upon three or four key competitors. By drawing together information with respect to their activities across these six dimensions, the buyer's own strategy can be informed in at least two ways. Firstly, it allows the buyer to identify the changes and developments in the trading environment that they perhaps must adopt in order to remain competitive. Secondly, and equally important, the analysis of the competition can also assist the buyer in the identification of the ways in which they can better the competition and differentiate their company within the market. A buying director for a leading French department store further explained the value of competitor monitoring:

> It helps us identify the competition's mistakes as they happen, and it also lets us exploit their mistakes. It should alert us not to make the same mistakes. Retailing is like warfare and competitor information is the key to success in the market.

Product trend tracking

The third dimension of a competent trend management strategy incorporates a comprehensive analysis of changes and developments with respect to products in the market. The extent to which buyers engage in this, as well as the other activities detailed above, is dependent upon the nature of the market in which they operate, as well as the size and resource availability of their companies. However, regardless of the extent to which buyers investigate product trends, their analysis will usually include three specific product trend dimensions; these include forecasted/pipeline developments, imminent and recent product launches, as well as upgrading/extension of current product range activities. Each of these will be considered below.

Forecasted/pipeline developments

Buyers draw from a variety of sources in order to obtain insights and information about forecasted new products and those that are currently in the development stage. Probably the most accessible and least expensive information source is that of trade publications, which continually report new product development trends. Often, the trade press will base their reports upon information obtained directly from manufacturers' press releases. In many instances, it is the role of the trade press to provide some form of technical evaluation of the feasibility of these new developments. Their reports may incorporate a prediction of the likely success of these developments in the market.

In markets that are very dynamic or which are technically advanced (such as the electronics sector), buyers will call upon the services of specialist forecasting agencies. Their role is to advise the company of their predictions with respect to how and where the market is likely to develop in the future. For example, within the fashion sector, specialist forecasting agencies advise buyers of their predictions for which colours, fabrics and designs will be strong in the forthcoming seasons. Drawing from these forecasts, buyers, working alongside their designers and merchandisers, will seek to interpret this information within the context of their understanding of their customer requirements by developing their own product concepts.

As well as using the services of individual forecasting agencies, retail buyers may also visit the various trade fairs and conferences that forecast market trends and innovations. Within the fashion sector, for example, buyers will visit events such as Premier Vision in Paris that predicts the colours and fabrics that will be in fashion in future seasons. Buyers may also visit events that promote new manufacturing technologies which may enable the creation and development of entirely new products or which allow for the manufacture of these goods in new and innovative ways.

In some circumstances (usually those where the retailer is in some way important to the manufacturer, typically because of their scale or market reputation), manufacturers may regularly present to the retailer their latest product concepts. In return for obtaining a retailer's reaction to the suitability of a product concept and a prediction of its likely market success, manufacturers are then willing to share their development secrets. This obviously provides the retail buyer with a first-hand account of market developments before these actually reach the market.

Imminent and recent product launches

An important means of obtaining information with respect to imminent product launches is for the retail buyer to attend trade fairs and other sorts of events that seek to showcase new products. The purpose of these events is typically to persuade buyers to stock these new products within their stores. Again, within the fashion sector, buyers for the world's most prestigious department stores, for example, will attend the many fashion shows held biannually in Paris, Milan, New York and London. These events not only showcase the designers' collections for the following year, but also serve as a sales forum, where buyers place their orders up to one year before they are launched on the market.

For those fashion buyers who operate outside the high fashion market, these may also use the designer fashion shows as a means of gaining insights into future trends that may filter into their markets. As such, these shows may provide a useful direction for the development of their own collections.

The direct marketing activity of manufacturers and distributors also serves as an important mechanism for communicating to buyers any information concerning imminent and recent product launches. This may be in the form of brochures, public relations events or through the canvassing of their representatives. In some companies, such as the British DIY chain B&Q, the buying department hosts events that invite manufacturers and suppliers to their headquarters in order that they may promote their new product ideas to buyers and inform the company of imminent launches. This sort of activity, which has become more popular in recent years, is a cost-effective method for buyers to be kept informed of new product developments either before or as they reach the market.

Other mechanisms for tracking imminent and recent product launches, which are accessible to most companies, include the reviewing of new product launch advertisements and editorial commentaries in the consumer or trade press. In addition, buyers may obtain intelligence from contacts within other companies and from general market gossip. Observing the new product launches of rivals is an obvious, but important, means of tracking these developments.

Another important source of information on new product launch activity is to be found in the retailer's own internal sales data. From an analysis of this data, the buyer can obtain insights into the level of customer receptivity to new product developments, particularly in terms of which new features appear to be of greatest interest to customers and which marketing communications campaigns have had the greatest impact. These studies also provide information with regards to the levels of product and brand switching that exists within their market. It also provides an opportunity to evaluate the levels of customer price sensitivity, especially if the new products carry with them a price premium.

Upgrading/extension of current product ranges

In reality, it is rare for a new product to be completely original and new to the market. Instead, there is every chance that it is an upgrade of some other existing, usually successful, product. Consideration of the nature and extent of these upgrades provides the buyer with useful information on how the market in general currently understands and responds to customers' needs and wants. Buyers can obtain information with respect to these upgrades from many of the sources identified above and especially from the marketing communications of suppliers and manufacturers, reports provided by the trade press, and the buying activities of their competitors.

The extension of current product ranges is motivated by the desire to maximize the sales potential of either a strong product idea or a successful brand name. For example, the Mars Confectionery Company extended their Mars Bar range beyond that of chocolate bars to also include Mars Bar ice-cream and soft drinks. This allowed the business to extend their brand into other product categories that would help harmonize the seasonality of demand for their core products. Similarly, the British fashion retailer Next recognized that their brand was trusted by consumers and this allowed for it to extend from clothing into other product categories, including home furnishings, jewellery and cosmetics.

An analysis of the various product range extensions undertaken by suppliers and retailers is important for the retail buyer for two particular reasons. The first is that it may provide direction for the buyer similarly to extend their product ranges. Secondly, it may instead encourage them not to extend their ranges in a similar way so that they can maintain a distinctive positioning by either retaining a precise product focus or by developing their ranges in another direction.

By undertaking this three-stage analysis of product trends, the buyer benefits from a comprehensive and inclusive understanding of current and future market trends. For those companies that market products under their own-brand name, this analysis is especially important. The significance of this activity to all retailers is perhaps best summarized by the comments of a buyer working for a British grocery retailer:

> As the market becomes more complex and competitive, product trend analysis becomes so much more important. Customers have high expectations and if they find that you do not have the latest and best products available for them, you will lose them. Retailers that are last to the market with products are last in the profit league too.

Having gathered together the details relevant to consumer, competitor and product trends, this information serves as a vital platform for decision making by the buyer. In particular, it is critical to the successful development of own-brand ranges. Later in this chapter, the integration of this information to the own-brand development process is explored in greater depth.

Box 6.1   Case example – Market data gathering in fashion

An American fashion retailer that is targeted towards male and female consumers, in their late twenties to late thirties, has developed a brand that represents a sense of fashion that is stylish, contemporary, but never radical. Their customers respect the attention to design detail that the company's product offers, as well as the inherent values of quality and value for money.

The product development team recognized the ever-increasing influence that European lifestyle trends and European brands have upon American fashion design. Therefore, in order to stay abreast of European fashion trends, in the mid-1990s the company established a marketing intelligence office in London.

The responsibility of researchers based in the London office is three-fold. Firstly, they search all of the key European fashion cities, especially London, Paris, New York, Madrid and Barcelona, for new fashion trends and the latest product ideas. These trends are then communicated back to buyers in the USA, through written reports but often in the form of the actual fashion products themselves. The American buyers then use these reports and the products themselves to inspire and direct the development of the product range. Secondly, the London-based researchers closely monitor the new product developments and other marketing activities of European retailers that compete directly with the company in the USA. This information allows the retailer to pre-empt the developments of their foreign competitors, since these initiatives are usually launched in Europe prior to their introduction in America. Thirdly, the researchers search for interesting new product developments in areas other than clothing, as well as new lifestyle brands and emergent lifestyle changes in Europe which may have a subsequent impact upon the life of their home market customers.

The European research team typically obtains their information by observing street fashions, visiting the key nightclubs, and by recording trends in retailing, specifically with respect to changing store environments and new visual merchandising methods. Their research monitoring encapsulates trends in music, literature and cinema. Reviews of the advertising and editorial included in lifestyle magazines also provide an important insight into consumer, competitor and product trends across Europe.

New supplier selection strategies

The nature of buyer and supplier relationships within retailing has changed significantly in the past 20 years. A variety of factors have contributed to this change, not least of which is the increased range and complexity of goods which are required in order to satisfy consumer requirements. Dawson and Shaw (1989) predicted that the nature of buyer and supplier relationships would change by necessity as a result of increased competition, particularly on an international basis, to supply and retail goods and services to customers. Furthermore, they suggested that the increased concentration of retail power with fewer but larger retail buyers, alongside the drive to improve gross and net margins in response to shareholder pressure, would be the catalyst for changed supply chain relationships. These factors, alongside the rising quality, presentation and design expectations of consumers, have meant that in many instances the nature of buyer and supplier relationships has changed from being adversarial to more collaborative in nature.

Evidence from the research with retail buyers suggests that buyers are at least trying to develop more collaborative relationships with their suppliers and they do so for a variety of reasons. Perhaps the most common, if not the most important, reason is the fact that establishing a new supplier has a learning cost factor. Considerable amounts of time are often taken upon in the process of searching, evaluating, selecting, negotiating and establishing a rapport with a new supplier. This process is resource intensive and also very costly. Therefore, in order to minimize these costs, buyers have sought to develop effective supplier selection strategies that provide for the successful identification and selection of suitable suppliers to the business.

As a corollary to the development of a new supplier selection strategy, there are a number of decisions which buyers must first consider. Again, drawing from the interviews with the retail buyers, one of the most important relates to the issue of how many suppliers a retailer should have. For example, a grocery buyer, responsible for the fresh produce buy, must ensure the availability, quality and competitive pricing of their range. From a price perspective, the buyer would be inclined to concentrate their buy to a small number of suppliers so as to obtain the benefits of economies of scale in their buy. However, by concentrating their buy to one or a small number of suppliers, the buyer faces a considerable risk. If the supplier's crops should fail, perhaps because of bad weather, the buyer is left in an untenable position.

In order to avoid an over-dependence upon a small and potentially vulnerable group of suppliers, buyers (particularly those that operate in product sectors which are in some way turbulent and unstable) are increasingly adopting a tiered supplier strategy. This involves their concentrating perhaps 70 per cent of their buy with a few, often larger suppliers, while the remainder of the buy is shared among a number of smaller companies. By adopting a tiered supplier strategy, buyers seek to combine the benefits of scale economies that are derived from the concentration of the buy, with the safety that spreading the buy across a number of sources can provide.

Looking specifically to the strategies that buyers adopt for new supplier selection, it is possible to identify four stages to the process. Each of these is listed below and will be considered in turn.

1 Identification of supplier selection criteria.
2 Supplier identification procedures.
3 Supplier evaluation processes.
4 Negotiation of trading arrangements.

Supplier selection criteria

In the past, price, and more specifically price competitiveness, was normally the defining criterion for supplier selection. However, in recognition of their need to develop a competitive advantage through the provision of added values from products and services, many buyers now acknowledge that an exclusive focus upon price is no longer sufficient to secure competitive advantage. Instead, buyers have extended their requirements of a supplier to be more inclusive. The criteria that they adopt vary depending upon the retailer and supplier size, and the nature of the sector and the product. However, in broad terms it is possible to identify five key areas for consideration, as detailed below.

Product
- Range of products available in the supplier's portfolio – a buyer may be more interested in a supplier that can provide a variety of different products at the same time.
- Quality of goods and services.
- Value for money of the range, principally in terms of the cost prices and the service benefits made available.
- Product development potential of the supplier.
- Exclusivity potential – which is especially important for those retailers that market their goods under their own brand.

Terms of trade
- Cost price levels.
- Payment cycle requirements – 30, 60 or 180 days.
- Range and conditions of discounts.
- Guarantees and other bonds – whereby the supplier will guarantee a minimum level of sales income. If this level is not reached, then the supplier will honour the sales shortfall, normally through a reduced invoice payment. This safeguard is specially important for prestigious retailers who require a minimum return on their investment.
- Level of investment required by the retailer in terms of their providing either financial or technical support to the supplier.

Reputation of the supplier
- Customer portfolio – as evidenced by the number and reputation of customers and the number of which that may be competitors.

- Reputation for ethical and safety standards – such as in relation to factory/workers' conditions.
- Reputation of the senior management and personnel within the supplier's company.
- Financial standing of the supplier – especially in terms of the risk of insolvency.
- Technical capability and reputation for quality management.

Systems support
- Communication systems for buyer–supplier relationship management.
- Stock management systems.
- Customer service systems – such as in relation to the handling of faulty goods and the crediting procedures that are to be used when these goods are returned.
- Administrative support for stock and financial processing.

Marketing support
- Reputation of the supplier's brand, if appropriate.
- In-store merchandising support available from the supplier.
- Promotional activities proposed by the supplier in order to support product in the market.
- Advertising support proposed by the supplier in order to communicate the product in the market.

Supplier identification procedures

For some retail buyers, the process of identifying new suppliers is an activity that they prefer to undertake infrequently because of the effort, cost and risk that this activity involves. In certain product sectors, such as in fashion, the buyer may delegate the responsibility of new supplier selection to an agent based overseas, such as in Hong Kong. An agent or a representative from the retailer's foreign buying office will identify new suppliers due to their geographic proximity, or because of their extensive contact with manufacturers. Regardless of whoever actually sources the new suppliers, most retailers have a standardized procedure for new supplier identification and this is presented in Figure 6.2.

Supplier evaluation process

In addition to the various techniques that buyers may adopt as part of the supplier selection process, it is also vital that they develop evaluation measures in order to monitor and review the performance of the supply base. There are a number of different measures that may be

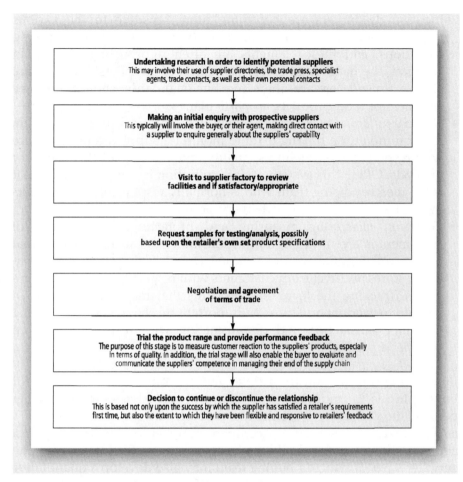

Figure 6.2 Procedures for new supplier identification.

adopted which cumulatively provide an invaluable insight into the performance of suppliers. These include the following:

● *Factory audits.* It is common for buyers, merchandisers and quality control specialists to visit the factories that supply these goods. These visits may, in some circumstances, be undertaken without prior warning. Often, the buying team will develop a standard document that records their findings with respect to a number of specific dimensions, and these documents serve as the basis for recording the ongoing performance of suppliers. It is common for factory visits to examine and compare the supplier's manufacturing techniques and the features of in-production samples against agreed buying specifications. The evaluation will also consider the quality control processes adopted, as well as the condition of relevant equipment.

Increasingly, buyers are becoming more sensitive to the various issues surrounding the conditions of the workforce and their working conditions, and these elements are often rigorously reviewed. In addition, the health and safety standards of suppliers' factories are also evaluated, as are their hygiene standards should they be suppliers of food products, in particular.

- *Delivery performance*. Where the volume of products supplied is high, it is common for a buying team to monitor a supplier's performance with respect to the timeliness, quality and accuracy of their delivery of goods. Often, this system of data collection is computerized and it is the merchandising team who is normally responsible for monitoring and assessing supplier delivery performance.

- *Complaint monitoring*. Assuring and protecting the goodwill of customers is a central buying responsibility. As such, it is vital that buyers collate, analyse and respond to complaints that arise from either stores or direct from customers with respect to every supplier's goods. Tracking the level of complaints that may arise, such as in relation to product quality, is an important mechanism for measuring customer satisfaction and dissatisfaction with respect to a given supplier's products.

By drawing information from these various sources, it is common for buying teams to undertake a regular and formal review of supplier performance. This may result, for example, in the production of a SWOT analysis that seeks to compare supplier performance against agreed performance levels. As well as generating a SWOT analysis of a supplier's performance, a buying team may also develop a quantitative form of supplier evaluation that identifies a number of criteria for which each supplier is awarded a particular rating. This enables the buyer to compare and contrast the performance of their whole supply base, as well as the relative performance of individual suppliers. Bailey (1987) provided a comprehensive review of the quantitative methodologies that buyers use and this work has retained its relevance and influence.

Having identified the mechanisms for evaluating suppliers for their performance, it is also important to consider the options or sanctions that are available to a buyer should the performance of the supplier fail to meet expectations. As a starting point for this process, it is necessary for the buying team to first precisely define the area of under-performance. Having done that, it is common to then measure the frequency of the under-performance and the impact that this has upon customer satisfaction. For example, it is rare for a buying team to terminate trading with a supplier over one incident of poor performance, unless that incident has significantly undermined the reputation and standing of the retailer in question. With this information to hand, the buying team can then assess the significance of the situation and decide upon their subsequent actions.

Before considering the various responses that a buying team may have in these situations, it is also important to note that their deliberations will have to take into account not only the gravity of the misdemeanour, but also the importance of the supplier to the company. Furthermore, the team must consider whether the supplier is a major or the only source in the market, and also whether substitute products, other brands or alternative suppliers are readily available in the market.

As to the course of action that a buyer will be able to take with respect to a supplier's poor performance, much of this is determined by the terms of the legal contract that binds buyers and suppliers. However, setting any specific contractual conditions aside, a buyer must first inform the supplier of a problem and expect an explanation for their under-performance. In some circumstances a formal or informal warning to the supplier may be issued and/or the goods may be returned to the supplier. In circumstances where the buying team can prove that the poor performance of the supplier has led to a loss of business, they may raise cash penalties against the supplier. Other sanctions may include reducing or cancelling an order or the imposition of supervision of the supplier's activities by the retailer. In extreme circumstances, non-performance may result in a cessation of trading. It is perhaps interesting to note that many buyers regard the cessation of trading as a failure on both sides, as one buyer from an electrical retailer explained:

> I think that if it gets to the stage that you have to act to cut a relationship with a supplier then the buyer has got to take some responsibility. Either the buyer has not done their job properly when selecting the supply base or they have failed to keep a close enough eye on the relationship.

Negotiation of trading arrangements

The ability to control supplier negotiations in order to protect and enhance the position of the buyer's company, irrespective of their position in the market and the stature of the supply base, is a critical buyer attribute. However, this does not mean that the buyer's negotiation position should be to undermine the supplier's position. While in the past the buyer's primary objective may have been to secure the best price and profit margin regardless of the effect upon the supplier's profitability, more recent practice underlines an increased commitment to collaborative forms of buyer–supplier relationships. This shift in the climate of buyer and supplier negotiations is evidenced by a commitment to long-term relationships through the mutual achievement of a reasonable profit. This change has been achieved through an increased shared understanding of the nature of both the buyer's and the supplier's businesses, and has been facilitated through a freer exchange of information between the two parties.

From a buyer's perspective, the starting point for successful negotiation necessitates that they have a competent understanding of the market, the product(s) and the issues associated with their delivery. The buyer must understand the specifications of their product(s), the manufacturing and technical processes required in creating it (them), as well as the pricing structure. Furthermore, an understanding of the price structure of the product's raw materials enables a more informed assessment of a supplier's cost price competitiveness, especially if their raw materials are susceptible to price fluctuations.

With this information, the buyer must then identify their requirements with regards to: the unit cost price of a product; their order quantity requirements; product lead times; delivery schedule requirements; exclusivity agreements; and marketing support requirements. Only in very rare cases will a buyer achieve all of their requirements in a negotiation. By its very nature, a negotiation, especially where the buyer and supplier seek to develop mutual, long-term relationships, necessitates that each side accommodate some of the needs of the other in the search for agreement.

However, the experienced buyer must also ensure that their accommodation of a supplier's demands is not detrimental to the profitability of their own company. As such, it is necessary for the buyer to identify, prior to a negotiation, what they might ideally obtain, what they would like to obtain and must obtain from a negotiation. The LIM acronym (Like, Ideal and Must) identifies the tolerances available to a buyer in terms of what they can concede in a negotiation with a supplier. The identification of the 'must have' elements is especially important prior to a negotiation in that it alerts the buyer to those dimensions that must be achieved to protect company interests. Table 6.1 presents an example of the LIM plan of a perfumery buyer for a prestigious London department store.

As a final point, it is worth noting that negotiations between buyers and suppliers, while not as comprehensive or as intense as those undertaken during the initial stages of their relationship, are nevertheless an ongoing activity. The activities of the competition, the introduction of new products and existing product enhancements, alongside changes in the macro environment (such as shift in oil prices, which may change transportation costs), all necessitate that buyers are

Table 6.1 An example of a perfumery buyer's LIM sheet

Dimension	Like	Ideal	Must
Product	Perfume and body range	Full range	Perfume range
Payment terms (days)	60	90	45
Distribution	Exclusive for 6 weeks	Exclusive for 6 months	Exclusive launch
Advertising	75% contribution from supplier	Full cost by supplier	50% contribution by supplier
Consultant staff	75% supplier/25% retailer pay contribution	Full pay contribution by supplier	50% pay contribution by supplier
In-store merchandising	50% contribution for fittings	100% contribution for fittings	25% contribution for fittings

in constant dialogue with suppliers. An electrical goods buyer further explains this:

> At the start of the relationship with a new supplier, it is important to be clear on price, delivery, replenishment systems, exclusivity and marketing deals. But it does not end there, because the market will change. So there are ongoing specific aspects of the deal. It is wrong to see negotiation as a one-off activity.

Procedures for managing the development of own-brand products

While the activities of new product development and brand management have traditionally been the responsibility of manufacturers, these activities have increasingly been assumed by retailers who seek to market products under their own brand name. The literature has identified a variety of reasons as to why retailers would wish to assume this responsibility, of which the most important is likely to be their desire to improve profitability through higher margins and cost-related benefits. Furthermore, own-brand development assists in the development of business loyalty and the creation of a distinct corporate identity (Webb, 2001; Murphy, 2001; McGoldrick, 2002). And while the development of a strong own-brand product range may provide the retailer

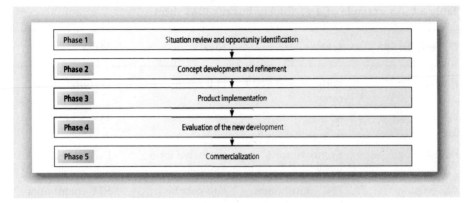

Figure 6.3 Phases in the development of an own-brand product.

with an early opportunity to seize new market opportunities and bargain more forcibly with suppliers over price and promotional support, it also increases their exposure to business risk. Consequently, it is important that retailers who are involved in own-brand development adopt a systematic and coherent approach to product management.

The following section will review the five significant phases in own-label product development. Typically, these phases occur sequentially, but on occasion, the phases may happen concurrently and modifications may occur with respect to the exact approach adopted by specific companies. Figure 6.3 delineates the five phases in the development of own-brand products.

Phase I: Situation review and opportunity identification

As part of this initial phase in the process, the buying team undertakes a full review of the market and, from their assessment, they ought to be able to identify opportunities for product development. Their initial analysis of the external environment will consider the various consumer, competitor and product trends within the market (as was delineated above in the section on 'Trend management strategies').

With a competent market understanding, it is necessary for the buying team to review the product situation in the company, specifically in terms of their current product portfolio. Each product category, and in some cases each product, is evaluated in terms of competitive position, stage on the product life cycle, and the rate of growth and decline. For those organizations with the relevant technology, it is also possible to identify specifically the direct profit contribution of a product category and even a specific product. Based upon these indicators, the strengths and weaknesses of the current offer can be located and the areas of development opportunity can be broadly identified.

In addition to this internal analysis, it is also useful for the buying team to review the capability of the existing supply base, with a view to identifying which supplier would be best placed to partner their future product development initiatives. As part of this appraisal, the buying team would consider the previous performance standards of individual suppliers, alongside an assessment of their advances in product and process innovation.

Finally, as part of this initial review of market trends, internal capability and supplier expertise, it is also useful for buyers to reflect, where possible, upon previous successful product developments. As well as identifying which actions and processes were most appropriate, this review may also locate opportunities whereby successful products could be extended, improved and relaunched.

Phase 2: Concept development and refinement

The inspiration for a new product concept may come from a variety of sources. As was indicated in the previous section that considered the methods of trend analysis that a buyer may use, visits to trade shows, exhibitions and fairs often provide the primary inspiration for a new product idea.

Ideas may also come from local competition that may have a product that the buying team may further develop and refine in order to suit the needs of their customers. In some cases, the buyers may simply replicate the competition's products with just sufficient modification in order not to fall foul of copyright infringement. These 'me too' products mean that the buyer can circumvent at least the first two stages of the product development process. For fashion buyers, new product inspiration may come from visits to foreign retailers. It is not unusual for them to purchase sample garments from these companies for their own designers to copy.

Finally, an important idea source for new products comes from customers themselves. It is common practice for buying teams to convene customer focus groups that serve, through the use of brainstorming techniques, to identify new product opportunities.

Drawing together ideas from these various sources, buyers will then brief designers, food development chefs or other specialist technicians on their ideas and request that they provide product concepts. In some circumstances, these designers and technicians will be employed directly by the buyer's company, often on a freelance basis. However, it could also be the case that the buying team brief technical personnel employed by their various suppliers. In some cases, suppliers may provide unsolicited product concepts for the buying team's consideration.

Whenever developments are felt to carry some form of risk to the retailer, it is common for buyers to first test the attitudes and responses of consumers to the product concept prior to moving to the implementation stage. One buyer explained the importance of consumer testing by stating:

> It is worthwhile spending two days testing customer reaction to a product idea rather as opposed to having a warehouse of unwanted product. If it is a bad idea, we can kill it off there and then.

Phase 3: Product implementation

The process of implementing the production, marketing, testing and distribution of a new product is complex and resource intensive. The starting point is inevitably the identification and briefing of suppliers. A buyer may choose to brief more than one supplier in order that they may then compare supplier performance in terms of quality, innovation and cost. In circumstances where the buying team believes that it has a product that is new and innovative, a confidentiality agreement will have to be signed by the suppliers. This will seek to prevent suppliers from providing information to the competition, often for a fixed period, normally of up to 5 years.

Having briefed suppliers, the buying team will expect suppliers to provide product samples and, from the samples, provisional product specifications will be created and initial costings agreed. In circumstances where the financial investment associated with a new product is relatively high, it is normally expected that the buyer will seek further assurance that the product will be commercially successful and has the support of senior management. As a means of testing the commercial viability of the product, buyers will undertake further consumer research, often in the form of 'user' studies. These will involve the customer using, wearing, eating or drinking the product. Based upon their experiences of the product, they are expected to feed back their levels of satisfaction with the product, and where necessary, identify areas for product improvement.

In certain organizations, senior management must first ratify any new product development and this is typically undertaken as part of the buying range review. As part of this process, the senior management will either accept or reject the buying teams' product, pricing and promotions proposals. Alongside these various management activities, product sample testing occurs, and this typically includes the assessment of quality and performance, and a review of the effectiveness, or otherwise, of care, maintenance and user's instructions.

Alongside the development of the actual product, it is also necessary for the buying team to manage the packaging requirements of each new product. In some cases, manufacturers may also take responsibility for the development of appropriate packaging, but this occurs in the minority of cases. Development lead times for packaging in particular can be significant, and buyers must work with technologists to develop the most appropriate packaging methods. As part of their analysis, they must consider not only how packaging may enhance the presentation and customer appeal of the product, but must also consider the practical requirements of packaging, especially in terms of protecting goods during transportation, storage and staff handling. In the food and gift sectors, in particular, the appropriate packaging selection can have a direct impact upon the success, or otherwise, of a product range.

Once the final specification of the product has been agreed, the buying team will then seek an agreement on the cost price with their suppliers. Given their intimate involvement in the development of these products, it is likely that the buyers will have a clear understanding of the new product's cost structure. In terms of agreeing the price, this will be dependent upon a number of factors, including the raw material costs, development costs (especially if the supplier had to invest in new plant and technology), handling and supply chain costs, and the supplier's mark-up policy. In most cases, buyers will agree a scale of prices that reflect different levels of volume demand for the products. Typically, this will mean that the unit price for an item will decrease as the order quantities increase.

Prior to the full launch of a new product, buyers may insist on a small pre-production trial to ensure that any problems with respect to the supply process or the product itself can be identified and rectified. When both the buyers and suppliers are satisfied with the results of the pre-production run, it is common for buyers to request a trial launch of the product. A pre-launch is especially likely if the product is totally new to the retailer's offer. As well as providing a means of assessing customer reaction, a product trial will also assist in the identification of future demand. By projecting forward estimates of customer demand, merchandisers can then calculate the volume of goods that they will commit for manufacture. Furthermore, a product trial provides the buying team with guidance as to the most effective means of merchandising the range and will also provide some indication as to the potential effect on the sales of other products.

Given that the purpose of a product trial is to evaluate the rate and nature of customer interest in a product range, where possible, it is beneficial if the range is made available within stores that differ in terms of customer profile, geographic location and store format type. Through this comprehensive coverage, merchandisers can make more informed decisions with respect to order quantities and product attributes, such as in relation to size, colour and materials/ingredients.

Phase 4: Evaluation of the new development

There are a variety of ways in which a buyer may evaluate the success of a new line. The most commonly used methods include measuring changes in sales and profit, monitoring the rate of product sell-thorough, as well as identifying changes in average customer transactions value, the number of transactions and the demand for substitute products. Drawing together this information, the buying team can then make a more informed assessment of a product's suitability.

As a result of a positive evaluation, an increase in production plans, delivery phasing and the required volume of packaging can be made. If the result is negative, initial actions may include re-merchandising the product range, altering the promotional support or adjusting the retail prices. If the product continues to under-perform against budget expectations, then a swift decision must be made to cease production so as to minimize losses. Having ceased production, the buying team must then assess the value of stock in the pipelines and develop a contingency for the liquidation of that stock. If raw materials have been purchased, it may be possible to divert these to alternative production lines.

Phase 5: Commercialization

The final phase in the process is the commercialization of the new product in the market. Typically, this will involve the merchandising team assuring its maximum availability within stores and controlling the supply chain so as to ensure there is a sufficient level of product availability in order to meet future demand. At this stage, it is especially important for the buying team to monitor the effectiveness, or otherwise, of relevant in-store point-of-sale materials and to ensure that visual merchandising standards are maintained. Furthermore, where necessary, it is vital that the buying team ensures that the staff has sufficient product knowledge so as to provide accurate and relevant information to customers.

At the early stages of full market commercialization, the buying team will closely monitor the sales of their new product. Furthermore, their attention will also extend to a consideration of the impact of the new introduction upon sales of existing lines. In certain circumstances, it may be necessary to eliminate a product or even products whose sales have declined sharply as a result of a successful new product introduction. In these circumstances, however, it is also important that the buying team consider the impact that eliminating a product may have upon the level of product choice that they offer to customers. For those retailers with a market positioning built upon having a wide product assortment, it may be necessary for the retailer to retain products principally as a support to their market reputation.

Finally, of the many dimensions of market and product performance that the buying team must monitor in the advent of a new product introduction, it is especially important that competitors' actions are constantly recorded. In situations where the newly launched product is innovative and new to the market, it is very likely that the competition will soon follow with their own version of the product. In these situations, buying teams will monitor the features and benefits of the

---

Box 6.2   Case example – Product evaluation in action

The buying team at one particular British fashion retailer undertake extensive trend analysis across the UK and in other countries. As well as exploring consumer attitudes to their new product ideas, the company also undertakes extensive research with respect to the quality performance of their goods. The company's in-house Quality Assurance Department rigorously tests a sample from every product range. As part of these tests, products are assessed for colour-fastness and durability. Furthermore, all products must satisfy European safety standard regulations.

In tandem with these technical tests, the company also conducts 'wearer trials' of their products. These trials involve ordinary members of the public wearing the products over a period of time. From their experience of wearing and using the product, the 'wearers' report back their assessment of the quality, value for money and levels of comfort that the products provide. In addition, they will assess how easy it is to care for the items and will consider whether the care instructions were easy to understand and accurate.

Drawing information from these two important sources, the buying teams then report their findings to the relevant suppliers. Where necessary, product specifications will be altered and modifications to the product features or to the method of manufacture will be made. It is through their investment in these forms of market research that has, according to the company, enabled the brand to develop and maintain a credible reputation for quality excellence in the British fashion market.

competitor's new product, in addition to their pricing and marketing communications tactics. Where it is believed some aspect of the competitor's offering may be detrimental to their own product, it may be necessary for the buying team to adopt measures to protect and positively differentiate their product from that of the competition.

As both a summation of the processes inherent to the development of own-brand products and an indicator of the inherent complexity of that process, a buyer working for an Italian fashion retailer made the following observation:

> For us, the process is quite linear, starting with the initial idea, through to launching in over 300 stores. But in my case, I am going through this with 240 lines at any one time, and these lines can be at any stage on the development line. To be a good buyer you have to be a good project manager and have a good memory for where you are at with each line. Own-brand products are complex, are high risk to manage. But they are worth the effort when you get it right.

Summary

This chapter reviewed the role of buying within retail organizations. Having recognized the central role that buyers play in the implementation of a retailer's positioning strategy, consideration was then given to the principle buying activities. These were identified as ranging from undertaking an analysis of market opportunity to the selection of the supply base. The measures that are used in order to measure the performance of the buying team were also reviewed.

The chapter sought to identify the defining issues relevant to retail buying in the twenty-first century.

As such, consideration was given to the trend management strategies that buyers adopt in order to appraise market opportunities, and this included a review of their consumer, competitor and product intelligence strategies.

Consideration was then given to the new supplier selection strategies that buyers adopt. Integral to this review was a full consideration of supplier selection criteria, supplier identification procedures, supplier evaluation measures and the methods that buyers adopt in order to negotiate with their supply base.

In recognition of the importance of own-brand development to the success of many retailers, the chapter reviewed the key procedures that buyers adopt for the creation of these ranges. The five key phases of development were considered, and these related to: the process of reviewing market opportunities; developing product concepts; implementing product plans; evaluating new developments and finally commercializing product ideas.

The chapter concluded by underlining the key fact that the process of own-brand development is inherently high risk but is one that provides the retailer with many significant opportunities.

Review questions

1 Identify the various participants who form a buying team within larger retailer companies. Describe the different roles that these perform within the buying team.
2 Outline the measures that can be used in order to review the performance of the buying team.
3 Review the strategies that a buyer could adopt in order to track trends within the market.
4 Identify and describe the criteria that a buyer could use in order to evaluate a new supplier.
5 What are the procedures that a buyer might adopt in order to develop an own-brand range of merchandise?

References

Bailey, P. J. H. (1987). *Purchasing and Supply Management*. Chapman & Hall, London.

Davidson, W. R., Sweeney, D. J. and Stampfl, R. W. (1988). *Retailing Management*. John Wiley, New York.

Dawson, J. A. and Shaw, S. A. (1989). The move to administered vertical marketing systems by British retailers. *European Journal of Marketing*, **23**(7), 42–52.

McGoldrick, P. (2002). *Retail Marketing*, 2nd edn. McGraw-Hill, London.

Murphy, R. (2001). B2C online strategies for fashion retailers. In *Fashion Marketing: Contemporary Issues* (Hines, T. and Bruce, M., eds). Butterworth-Heinemann, Oxford.

Varley, R. (2001). *Retail Product Management – Buying and Merchandising*, 1st edn. Routledge, London.

Webb, B. (2001). Retail brand marketing in the new millennium. In *Fashion Marketing: Contemporary Issues* (Hines, T. and Bruce, M., eds). Butterworth-Heinemann, Oxford.

7

Retail logistics

Introduction

The principles behind logistics and supply chain management are not new. Managing elements of the supply chain has been encapsulated within organizations for centuries. Decisions such as where to hold stock, in what quantities and how it is distributed have been part of the 'trade-off' analysis that is at the heart of logistics management. It is only in the last 10–15 years, however, that logistics has achieved prominence in companies' boardrooms, primarily because of the impact which the application of supply chain techniques can have on a company's competitive position and profitability. Retailers have been in the forefront of applying best practice principles to their businesses, with UK grocery retailers being acknowledged as innovators in logistics management. This chapter discusses:

- the theoretical framework which underpins logistics and supply chain management (SCM) concepts;
- efficient consumer response (ECR) and managing supply chain relationships;
- the application of supply chain concepts in different international markets;
- future trends, most notably the impact of e-commerce upon logistics networks.

Supply chain management: theoretical perspectives

The roots of supply chain management as a discipline are often attributed to the management guru, Peter Drucker, and his seminal article in *Fortune* magazine in 1962. At this time he was discussing distribution as one of the key areas of business, where major efficiency gains could be achieved and costs saved. Then, and through the next two decades, the supply chain was still viewed as a series of disparate functions. Thus logistics management was depicted as two separate schools of thought; one dealing with materials management (industrial markets), the other with physical distribution management (consumer goods markets) (see Figure 7.1). In terms of the marketing function, research has focused upon buyer–seller relationships and the shift away from adversarial relationships to those built upon trust (see Ford, 1997). At the same time a body of literature was developing, mainly in the UK, on the transformation of retail logistics from a manufacturer-driven to a retail-controlled system (McKinnon, 1989; Fernie, 1990; Fernie and Sparks, 1998).

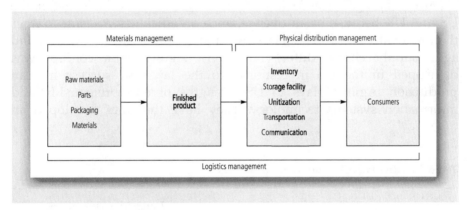

Figure 7.1 Logistics management.

In both industrial and consumer markets, several key themes began to emerge:

1 The shift from a push to a pull, i.e. a demand, driven supply chain.
2 The customer is gaining more power in the marketing channel.
3 The role of information systems to gain better control of the supply chain.
4 The elimination of unnecessary inventory in the supply chain.
5 The focusing upon core capabilities and increasing the likelihood of outsourcing non-core activities to specialists.

To achieve maximum effectiveness of supply chains, it is imperative that integration takes place by 'the linking together of previously separated activities within a single system' (Slack et al., 1998, p. 303).

This means that companies have had to review their internal organization to eliminate duplication and ensure that total costs can be reduced rather than allow separate functions (including marketing) to control their costs in a suboptimal manner. Similarly, supply chain integration can be achieved by establishing ongoing relationships with trading partners along the supply chain.

Throughout the 1970s and 1980s, attention in industrial marketing focused upon the changes promulgated by the processes involved in improving efficiencies in manufacturing. Total quality management, business process re-engineering and continuous improvement brought Japanese business thinking to western manufacturing operations. The implementation of these practices was popularized by Womack et al.'s (1990) book on the machine that changed the world. Not surprisingly, much of the literature on buyer–seller relationships focused upon the car manufacturing sector.

During the 1990s, this focus on lean production was challenged in the US and UK because of an over-reliance on efficiency measures rather than innovative responses. Harrison et al. (1999) showed how lean and agile supply chains differ (Table 7.1). Agility as a concept was developed in the US in response to the Japanese success in lean production. Agility plays to US strengths of entrepreneurship and information systems technology. They have therefore developed an

Table 7.1 Alternative supply chain processes

	Efficient/function (lean)	Innovative/responsive (agile)
Primary purpose	Supply predictable demand efficiently at lowest cost	Respond quickly to unpredictable demand in order to minimize stockouts, forced mark-downs and obsolete inventory
Manufacturing focus	Maintain high average utilization rate	Deploy excess buffer capacity
Inventory strategy	Generate high turns and minimize inventory	Deploy significant buffer stock of parts
Lead-time focus	Shorten lead time as long as it doesn't increase cost	Invest aggressively in ways to reduce lead time
Approach to supplier selection	Select primarily for cost and quality	Select primarily for speed, flexibility and quality

Source: Harrison et al. (1999).

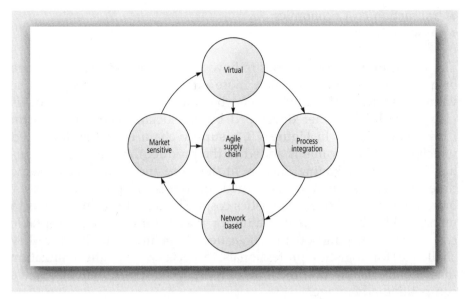

Figure 7.2 The agile supply chain. *Source*: **Harrison et al. (1999).**

agile supply chain model (Figure 7.2) which is highly responsive to market demand. They argue that the improvements in the use of information technology to capture 'real time' data mean less reliance on forecasts and create a virtual supply chain between trading partners. By sharing information, process integration will take place between partners who focus upon their core competencies. The final link in the agile supply chain is the network where a confederation of partners structure, co-ordinate and manage relationships to meet customer needs.

From this background to the evolution of supply chain management, it is clear that SCM draws upon a range of disciplines with regard to theoretical development. Initially, much of the research was geared towards the development of algorithms and spatial allocation models for the determination of the least-cost locations for warehouses and optimal delivery routes to distribute to final customers. The disciplines of geography, economics, operational research and mathematics provided solutions to management problems.

As SCM has developed into an integrated concept seeking functional integration within and between organizations, the theories to explain empirical research have been increasingly drawn from the strategic management or economics literature.

The key concepts and theories in SCM are:

- the value chain concept;
- resource-based theory (RBT) of the firm;

- transaction cost economics;
- network theory.

The thrust of all these theories is how to gain competitive advantage by managing the supply chain more effectively. The concept of the value chain was originally mooted by Michael Porter (1985) and his ideas have been further developed by logisticians, especially Martin Christopher (1997). In Figure 7.3, a supply chain model is illustrated which shows how value is added to the product through manufacturing, branding, packaging, display at the store and so on. At the same time, at each stage cost is added in terms of production costs, branding costs and overall logistics costs. The trick for companies is to manage this chain to create value for the customer at an acceptable cost. The managing of this so-called 'pipeline' has been a key challenge for logistics professionals, especially with the realization that the reduction of time not only reduced costs, but also gave competitive advantage.

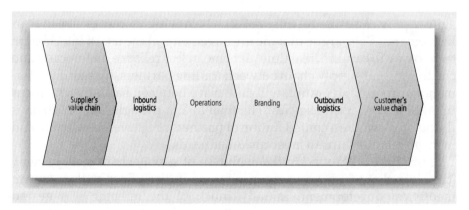

Figure 7.3 The extended value chain. *Source*: **Christopher (1997).**

According to Christopher, there are three dimensions to time-based competition which must be managed effectively if an organization is going to be responsive to market changes. These are:

1 *Time to market* – the speed at bringing a business opportunity to market.
2 *Time to serve* – the speed at meeting a customer's order.
3 *Time to react* – the speed at adjusting output to volatile responses in demand.

He uses these principles to develop strategies for strategic lead-time management. By understanding the lead times of the integrated web of suppliers necessary to manufacture a product, he argues that a 'pipeline map' can be drawn to represent each stage in the supply chain process from raw materials to customer. In these maps it is useful to differentiate between 'horizontal' and 'vertical' time.

- Horizontal time is time spent on processes such as manufacture, assembly, in-transit or order processing.
- Vertical time is the time when nothing is happening, no value is added but only cost and products/materials are standing as inventory.

It was in fashion markets that the notion of 'time-based competition' had most significance in view of the short time window for changing styles. In addition, the prominent trend in the last 20 years has been to source products offshore, usually in low-cost Pacific Rim nations, which lengthened the physical supply chain pipeline. These factors combined to illustrate the trade-offs which have to be made in supply chain management and on how to develop closer working relationships with supply chain partners. Christopher has used the example of The Limited in the US to illustrate his accelerating 'time to market'. The company revolutionized the apparel supply chain philosophy in the US by designing, ordering and receiving products from South-East Asia to stores in a matter of weeks rather than the months of its competitors. New lines were test marketed in trial stores and orders communicated by EDI to suppliers, which also benefited from CAD/CAM technology in modifying designs. The products, already labelled and priced, were consolidated in Hong Kong, where chartered 747s air-freighted the goods to Columbus, Ohio, for onward despatch to stores. The higher freight costs were easily compensated for by lower mark-downs and higher inventory turns per annum.

Along with The Limited, another catalyst for much of the initiatives in lead-time reduction came from work undertaken by Kurt Salmon Associates (KSA) in the US in the mid-1980s. KSA were commissioned by US garment suppliers to investigate how they could compete with Far East suppliers. The results were revealing in that the supply chains were long (one and a quarter years from loom to store), badly co-ordinated and inefficient (Christopher and Peck, 1998). The concept of quick response was therefore initiated to reduce lead times and improve co-ordination across the apparel supply chain. In Europe, quick response principles have been applied across the clothing retail sector. Supply base rationalization has been a feature of the last decade as companies have dramatically reduced the number of suppliers and have worked much closer with the remaining suppliers to ensure more responsiveness to the marketplace.

The resource-based perspective builds upon Porter's models by focusing upon the various resources within the firm which will allow it to compete effectively. Resources, capabilities and core competences are key concepts in this theory. As a supply chain perspective to competitive advantage increases the resource base within which decisions are taken, this theory links to transaction cost analysis and network theory. Thus, firms have to make choices on the degree of vertical integration in their business, to 'make or buy' in production and the extent of outsourcing required in logistical support services. Building upon Williamson's (1979) seminal work, Cox (1996) has developed a contractual theory of the firm by revising his ideas on high-asset specificity and 'sunk costs; to the notion of core competences' within the firm. Therefore, a company with core skills in either logistics or production would have internal contracts within the firm. Complementary skills of medium-asset specificity would be outsourced on a partnership basis and low-asset specificity skills would be outsourced on an 'arm's-length' contract basis.

The nature of the multiplicity of relationships has created the so-called network organization. In order to be responsive to market changes and to have an agile supply chain, flexibility is essential. Extending the resource-based theory, the network perspective assumes that firms depend on resources controlled by other firms and can only gain access to these resources by interacting with these firms, forming value chain partnerships and subsequently networks. Network theory focuses on creating partnerships based on trust, cross-functional teamwork and inter-organizational co-operation.

In industrial markets, especially the automobile and high technology sectors, a complex web of relationships has been formed. This has led Christopher (1997) to claim 'that there is a strong case for arguing that individual companies no longer compete with other stand-alone companies, but rather, that supply chain now competes against supply chain' (p. 22). Tiers of suppliers have been created to manufacture specific component parts and other supplier associations have been formed to co-ordinate supply chain activities. In these businesses the trend has been to buy rather than make and to outsource non-core activities.

Benetton, which has been hailed as the archetypal example of a network organization, is bucking the trend by increasing vertical integration and ownership of assets in the supply chain (Camuffo et al., 2001). While it is retaining its network structure, it is refining the network from product design through to distribution to its stores (see Box 7.1).

Box 7.1   The Benetton Group

The Benetton Group has around 5500 shops in 120 countries, manufacturing plants in Europe, Asia, the Middle East and India and revenues of more than $1.8 billion. Its interests are in two main areas:

- casual wear, accounting for around three-quarters of its total revenue. Key brands are United Colors of Benetton and Sisley.
- sportswear, accounting for one-fifth of total revenue. Key brands are Nordica, Prince, Killer Loop and Rollerblade.

Much of Benetton's success until the 1990s could be attributed to its innovative operations techniques and the strong network relationships that it has developed with both its suppliers and distributors. Benetton pioneered the 'principle of postponement', whereby garment dyeing was delayed for as long as possible in order that decisions on colour could be made to reflect market trends. At the same time, a network of subcontractors (small to medium-sized enterprises) supplied Benetton's factories with the labour-intensive phases of production (tailoring, finishing and ironing) while continuing to manufacture the capital-intensive parts of the operation (weaving, cutting, dyeing, quality control) in Treviso in north-eastern Italy. In terms of distribution, Benetton sells its products through agents, each responsible for developing a market area. These agents set up a contract relationship, similar to a franchise, with the owners who sell the products.

Benetton is now beginning to transform its business by retaining its network structure but changing the nature of the network. Unlike most of its competitors, it is increasing vertical integration within the business. As volumes have increased, Benetton set up a production pole at Castrette nears its headquarters. This large complex is responsible for producing around 120 millions items per year. To take advantage of lower labour costs, Benetton has located foreign production poles, based on the Castrette model, in Spain, Portugal, Hungary, Croatia, Tunisia, Korea, Egypt and India. These foreign production centres focus on one type of product utilizing the skills of the region, so T-shirts are made in Spain, jackets in Eastern Europe.

In order to reduce time throughout the supply chain, Benetton has increased upstream vertical integration by consolidating its textile and thread supplies so that 85 per cent is controlled by the company. This means that Benetton can speed up the flow of materials from raw material suppliers through its production poles to ultimate distribution from Italy to its global retail network.

The retail network and the products on offer have also experienced changes. Benetton had offered a standard range in most markets but allowed for 20 per cent of its range to be customized for country markets. Now, to communicate a single global image, Benetton is only allowing 5–10 per cent of differentiation in each collection. Furthermore, it has streamlined its brand range to focus on the United Colors of Benetton and Sisley brands.

The company is also changing its store network to enable it to compete more effectively with its international competitors. It is enlarging its existing stores, where possible, to accommodate its full range of these key brands. Where this is not possible, it will focus on a specific segment or product. Finally, it is opening more than 100 megastores worldwide to sell the full range, focusing on garments with a high styling content. These stores are owned and managed solely by Benetton to ensure that the company can maintain control downstream and be able to respond quickly to market changes.

Efficient consumer response (ECR)

The notion of time-based competition through just-in-time (JIT) and quick response (QR) principles was given further credence in the fast-moving consumer goods (FMCG) sector with the advent of efficient consumer response (ECR).

ECR arrived on the scene in the early 1990s, when Kurt Salmon Associates produced another supply chain report, Efficient Consumer Response, in 1993 in response to another appeal by a US industry sector to evaluate its efficiency in the face of growing competition to its traditional sector. Similar trends were discerned from their earlier work in the apparel sector; excessive inventories, long unco-ordinated supply chains (104 days from picking line to store purchase) and an estimated potential saving of $30 billion, 10.8 per cent of sales turnover.

During the last decade the ECR initiative has stalled in the US; indeed, inventory levels remain over 100 days in the dry grocery sector. Nevertheless, ECR has taken off in Europe from the creation of a European Executive Board in 1994 with the support of European-wide associations representing different elements of the supply chain – AIM, the European Brands Association; CIES, the Food Business Forum; EAN International, the International Article Numbering Association; and Eurocommerce, the European organization for the retail and wholesale trade.

It was in 1994 that initial European studies were carried out to establish the extent of supply chain inefficiencies and to formulate

Table 7.2 Comparisons of scope and savings from supply chain studies

Supply chain study	Scope of study	Estimated savings
Kurt Salmon Associates (1993)	US dry grocery sector	10.8% of sales turnover (2.3% financial, 8.5% cost)
		Total supply chain $30 billion, warehouse supplier dry sector $10 billion
		Supply chain cut by 41% from 104 to 61 days
Coca-Cola Supply Chain Collaboration (1994)	127 European companies	2.3–3.4 percentage points of sales turnover (60% to retailers, 40% to manufacturer)
	Focused on cost reduction from end of manufacturer's line	
	Small proportion of category management	
ECR Europe (1996 ongoing)	15 value chain analysis studies (10 European manufacturers, 5 retailers)	5.7 percentage points of sales turnover (4.8% operating costs, 0.9% inventory cost)
	15 product categories	Total supply chain saving of $21 billion
	7 distribution channels	UK savings £2 billion

Source: Fiddis (1997).

initiatives to improve supply chain performance (Table 7.2). ECR Europe defines ECR as 'a global movement in the grocery industry focusing on the total supply chain – suppliers, manufacturers, wholesalers and retailers, working close together to fulfil the changing demand of the grocery consumer better, faster and at less cost'.

One of the early studies carried out by Coopers & Lybrand identified 14 improvement areas whereby ECR principles could be implemented. These were categorized into three broad areas of product replenishment, category management and enabling technologies (Figure 7.4). Most of these improvement areas had received management action in the past; the problem was how to view the concepts as an integrated set rather than individual action areas.

As the ECR Europe movement began to gather momentum, the emphasis on much of the work conducted by the organization tended to shift from the supply side technologies (product replenishment) to demand-driven initiatives (category management). This is reflected in

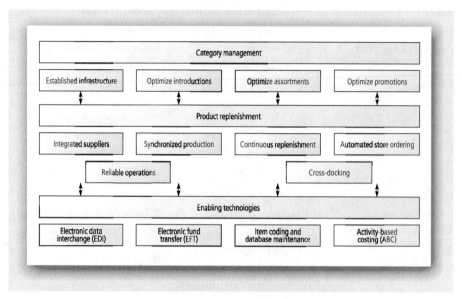

Figure 7.4 ECR improvement concepts. *Source*: **Coopers & Lybrand (1996).**

the early ECR project reports which dealt with efficient replenishment and efficient unit loads. While the supply side is still important as reflected in projects on transport optimization and unit loads identification and tracking, the majority of recent projects have focused upon consumer value, efficient promotion tactics, efficient product introductions and collaboration in customer-specific marketing.

Commensurate with this change in emphasis has been the topics under discussion at the annual ECR Europe conference. At its inception in Geneva in 1996, the concept was being developed and efficient replenishment initiatives were prominent on the agenda. Subsequent conferences have tended to emphasize demand-driven initiatives and emerging issues such as e-commerce.

It can be argued that the early work focused upon improving *efficiencies* within the supply chain and later collaborations have stressed the *effectiveness* of the supply chain. Thus, the focus now is on how to achieve profitable growth, as there is little point in delivering products efficiently if they are the wrong assortment, displayed in the wrong part of the store!

The ECR Europe prime objective is to develop best practices and to disseminate these benefits to all members of the food supply chain in Europe. To date, it has been highly successful in moving towards this objective. The early conferences were well attended (over 1000 delegates) but events in the twenty-first century have attracted over 3000 people. ECR initiatives are now formally organized in 14 European countries and the work in these countries is formally recognized through representation on the Executive Board. The Board itself is comprised of 30 senior executives from leading retailers and branded manufacturers in Europe who established the policy agenda to initiate new pilot projects and develop demand and supply strategies.

It is clear, however, that ECR will not be a panacea for all companies. The improvement areas suggested in Figure 7.4 provide a tariff of initiatives from which companies will choose according to their own particular objectives. Each company will have a different starting point and a different agenda depending upon the current nature of supplier–retailer relationships. Nevertheless, a common theme applicable to all retailers is the limited number of relationships which are established with suppliers. The large grocery retailers deal with thousands of suppliers and have only formal partnerships or initiated pilot projects with a small number of suppliers – for example, J Sainsbury has supply chain forums that bring together senior supply chain staff with 19 of their counterparts (suppliers), which account for a large part of Sainsbury's volume business. A criticism of ECR Europe conferences and in those held in the UK is that these venues are packed with representatives from the largest retailers and their multinational FMCG suppliers. Such concentration, the argument goes, can only lead to restricting consumer choice, high profit margins and higher prices. So much for the consumer in ECR! With Wal-Mart's entry into the European market, this is hardly true in view of the intense price competition in Germany and the UK, the initial target markets. ECR can in fact enable companies to compete better in such competitive markets. It is true, however, that smaller companies have been slower to hop on the ECR bandwagon because of the time and resource commitments required to carry out ECR initiatives. Nevertheless, smaller companies such as those operating convenience stores have achieved significant increases in sales through working with key suppliers which have acted as 'category captains' in developing assortments within stores.

The retail supply chain

The implementation of ECR initiatives has been identified as the fourth and final stage of the evolution of grocery logistics in the UK. Fernie et al. (2000) classify this as the relationship stage which relates to a more collaborative approach to supply chain management after decades of confrontation. The UK is often mooted to have the most efficient grocery supply chain in the world and a key contributor to the healthy profit margins of its grocery retailers.

The four stages are:

- supplier control (pre-1980);
- centralization (1981–1989);
- just in time (1990–1995)
- relationship (1995–the present).

The first stage, supplier control, is widespread in many countries today and was the dominant method of distribution to stores in the 1960s and 1970s in the UK. Suppliers manufactured and stored products at the factory or numerous warehouses throughout the country. Direct store deliveries (DSDs) were made on an infrequent basis (7–10 days), often by third party contractors that consolidated products from a range of factories. Store managers negotiated with suppliers and kept this stock in 'the backroom'.

Centralization, stage 2, is now becoming a feature of retail logistics in many countries and was prominent in the UK in the 1980s. The grocery retailers took the initiative at this time in constructing large, purpose-built regional distribution centres (RDCs) to consolidate products from suppliers for onward delivery to stores. This stage marked the beginning of a shift from supplier to retailer control of the supply chain. There were clear advantages from a retailer perspective:

- reduced inventories;
- lead times reduced from weeks to days at stores;
- 'backroom' areas released for selling space;
- greater product availability;
- 'bulk discounts' from suppliers;
- fewer invoices, lower admin. costs;
- better utilization of staff in stores.

Centralization, however, required much capital investment in RDCs, vehicles, material handling equipment and human resources. Centralization of distribution also meant centralization of buying, with store managers losing autonomy as new headquarter functions were created to manage this change. This period also witnessed a boom in the third party contract market as retailers considered whether to invest in other parts of the retail business rather than logistics. All of the 'big four' grocery retailers, Sainsbury, Tesco, ASDA and Safeway, contracted out many RDCs to logistics service providers in the mid to late 1980s.

In stage 3, the just-in-time phase, major efficiency improvements were achieved as refinements to the initial networks were implemented. The larger grocery chains focused upon product-specific RDCs, with most temperature-controlled products being channelled through a large number of small warehouses operated by third party contractors. By the early 1990s, temperature-controlled products were subsumed within a network of composite distribution centres developed by superstore operators. Composites allowed products of all temperature ranges to be distributed through one system of multi-temperature warehouses and vehicles. This allowed retailers to reduce stock in store as delivery frequency increased. Furthermore, a more streamlined system not only improved efficiency, but also reduced waste of short shelf-life products, giving a better quality offer to the customer.

Whilst efforts were being made to improve secondary distribution networks, initial projects were established to integrate primary with secondary distribution. When Safeway opened its large composite in 1989 at Bellshill in Scotland, it included a resource recovery centre which washed returnable trays and baled cardboard from its stores. It also established a supplier collection programme which was to save the company millions of pounds during the 1990s. Most secondary networks were established to provide stores with high customer service levels; however, vehicle utilization on return trips to the RDC were invariably poor and it was efforts to reduce this 'empty running' that led to initiatives such as return trips with suppliers' products to the RDC or equipment/recycling waste from stores.

Although improvements to the initial networks were being implemented, RDCs continued to carry 2 weeks or more of stock of non-perishable products. To improve inventory levels and move to a just-in-time system, retailers began to request more frequent deliveries from their suppliers in smaller order quantities. Whiteoak, who represents Mars, and therefore suppliers' interests, wrote in 1993 that these initiatives gave clear benefits to retailers at the expense of increased costs to suppliers. In response to these changes, consolidation centres have been created upstream from RDCs to enable suppliers to improve vehicle utilization from the factory.

The final stage, the relationship stage, is ongoing but is crucial if further costs are going to be taken out of the supply chain. In the earlier third stage, Whiteoak had noted that the transition from a supplier- to a retail-controlled network had given cost savings to both suppliers and retailers *until* the just-in-time phase in the early 1990s. By the mid-1990s, retailers began to appreciate that there were no 'quick wins' such as that of centralization in the 1980s to improve net margins. If another step change in managing retail logistics was to occur it had to be realized through supply chain co-operation. The advent of ECR and its promotion by the Institute of Grocery Distribution fostered further co-operation between supply chain members. By the early part of the 2000s, however, increased competition in the retail marketplace fuelled by Wal-Mart's entry into the UK in 1999 has led to a drive for greater operation efficiencies and diversification into non-food areas, where margins are greater. The latter has led to a transformation of distribution networks as indicated by recent changes in ASDA's network (see Box 7.2).

Box 7.2   ASDA's changing distribution network

ASDA was the last of the major grocery retailers to centralize its distribution. As the superstore pioneer in the UK, the company stocked more lines, including non-food lines, than its competitors. It also focused on branded products and suppliers delivered them direct to their nationwide network. By the mid-1980s, however, ASDA reviewed its marketing and distribution strategy. Backdoor congestion at stores where 50–60 vehicles per day jostled to unload, coupled with the huge administration costs of each store manager dealing with thousands of suppliers, led to the decision to centralize its buying and distribution functions. The increase in own-label penetration of its product mix reinforced the centralization decision. By centralizing late, ASDA gained experience from a maturing distribution industry which had implemented networks for other retailers. Because of the size and distribution of the ASDA store network, a small number of large distribution centres were built: six RDCs and two national distribution centres stocking slow-moving grocery lines and non-food merchandise. Most of these distribution centres (six) were contracted out to logistics service providers (LSPs).

Throughout the 1990s, ASDA developed more distribution centres and restructured its network as store numbers increased from 130 to 230 in a decade. The success of the George brand led to the opening of a new state-of-the-art automated clothing centre in 1999. Although this depot was contracted out, the new grocery additions to the network were run 'in-house' by ASDA. Nevertheless, with its creation of seven consolidation centres to co-ordinate the fresh produce chain, it contracted out the management of these freight movements to an LSP. It was in this year that Wal-Mart purchased ASDA and embarked upon the further development of general merchandise products. By 2005, 20 supercentres are planned, with 50 per cent of sales space being devoted to non-food lines. Furthermore, by implementing Wal-Mart's Retail Link systems into ASDA, it was anticipated that existing stores would release more space for selling these higher margin lines. For example, in September 2001 ASDA relaunched its Home and Leisure business, introducing up to 5000 new lines, around 2000 of which were sourced through Wal-Mart's global network.

The existing network is as follows:

- National Distribution Centres – Brackmills, Chepstow, Corby, Ince, Lutterworth, Newcastle-under-Lyme, Wakefield, Whitwood.
- Composite RDCs – Dartford, Grangemouth, Lutterworth, Washington, Wigan.
- Other RDCs – Bedford, Bristol, Chepstow, Didcot, Wakefield, Washington.

This network of 21 distribution centres from 15 sites services 256 ASDA stores on a daily basis. The national centres hold slow-moving grocery (Lutterworth, Wakefield) or non-food lines (Brackmills, Newcastle-under-Lyme and Ince for clothing; Whitwood, Chepstow and Corby for home and leisure).

The most radical initiative to impact upon the grocery supply in the 2000s is the implementation of factory gate pricing (FGP) by the major multiple retailers. Initiated by Tesco and Sainsbury, FGP is the price retailers are willing to pay excluding transport costs from the point at which the product is ready for shipment to the retailers' RDC. In essence this is the next step on from 'ad hoc' backhauling and the consolidating of loads. In theory, FGP optimizes the entire transport network throughout the supply chain. Instead of a series of bilateral transport contracts between logistics service providers (LSPs) and retailers/manufacturers, transport resources would be pooled to maximize vehicle utilization. The larger retailers and logistics service providers can see the major benefits of FGP. With increased international sourcing, LSPs have been keen to offer services in managing product flows across countries and continents. Technologies are now available to track such movements and cost visibility should enhance openness in negotiations. Suppliers, however, have shown most concern with FGP. Whilst the disaggregation of product price from transport price leads to dislocation of current practices, many suppliers fear that retailers will then scrutinize product cost, demanding further price reductions.

Differences in logistics 'culture' in international markets

ECR initiatives launched throughout the 1990s have done much to promote the spirit of collaboration. Organizations are having to change to accommodate and embrace ECR, and to dispel inherent rivalries which have built up over decades of confrontation. The UK has been in the vanguard of implementing ECR, with Tesco and Sainsbury claiming to have saved hundreds of millions of pounds in the late 1990s/early 2000s. The rate of adoption of ECR initiatives has varied between companies within international markets. Table 7.2 shows that the Kurt Salmon report hoped for an improvement of supply chain time from picking line to consumer from 104 to 61 days in the USA. A comparative study of European markets by GEA (1994) showed that all of the major countries hold much less stock within the supply chain. Indeed, the UK figure is now around 25 days. Mitchell (1997) argues that few of the largest European retailers (mainly German and French companies) have proven to be ECR enthusiasts. Many of those French and German retailers are privately owned or franchise operations and they tend to be volume- and price-driven in their strategic positioning. By contrast, UK and Dutch firms are essentially publicly quoted, margin-driven retailers who have had a more constructive approach to supplier relations. Whilst accepting that there are key differences in European markets, in general there are differences between the US and Europe with regard to trading conditions. Mitchell (1997, p. 14) states that:

- The US grocery retail trade is fragmented, not concentrated as in parts of Europe.
- US private-label development is primitive compared with many European countries.
- The balance of power in the manufacturer–retailer relationship is very different in the US compared with Europe.
- The trade structure is different in that wholesalers play a more important role in the US.
- Trade practices such as forward buying were more deeply rooted in the US than Europe.
- Trade promotional deals and the use of coupons in consumer promotions are unique to the US.
- Legislation, especially anti-trust legislation, can inhibit supply chain collaboration.

While legislation has imposed controls on US retailers in terms of pricing and competition policy, there are significantly fewer controls on location, planning and store choice issues. This has resulted in US retailers being able to operate profitably on much less sales per square metre ratios than the higher priced, fixed costs associated with the more 'controlled' markets of Europe.

To understand how different country logistics structures have evolved it is necessary to understand the nature of consumer choice and the range of retail formats prior to seeking explanations for the nature of logistical support to stores through supplier relations, cost structures and other operational factors.

Consumer choice and retail formats

US tourists coming to Europe are probably puzzled at store opening hours and the restrictions on store choice compared with their own country. Although liberalization of opening hours is beginning to happen across Europe, the tight planning restrictions on store sizes and location have tended to shape format development. Furthermore, cross-national surveys of attributes influencing a consumer's choice of store has shown the strong influence of price in France and Germany compared with the UK, where price tends to be ranked behind convenience, assortment range, quality and customer service. (It can be argued, however, that as Wal-Mart becomes more established in the UK, the price spread between it and the UK competition may lead consumers to revalue these store attributes.) In the US, price and promotion are also strong drivers of store choice; however, US consumers spend their food dollar in a variety of ways, including eating out, which has always been more common than in Europe. Indeed, the KSA survey on ECR was initiated because of the competition from warehouse clubs and Wal-Mart into the traditional supermarket sector.

A partial explanation for the high inventory levels cited by KSA in their survey is that US consumers do buy in bulk. With such an emphasis on price and promotion, consumers shop around and stockpile dry goods in garages and basements. Compared with their European counterparts, who neither have the space nor the format choices, US consumers have their own household 'backroom' warehouse areas.

In Europe, the pattern of format development follows a broad north–south division. The southern Mediterranean and eastern European markets continue to have a predominance of small, independent stores and the supply chain is manufacturer controlled. This is changing, however, as northern European retailers enter these markets. In northern Europe, retailers have developed large store formats, but in different ways. For example, it is not surprising that Wal-Mart chose Germany as its entry market for Europe because of its strong discounter culture. This is reflected in its large number of hypermarkets and hard discounters, but the German consumer also shops at local markets. In France, the home of the hypermarket, large-scale formats coexist with 'superettes' and local markets, whereas in the UK and the Netherlands fewer formats are evident, with superstores and supermarkets respectively dominating their markets.

In these northern European countries, different logistics networks have evolved in response to format development. As discussed earlier in the chapter, many of the largest supermarket chains in the UK that have a portfolio of superstores have developed composite distribution to improve efficiency throughout the supply chain. Here all product categories – produce, chilled and ambient – are consolidated at a regional distribution centre for onward distribution to stores in composite trailers which also can carry a mix of products. In the Netherlands, Albert Heijn has utilized cool and ambient warehouse complexes to deliver to their smaller-sized supermarkets, whereas the German and French retailers have numerous product category warehouses supplying their wide range of formats (with hypermarkets, depending on spread of stores, products may be delivered direct by suppliers).

Manufacturer–retailer relationships

A major feature of retail change in Europe has been the consolidation of retail activity into fewer, large corporations in national markets. Many grocery retailers in Europe were small, privately owned family companies 30 years ago and they were dwarfed by their multinational branded suppliers. This is no longer the case. Some may remain privately owned, but along with their PLC counterparts they are now international companies which have grown in economic power to challenge their international branded suppliers. Although the largest companies are predominantly German and French in origin, a high degree of concentration also exists in the Netherlands and the UK. Indeed, the investigation by the Competition Commission on the operation of multiple retail grocery companies in the UK illustrates this shift in power from manufacturer to retailer.

An indication of the growth of these European retailers has been the way in which they have been able to dictate where and when suppliers will deliver products to specific sites. Increasingly, the product has been of the distributor label category. This is of particular significance in the UK, where grocery chains have followed the Marks & Spencer strategy of premium value-added brands that compete directly with manufacturers' brands.

The implications of these changes in power relationships between retailers and their suppliers have been that manufacturers have been either abdicating or losing their responsibility for controlling the supply chain. In the UK, the transition from a supplier-driven system to one of retail control is complete compared with some other parts of Europe. As mentioned earlier, most grocery retailers in the UK not only have centralized over 90 per cent of their products through regional distribution centres, but have created primary consolidation centres further back up the supply chain to minimize inventory held between factory and store. The implementation of factory gate pricing further reinforces the trend to retail supply chain control. Although this degree of control is less evident in other European markets and in the US, the spate of merger activity in the late 1990s and the expansion of retail giants (Wal-Mart, Carrefour, Tesco, Ahold) with their 'big box' formats into new geographical markets is leading to internationalization of logistics practice.

Despite these shifts in the power balance, it is generally accepted that to apply ECR principles, the greatest challenge for European retailers is the breaking down of cultural barriers within organizations to move from a confrontational culture to one of collaboration. Organizations will change from a traditional functional 'internal' structure to that of a multifunctional 'external' structure. The changing organizational forms are shown in Figure 7.5, which depicts the traditional 'bow tie' and the new cross-functional team approach.

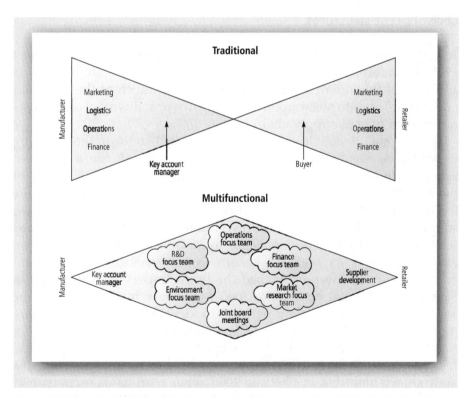

Figure 7.5 Transformation of the interface between manufacturer and retailer. *Source:* **Fiddis (1997).**

To achieve the significant supply chain savings mooted in ECR reports, companies are having to change their attitudes, although the politics and inherent rivalries built up over the decades will take years for this cultural revolution to take place. It was significant that J Sainsbury was *the* retailer represented at the ECR session in Paris in 1999 in 'ECR – the human side of change'. Sainsbury was initially cynical about the benefits of ECR, but have made significant progress in recent years and are aware of the time and resources required to modify working practices. One of the Roland Berger consultants represented at this session commented that the Anglo-Saxon countries were more proactive in implementing cultural change to move to a trusting partnership approach than the French or German companies.

Despite these possible drawbacks, the speed of change is remarkable. Surveys conducted throughout the 1990s on manufacturer–retailer relationships in the UK initially showed that partnerships would not work. By 1997, a sea change in attitude was happening. Who would have thought even then that the main grocery retailers would be sharing EPOS data?

Logistics cost structures

A critical aspect of these organizational changes that have been evolving in response to ECR initiatives is how to share both the benefits and *costs* of the initiatives. Until the mid-1990s, much of the emphasis on logistics costs focused upon the company or industry channel costs rather than overall supply chain costs.

The advent of activity-based costing (ABC), one of the enabling technologies identified in Figure 7.4, has allowed for a 'process' approach to be taken to supply chain activities. For example, many of the initiatives undertaken on product replenishment had clear benefits for retailers but required extra work (i.e. extra costs) further up the supply chain. Thus, the cultural revolution referred to in the previous section is necessary for retailers to establish 'ground rules' on attributing costs as well as benefits when seeking supply chain efficiencies. ECR Europe launched the Profit Impact of ECR project in September 1997 and have developed a software modelling tool, 'the wizard', which helps trading partners to identify the activities that are impacted upon when applying ECR initiatives.

Although the tools are being developed to improve existing practice, logistics costs do vary considerably in different countries. This was aptly shown in the UK in 1999 and 2000, when road-haulage companies and other supporting businesses organized blockades in major cities and oil refineries in protest at hikes in fuel duty after successive budgets had made fuel costs the highest in Europe. Fuel costs are only part of the cost equation; labour costs in warehousing and transport, property prices and interest rates lead to differences in European markets. With the implementation of the EMU and standardization of interest rates, distortions created by national governments' fiscal policies should be less significant than in the past. For example, high relative interest rates in Britain were often the reason cited for destocking by British retailers and innovations pertaining to JIT distribution. Also, the cheaper land costs in France and Spain have been responsible for more speculative forward buying of stock and for holding more inventory in hyper-markets. This is similar to the US, where the cost trade-offs in the logistics mix differ because of relatively cheaper fuel and land costs but greater geographical distances to cover.

Role of the logistics service provider

One area of collaboration that is often overlooked is that between retailer and professional logistics contractors. Historically, the provision of third party services to retailers varied markedly from country to country. In the UK, where centralization of distribution occurred early, a major market was created for third party providers to manage RDCs. In the rest of Europe, less enthusiasm for 'contracting out' was initially shown, with a tendency for companies to retain warehousing 'in-house' and possibly contract out the transport. Financial conventions differ by country and in Germany, for example, strong balance sheets are viewed positively compared with the UK; also, the opportunity cost of capital (investing in logistics infrastructure compared with retailing assets) may result in retaining rather than outsourcing these functions.

In recent years, however, the role of logistics service providers has been enhanced. This can be attributed to the internationalization of retail and transport businesses and the need for greater co-ordination of supply chain activities. The supply chain is now more complex than before. Retailers are optimizing traffic loads to minimize empty running and are backhauling from suppliers and recovering packaging waste from recycling centres. As efficient replenishment initiatives are implemented, consolidation of loads is required within the primary distribution network. Logistics service providers are better placed to manage some of these initiatives than manufacturers or retailers. Furthermore, the internationalization of retail business has stretched existing supply chains and third party providers can bring expertise to these new market areas. Some British companies have utilized British logistics companies as they opened stores in new markets. Similarly, the world's largest retailer has utilized the expertise of a British logistics company (Tibbet & Britten) to provide logistical support to stores acquired in Canada and Germany. Indeed, the internationalization of Tibbet & Britten from its UK base has been significant in the 1990s in that it could report in the early 2000s that over a third of its sales was now in North America, where major structural changes are occurring in the grocery market.

The internationalization of logistics practice

The gist of our discussion on differences in logistics cultures was to show that implementation of best practice principles has been applied differentially in various geographical markets. Nevertheless, the impetus for internationalization of logistics practice has been achieved through the formal and informal transfer of 'know-how' between companies and countries. ECR Europe conferences, their sponsoring organizations, and national trade associations have all promoted best practice principles for application by member companies. Many of the conferences initiated by these organizations have included field visits to state-of-the-art distribution centres to illustrate the operational aspects of elements of ECR. At a more formal level, companies transfer 'know-how' within subsidiaries of their own group or through formal retail alliances.

To illustrate how logistics expertise is being transferred across international boundaries, we will look at two European case studies, Tesco and Ahold. Both are global players, although their history of internationalization is very different. Tesco internationalized late and concentrated primarily in Europe; Ahold has around 60 per cent of its sales in the USA and is only beginning to refocus its attention on the European market.

Tesco in Ireland and Poland

Tesco's most recent acquisitions in Europe (in Ireland and Poland) offer an insight into how changes in logistics practice can be implemented in different markets. In the wake of its acquisition of Wm Low in Scotland, Tesco plc turned its attention to Ireland in 1997 with the acquisition of 110 supermarkets from Associated British Foods. In the South, Power Supermarkets were part of this acquisition and at the time Power had plans to consolidate distribution. With the takeover, Tesco inherited a 'push' logistics system:

- only 12 per cent of volume was centralized;
- high stockholding levels at store (2 weeks);
- high stockholding levels at depot (4+ weeks);

- up to 600 deliveries per week per store;
- unknown supply chain costs.

Tesco initiated a 3-year plan to transfer Tesco UK 'know-how' to Tesco Ireland. This involved:

- consolidation of all product categories, initially through third party contractors (except one inherited warehouse);
- move to a composite 'chilled' distribution facility by 2000;
- the use of best practice ECR principles developed in the UK to Ireland;
- the upgrading of systems technology to achieve this.

In essence, Tesco Ireland is focusing upon replenishment areas of ECR in the first instance before tackling the demand side of ECR with regard to product assortments, promotion and new product launches.

What is interesting about Tesco's entry into Ireland is that it has speeded up the process of consolidation throughout Ireland. Super-quinn also had a supplier-driven logistics system and in a matter of 2 years began to put in place centralized distribution. The Musgrave Group, which operates franchised convenience stores and supermarkets in both Northern and Southern Ireland, had centralized ambient products prior to Tesco's entry. Since 1997, Musgraves has taken the lead in Ireland in implementing a supply chain strategy. Two new chilled distribution centres have been opened and the company has been active in ECR projects, which has resulted in organizational changes within the company.

Tesco's entry into Poland has posed a very different set of challenges to logistics managers. The acquisition of the Savia supermarket chain in 1995 followed on from a series of acquisitions in Hungary, the Czech Republic and Slovakia a few years earlier. In all of these cases, Tesco has adopted a similar strategy – gradually introducing the Tesco brand and opening larger supermarkets and hypermarkets. Whereas the supply chain is supplier led, this has a different meaning to the push system pre-1997 in Ireland. In Ireland, much of the discussion on Tesco's entry to the market was about the possible fate of Irish suppliers. In Poland, this is not the case in that most goods will be locally sourced; however, there is a need to improve operational relationships with respect to quality, packaging and delivery. ECR is not an agenda item for management!

Ahold in Europe

Ahold has benefited from the transference of logistics practice because of its relationships in retail alliances in addition to synergies developed with its expanding web of subsidiaries. During the 1990s, Ahold partnered with Casino of France and Safeway of the UK in the European Retail Alliance. In 1994, a 'composite' distribution centre was very much a UK phenomenon; now it has been developed by Safeway's European partners. Not only have these logistics practices been applied in France and the Netherlands, but also in the parent companies' subsidiaries in the US, Portugal and the Czech Republic.

In the Netherlands, Albert Heijn (Ahold's Dutch subsidiary) has developed a state-of-the-art distribution system based on a modified UK 'composite' model. Because Heijn's stores are much smaller than those of the superstore operators in the UK, these composite distribution centres are comprised of three independent units, unlike in the UK, where all products are stored in one facility. The three centres are a fresh centre dealing with the cool chain, a regional distribution centre for ambient and non-food products, and a returns centre for reallocation and recycling of returned products and handling materials.

ECR initiatives, especially those pertaining to efficient replenishment, have been a feature of Albert Heijn's supply chain strategy, with cross-docking and continuous replenishment being a feature of their relationships with key suppliers such as Coca-Cola and Heineken. On a global basis, Ahold attempts to synchronize best logistics practices across its operating subsidiaries. Clearly, this is quite a challenge as the company operates in Latin America, Asia Pacific and the US. Like J Sainsbury, Ahold has retained the local store names in the US post-acquisition, but has initiated best practice principles to achieve supply chain efficiencies.

Future challenges

Clearly, there has been a transformation of logistics within retailing during the last 25 years. Centralization, new technologies, both in materials handling and information handling, ECR and the implementation of best practice principles have resulted in logistics becoming a key management function within retailing. But what of the future? Are we about to experience evolution or revolution of retail logistics? Much depends upon the pace of retail change in the two areas identified in earlier chapters as drivers of change in the future – namely, the extent of the internationalization of retail businesses and the eventual size of the e-commerce market. These two key strategic factors are interlinked, however, as the Internet brings together consumers seeking products and services in international markets, and retailers join with their suppliers in global exchanges such as WorldWide Retail Exchange (WWRE) to reap the benefits of reduced costs by streamlining procurement. Much of what was discussed in the previous section will continue. The large global retailers will force further consolidation of retail markets in North America, Europe and South-East Asia. Their presence in these markets will necessitate a review of their supply chains on how to provide logistics support to new markets as they develop.

The biggest challenge facing retailers is how to respond to the market opportunities offered by e-commerce. Shopping from home is hardly a new experience for consumers. Mail order shopping arose in many markets because of the lack of fixed stores in rural communities, and catalogue and other non-store offerings have developed throughout the twentieth century. Compared with the US, however, where 'specialogues' for upscale consumers became the norm 20 years ago, the bulk of the mail order business in the UK is still rooted in traditional catalogues targeted at lower socio-economic group consumers (it was the lure of cheap credit which provided a catalyst for growth in this market in the first place). The traditional players such as GUS and Littlewoods have the logistical infrastructure in place, but until digital TV takes off as the medium for e-commerce ordering, Internet consumers are the 'wrong' segment for traditional catalogue shopping.

Success in the e-commerce market will be largely dependent upon getting fulfilment and therefore logistics right. If time-constrained consumers are to be lured to e-commerce shopping, they have to be persuaded that the retail offer is better in terms of quality, value and *customer service* – that is, getting the product delivered when specified (Christopher's 'time to serve'). Take, for example, the situation in the US between Thanksgiving and Christmas, the period when Internet ordering is at its peak. In 1999, 40 per cent of online shoppers reported problems from finding products to late delivery and high shipping costs (*Retail Week*, 21 July 2000). The creation of a healthy third party market in the UK using the logistics infrastructure of traditional mail order companies (N. Brown, GUS) and more recent specialists (Zoom) offers a solution to the fulfilment problem.

Much of the recent attention on e-commerce has focused upon the grocery sector, which is coming through the experimental phase with a greater commitment to online retailing. The initial reticence is understandable in that major supermarket operators invest heavily in property assets and they did not wish to cannibalize their existing store customers with a competing e-commerce offer. Over time it has been shown that online retailing can complement the store offer and can indeed lead to switching of customers from one chain to another. The development of the online grocery market with a profile of Tesco.com can be found in Chapter 13. Here, we will focus upon fulfilment models. Currently, there are two main logistics models for grocery e-commerce: the store-based order picking and the dedicated order picking models, as illustrated in Figures 7.6 and 7.7. The store-based system used by Tesco makes use of

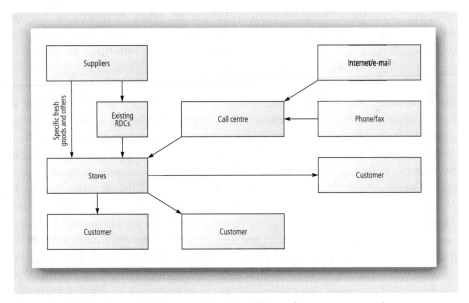

Figure 7.6 Logistics model for store-based picking of e-commerce orders.

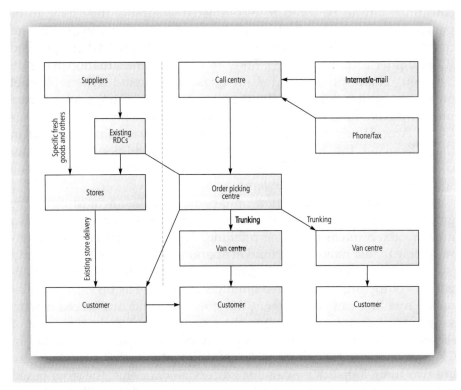

Figure 7.7 Logistics model for dedicated picking of e-commerce orders. *Source*: Retail Logistics Task Force (2000).

existing distribution assets in that products pass through RDCs to stores and their store staff pick and distribute orders to customers. The advantages of this system are the speed of implementation and the relatively low initial investment costs. This system offers customers the full range of goods available in the local store; however, 'out of stocks' occur because the online shopper is competing with in-store customers. It also permits the pooling of retail inventory between conventional and online markets, improving the ratio of inventory to sales.

Tesco's approach is interesting because it is reminiscent of ASDA's late acceptance of centralized distribution. ASDA's decision not to centralize in the 1970s like some of its regional competitors meant that it could achieve national penetration quickly (compared to the national leader of the time, J Sainsbury, which has only opened an RDC in Scotland in 2000!). Now Tesco is delivering 'direct' from stores rather than centralizing its e-commerce operation because it gives greater market penetration.

Conflicts between conventional and online retailing are likely to intensify at the back of the store as well as at the 'front end'. Back storeroom areas, where much of the assembly and packing of home orders is undertaken, will become increasingly congested. Over the past 20 years, the trend has been for retailers to reduce the amount of back storage space in shops as in-store inventory levels have dropped and quick-response replenishment has become the norm. This now limits the capacity of these retail outlets to assume the additional role of online fulfilment centre.

Furthermore, it has been estimated that 50 per cent of distribution costs is tied up in-store. Our discussion on delivery options has been the so-called 'last mile' problem. In the case of Tesco, 5 per cent of sales is tied up in the last 50 yards (*The Grocer*, 14 September 2002). Out of stocks on the shop floor are getting worse, despite JIT replenishment techniques, because of the haphazard nature of backstores. Shelf stackers are having difficulty finding products now – what will the situation be like as online fulfilment competes for the same space. Where sufficient land is available, shops can be enlarged to accommodate a higher volume of home shopping business. New shops can also be purpose-built to integrate conventional retailing and online fulfilment. The Dutch retailer Ahold has coined the term 'wareroom' to describe a dedicated pick facility co-located with a conventional supermarket.

Most of the purpose-built fulfilment centres so far constructed are on separate sites. They overcome most of the problems of fulfilling orders from existing shops. They can be designed specifically for the multiple picking of online orders, incorporate mechanized picking systems and provide much more efficient reception facilities for inbound and outbound vehicles. As their inventory is assigned solely to the online market, home shoppers can have greater confidence in the availability of products at the time of ordering. All of this comes at a high price, however, both in terms of capital investment and operating costs. It is estimated, for instance, that Webvan's fulfilment centres cost an average of $36 million. Dedicated pick centres must generate a high throughput to earn the e-tailers an adequate rate of return. They also require a high throughput to support a diverse product range. It is very costly to offer a broad range in the early stages of an e-tailing operation when sales volumes are low. Offering a limited range, however, can significantly reduce the appeal of online shopping and retard market growth. The collapse of Webvan, which tried, from an early stage, to offer a range of 55 000 items through purpose-built centres, provides a salutary warning to other new entrants to the e-grocery market.

In summary, the shop-based fulfilment model has low start-up costs but is likely to prove more expensive in the longer term as retail outlets become more congested and service quality for both conventional and online shoppers deteriorates. The fulfilment centre model, on the other hand, has high initial capital and operating costs, but is likely to prove more cost effective in the longer term.

The relative efficiency of the two fulfilment models is likely to vary geographically. Companies might find it more cost effective to serve home shoppers in some areas from shops and in other areas from pick centres, depending on sales densities and local competition.

Other complicating factors are the size and service area of the fulfilment centre. There has been much debate about the optimum size of pick centres and, by implication, the number of centres required to serve the national market. One large UK supermarket estimated that it would require 18 such centres to provide national coverage, while another e-grocery business has indicated that five or six strategically located centres might suffice. Similar principles of warehousing planning apply to pick centres as to distribution centres at a higher level in the supply chain. The more centralized the system, the lower will be the capital investment and inventory levels. Fewer pick centres, however, means longer average distances to customer's homes and higher delivery costs. The cost of transporting orders over longer distances can be reduced by inserting an extra tier of satellite depots between the pick centre and the home (Figure 7.7). Orders bound for the same district can be trunked in a consolidated load to a local 'satellite' depot (or 'van centre'), where they are broken down for onward delivery in small vans (Retail Logistics Task Force, 2001). Webvan operated a hub-satellite system of this type, with each pick centre supplying orders through a network of 10–12 satellites. The satellites do not need to be separate buildings. The use of demountable vehicles, as proposed by the UK e-grocer Ocado for

South-East England, allows the local break-bulk operation to be 'depot-less' and thus more cost effective.

Solutions to the last mile problem

In the UK, it has been estimated that the average cost of order processing, picking and delivery for groceries is around £13 per order. As the charge to the customer is normally £5 per order, it is clear that unless the order value is high, retailers will make a loss on every delivery they make.

The cost of the delivery operation is strongly influenced by time constraints, in particular the width of the 'time windows' when orders are dropped at customers' homes. In deciding how wide a time window to offer online shoppers, e-tailers must strike a competitive balance between customer convenience and delivery efficiency. From the customer's standpoint, the ideal would be a guaranteed delivery within a very narrow time interval, minimizing the encroachment on his or her lifestyle. It is very costly, however, to provide such 'time-definite' deliveries. Nockold (2001) modelled the effect of varying the width of time windows on home delivery costs in the London area. The window was initially set at 3 hours. He then reduced it by 25 per cent, then 50 per cent, and finally eliminated this time constraint. These options had the effect of cutting transport costs by, respectively, 6–12 per cent, 17–24 per cent and 27–37 per cent. His conclusion was that by having completely open delivery times, cost savings of up to a third were attainable.

Normally, to achieve this degree of flexibility, it must be possible to deliver orders when no one is at home to receive them. Unattended delivery can take various forms. According to market research, the preferred option for around two-thirds of British households is to leave the goods with a neighbour (Verdict, 2000). This applies mainly to non-food items, however. Because of their bulk and the need for refrigeration, few online grocery orders are left with neighbours. Instead, home-based reception (or 'drop') boxes are being promoted as a technical solution to the problem of unattended delivery. These boxes can be divided into three broad categories:

1 *Integral boxes* – generally built into the home at the time of construction.
2 *External fixed boxes* – attached to an outside wall.
3 *External mobile (or 'delivery') boxes* – moved to and from the home and secured there temporarily by, for example, a steel cable linked to an electronic terminal.

These boxes come in various sizes and offer different types of electronic access. Most are well enough insulated to maintain the temperature of frozen and chilled produce for 6–12 hours. In a comparison of fixed and mobile boxes, Punakivi et al. (2001) concluded that their operating costs are similar, assuming that the latter are only collected at the time of the next delivery. Mobile boxes, however, have a capital cost advantage because they are shared between many customers and can achieve much higher utilization rates.

In the US, unattended reception was pioneered, unsuccessfully, by Streamline. Their Stream Boxes were generally located in customers' garages, which were equipped with keypad entry systems. Home access systems do not require the use of a reception box. One system that is currently being trialled in 50 homes in the English Midlands uses a telephone-linked electronic keypad to provide delivery staff with controlled access to garages and outbuildings. The keypads communicate with a central server, allowing the 'home access' agency to alter the pin codes after each delivery. It is claimed that this system cuts average drop times from 10 to 4 minutes and, if coupled with a 5-hour time window, would allow delivery productivity (measured in drops per vehicle per week) to improve by 84 per cent. Home access systems offer greater flexibility than drop boxes and are much cheaper to install than an integral reception unit. Their main disadvantage is that they pose a significant security risk, both to the goods being delivered and the home itself.

A more radical means of cutting transport costs is by delivering to local collection points rather than to the home. These collection points can be existing outlets, such as corner shops, post offices or petrol stations, purpose-built centres or communal reception boxes. Few existing outlets have the capacity or refrigeration facilities to accommodate online grocery orders. This has led one property developer to propose the development of a network of specially designed collection centres (or 'e-stops') to handle a range of both food and non-food products. A much cheaper option is to install banks of reception boxes at central locations within neighbourhoods where orders can be deposited for collection. One company has adapted left luggage lockers into pick-up points for home-ordered products. Their size, shape and lack of refrigeration limits their suitability for the collection of online grocery orders. As e-grocery sales expand, however, there will be an increasing demand for communal reception facilities at apartment blocks.

The use of collection points economizes on transport by sharply reducing the number of delivery locations and increasing the degree of load consolidation. It achieves this, however, at the expense of customer convenience, by requiring the online shopper to travel to the collection point to pick up the order. If the collection can be made in the course of an existing trip, say from work or to a petrol station, the loss of convenience may be acceptable. For most online grocery shoppers, however, this is unlikely to prove an attractive option.

Table 7.3 Comparison of home delivery concepts

Case	Home delivery concept and description	Example
1	**Attended reception with 2-hour delivery time windows** Delivery hours 08.00–22.00 Customer locations based on POS data Number of orders per day varies from 20 to 720	Peapod.com, USA Tesco.com, UK
2	**Home-based reception box concept** Delivery time window 08.00–16.00 Customer locations based on POS data Number of orders per day varies from 20 to 720	SOK, Finland Streamline, USA
3A	**Delivery box concept, with pick-up of the box on the next delivery** Delivery time window 08.00–16.00, pick-up on next delivery Customer locations based on POS data Number of orders per day varies from 20 to 720	Homeport, UK
3B	**Delivery box concept with pick-up of the box on next day** Delivery time window 08.00–16.00, pick-up next day Customer locations based on POS data Number of orders per day varies from 20 to 720	Homeport, UK Sainsbury, UK Food Ferry, UK
4	**Shared reception box concept** Time window 08.00–16.00, 'by end of working hours' 5, 10, 20, 30 selected central locations of the shared reception box units Capacity of the shared reception box units varies: 8, 16, 24 and 32 customer-specific lockers per unit Utilization rate of shared reception box units in the analysis: 50% and 75% Number of orders (20–720) per day varies according to a combination of the above elements	Hollming, Finland Boxcar Systems, USA ByBox Holdings, UK

Source: Punakivi and Tanskanen (2002).

Punakivi and Tanskanen (2002) have made a comparative study of the delivery costs for several 'last mile' options, using point-of-sale (POS) data from one of the largest supermarket chains in Finland. The data set contained 1639 shopping baskets of 1450 anonymous household customers. In their analysis, five home delivery concepts were modelled (see Table 7.3). These ranged from the standard Tesco model of attended reception within 2-hour delivery slots, to unattended delivery, to shared reception boxes in 'central locations'. Not surprisingly, the more the customer controlled the delivery time windows, the higher were the delivery costs. The results of the modelling exercise show that transport costs for unattended delivery to shared reception boxes were 55–66 per cent lower than attended delivery within 2-hour windows.

Outsourcing of home delivery operations

Most deliveries of online grocery orders are currently made on a dedicated basis either by the e-tailers themselves or third party distributors working on their behalf. Most of the larger e-grocers have been keen to retain direct control of the 'last mile' to ensure a high level of service and maintain customer contact. This carries a transport cost penalty, however. By outsourcing home deliveries on a shared-user basis, e-grocers could collectively reduce their transport costs by increasing drop densities and consolidating loads. A 'common distribution system' for grocery home deliveries would have to interface with different company IT systems and probably require the insertion of an additional consolidation point in the home delivery channel (Retail Logistics Task Force, 2001). Adding another node and link would offset some of the consolidation benefits. It is worth noting, though, that the Swiss online grocer LeShop manages to provide a low cost, next-day delivery across Switzerland by channelling home orders through the national postal service.

Summary

This chapter has outlined the theoretical constructs underpinning supply chain management and their applications to the retail sector. It was shown that the notion of time as a driver in competitive advantage is reflected in concepts such as just in time (JIT) in manufacturing, and quick response (QR) and efficient consumer response (ECR) in fast-moving consumer goods. If the aims of ECR are to be realized by meeting consumer demand better, faster and at less cost, supply chain integration will be necessary between and within companies.

Considerable progress has been made to realize these objectives in the last 10–15 years. Fashion retailers such as The Limited, Zara and Benetton have gained competitive advantage through efficient management of their supply chains. The traditional adversarial approach between grocery retailer and supplier has also weakened as ECR initiatives were implemented throughout the 1990s. In the evolution of grocery logistics in the UK, this has been identified as the relationship stage since 1995. Whether factory gate pricing initiated by leading retailers will lead to conflict and mistrust again remains to be seen.

What was clear from the discussion on international markets was that collaboration and the implementation of ECR are more advanced in the UK than in other countries. Differences in logistics networks across markets can be explained by factors other than the nature of manufacturer–retailer relationships – for example, the range of retail formats and their spatial distribution, variations in logistics costs in relation to land, labour and freight costs, and the relative sophistication of the logistics service provider market.

Nevertheless, the consolidation of retail markets throughout the world and further internationalization by the retail giants will result in more global sourcing and the adoption of logistics best practice principles across international markets, as illustrated by the cases of Tesco and Ahold.

Finally, the main challenge facing retailers in the future is how they unlock the potential of e-commerce. Chapter 13 shows how this market was developing, but most dot.com failures resulted from fulfilment problems. The two models discussed here outlined the pros and cons of the store-based model compared to the picking centre model for meeting consumers' orders. Although the store model is currently the most successful, increased back-door congestion in store warehouses will ultimately lead to the development of picking centres in the future. Regardless of which model is adopted, the 'last mile' problem remains unsolved. The standard 2-hour delivery window offered by most retailers does not maximize the utilization of their vehicle fleets. Thus, a variety of technical solutions, involving unattended reception boxes, have been mooted to reduce these costs. The relative success of unattended delivery options will depend upon their acceptability by customers, who will have to be persuaded to switch from attended delivery within narrow time windows.

Review questions

1 Discuss the key concepts and theories of SCM and their application to fashion retailing.

2 Outline the history of ECR and discuss its implementation in the markets of different countries.
3 Comment upon the four stages of the evolution of grocery logistics in the UK. To what extent will factory gate pricing (FGP) negate the collaborative efforts by suppliers and retailers in the relationship (fourth) stage?
4 With the aid of examples, show how logistics best practice principles are being applied internationally.
5 Review the advantages and disadvantages of the two main fulfilment models for grocery e-commerce and discuss some of the solutions proposed to overcoming the 'last mile' problem.

References

Camuffo, A., Romano, P. and Vinelli, A. (2001). Back to the future: Benetton transforms its global network. *MIT Sloan Management Review*, Fall, 46–52.

Christopher, M. (1997). *Marketing Logistics*. Butterworth-Heineman, Oxford.

Christopher, M. and Peck, H. (1998). Fashion logistics. In *Logistics and Retail Management* (Fernie, J. and Sparks, L., eds), Chapter 6. Kogan Page, London.

Coopers & Lybrand (1996). *European Value Chain Analysis Study – Final Report*. ECR Europe, Utrecht.

Cox, A. (1996). Relationship competence and strategic procurement management. Towards an entrepreneurial and contractual theory of the firm. *European Journal of Purchasing and Supply Management*, **2**(1), 57–70.

Drucker, P. (1962). The economy's dark continent. *Fortune*, April, 265–70.

Fernie, J. (1990). *Retail Distribution Management*. Kogan Page, London.

Fernie, J. and Sparks, L. (1998). *Logistics and Retail Management*, Kogan Page, London.

Fernie, J., Pfab, F. and Marchant, C. (2000). Retail grocery logistics in the UK. *International Journal of Logistics Management*, **11**(2), 83–90.

Fiddis, C. (1997). *Manufacturer–Retailer Relationships in the Food and Drink Industry. Strategies and Tactics in the Battle for Power*. FT Retail and Consumer Publishing, Pearson Professional, London.

Ford, D. (ed.) (1997). *Understanding Business Markets*. Academic Press, London.

GEA Consultia (1994). *Supplier–Retailer Collaboration in Supply Chain Management*. Coca-Cola Retailing Research Group Europe, London.

Harrison, A., Christopher, M. and van Hoek, R. (1999). *Creating the Agile Supply Chain*. Institute of Logistics and Transport, Corby.

McKinnon, A. C. (1989). The advantages and disadvantages of centralised distribution. In *Retail Distribution Management* (Fernie, J., ed.), pp. 74–89. Kogan Page, London.

Mitchell, A. (1997). *Efficient Consumer Response: A New Paradigm for the European FMCG Sector*. FT Retail and Consumer Publishing, Pearson Professional, London.

Nockold, C. (2001). Identifying the real costs of home delivery. *Logistics and Transport Focus*, **3**(10), 70–1.

Porter, M. (1985). *Competitive Advantage: Creating and Sustaining Superior Performance*. Free Press, New York.

Punakivi, M. and Tanskanen, K. (2002). Increasing the cost efficiency of e-fulfilment using shared reception boxes. *International Journal of Retail and Distribution Management*, **30**(10), 498–507.

Punakivi, M., Yrjola, H. and Holmstrom, J. (2001). Solving the last mile issue: reception box or delivery box. *International Journal of Physical Distribution and Logistics Management*, **31**(6), 427–39.

Retail Logistics Task Force – DTI Foresight (2000). *@Your Service: Future Models of Retail Logistics*. DTI, London.

Retail Logistics Task Force – DTI Foresight (2001). *@Your Home: New Markets for Customer Service and Delivery*. DTI, London.

Slack, N., Chambers, S., Harland, S. C., Harrison, A. and Johnson, R. (1998). *Operations Management*, 2nd edn. Pitman, London.

Verdict Research (2000). *Electronic Shopping, UK*. Verdict, London.

Williamson, O. E. (1979). Transaction cost economics; the governance of contractural relations. *Journal of Law and Economics*, **22**, October, 223–61.

Womack, J. P., Jones, D. and Roos, D. (1990). *The Machine that Changed the World: The Story of Lean Production*. Harper Collins, New York.

Part 3

Managing Retail Operations

8

Adding value through customer service

Introduction

There are two main roles in a retail organization: 'directly serving customers, or serving the people who do, so they can serve customers better' (Daffy, 1999). Definitions of customer service show the wide-ranging nature of a subject, which many, if not most, customers equate merely with a positive and easy-to-use returns process and complaints procedure. In addition to the growing breadth of extra services offered by retailers, from bag packing to crèches, information to installation, customer service is also linked to customer perception of service quality. It is, in one definition, the reason for retailers' existence.

The intangibility of services together with other service characteristics, inseparability, ownership, heterogeneity and perishability, create challenges for retailers, especially to deliver over time, clear customer expectations and experience of service quality. These can be used for purposes of organization or store brand differentiation in an intensely competitive market facing slow growth of the customer base. Where this is coupled with an ageing population, customer retention through customer service is deemed essential as the pool of new customers will decline over time (Rust and Oliver, 1994).

Service quality has been defined as 'the ability of the organization to meet and exceed customer expectations' (Christopher et al., 1991). If the main difference between service quality and customer satisfaction is that the former relates to managing the quality of the service and the latter to customers' expectation and experience of the quality of service delivery, then improving customer service means delivering service quality improvements which are customer defined.

The SERVQUAL model, a useful tool for retail managers to use in the quest for service quality improvement and enhanced customer satisfaction, explores the sources of the gap between service expectation and perceived service experience.

The management of consumer services involves:

1 Renewing the service offering.
2 Localizing the point-of-service system.
3 Leveraging the service contract.
4 Using information power strategically.

It also involves planning, organizing, implementing and controlling customer service within the organization.

Customer service defined

Customer service can be defined in four ways (Baron et al., 1991, p. 55):

1. The reason for the existence of a retail business.

Retailers exist to provide service to customers – at a profit. All the functions of retailing – location, assortment, breaking bulk, providing inventory, marketing, and so on – *add value* to the products purchased by customers. Each function, in adding value, provides a service to customers. It is the retailer's role in adding value which creates profit for retail organizations.

Efficiencies in supply chain management which can be generated by logistical streamlining through systems such as just in time (JIT) and electronic data interchange (EDI) can be passed on to customers in terms of better service at lower prices. However, few retailers would argue that investment in such systems is aimed at increasing profit margins. Generally, the higher the level of customer service provided, the higher the price customers are willing to pay, and the greater the profit margin is made by the retail organization.

2. The provision of facilities, activities, benefits, environments etc. by a retailer as an augmentation of the fundamental exchange relationship between merchandise supplied and money taken.

There is an enormous range of services and facilities offered by retailers today. They include:

- Accepting credit cards   Offering credit   Cashing cheques
- Altering   Assembling   Delivering
  merchandise   merchandise   merchandise
- Trolleys   Bag packing   Bag carrying
- Child care   Changing rooms   Restaurants
- Demonstrating goods   Merchandise display   Sampling of goods
- Information services   Financial services   Associated services

---

Box 8.1   Retailer profile – J Sainsbury plc

Many large retailers operate a number of formats under different names. For example, J Sainsbury plc operate six store formats designed to appeal to various market segments:

- Savacentres.
- Superstores.
- Supermarkets.
- Country Town.
- Sainsbury's Central.
- Sainsbury's Local.

They also operate two trial formats:

- Sainsbury's Assisting Village Enterprises.
- Orderline.

Sainsbury's aim is to '*make the Sainsbury's brand accessible to as many customers as possible, and so maximize its value and achieve a competitive advantage. Our approach to store development is driven by a combination of the desire to improve our geographical spread and to changing lifestyles ... so we have introduced a variety of formats to meet different customer needs.*'

   With this in mind, Country Town stores have been developed to suit the needs of shoppers in small towns, Sainsbury's Central to suit the needs of city shoppers, and Sainsbury's Local is the group's convenience store format. The merchandise range and the range of services in each format are tailored to the demands of the target customer.

Source:
http://www.j-sainsbury.co.uk/finres/1999_final/o_andfin/o_f_review.html

The environments presented by retailers for shoppers have diversified as successful retailers have used the technique of market segmentation to identify target markets, to develop customer profiles, and to create merchandise mixes which suit the needs of each customer group. This has led to new retail formats such as forecourt retailing, airport retailing and limited range supermarkets in town centres.

At the same time, the internal retail environments in the UK presented to consumers have moved upmarket. In addition to choice, most multiple retailers offer the customer a pleasant or enjoyable atmosphere in which to shop.

Profiling customer behaviour has also led to the development of category management. For customers, category management reduces the time taken to make choices, while for retailers it rationalizes the plethora of products and brands available in the market (Molla et al., 1997).

Customer service, if it is about augmenting the basic exchange relationships between retailers and customers, is therefore a key element in the way retailers can differentiate themselves from their competitors – through the range and quality of services and environments offered to customers.

> **3.** The perception held by a (potential) patron of the likely provision of facilities, activities, benefits, environments etc. by a retailer in support of the exchange relationship and its continuation, or a patron's experience of this 'total purchase package'.

The expectations of customers will affect the service they receive from a retailer. For example, a shopper in J Sainsbury plc will expect space, cleanliness, a welcoming, bright environment, well-trained helpful staff, shelves well stocked. They expect to be able to park, have a trolley available, and bags packed on demand. In return, they are willing to pay a bit more but if the service is not up to standard the customer will be disappointed, or even angry. A shopper in Lidl will have lower expectations. They will expect to be able to park, but will be satisfied with a restricted range of goods and associated services, with basic shopfittings, and more restrictions on when they can shop.

A customer's perception of the service they receive is affected by several factors, including:

- previous experience of shopping with the retailer;
- information from the retailer in the form of corporate image, advertising and other promotions, and word of mouth.

This means that retailers have to be careful to maintain the standard of service and merchandise over time to avoid disappointed customers.

Marks & Spencer, a retailer whose reputation and premium prices were built on quality merchandise, began to suffer when the lower quality of products meant that customers were disappointed and began to shop elsewhere. Marks & Spencer also refused to take credit cards, despite the rise in the number of people who habitually use them for shopping and managing their cash flow. They also lost the custom of visitors from overseas because credit cards have been largely replacing traveller's cheques as the main means of taking spending money abroad.

It also means that the image and promotion of the retailer must give a true reflection of the quality of service and merchandise offered. Otherwise, again, customers will be disappointed. Marks & Spencer, until 1999, relied mainly on its image, reputation and word of mouth to convey the level of quality of the products and service offered. When the level of quality dropped and the image was damaged, the retail organization had to take steps to improve the quality and range of merchandise, but also had to invest heavily for the first time in advertising to its customers – to get them back into the shops.

4. The explicit provision by a retailer of:

  1 Post-purchase facilities for the alteration, customization, after-care etc. of products sold.
  2 A complaints handling procedure.

Many people equate good customer service with a no-quibble goods returns policy. This type of policy encourages customer confidence in making the purchase decision, and will tend to increase repeat purchases.

Retailers may also give customers confidence in their purchase of larger items by offering a warranty, a fitting service (for example, in the purchase of kitchen, bathroom, bedrooms) and a technical help line (for example, in the purchase of computers).

These retailers recognize that customer service does not end when the customers leave the store. By recognizing post-purchase needs and behaviour, retailers encourage the purchase decision, and profitably extend their relationship with customers.

The complaints handling procedure extends the returns policy – both returns and other complaints are often handled at a customer service counter. A customer-focused retailer should encourage customers to complain when they are dissatisfied. This is because it is a good way of finding out what customers think of the service offered. By *listening* to customers, retailers can improve their operations and service. Customer complaints, if handled politely and promptly, can improve customer relations.

Service characteristics and their implication for customer service

Services and products differ in a number of important ways, which have implications for purchasers and for customer service itself. By understanding the characteristics of services, retailers can learn to *overcome* the problems they pose for service providers. Retailing is itself a service – retailers make a variety of goods available for the customer in a single location, offer information, display merchandise, provide finance and an array of additional services.

The characteristics of services include:

- Intangibility.
- Heterogeneity.
- Perishability.
- Ownership.
- Inseparability.

Intangibility

Intangibility means not being able to feel by touch – services cannot be touched or held. While store customers buy tangible (touchable) goods, the service of providing them, selling them, giving information about them and delivering them *cannot* be touched.

While you can hold, eat and taste the shiny apple you have bought, and gauge its quality and value for money in that way, the quality of the service the retailer has provided in sourcing, displaying and selling the product is assessed through perception, observation and communication. That is why retailers provide a pleasant environment in which to buy the product, and why staff attitude and communication are so important in conveying the quality of service the retailer intends his or her customers to experience.

Heterogeneity

Heterogeneity is defined as *'different in kind'* or *'composed of parts of different kinds'*. Services are experienced in different ways on different occasions by the same consumer. Similarly, different consumers will have dissimilar experiences of the same service at the same time.

As a customer, when you go into a store, on different occasions, the experience will differ in terms of display, staff, goods, communication and so on, but also because you will be in a different mood, or may have had more or less difficulty in parking, and may be in different company. It is probable that *every* experience you have of service in the same store will vary in some way from all the other experiences.

Retailers, wanting their customers to experience quality customer service, will try to reduce the amount of *heterogeneity* by making every experience of their store a positive one. One of the means of doing this is by reducing heterogeneity through standardization of processes where possible. Equipment can be used to standardize selection and transactional processes, for example. Staff are often trained to use standard techniques in dealing and communicating with customers. Dress codes and décor standardize appearances to enhance corporate image and reinforce the retail brand.

Perishability

Perishability can be defined as *'the ability to waste away or the ability to be lost'*. The opportunity to experience or to provide a service, once passed, is lost forever.

As a customer you can buy a good and store it, use it and often reuse it. Not so with a service. If you go to a store to buy an apple you occupy a *service experience*, in a certain location at a certain point in time. That opportunity will never recur. You cannot go in to buy the same apple at a different time, or go to buy another and experience exactly the same service. If you, or other customers, decide not to buy, or to buy elsewhere, then the retailer has lost these particular service opportunities forever.

Retailers deal with the characteristic of perishability through trying to maximize customer service opportunities. Their time for providing service is finite. Hence, longer opening hours provide more service opportunities, as do reducing prices at the end of the day and providing extra services such as delivery for customers who could not otherwise shop with them.

Ownership

Ownership is *'the ability to possess'* and in terms of retail service provision, this means that while a customer can own a product, they cannot own the service provided in making the product available – or any of the other related services which retailing entails.

When you buy your shiny apple you can take it away with you, and do what you want with it. You can't own the service the retailer provides you with in sourcing and selling the apple. You cannot own the service provided by staff who have directed you to the display, or the information conveyed by the display.

The goods you take home, and sundry other associated items such as bags, receipts and guarantee documents (these are named 'peripheral evidence' when referring to the service marketing mix), *represent* the quality of service experienced. Retailers try to reliably provide goods which accurately represent the quality of service they want to provide for their customers. The peripheral evidence of purchase is also used to reinforce brand image. Reliability of goods and service quality is a key means of developing trust between customer and retailer. If the quality of either over time reduces, customers will be dissatisfied and shop elsewhere.

Inseparability

Inseparability is defined as *'the inability to be separated'* and in terms of service it means that the service you experience as a customer is inseparable from the service being provided by the retailer.

When you buy your apple, the service you experience is intrinsically related to the people providing the service, most notably the personnel who communicate with you in the store, but also linked into the personnel who, though invisible to the customer, help to make the product and service available.

For retailers, this is why their staff are so important a cog in the wheel of service provision. Shop-floor staff's attitude and training improve the customer service experience, while the teamwork required in providing goods for sale to the customer needs to focus on the quality of service to the end customer. The characteristic of inseparability is the reason why customer service training is a key requirement for staff and management in retailing today.

Improving the quality of customer service

Customers' perception of the quality of service provided by retailers depends upon the level of satisfaction they experience in the process of shopping (Oliver, 1981). Their satisfaction is affected by both their *expectations* of the shopping experience and the *actuality* of the experience. If customers experience higher levels of service than expected over time, then they will perceive the retailer as offering a high quality of service. If the level of service is lower than expected over time, the retailer will be perceived as offering a low level of service quality (Bell et al., 1999). The main difference between service quality and customer satisfaction is that the former relates to managing the quality of the service and the latter to customers' expectation and experience of the quality of service delivery. Therefore, improving customer service means delivering service quality improvements which are customer defined. The SERVQUAL model can be used as a basis for considering how to do this.

SERVQUAL – a model for improving service quality

The SERVQUAL model has been widely applied as a means to measure service quality (Parasuraman et al., 1985). In this model, the 'service gap' – that is, the difference between the level of service quality which customers expect and the level they experience – is the result of four main criteria (see Figure 8.1). These are:

1 The gap between what customers expect and what managers think they expect – the knowledge gap.
2 The gap between what managers think customers expect and the standards of service they specify – the standards gap.
3 The gap between standards of service set by managers and standards of service delivered – the delivery gap.
4 The gap between standards of service delivered and those communicated to the customer (which create the customer's initial expectations of the level of service which they will experience) – the communication gap.

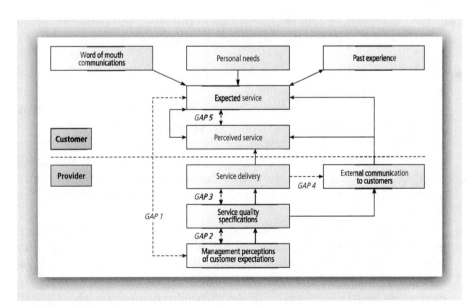

Figure 8.1 Service quality gaps. *Source*: **Parasuraman et al. (1985).**

The size of the service gap – between perceived and experienced quality of service – affects the level of satisfaction experienced by customers of a retail organization.

According to this model, retailers can improve their service quality – and hence improve the level of customer satisfaction, by closing or reducing the four gaps. This theory has been criticized, not least because it:

- oversimplifies the relationship between customer and service provider;
- does not allow for the relationship between customer and service provider which is an integral part of the service experience.

However, SERVQUAL is a useful model for retail practitioners because it provides an easy to use framework for improving their customer service and overall service quality.

Closing the knowledge gap

Retail managers very often overlook this potential gap because the measure of meeting customer needs lies directly in successful sales figures. If sales dip below expectations, the action taken is often to create economies in the organization by restructuring, by sourcing cheaper suppliers, or by creating further efficiencies in the supply chain.

In fact, the problem will frequently lie in the changing expectations of customers. These are affected by a range of factors, including:

- The customers' experience of the retailer over time – even if service quality is meticulously maintained over time, customers will become used to the level of service quality on offer. It will become the norm. The route to customer satisfaction is to raise the *experience* of shopping above the *expectation* of the experience of shopping, to maintain a state of *customer delight* (Piercy, 1997) with the retail offering. Then the retailer has to take care to substantially *raise* service quality levels periodically, or to *continuously improve* service quality levels.

  This may take the form of increasing the range of services on offer, of altering the product/service mix available, of changing the quality of the retail environment or of raising the level of post-purchase service. Homebase, for example, offers an additional service to customers by having a list of tradesmen who can help with or install merchandise bought in-store.

- Their perception of the level of product and service quality offered by the retailer relative to those of competing organizations. Service quality is very frequently used by retailers as a means of differentiating their retail offer from those of their competitors. Certainly, this has been the case with Marks & Spencer and Sainsbury.

However, customer expectations of service quality have risen over time. At the turn of the millenium shoppers are well travelled, media literate, and able to compare the product/service offerings not just of competing local retailers, but to compare these with the quality of merchandise and services offered by national and international retail organizations.

The raised expectations of sophisticated customers means that in the future high levels of customer care will be standard in retailing – to differentiate their service quality, retailers will have to be innovative in surprising or delighting the customer with the level of service quality.

Managers can learn more about customers' expectations and perception of service levels through market research, including analysis of customer service data. They can spend time on a daily basis in direct contact with customers and shop-floor staff. They can facilitate communication routes for shop-floor staff upwards through the organization. They also need to act rapidly to implement improvements suggested as the result of research and communication.

Closing the standards gap

Meeting the changing and increasingly sophisticated expectations of customers through the development of service standards can be difficult for retailers. Management training for retail managers is largely organizationally based or non-existent. In the first instance, there is an internal bias in the management techniques acquired; in the second, staff acquire management skills on an ad hoc basis. Under either circumstance, the development of performance standards for service quality which will deliver the service desired by external customers can be difficult for managers. In addition, many retail organizations have to deliver short-term profit levels to satisfy shareholders, which will preclude setting of levels of service which retail managers and customers desire.

To close the standards gap, therefore, there has to be a commitment from the senior management team towards service quality. Only then will the human, financial and material resources be made available for the development of a formal quality system. The quality system should establish the formal processes for setting service quality objectives, and should establish the roles of staff within these processes. Only if there is a *visible* commitment to quality service at senior level will managers be confident in setting and implementing the service quality standards within their remit. A reward system for service quality achievement will enhance staff and management commitment to implementing, meeting or exceeding the standards set (Zeithaml et al., 1988).

The achievement of standards of quality can be made easier through the use of technology to standardize processes. Hard technology has been used widely in retailing in checking in, display and checkout procedures, whereas soft technology includes refinement of work methods – for example, use of teamwork to solve customer problems quickly, bag packing by checkout operators.

Closing the delivery gap

The gap between standards set and those delivered arises for a variety of reasons – for example, unrealistic standards, lack of clarity in standards, poor communication of standards and their purpose, weak staff motivation, poor supervision, lack of human, financial or material resources.

To reduce this gap, managers can focus on the following (Lovelock, 1991):

- Clarification of standards and staff roles so that staff understand the context of their work.
- Involvement of staff in setting standards so that they own and commit to quality.
- Communication of standards to staff.
- Selection and training of staff so that they are capable of delivering the set standards.
- Encouragement of teamwork to deliver quality.
- Motivation of staff.
- Regular and spot measurement of performance so that staff become accustomed to performing and to being assessed to the set standards.

Closing the communication gap

The communication gap is the difference between the standard of service delivered to customers and that communicated by the retailer to customers through their external marketing communications.

The information communicated to customers should accurately reflect the quality of service to be offered. Merchandise should be accurately represented, available, prices accurate, delivery times adhered to. It is very easy to cause inadvertent dissatisfaction in providing for the disparate needs of customers in a national or international context. For example, Safeway, in its customer magazine for loyalty card customers, offered discounted products and services in return for card points. However, some of the services – for example, crèche and laundry – are unavailable in many stores and this lead to dissatisfaction among a percentage of regular, 'loyal' customers.

The reason why the communication gap exists in many organizations is because promotion is undertaken by a marketing department or agency. Therefore, the staff drawing up promotional materials and messages are doing so in isolation from the realities of the shop-floor. By reducing this internal communication gap, it is possible to portray the retail offering more accurately to customers.

One way of doing this is for shop-floor staff to be involved in the creation, content or approval of promotional materials. Another is to involve marketing staff in operational duties. A third is improved internal communication through internal marketing, cross-functional teams or shared training programmes.

Other ways to reduce the communication gap include: focusing the content of promotional programmes on key aspects of the retail offering – those of most importance to customers; standardizing service levels across the retail organization; offering and promoting different levels of service for different price bands.

While the closure of the service gap between perceived and experienced service, is a desirable focus for service quality management, it does not address the spiral of rising customer expectations of service quality. To compete successfully on the service quality front, exceptional service is required – which means the closure of a further gap – between what customers experience in terms of service quality and what they really want. For this, retailers have to listen closely and respond rapidly to customers' desires.

Box 8.2   Research focus

Bell et al. (1999) carried out a research study on service quality in food retailing. Over 1000 interviews were carried out with customers in two superstores in South-East England. Customers were asked to recall recent occasions when they had been particularly satisfied with service, and when they had been particularly dissatisfied with service. The incidents collected were categorized under the headings:

- Physical.
- Price.

- Interpersonal.
- Merchandise.
- Process.
- Non-core services.

The researchers found that over 50 per cent of negative incidents were generated by the retail process. Process was divided into subcategories:

- Travel.
- Arrive and enter.
- Select items.
- Checkout.
- Leave with goods.
- Appraisal.

They concluded that improvements in store design, together with a proactive focus on service delivery, could gain a retailer competitive advantage. Their conclusions include the following:

- Since the shopping experience begins outside the store (travel), there needs to be a focus on entry roads, car parking, security and cleanliness.
- On entry to the store, customers like to be greeted or acknowledged in some way. Also on entry, customers appreciate a 'decompression' area where they can relax into the shopping experience.
- Extra space is needed round areas where customers congregate – e.g. special displays, in-store bakeries – so that the flow of customers is not impeded.
- Poor product availability is a distinct problem for customers, and one which is recalled even after a long period of time. The authors suggested that out-of-stocks corrupt sales data in just-in-time systems because replenishment is based on sales rather than demand.
- Extended shopping hours have created problems for high volume replenishment during closed hours. Customers don't like trolleys and boxes blocking the aisles.
- Switching staff from stocking to checkout activities to meet variable customer demand causes problems with a stocking backlog to the end of the day – again exacerbated through extended opening hours.
- Customers really like quick, efficient checkout operation. Bag packing and help with bags are currently a route to 'customer delight', although it is liable to be accepted as standard in the future.
- Whole trolley scanning would be a means of speeding up checkout and replenishment, and therefore the expense could be justified.

Source: Bell et al. (1999).

Managing customer service

Strategic options: standardization and customization strategies

While standardized methods and machinery can improve the efficiency and effectiveness of the service experience, customers want to feel special and hence customization of service to the needs of the individual is seen as the route to building and maintaining a secure customer base. Standardization and customization of service can be viewed as a continuum (Figure 8.2).

Many retail businesses are built on the premise of standardization. The main UK grocery retailers have developed standardized formats to build market share. Customers are guided round the store in a pre-set flow pattern, greeted and dealt with according to standardized procedures. Automation and standardization are fundamental to the high levels of service retail customers experience in their shopping today.

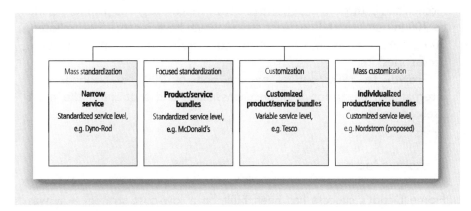

Figure 8.2 Standardization and customization of service as a continuum.

Customized service

If standardization is the cornerstone of retail excellence, then customization is the key to retail differentiation. Customized services – service experiences customized to the needs of the customer – have always existed in retailing (for example, couture clothing and quality dining). In addition, the range of extra services available in some stores allows a degree of customization to be available to self-service shoppers – for example, dropping off the laundry in the grocery store, having a meal, buying petrol, child care, bag packing and so on. With home delivery and Internet shopping, the range of customization is expanding.

In recent years, supported by information technology and the integration of organizations in the supply chain, mass customization

Box 8.3   Retailer profile – Home Depot

With sales growth of over 25 per cent and 9.9 per cent growth in profit in 1999, Home Depot has a success profile any retailer would envy. The world's largest home improvement retailer, Home Depot's performance was fuelled by growth in both number and value of transactions.

Merchandise and formats

Home Depot has 914 stores across the US, with the standard store format 1200 square metres in size. Merchandise includes the normal DIY range, including timber, floor and wall coverings, plumbing goods, lighting and electrical supplies, ironmongery, tools and machinery, garden areas and accessories. The range has recently been extended into home appliances. Two other formats are operated – Expo Design Centres – kitchen and bathroom design showrooms, which the group plan to expand to 200 in number, and compact stores which have recently been piloted, 300 square metres in size, which stock household goods and home accessories.

Growth to 1900 outlets by the end of 2003 is planned, with international expansion a distinct possibility, and acquisition the most likely route.

Customer focus

Home Depot's success has been built on a low-cost strategy – it was the first discount shed DIY operator in the 1970s – and led the way for DIY retailers in the UK and Europe. It operates large stores, maintains a low-price strategy and builds value for customers through exceptional customer service. The CEO claims its recent success is the result of customer focus, providing the customer with the highest level of customer service together with quality products at the lowest prices. Profitability comes from the increasing volume of transactions. The boom in personal wealth has meant an increasing level of house moves and improvements.

The retailer's website, originally used as a customer information and marketing tool, was developed for selling during 2000, with orders being processed and delivered from local stores. Online prices and range are the same as in the local stores. The website offers advice to customers on basic DIY skills and techniques, and offers projects for customers to work on, such as building a porch or garden swing.

Beyond customer service

Home Depot is committed to community involvement, with $15 million spent on community projects such as low-cost housing, at-risk youth support and environmental programmes. At a national level, in 1999 donations of tools, materials and expertise from Home Depot helped to build emergency homes for hurricane victims. Community involvement helps embed organizations in the community they serve, building up a loyal customer base. It is also a means of creating a continuous stream of publicity.

Source: Clements (2000).

has become a possibility for retail organizations because the costs of customization have been reduced. Mass customization means that every customer can receive a unique service tailored to individual needs. As communication and information technology develop and converge, without doubt some retailers will implement a mass customization strategy in the near future.

Customer service strategies: key aspects of managing a consumer organization

Four key aspects of managing a consumer business are (Allen, 1991, p. 145):

1 Renewing the service offering.
2 Localizing the point-of-service system.
3 Leveraging the service contract.
4 Using information power strategically.

Renewing the service offering

The need to revise and renew the service offering stems from the investment in premises and infrastructure, which contrasts with the perishable nature of services. Therefore, the high fixed costs of premises and supply chain infrastructure contrast with the fluctuating flow and demands of customers.

Retail operators have to be creative in maximizing customer opportunities to shop, and be both sensitive and responsive to changing customer and market demands. Service extension and enhancement are the means to consider in responding to opportunities offered by the changing marketplace. Retail examples of service extension include: Internet information and advice; direct delivery; and financial services. While these extend the service retailers provide, service is enhanced by associated services such as childcare, changing rooms, toilets, bag packing and credit.

The route to innovative service extension and enhancement lies in understanding consumers' problems through proactive market research, and in altering the service in response. This is because consumers are more able to articulate their complaints and problems than they are able to express the benefits they want from a service. For this reason, retailers should not only deal rapidly with customer complaints and put in process the means for preventing their recurrence, but should also encourage customers to express their problems, as this can be the basis for enhancing and differentiating the service they provide. For example, the problem of delivery receipt of Internet or telephone orders to busy workers can, for example, be overcome through delivery to work or to pick-up points.

If the development and revision of procedures for reviewing and upgrading service provision is the key to creative response in a changing market, then localizing the point-of-service is the means of increasing the rate of customer interception, which helps to increase numbers and the value of customers to the organization.

Localizing the point-of-service system

According to service management theory, if customers are intercepted at the time and place when a service is needed they will purchase the service. Hence, a convenience store will attract custom if it is located near the customer, open at the time the customer wants to shop and premium prices can be charged. Another example is fast food delivery, in which the distance barrier to purchase is overcome through reliable and speedy delivery.

Retailing is polarizing into destination and proximity formats (Dawson, 1995). The former is based on a merchandise mix, merchandise selection, and associated quality and service levels which will attract customers from a distance – for example, Jenners, the Edinburgh department store. The latter is based on customer interception through locating where potential customers naturally congregate – for example, forecourt and shipping, rail and airport terminal retailing. Major grocery retailers have successfully used forecourt outlets to localize their point-of-service and increase market penetration – for example, Tesco Express.

Direct mail retailers intercept home-bound customers and workers, and more recently, interactive television and Internet retailing have allowed the ultimate in localizing point-of-service to customers through entering the home environment in an interactive mode. However, because services are consumed without ownership (see service characteristics section above), this means that the service a retailer provides across the Internet has to also incorporate the delivery of the goods. So, unlike the service provided within a shop, which is consumed within and close to the premises, the service provided by an Internet retailer cannot be focused entirely on website design and content, but has to focus on delivery of the goods.

In one study, website users rated convenience, reliability, content and responsiveness the most important factors in meeting their needs, but other significant factors were a user-friendly interface, marketing communication, and information management and maintenance (McGoldrick et al., 1999). These factors can be incorporated into website design and management and will enable retailers to intercept customers. However, to localize the point-of-service, Internet retailers have to streamline logistics and delivery services.

Leveraging the service contract

The third key aspect of managing a consumer service is leveraging the service contract – this means establishing the basis for retention of customers, and raising barriers against customers switching to competing service deliverers.

The large retail groups in the UK have extensively implemented leverage strategies. In order to retain customers and increase their spend, retailers in the competitive UK retail market have had to minimize reasons for customers to switch to competitors, and build and maintain barriers to defection.

Service extension and enhancement can build share and loyalty among customers, as can loyalty card schemes, and loyalty card scheme extensions such as catalogues, mailings and direct delivery. However, in areas with extensive coverage of competing retailers, customers tend to be promiscuous, with loyalty cards to many stores. In this case, managers have to focus on barriers to switching, such as extra point values, double points and bonuses. Other barriers include promotional activities – advertising and sales promotions – and partnerships with, or acquisition of, competing retail organizations.

Loyalty card schemes reward all members equally according to the amount spent. While this can increase customer spend, it is expensive to administer and retailers also need to focus on finding and retaining those customers who spend the most – their key customers – and establish retention strategies specifically designed for them. This type of strategy has been implemented successfully by airlines, which reward different levels of loyalty with different service contracts – executive and premier club membership, for example.

It has been argued that loyalty schemes create loyalty to the scheme not the retailer. They are costly to administer, and some retailers have withdrawn from them. Safeway, for example, used the savings from abandoning their ABC card to fund their high/low promotional strategy. True loyalty exists when a customer remains loyal to the retail organization over an extended period of time, despite price and other incentives to change. This type of loyalty costs time, effort and expenditure. It was achieved by Marks & Spencer, for example, over decades, before dissipating in the late 1990s as product and service quality declined below the threshold offered by competitors and acceptable to loyal customers.

Using information power strategically

The characteristics of services – inseparability, heterogeneity, perishability and intangibility – are reasons why the quality of the customer's service experience is so closely allied with the quality of services provision and services personnel.

Fergal Quinn (Superquinn) thinks that retailers should encourage a listening culture using a variety of listening systems. Observing the customer's point of view is essential and there are a variety of ways of doing this, from market research to focus groups, comment forms and complaints procedures. Superquinn, for example, has a rule that managers should do their household shopping there once a month to see the shops through the eyes of the customer, and there should also be encouragement of shop-floor staff to feed back information from customers. Other feedback routes include market research, focus groups, customer complaints and 'walking the floor'. In order to achieve service superiority, quick response should not just be applied to the supply chain but also to the implementation of customer-derived service improvements.

The close relationship between customer and provider means that service businesses are well placed to benefit from the exponential growth of communication and information technologies. These can be used to help personalize service, manage service quality and extend the service offering. Tesco, one of the first UK grocery retailers to go online in the mid-1990s, offers a wide range of products and services through its Internet provision (see Box 8.4).

The large UK retailers have had a presence on the Internet for a number of years, and are now in a position to exploit the opportunities

Box 8.4 Tesco Internet services 2000

Tesco Online – http://www.texco.co.uk
Shopping for fashion, music, sporting, electrical goods, wine, spirits, fragrances, toiletries, flower delivery UK wide.

TescoNet – http://www.tesco.net
Free Internet service provider offering website hosting, web page design information, POP e-mail, dial-up and ISDN Internet access.

TescoDirect – http://www.tescodirect.com
Order and delivery of fresh groceries within selected areas.

Tesco SchoolNet – http://www.tesco.schoolnet2000.com
Information about UK schools, history and environment.

Tesco – http://www.tesco.co.uk/software
Free cooking software including recipe collection and wine selector.

Tesco – http://www.tesco.co.uk
Web home (company and investor services) – shopping and financial services.

Tesco Internet Superstore – http://www.tesco.co.uk/homeshop
Online superstore.

Tesco: Job Opportunities – http://home.tesco.co.uk/recruit
Job information and company details.

Tesco: Investment Information – http://www.tesco.co.uk/information/investor
Company's annual report and financial statements.

Tesco: Corporate Homepage – http://www.tesco.co.uk/indexn.thm
Customer service information, graduate recruitment and financial data.

It is clear that Tesco is using the Internet to communicate to customers, to offer extensions of existing services and to offer new services. The Tesco Homepage lists the services offered under the heading Personal Finance (AD2000):

- Personal loan.
- Visa card.
- Savings.
- Isa.
- Pension.
- Car insurance (new service).
- Home insurance.
- Pet insurance (new service).
- Travel insurance.
- Online banking (new service).

Source: http://www.tesco.co.uk/indexn.thm, 2000.

afforded by this new medium. At the same time they have developed and implemented their loyalty card schemes, gathering personal and purchase information from their regular customers. On the one hand, they are developing the infrastructure and methods for quality service delivery to distant customers; and on the other, they are developing their strategic use of information power.

The development of communication media is fast paced, offering diverse means and routes to communicate with customers. It is interesting to note that e-tailers still need to use traditional media such as television, newspapers, magazines and even bus shelters to build brand awareness.

The large UK retailers have extremely strong brands already, and therefore can concentrate on the use of new media in developing, customizing and communicating service and market extensions.

Information and communication technology developments have also afforded opportunities to smaller retailers, allowing them to broaden the range of services offered and widening their market potential. Lacking the financial muscle to build brand awareness using traditional mass media, small retailers instead are more focused in communicating with their customers.

However, many small retailers lack information and communication technology skills, many do not collect information on customers and some well-established small retailers, even in 2000, were operating without computers.

Implementing good customer service in retailing

The successful implementation of good customer service as a differentiation strategy requires recognition that it has to apply within as well as outside the organization. The previous section highlighted the importance of listening to customers and incorporating feedback routes within the organization – from customers and staff. Implementation of good customer service requires management to view staff as internal customers (and vice versa), and that staff are given the resources to meet customers' needs effectively and competitively.

Managing in a retail organization includes developing both the 'hard' factors – the formal structure, processes and procedures – which comprise the business and managing the 'soft' factors – the informal style of doing business. The 'hard' and 'soft' factors include the following:

Hard factors
- Formal statements of objectives and strategies, formal planning process.

- Organizational structure.
- Formal communication system.
- Formal processes.
- Formal procedures.

Soft factors
- Shared norms and aspirations.
- Organizational 'culture'.
- Informal networks of communication which modify formal policies and information flows.
- The established style of doing work.
- The skills, knowledge and expertise of the workforce.

The soft factors are 'people related' rather than 'process related', and because customers' perception of good service is so closely related to their interaction with the workforce, it is especially important that retail managers recognize and manage the 'fit' of the informal culture of the organization with the formal strategy and structure. Where the 'fit' is poor – for example, when the workforce are faced with changed processes and procedures which conflict with the established style of doing work, or which undermine their skills and expertise – stress will occur, and workforce stress will impact on customer service.

Of course good communication, training and involvement of staff in the development of plans and policies will tend to reduce conflict. Implementing the formal strategies, policies, processes and procedures (Stone and Young, 1994) requires managers to:

- Communicate with staff – tell them your objectives and policies; not just what they are, but *why* they are.
- Train staff – make sure they know what the processes and procedures are and how to do them.
- Give your staff the support they need to succeed.
- Give them the right equipment and other resources to succeed.
- Give them adequate time to complete the set work.

Through applying this framework for implementation to customer service within the organization, it is clear that where excellence in customer service is an organizational priority, it has to be championed by the senior management team – embedded within the organization at the highest level. This should take a visible form – managers serving customers, interacting with customers and staff, listening to views and demands, implementing change as a result of their findings.

There should be customer service objectives set and strategies set in place for these to be achieved. A written customer service policy and/or charter should be created. This needs to be shared with staff and customers to establish the level of service of the organization – to establish customer and staff expectations.

A formal planning cycle for customer service should be established (Figure 8.3). The organizational structure for customer service has to be set up – establishing the roles and spans of control for dedicated customer service staff, and for the rest of the staff. Standards for key customer service tasks have to be developed and implemented through communication with the staff concerned. Indeed, communications regarding customer service, lateral, diagonal, up and down the organization can help to implant a customer service philosophy throughout.

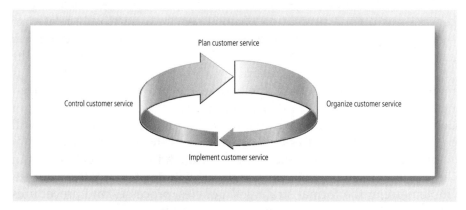

Plan customer service

Control customer service

Organize customer service

Implement customer service

Figure 8.3 Planning cycle for customer service.

Training of staff in customer service processes and procedures should be arranged. Staff have to be clear regarding how and when their performance will be measured and controlled. In addition, a system of reward will help to embed the required levels of customer service throughout the organization. Feedback on performance should be used in the development of new objectives at the end of the planning cycle.

Nordstrom, one of the leading fashion retailers in the US, whose customer service is recognized for its excellence, believe in employing staff who are customer driven, entrepreneurial and motivated, then training and empowering them to make decisions which ensure every customer leaves the stores satisfied (see Box 8.5).

The management input to good customer service includes:

● Adding value – encouraging staff to add value to everything they do, and leading by example.

- Giving ownership – where possible, assign responsibilities and ownership for offering customers excellent service to the relevant staff so that progress can be easily monitored by all.
- Increasing staff creativity by encouraging them to take initiative and by allowing mistakes in the pursuit of real progress and improvement.
- Encouraging teamwork because it improves communication and harnesses the abilities and knowledge of staff to create synergy.
- Investing in people – in addition to dedicated customer service training, all staff, including managers, will benefit in terms of confidence and capability from constructive appraisal and self-development opportunities.
- Communicating – good formal and informal communication routes generate better relationships among staff, between staff and managers, and help staff to develop a better dialogue with customers. Use direct communication where possible because feedback is instantaneous.

Service excellence requires more than management dexterity, however. According to Zeithaml et al. (1990, p. 5):

> People in service work need a vision in which they can believe, an achievement culture that challenges them to be the best they can be, a sense of team that nurtures and supports them, and role models that show them the way. This is the stuff of leadership.

Box 8.5   The Nordstrom route to exceptional customer service

In the last century, Nordstrom has grown from modest beginnings to become one of America's foremost fashion retailers, with shops across the country selling clothing, shoes, cosmetics and accessories for the whole family, aimed at customers in middle/upper income levels. The company is committed to principles of service, quality, selection and value for money.

> The best Nordstrom sales associates will do virtually everything they can to make sure a shopper leaves the store a satisfied customer, carrying home *the right item in the right size in the right colour at the right price...*
>
> (Spector and McCarthy, 1995, p. 25)

Value is created by the entrepreneurial style of buying. Strong negotiation secures best value, buyers work with manufacturers to secure a wide variety of styles which can sell at various price points and quality is closely inspected. Buyers also have freedom to source stock close to the store, which allows for regional variations in taste, while buying for a limited number of outlets reduces the potential for large-scale failure of any item of stock. Buyers are also expected to spend time on the shop-floor to keep tabs on customer-based market information.

Nordstrom's reputation for the depth and breadth of its inventory has grown out of the belief that customer service and satisfaction are related to the availability of stock for every customer. Therefore, a wide range of styles from economical to expensive needs to be available in a wide variety of sizes. If a customer likes a style of merchandise but it is not available in the right size, the customer will leave the store dissatisfied.

As a customer-driven organization there is a strong service culture, and employees are given freedom to make customer- and stock-related decisions, to serve the customer throughout the store and to operate '*like entrepreneurial shopkeepers*' (Spector and McCarthy, 1995, p. 100). Store managers have the autonomy to employ staff and buy inventory. Nordstrom believe in a 'hands-on' management style in which managers are visible on the shop-floor, serving customers and encouraging staff. All staff are expected to put the customer before the organization in making decisions, with the organization bearing the consequences.

Employee selection is regarded as crucial to the success of the organization. Employees need to genuinely like people, and to find satisfaction in serving people. Ideas and innovations are required from shop-floor staff, who must also be happy to work in an unconfined environment in which they are expected to take the initiative. Nordstrom believe that staff work best when there are few restrictions and bureaucracy is minimized.

Staff pay is based on commission to reward for ability, and success is further rewarded with more responsibility and promotion – the organization believes in promoting from within as a motivational tool. Sales targets are net of returns and there is a generous returns policy which guarantees that if a customer is dissatisfied with a purchase, for whatever reason, it can be returned to the store. This means that salespeople are not induced to hard-sell to make targets but to meet customers' needs so that returns do not occur. Successful staff build up a database and profile of customers they serve in order to serve them better over time. Therefore, staff stand to increase their own income through managing relations with their own customers. Staff who fail to meet sales targets, on the other hand, are given special coaching to help them achieve.

The culture is spread to new stores by involving established Nordstrom staff in new store openings. Acquisition or merger are rejected as expansion strategies because of the difficulties involved in culture change. The organization is structured like an inverted pyramid, with management supporting the sales associates who serve the customers.

The threat posed by discount and value retail competitors has been tackled in a number of ways. Firstly, entrepreneurial buying allows fashion items to be stocked which cannot be replicated by discounters. Secondly, Nordstrom has used its private-label brands to achieve value for customers rather than higher profit margins. Thirdly, the organization has developed its own self-service value outlets to dispense clearance merchandise and special buys not carried in its normal stores – Nordstrom Rack. These stores also serve to introduce customers and staff to Nordstrom, and provide entry-level training for staff.

Further innovations are regarded as necessary to meet the needs of shoppers in the future. Experimentation with personalized interactive shopping has been undertaken in which customers using diverse communication media are dealt with directly by Nordstrom salespeople and given the same kind of service as in-store customers. Mail order, previously regarded as an additional means of advertising, has been extended as a direct sales medium.

Summary

In retailing, customer service can be defined in four ways. Firstly, retail organizations exist in order to provide products to customers, adding value to the products through bringing them together in one place, providing information about them, enabling customers to buy. Secondly, the wide range of services that retailers have put together to add value to the fundamental exchange relationship (money for products) has become an intrinsic part of customer service. Thirdly, the customer's perception and experience of the service retailers provide affect the level of customer satisfaction. Fourthly, customer service involves post-purchase facilities and services plus the complaints and returns policies.

The five service characteristics – intangibility, heterogeneity, perishability, ownership and inseparability – inherently frame the customer service experience. By considering each in turn, retailers can improve the customer service experience.

The intangibility of the service means retailers have to focus on tangibilizing the brand – for example, by giving customers loyalty cards and carrier bags. The heterogeneity of the retail experience can be overcome through standardization of procedures, training and dress –

although this can also be exploited through using new information and communication technologies to customize the retail offering to individual or small group needs. The perishability of the service has led retailers to maximize the opportunities for their customers to shop. Ownership is a characteristic which means that retailers have to strive for consistency – in service terms and in reliable provision of products. Inseparability is the characteristic which requires retailers to ensure their staff have positive attitudes and behaviour, are well trained and informed, because the staff–customer interaction is so important in ensuring customer satisfaction.

The SERVQUAL model is a useful tool retailers can use to focus on areas in which their service quality can be improved. By analysing the knowledge, standards, delivery and communication gaps in the service they provide, they can reduce the gap between what customers expect in terms of service and their perception of level of service they receive. In this way, they can improve the level of satisfaction their customers experience.

Customer service strategies range from standardization to mass customization – retailers have to decide which strategy to implement. However, as the costs of customization reduce with the convergence of communication and information technologies, the opportunities for mass customization will increase.

There are four key aspects in managing a consumer business. Firstly, retail managers should renew the service offering to generate customer interest and build customer relationships. Retailers do this through service extension and service enhancement. Secondly, retailers should localize the point-of-service system – that is, consider ways and means of intercepting customers beyond the confines of their traditional outlets, and making it easy for them to shop. Leveraging the service contract is the third factor. Retailers need to consider how to boost both loyalty and spend – focusing on delivering exceptional service to their key customers is one way of doing this. Finally, retailers are well positioned to make use of the information and communication technology advancements in order to manage customer information to personalize services, develop service extensions/enhancements and manage service quality.

Review questions

1 How well do the definitions of customer service encapsulate the main customer service issues facing retailers?
2 Describe five characteristics of services and explain why these need to be addressed by retail organizations.

3 Explain the difference between service quality and customer service.
4 To compete successfully on the service quality front, exceptional service is required. What steps can a retailer take to drive exceptional service in the organization?
5 Explain the main factors which have to be considered in implementing good customer service in an organization.

References

Allen, M. (1991). Strategic management of consumer services. In *Services Marketing* (Lovelock, C. H., ed.). Prentice-Hall, London.

Baron, S., Davies, B. and Swindley, D. (1991). *Macmillan Dictionary of Retailing*. Macmillan Press.

Bell, J., Gilbert, D., Lockwood, A. and Dutton, C. (1999). Getting it wrong in food retailing: the shopping process explored. 10th International Conference on Research in the Distributive Trades, Stirling, August.

Christopher, M., Payne, A. and Ballantyne, D. (1991). *Relationship Marketing*. Butterworth-Heinemann, Oxford.

Clements, A. (2000). *Retail Week*, 21 January.

Daffy, C. (1999). *Once A Customer Always A Customer*. Oak Tree Press.

Dawson, J. (1995). Retail trends in Scotland: a review. *International Journal of Retail Distribution Management*, **23**(10), 4–20.

http://www.j-sainsbury.co.uk/finres/1999_final/o_andfin/o_f_review.html.

http://www.tesco.co.uk/indexn.thm.

Lovelock, C. H. (ed.) (1991). *Services Marketing*. Prentice-Hall, London.

McGoldrick, P., Vazquez, D., Lim, T. Y. and Keeling, K. (1999). Cyberspace marketing – How do surfers determine website quality? 10th International Conference on Research in the Distributive Trades, Stirling, August.

Molla, A., Mugica, J. and Yague, M. (1997). *Category Management and Consumer Choice*, 9th International Conference on Research in the Distributive Trades, Leuven, July.

Oliver, R. L. (1981). The measurement and evaluation of the satisfaction process in retail settings. *Journal of Retailing*, **57**, Fall, 25–48.

Parasuraman, A., Zeithaml, V. A. and Berry, L. L. (1985). A conceptual model of service quality and its implications for future research. *Journal of Marketing*, **49**, Fall, 41–50.

Piercy, N. (1997). *Market-Led Strategic Change: Transforming the Process of Going to Market*. Butterworth-Heinemann, Oxford.

Rust, R. T. and Oliver, R. L. (1994). *Service Quality, New Directions in Theory and Practice*. Sage.

Spector, R. and McCarthy, P. D. (1995). *The Nordstrom Way: The Inside Story of America's No. 1 Customer Service Company*. John Wiley, New York.

Stone, M. and Young, L. (1994). *Competitive Customer Care: A Guide to Keeping Customers*. Croner, Kingston-upon-Thames.

Zeithaml, V. A., Berry, L. L. and Parasuraman, A. (1988). Communication and control processes in the delivery of service quality. *Journal of Marketing*, **52**, 35–48.

Zeithaml, V. A., Parasuraman, A. and Berry, L. L. (1990). *Delivering Service Quality*. Free Press, New York.

9

Retail selling

Introduction

An increasingly competitive market means that retail selling is growing in importance for all retailers, not just retailers of high-value, complex products. Retailing is a service, and retail selling is as essential a function as customer service. Indeed, the two are interlinked, not just because both functions are undertaken by the same staff in many retail organizations, but also because both customer service and sales staff have the prime role as interfacers between the retail organization and its customers. The customers' interpretation of the organization's image and ethos are affected by the nature of their relationship and encounters with retail staff.

Retailers, operating market-focused service businesses, need to tailor their retail selling to the customers' requirements with regard to the type of product being bought and the type of purchase decision. They also need to take into consideration their customers' shopping motives and their stage in the process of making the buying decision (Merrilees and Miller, 1996).

Retail selling requires, therefore, a good knowledge of the products being sold, an understanding of the profile of target customers, and further, comprehension of customers' needs, in terms of both merchandise being sold and the shopping experience.

The nature and depth of retail selling is related to a variety of factors, including type of product, the customer's understanding of its qualities, uses and attributes, the complexity and value of the product, brand loyalty, and the extent to which the customer desires involvement in the buying process.

Retail selling, as only one element of the retail promotional mix, is dependent on successful deployment of selected other elements, and should be integrated into a full promotional programme in order to nurture customer satisfaction.

Retail selling and product classification

The amount and quality of time a retail salesperson will spend actively selling depends firstly on the type of merchandise stocked by the retail organization. Merchandise can be classified as follows:

- *Convenience goods* – relatively inexpensive goods which are bought on a regular basis, without much thought going into the purchase, as customers are confident in product qualities, uses and attributes. Examples of convenience goods include items such as milk, eggs, bread, toilet rolls, clingfilm, floor cleaner and other 'everyday' items for which buyers tend to have low brand loyalty. The customer usually buys convenience goods at a supermarket or convenience store and needs little help to buy from the retail salesperson, although they can be encouraged to buy extra or associated items through suggestion and reminder. For example, cakes or pies can be suggested with bread, cream or cheese with milk; or the customer can be reminded of a special promotion on a larger size, or on two-for-one in a non-pressurizing manner.
- *Preference goods* – relatively inexpensive goods which are bought without much thought on a regular basis, for which the customer may have a reasonable amount of brand loyalty, but is less certain about desired product attributes. Goods such as tea, coffee, cigarettes, soft drinks and shampoos tend to fall into this category, and they are normally bought in grocery or convenience stores. Brand preference may have been established over time through other promotional activities such as advertising and sales promotion, and branding makes such stock highly visible within the store. Again, little help is required from the salesperson, although brand extensions and associated items can be suggested or new alternatives demonstrated.
- *Shopping goods* – more expensive and normally more complex goods which the customer wants to compare and contrast with competing or complementing goods within and outside the store. The customer is normally relatively confident about the attributes, qualities and uses of these goods, but is not strongly brand loyal and therefore wants to 'shop around' to compare quality, price and features. Although customers are willing to spend time shopping for these

goods, they are not always keen to travel to make comparisons. These goods are often bought from small specialist retailers. Goods such as clothes, shoes, accessories and cards often fall into this category. Salespeople can help customers to make a decision by giving information on comparative features, benefits and qualities for the price.

- *Speciality goods* – more expensive and complex goods, for example many electronic goods, in which customers experience uncertainty regarding attributes, qualities and uses, but for which they are willing to spend time and effort in shopping, including willingness to travel to buy from specialist retailers. Salespeople have an important role in helping customers to make a selection and come to a buy decision.

- *Unsought goods* – normally more expensive and complex goods which the customer would not necessarily think of buying, and therefore for which there is both uncertainty regarding attributes and low brand loyalty. Many unsought goods are sold door-to-door, although increasingly they are offered through traditional retail outlets. Examples are insurance, windows, conservatories and kitchens. Salespeople have a relatively important role in helping customers to make a buy decision. However, unlikely items which are occasionally juxtaposed with convenience and preference items also could be said to fall into the 'unsought' category. In this case the buy decision can be encouraged through strong promotional pricing or by information given to the customer through the sales process. In both cases the decision process will be aided by assurance through guarantee/ returns policy.

The classification above is general and retail sellers need to understand how their target customers regard the products they are selling, something which is influenced by factors such as age, income, wealth and buying experience. Some buyers will have strong preferences for some convenience items for example, and others will regard some shopping goods as speciality goods. Direct communication between customer and salesperson allows rapid determination of the amount of help needed.

Retail selling and types of buying decision

The complexity of the buying decision is related to the variety of factors introduced in the sections above. The range of buying decisions can be classified as follows:

- *Routine decision making* – tends to be associated with repeat buying of convenience or preference products, either because of habit, low involvement in the purchase or because a strong preference for brand has been established, which aids decision making.
- *Limited problem solving* – in this situation the customer tends to have a higher level of involvement with the decision and will take more time to buy. Some information or incentive is needed to help make the buy decision. For example, a new brand or brand extension may have entered the market, or for a relatively simple, inexpensive item, the buyer may be new to the product category.
- *Extensive problem solving* – here the customer is willing to spend time and effort in shopping, either because the product is complex or new to the market, is expensive, has high value to the customer in some other way, or the customer has little experience in the product category.

The role of the retail salesperson is closely related to the complexity of the buying process. The complexity of the process can vary for individual customers and a knowledge of the target segment customer profile will help to determine the degree of personal selling needed. For example, a computer is a complex and expensive product for which many customers will need help to buy. However, many people are now computer literate, confident in buying or have established strong brand preference.

Retail selling and shopping motives

People have a wide variety of motives for shopping:

- Necessity.
- Recreation.
- Fun/entertainment.
- Stimulation.
- Social.
- Exercise.

This is why, though the merchandise being bought is the main reason for the shopping experience, for most customers the total shopping experience will affect customer satisfaction. The total shopping experience includes peripheral aspects such as atmospherics, display, price, location, assortment and the dynamics of shopping, which will vary from customer to customer and on each shopping occasion. In addition to the variation of peripheral elements across shopping occasions there will exist differences in mood, staff encounters, number of other shoppers and so on. Even where the motive for shopping is necessity, it is widely recognized that the total shopping experience, rather than the merchandise itself, influences sales levels. Where shopping is for motives such as entertainment, recreation or social interaction, the dynamics of the shopping experience are more important, and the creation of a fun, exciting, interesting and diverting shopping environment are even more important.

Shopping motives vary from person to person and from occasion to occasion. Again, from a retail sales perspective, this illustrates the necessity to profile target customer groups. Almost every person who enters a store is a potential customer, however, and the role of selling in contributing to the total shopping experience should not be overlooked. Retail salespeople can quickly gauge shopping motives and respond accordingly. They can also help to create an 'exciting' shopping experience by exhibiting products or offering merchandise to customers to sample. Even if they only help in redirecting the customer to another store or destination, then they are contributing to the image of the organization as customer friendly – which may bring in future custom.

Retail selling and the buying process

Two models illustrate the buying process. The AIDA model is the simplest to remember and is useful to consider here because it is widely used in developing promotional campaigns that include selling as one contributory element.

> **A**wareness
> **I**nterest
> **D**esire
> **A**ction

Potential buyers first become aware that they have the need for a specific product, brand or product group. Awareness can be stimulated by immediate lack of the product – running out of milk, for example – or by a growing awareness, such as a large car bill which heralds the onset of the need to start looking for another. Awareness means that the potential buyer consciously or subconsciously begins the search for product.

The next phase is growing interest in finding the product required and is characterized by the search for and collection of information on the product. The type and extent of information looked for varies with product classification, with the type of buy decision, and even with the nature, confidence, experience and intelligence of the potential buyer. However, more information will be collected for shopping and speciality goods, which may include items such as product attributes, competing brands, competing outlets, prices, features and sources of finance. The potential buyer will collect information from the media, outlets, friends and family.

Studying the information and refining the data collected leads the potential buyer to gain a clearer picture of the product or brand required. One of the ways in which consumers reduce and refine the desired data from the plethora of information available is illustrated by a concept known as the 'evoked set'. For each product category, consumers will develop over time a set of brands from which they are most likely to choose an alternative. Hence, for example, a consumer in the biscuit aisle of the supermarket may decide between McVitie's Ginger Snaps, Rich Tea Biscuits, Hob Nobs, Nestlé's KitKats and Traidcraft Geobars, automatically filtering out supermarket own-brands and other varieties. Further, for each member of the evoked set, customers learn and compare the various features and benefits (price, calories, taste, size) so that choice of alternative is facilitated. Desire has been defined as need plus ability to buy – so for expensive products, sources of finance will have been found. This customer is ready to buy. There may still be some doubts regarding brand, model, alternative finance sources and product features.

Action is when the potential customer makes the buy decision. Payment methods, terms and contracts need to be settled, but the decision has been made.

The weakness of the AIDA model is that it does not recognize what happens after the buy decision. The consumer buying process addresses this by dividing the process into five steps, the first four of which are comparable with the AIDA model:

1 Problem recognition.
2 Informaton search.
3 Alternative evaluation.
4 Alternative choice.
5 Post-purchase evaluation.

Post-purchase evaluation is the phase after the buyer has committed to the buy decision and seeks reassurance that the right decision was made through continuing to scan for alternatives, asking friends, checking items out in other shops and so on. Post-purchase dissonance is the term used for the vague unease regarding whether the right decision has been made, and post-purchase evaluation helps to reduce

Table 9.1 Salesperson activities in relation to the buying decision process

Problem recognition	Introduce new models or forthcoming product developments, can contact previous buyers to indicate current model is ageing or out of date; approach in-store customers to assess needs
Information search	Give information on alternative models, outlets; indicate sources of information
Alternative evaluation	Highlight particular features and benefits of alternative models, illustrations of satisfied customers
Alternative choice	Indicate special offers, finance, guarantees to help the decision to buy
Post-purchase evaluation	Telephone or write to check satisfaction; can invite back to exhibitions, previews and other special events; can remind the customer it is time to buy again

the dissonance until the buyer is certain that the buy decision was, if not correct, good enough in the circumstances.

One of the benefits of retail selling is the potential of the seller to take the potential buyer through all the steps of the buying decision process, sometimes in a single visit, speeding and facilitating the decision to buy. Depending, of course, on the type of merchandise being sold and the type of buying decision, the retail salesperson has a role to play at every stage of the buying process (see Table 9.1).

However, because retail selling is primarily a one-to-one activity, and therefore expensive, the most effective use of the salesperson's time is during the alternative evaluation and alternative choice stages. In many selling situations the successful deployment of the other promotional mix elements can abbreviate the sales time spent on customers in the other stages of the buying process.

Retail sales roles

Retail salespeople have a major role to play in facilitating and enhancing the process of purchase decision making. Additionally, they can represent and reinforce store image, provide a dynamic shopping experience and build immediate relations with customers and potential customers.

There are two main roles which retail salespeople undertake:

- Order taking.
- Order getting.

Very many retail salespeople are order takers. That is, they process customers' decisions on products bought, at the very simplest merely running the item through checkout. This tends to happen with convenience and preference goods, and in shopping situations where routine decision making is the norm. These staff, nevertheless, have an important role in maintaining processing speed, and can influence sales through efficiency (or lack of it). Other order takers may show customers the location of goods, get them from stock, and give some limited information to aid evaluation and choice.

Stores which stock shopping and comparison goods, but which specialize in providing value at the expense of customer service, often operate staffing levels which preclude any but the most basic order-processing sales activities. These retailers rely on discounting, price, sales promotions and value to stimulate the decision to buy.

Increasingly, order takers will be encouraged to increase sales through means such as suggesting additional items to buy at the checkout, offering delivery service, or passing on information on deals and offers.

Order getters are retail salespeople who deal primarily with shopping and speciality goods where the decision to buy is not routine. The great benefit of salespeople in this role is their capability for direct customer communication, gauging shopping motive, relationship with merchandise and stage in the buying process. These sellers will engage potential customers in the selling process, informing them, guiding them and helping them make the decision to buy on the spot, or at some time in the future (Levy and Weitz, 1995). Sometimes termed sales associates, order getters may be paid partly (or even wholly) in commission, which can lead to a pressurized selling environment that can conflict with customer preferences. One way round this is to relate commission not only to sales but to the value of returned products. Customer-orientated selling places customer focus at the heart of the selling process and aims at building a long-term customer relationship, which increases satisfaction with the product bought, salesperson, retailer and manufacturer (McGoldrick, 2002). Due to their more extensive involvement in directly communicating with customers, order getters have a prime role in influencing customer perceptions of the retail organization and levels of customer satisfaction.

The retail sales process

The selling process includes the stages summarized in Table 9.2. Although stages of the selling process are most actively engaged by 'order-getting' retail salespeople, they also form a useful checklist for core retail activities.

Table 9.2 The selling process (and the buying process)

Buying process stages	Selling process stages	Salesperson activities
Problem recognition	Prospecting	Developing a list of prospective customers
	Preparing	Learning customer profiles; learning features/benefits of products and other relevant information; matching to profiles
Information search	Approach	Approaching customer to determine shopping motives and needs; finding out desired product(s), benefits
Alternative evaluation	Presentation	Presenting information on product or products under consideration; showing demonstrating features and benefits
	Overcoming objections or reservations	Finding out reservations and barriers to the buy decision for products under consideration; answering questions
Alternative choice	Close	Asking for a buy decision
Post-purchase evaluation	Follow-up	Suggesting additional or complementary items; checking the customer's satisfaction with the product

A 'prospect' can be defined as any person who has the potential to purchase your goods or services. Sources include:

- Previous customers.
- Customer and employee referrals.
- Lapsed customers.
- Direct mail and other promotional methods.
- Exhibitions and demonstrations.
- Centre of influence method – use of local/regional/national celebrities to endorse store/organization.

Preparation includes learning about the target customer group, and how to handle different types of customer, including difficult customers. It also includes learning about the merchandise, its make-up, uses, performance, care, background and associated services. Retail salespeople also need to know about store policies on opening hours, payment, returns and delivery (Dunne and Lusch, 1999).

Customers who ask for help, try to catch the eye, or who are inspecting merchandise closely are the salesperson's best prospects, and a friendly outgoing approach with a direct greeting is recommended. The salesperson has to quickly determine the customer's needs through open questioning, but should remember to allow the customer time to talk freely, while listening, understanding, responding and summarizing. During the approach the salesperson has to indicate extensive product knowledge, show a genuine desire to meet the customer's needs and show a positive service attitude.

Once the customer's needs and price range have been defined, the salesperson presents the merchandise. The AIDA model (Awareness, Interest, Desire, Action) can serve as a structure for the presentation, as the salesperson outlines or demonstrates merchandise features, advantages and benefits to the prospect, relating these to the customer's specific needs. Allowing the customer to try or handle the merchandise helps to build desire, as does showing that a particular product will save money or exceed customer needs. Open questions allow the customer to express reservations or further needs, and closed questions allow the salesperson to determine understanding, facts and level of interest. The aim is not to 'sell' the customer, but to help the customer buy the merchandise which will give most satisfaction.

Reservations and objections are barriers to the buy decision and, if they are genuinely important to the customer, they have to be overcome to make a sale. It is best to anticipate common objections early in the presentation to prevent negativity later in the process. Other means of handling reservations include:

- Pass up the objection – skirt around the issue. If it comes up again it is important and needs to be addressed.
- Ask questions – find out the prospect's concerns.
- Rephrase the objection – summarize understanding of the customer's reservation. This buys thinking time.
- Compensate for the objection – outline the features and benefits which make the product worth buying.
- Deny the objection – where the customer reservation is based on a misconception, acknowledge their views and concern, then explain the correct situation.
- Use a testimony or third party – explain or demonstrate an instance in which the objection was previously made and the customer subsequently satisfied.

As each objection is answered, the salesperson should check that it has been overcome, using a closed question to determine the customer's agreement. This is sometimes called a 'trial close'. Where the objection cannot be overcome, this has to be acknowledged, followed by an indication of how the benefits of the product outweigh the disadvantages, or if appropriate, presentation of an alternative product.

Closing the sale is the point at which the customer is directly asked whether they want to buy. Buying signals are those behaviours which indicate genuine interest in purchase, such as reading the warranty or user manual, trying the product, examining the item in detail, asking questions about colours, styles, delivery, accessories, and making positive comments about the product. If the buying signals have been misinterpreted and the customer refuses to close, it is possible that there is a further reservation which requires to be determined and met. Alternatively, there may be another product or model which will meet their needs. It is, however, important not to pressurize the customer into buying.

Following up the sale can lead to extra sales in a number of ways, such as: supplementary and complementary items can be suggested to the buyer; a discount can be offered for the next purchase, or for a referral; the buyer can be added to a list of future prospects. It is good practice to enquire by telephone or card about customer satisfaction with any expensive or complex purchase.

Retail selling and the promotional mix

Retail selling should form part of an integrated promotional plan, encompassing a variety of promotional mix elements and clear promotional objectives, which need to be communicated to those undertaking sales roles. Integration is required due to the nature of the consumer buying process. Consumers engaged in the 'information search' and 'alternative evaluation' stages of the buying process will be consciously or unconsciously acquiring and absorbing information put out by the retailer in the form of advertising, publicity, sales promotions and/or sponsorship (in addition to information from other agencies such as the media, competitors and friends). This information feeds into their expectations regarding the product(s) sought, the retail experience and the sales experience. Where there is a divergence between expectation and actuality, there is likely to be dissatisfaction.

For example, where an advertisement indicates a price reduction, the buyer will expect the salesperson to know about it, and to be offered it. Where a retailer advertises certain products for sale, the buyer will expect them to be in stock. When a retailer advertises in a magazine associated with high-quality, high-price merchandise, the buyer will expect an equally polished retail and sales experience.

The other promotional tools act together to form the foundation of the sales experience – they will bring in the potential customers, and the more successful they are, the less 'selling' will be required. However, the sales role undertaken by staff, the selling process itself, has to be tailored to accommodate the customer expectations raised through other promotional efforts. The knowledge salespeople have, their sales targets, the way they dress, the way they act and how they sell have all to be related to the other elements of the promotional mix and to the overall promotional objectives of the retailer.

Summary

There is a strong relationship between retail selling, customer service and customer satisfaction. Retailers, operating market-focused service businesses, need to tailor their retail selling to customers' requirements with regard to:

- the type of product being bought;
- the type of purchase decision;
- customers' shopping motives;
- stage in the process of making the buying decision.

The nature and depth of retail selling required are related to the type, complexity and value of the product, the customer's understanding of its qualities, uses and attributes, brand loyalty and the extent to which the customer desires involvement in the buying process.

Merchandise can be categorized into convenience, preference, shopping, speciality and unsought goods, although the category for any one product may vary according to the customer's attributes, such as age, wealth and buying experience. The role of retail salespeople and the nature of the selling process will vary according to merchandise category and target customer profile.

The nature of retail selling also varies according to the extensiveness of the customer decision-making process. Less involvement is required in selling convenience items, or those for which a strong brand preference has been established. More extensive selling is required for complex and expensive products which engage customers in extended problem solving.

The role and activities of retail salespeople also depend on the shopping motives of customers; where shopping is for social reasons, or for fun and entertainment, salespeople can contribute to a dynamic and changing retail experience.

The customer buying process can be summarized within the Awareness, Interest, Desire, Action (AIDA) model, or more commonly within the five stages of the buying process.

The speed at which customers proceed through the stages depends on individual characteristics such as age and background, merchandise category and type of buying decision. The role of retail salespeople as direct communicators with customers allows them unique capability in rapidly determining, through simple questioning, which stage any individual customer has reached. The activities of retail salespeople will vary according to each stage of the buying process, but the most effective use of salespeople's time is to contribute to alternative evaluation and choice.

Most retail salespeople have an order-taking role – processing customers' orders once they have selected the merchandise. However, these staff can increase sales through their own efficiency and by suggesting supplementary and complementary merchandise to customers. Order getters have a more extensive sales role, usually associated with more complex and expensive merchandise, and these salespeople will engage potential customers in the selling process, informing them and helping them make the decision to buy.

The sales process undertaken by order getters includes seven stages: prospecting, preparing, approach, presentation, overcoming objections, close, and post-purchase evaluation and follow-up. These can be linked to the stages of the buying process so that the salesperson has a more informed basis for the activities to be undertaken during each stage.

Retail selling is one element of the promotional mix and contributes to the achievement of promotional objectives. The integration of selling and other promotional mix elements is required to meet in-store customer expectations built through promotional activities during the information search of the buying process.

Review questions

1 Explain how the nature of retail selling will vary with the classification of merchandise sold by a retailer.
2 How does the selling process relate to the buying decision process?
3 How will the roles undertaken by salespeople differ according to customers' shopping motives and types of buying decision?
4 Explain how retail selling forms part of an integrated promotional mix.

5 Why is it useful for order-getting salespeople to investigate and respond to customers' reservations about making the buy decision?

References

Dunne, P. and Lusch, R. F. (1999). *Retailing*, 3rd edn. Dryden Press, Orlando.

Levy, M. and Weitz, B. A. (1995). *Retailing Management*. Irwin, USA.

McGoldrick, P. (2002). *Retail Marketing*, 2nd edn. McGraw-Hill, Maidenhead.

Merrilees, B. and Miller, D. (1996). *Retailing Management: A Best Practice Approach*. RMIT Press, Victoria.

10

Retail security

Introduction

Retail crime has long been trivialized in the eyes of the general public. The stereotypical shoplifter is envisaged as a 'naughty teenager' enacting a dare, a poor pensioner lifting a few items or a poorly paid member of staff supplementing their income. The general view is that retail theft is a minor misdemeanour at the expense of organizations making large profits from their customers. This perception is enhanced by low levels of conviction – in 2000, for example, of 292 000 customer thieves apprehended in the UK, less than half were found guilty in court (British Retail Consortium, 2001).

Less than 50 per cent of thieves apprehended by retailers are handed to the police (Centre for Retail Research, 2002a), the main reasons being:

- it takes up too much staff time (particularly in owner-operated stores);
- a preference not to prosecute the elderly, juveniles or the mentally ill;
- a low level of conviction;
- poor deterrence by fine/penalties;
- a low prosecution rate.

Retail security has relatively recently become a major issue for the retail industry as a whole. This major sector of the economy wanted reliable and comparative data on crime and security to underpin increased, co-ordinated action in combating crime.

The British Retail Consortium (BRC) established its Retail Crime Initiative in 1993, financed by some of the major retail companies in the UK, carrying out the first of its annual surveys into retail crime the same year. This would establish and publicize the scale of retail crime, raising the profile of the subject, and forming a basis for analysis and action. The sharing of information on retail crime informed retailers themselves, government, police and the justice system of the size of the retail crime problem. The annual surveys can be used by retailers as a benchmark against which to measure shrinkage and crime in their own operations, and to influence sector-wide schemes for crime prevention (May, 1996).

In 2002, the first European Retail Theft Barometer was published with a view to establishing international comparison of shrinkage, crime statistics and crime prevention. The first of these six-monthly studies of retail crime within Europe was based on a survey of 424 major European retailers across 15 countries (Centre for Retail Research, 2002a).

Causes of shrinkage

Shrinkage is normally expressed as a percentage of turnover. It is the difference between the recorded value of inventory at retail prices, based on purchase and receipt of inventory, minus the value of inventory at retail prices in stores and distribution centres, divided by retail sales during the period of calculation. In Europe, the average shrinkage rate in 2001 was 1.42 per cent of turnover, with the UK above average at 1.76 per cent. The top retail sectors for shrinkage across Europe were department and general stores (1.96 per cent), clothing and textiles (1.73 per cent), and other non-food (1.94 per cent).

The Centre for Retail Research (CRR) defined four main causes of retail loss in its national survey of retail crime and security:

- Customers.
- Employees.
- Vendors.
- Administration.

The percentage of losses caused by small retailers, multiples and large multiples was also compared (see Figure 10.1).

Although total shrinkage was found to account for nearly a quarter of retail profit, only 83.3 per cent of shrinkage was due to crime, with administrative error the cause of a sizeable percentage. When the British Retail Crime Survey requested retailers to give a value for unexplained

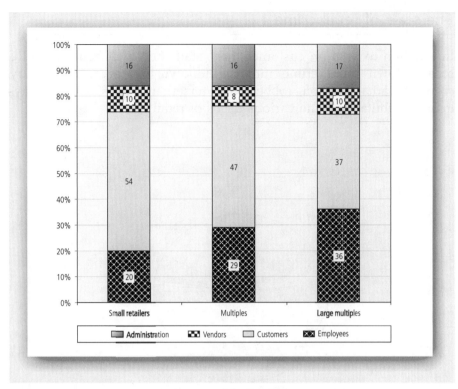

Figure 10.1 Causes of comparative shrinkage among small, multiple and large multiple retailers. *Source*: Centre for Retail Research (2002a).

stock losses which were attributed to unrecorded crime (excluding unexplained losses due to administrative error, breakages and vendor (supplier) fraud), it was found that 50 per cent of unexplained stock loss was attributed to customer theft and 39 per cent to staff theft. The major source of shrinkage experienced by retailers is theft – by customers and by employees.

It has been found in both the UK and the US that high shrinkage is associated with:

● low rates of pay;
● non-existence of profit-sharing schemes;
● high staff turnover;
● high proportion of part-time staff;
● poor store management.

All are widespread features of the retail industry, and therefore it would seem apparent that human resource management in UK retailing is as important an issue as increasing security measures.

The scale of retail crime

In addition to data on customer theft, staff theft and fraud, the BRC breaks down retail crime into the following categories: burglary, criminal damage, arson, robbery and terrorism. Figure 10.2 displays losses attributable to the various forms of retail crime.

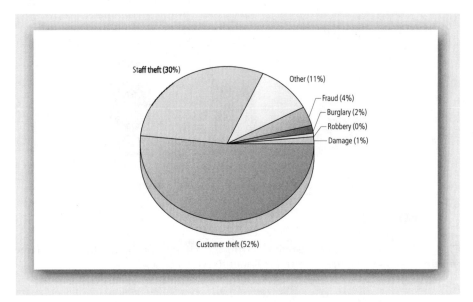

Figure 10.2 Relative size of causes of UK retail crime – year 2000. *Source*: **British Retail Consortium (2001).**

According to the British Retail Crime Survey, retail crime costs for the UK in 2002 were estimated at £2044 million, comprising £626 million spent on crime prevention and £1418 million lost value due to crime. This represents 0.91 per cent of retail turnover and represents an average loss of £85 per year per household.

The survey also published risk rates by retail category of various forms of crime, which show that above average risk of customer theft (per 100 outlets) is assumed in the following sectors:

● Department stores.
● Food and drink retailers.
● Mixed retail businesses.
● Other non-food (including photographic, optical and office supplies).

Above average risk of staff theft occurred in:

- Department stores.
- Booksellers and CTNs.
- Chemists.
- DIY and hardware.
- Food and drink retailers.

The relative proportions of the non-theft causes of retail crime are detailed in Figure 10.3.

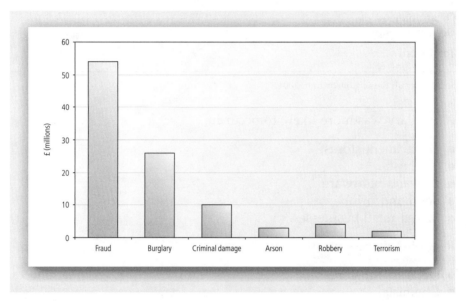

Figure 10.3 Relative size of the causes of non-theft retail crime in 2000. *Source*: **Centre for Retail Research (2002a).**

Both the BRC and CRR statistics show that fraud is the major source of non-theft retail crime, followed by burglary, criminal damage and robbery.

The BRC study recorded risk of fraud experienced by various forms of retailer. The results are shown in Table 10.1. Risk of cheque fraud was highest in furniture, textiles and carpets, and electrical, gas and electrical hire retailers. The first also featured in the list of retail categories which experience more than twice the average risk of payment card fraud, together with mixed retail businesses, footwear and leather goods, and department stores.

Table 10.1 Risk rates by retail category – fraud (per £million turnover)

Survey category	Cheque fraud (£)	Payment card fraud (£)
Booksellers and CTNs	19	32
Chemists	55	27
Clothing	79	61
DIY and hardware	16	20
Electrical, gas and electrical hire	144	62
Food and drink	83	39
Footwear and leather goods	89	103
Furniture, textiles and carpets	184	173
Mixed retail businesses	71	209
Other non-food	133	78
Department stores	88	115
Total retail	79	54

Source: British Retail Consortium, 2001.

Burglary was more likely to occur in:

- Department stores.
- Chemists.
- DIY and hardware.
- Food and drink.
- Mixed retail businesses.

Risk of damage was above average in:

- Department stores.
- Chemists.
- DIY and hardware.
- Food and drink.
- Furniture, textiles and carpets.
- Mixed retail businesses.

Only one category of retail business experienced an exceptional rate of robbery – food and drink retailers. Two categories – booksellers and CTNs, and food and drink retailers – experienced more than double the average rate of till snatches. The lowest crime risk category overall was furniture, textiles and carpets.

As retailers add or decrease the varieties of merchandise they offer, the focus and extent of their expenditure on security will also change. For example, a grocery business expanding into clothing and footwear should expect to experience the higher levels of payment card fraud and customer theft associated with mixed retail businesses.

Types of retail crime

Customer theft

The percentage of known incidents of customer theft in the UK jumped 56 per cent from 1999 to 2000, with department stores the most susceptible to theft. The value of goods stolen also rose (British Retail Consortium, 2001). Shoplifters tend to target merchandise for their own consumption or for quick conversion to cash. The items most frequently stolen tend to be high-value/high-demand items such as brand name clothing and shoes, CDs, videos and games (DiLonardo, 2002).

Thieves are more likely to be male than female (ratio 66:34) and merchandise stolen tends to be gender related. In the UK, 22 per cent of thieves were minors (17 and under); in Scotland the figure was 31 per cent, similar to that in the United States. Youth crime accounts for an even more disproportionate amount of theft because of the low percentage of the population under the age of 18. One study showed that most adult theft was also committed by young adults (under age 30). In the UK, the most common categories of store targeted by youths are department stores and electrical stores.

One of the considerable underlying causes of retail theft is drug addiction. The BRC study established that drug-related crime accounts for the majority of retail and other crime in city centres, with £22 000–£44 000 per year required to fund an average drug addict's £11 000 per year habit. In 1998, a Home Office study showed that 80 per cent of people arrested tested positive for at least one drug, while 47 and 30 per cent tested positive for opiates and cocaine respectively. Where crime in city centres is combated successfully, it has been found that other crimes such as domestic burglary increase in other areas. Handling of drug abusers by drug courts with the power to impose drug treatment orders and regular drug testing of offenders is a potential means of reducing drug-related crime.

Customer theft is frequently planned by professional shop thieves, who steal to order, operate in gangs and move from town to town. Targets are carefully monitored, with lunch-times, tea breaks and shift changes noted, and the layout of the store investigated. Sometimes a groups of thieves will enter a store at a time when there is low staffing, fanning out through the store to prevent apprehension.

Stock near the entrance to stores is at most risk of theft, the very displays used to attract customers into the store proving the most vulnerable to shoplifters. Many professional shop thieves dispose of the items to their customers almost immediately on leaving the store, exiting the scene by prearranged routes and transport.

Employee theft

The cost of the second largest source of retail shrinkage, employee theft, increased by 41.3 per cent between 1997 and 1999, with 43 staff thefts occurring per 100 retail outlets. In 2000, employees stole £538 per incident compared with just £74 for customer theft. The type of retail outlet in which employee theft is most prevalent is chemists, both in terms of number of incidents and in value of goods stolen. Department stores and DIY/hardware stores are also sectors experiencing a high number of employee thefts (British Retail Consortium, 2001).

Internal theft is difficult to detect and deal with because of the wealth of opportunity for theft and the degree of trust that must rest with employees, and this is particularly the case where managers are involved. There are a wide variety of ways employees can steal from retailers, including:

- Under-ringing sales at the till.
- Taking cash from the till.
- Taking a cheque without registering the sale, later taking out the equivalent in cash so the till balances.
- Throwing merchandise into waste bins and returning to remove them later.
- Collusion with customers – handing out merchandise to relatives or friends, or by including free items with legitimate purchases.
- Collusion with suppliers – for example, fraudulent deliveries made with forged slips.
- Retention of receipts to gain fraudulent refunds or voids.
- Stockroom theft.
- Display theft.
- Delivery theft, including use of company vehicle for personal use, false declaration of mileage and overtime.

Where retailers are using their staff and store to fulfil online orders and deliveries, there is the additional risk of collusion among store-based and delivery management and staff.

Many employers condone small infringements of their code of employee conduct, such as appropriation of small items like pencils and pens for personal use, and personal use of the photocopier, e-mail, phone or Internet, all of which can foster a culture in which daily theft by employees is regarded as acceptable and the level of acceptable theft difficult to determine.

Fraud

Retail fraud is the largest source of non-theft retail crime, accounting for 3.6 per cent of retail crime losses in the UK in 2000; the amount of loss to fraud is increasing rapidly. While with theft property is taken without the owner's consent, with fraud the owner consents to part with the property; however, the consent is obtained by deceit, falsehood or other fraudulent means.

The three biggest sources of fraud are:

- Cheque fraud.
- Payment card fraud.
- Counterfeit money.

Together, these account for 77 per cent of total fraud. According to the BRC study, the biggest and fastest-growing loss is from cheque fraud, because fraud which occurs on a purchase made by cheque that is over the guarantee level is charged back to the retailer. As cheque guarantee levels have not been changed since the 1980s, clearly the opportunity for such fraud has risen significantly, and this is compounded by the development of sophisticated anti-fraud measures applied to payment card purchases. In Scotland, where shopping trips are made more frequently, with less purchased per trip, cheque fraud is substantially less of a problem.

Cheque fraud can occur in a number of ways:

- No-account cheques cashed by people who use fictitious names or make no effort to conceal identity and rely on cashing a sufficient number of cheques to make it worthwhile.
- Non-sufficient funds cheques passed by a criminal who has opened a bank account with a small deposit.
- Forged cheques.

Electrical, furniture and carpets are the two retail sectors in the UK most at risk from cheque fraud, with more than double the average for all retailers.

Payment card fraud is also increasing (32 per cent from 1999 to 2000), and involves the use of stolen, forged or expired credit and store cards. Mixed retail, furniture and carpet sectors experience three times the UK retail average payment card fraud. The growth of Internet, catalogue, telephone and TV shopping has increased the use of 'card not present' transactions, which exposes both retailers and customers to fraud on a larger scale.

Counterfeit money is the third commonest type of fraud, accounting for 17 per cent of retail fraud in the UK, and is also on the increase, particularly among notes of larger denominations such as £20 and £50 (British Retail Consortium, 2001).

There are two further common methods of fraud:

- Fraudulent refunds – for example, claimed by staff who have retained receipts, or by customers who claim refunds for merchandise which has been bought and used.
- Price switch – in which the price of a lower-priced item is switched to a higher-priced item, the lower price being paid.

Supplier fraud and supply chain theft are also a significant issue for retailers (see Figure 10.1 and Chapter 7).

External threats to retail security

Burglary. In the UK, 17 per cent of retail outlets are burgled per annum, with the rate of attempted burglary a further 9 per cent. Most occur in the DIY and hardware sector, and food and drink stores, with over 50 per cent of outlets burgled per annum. Although burglary is much less common than theft, the amount of loss per incident is much higher – in 2000 this was £1800, with an extra £1200 average repair costs per incident. Burglary and attempted burglary are higher than average for small retailers in terms of the number of incidents and stock loss per incident, with small food and drink outlets most susceptible.

Criminal damage. This is a declining form of retail crime, but nevertheless accounts for a significant external threat to retail security, particularly for small retailers. Twenty-four cases occurred per 100 outlets, but the level for small retailers is nearly double. Again, small food and drink outlets are most susceptible with more than double the average rate.

Robbery and till snatches. Robberies averaged 3 per 100 outlets in 2000, and till snatches 6 per 100 outlets. The rate of till snatches increased by 33 per cent, with food and drink retailers most at risk. Small food and drink outlets are twice as likely as other retailers to experience robbery and till snatches.

Arson and terrorism. Incidents in these categories of crime are reasonably numerous. In 2000, 2.5 cases of arson and 3 cases of terrorism occurred per 100 outlets. The cost per incident in these two categories doubled within a year from 1999. Terrorism includes use of explosives, hoax calls and evacuations.

Violence and threats. Retail staff are at risk of physical violence, threat of physical violence and verbal abuse which can injure them physically and psychologically. The main cause of physical violence to staff is theft.

On average, 5 in every 1000 retail employees experience physical violence, and a further 14 experience threats of violence. Staff in small retail organizations, and in large food and drink retail outlets, are much more at risk. Nearly 70 out of every 1000 SME staff experience physical violence per year. (British Retail Consortium, 2001.)

Dealing with crime – UK

Due to differences in the legal systems, there are slight variations across the UK in definitions of the crime experienced by retailers, and in how retailers and the legal process interpret and deal with crime. Definitions of the crimes most commonly suffered by retailers in Scotland are listed in Box 10.1. In England, theft is dealt with by statute under the Theft Act 1968. It is defined as *dishonest appropriation of property belonging to another with the intention of permanently depriving the other of it*. In Scotland, theft is a common law offence, defined as '*the felonious taking or appropriation of the property of another without the consent of the owner and with intent to deprive him of that property*'. Both definitions include the same basic elements:

- the thief acted dishonestly;
- the property was appropriated by the thief;
- the property belongs to another;
- the intention was to permanently deprive the owner of the property.

In both England and Scotland the law allows ordinary citizens the power to arrest anyone who has committed an offence for which they may be sentenced on first indictment to 5 or more years in prison. Theft belongs in this category of offence and therefore ordinary citizens have the power to arrest any individual who has committed a theft. Again, power to arrest is slightly different in each country. In England, the Police and Criminal Evidence Act 1984 states that '*any person may arrest without warrant anyone who is, or whom he with reasonable cause suspects to be, in the act of committing an arrestable offence*'. In Scotland, the power of arrest is provided under common law and under the Civic Government (Scotland) Act 1982, section 7 – '*any citizen witnessing a crime may apprehend the criminal, but must not do so on suspicion or information*'. In Scotland, therefore, the power to arrest is more limited than in England. Whereas in England a citizen's arrest for theft can be carried out '*with reasonable cause suspects to be in the act of committing an ... offence*', in Scotland only persons who have actually *witnessed* the offence being committed can make an arrest.

Box 10.1   Definitions of crime – Scotland

Theft: a crime at common law committed by any person who feloniously takes and appropriates the property of another without the consent of the owner or other lawful authority.

Reset: a crime at common law committed by any person who, with intent to deprive the owner, receives and keeps property knowing that it was appropriated by theft, robbery, embezzlement or fraud.

Malicious mischief: a crime at common law constituted by the wilful, wanton and malicious destruction of, or damage to, the property of another.

Vandalism: Section 78(1) Criminal Justice (Scotland) Act 1980 – an offence in which any person wilfully or recklessly destroys or damages the property of another, without reasonable excuse.

Assault: a crime at common law committed by any person who makes a criminal attack intended to take effect physically upon the person of another.

Categories of assault:

1 Direct.
2 Indirect.
3 Menaces.

Breach of the peace: a crime at common law constituted by one or more persons who conducts himself, or themselves, in a riotous or disorderly manner, anywhere, to the alarm, annoyance or disturbance of the lieges.

Fraud: a crime at common law; the term fraud is used to include all offences which consist of fraudulent deception.

Essential elements:

1 Falsehood – false representation by word of mouth, conduct or writing.
2 Fraud – intention to deceive.
3 Wilful imposition – the cheat designed has been successful.

Forgery and uttering: a crime at common law consisting of the making and publishing of a writing feloniously intended to represent and pass for the genuine writing of another person.

Larger retail organizations have clear guidelines for staff regarding what to do when dealing with a person suspected of shoplifting. However, general guidelines for dealing with a suspect include:

- Be sure the person has the item(s) still with them.
- Be sure you witnessed the theft and kept the suspect under continuous observation.
- Be careful to have a second member of staff there to assist, and to act as a witness to what is said and done when you deal with the suspect.
- Wait until the suspect has passed all points of payment and/or left the store.
- Tell the suspect who you and your witness are. State your job title and show an ID if possible. Take care that the suspect is given no reason to complain about assault.
- Say '*I am employed by . . . . I have reason to believe that you have goods in your possession which you have not paid for. Will you please return to the store.*' Describe the article(s) and clearly state the name of the store.
- If he/she refuses, you can carry out a citizen's arrest. Tell the suspect you are '*making a citizen's arrest for theft*'.
- If the suspect tries to escape you can use the minimum amount of force necessary to restrain him/her.
- Note that if you do not inform the suspect of the citizen's arrest and the reason, he/she could bring a charge of assault against you.
- Return to the store. One member of staff should lead the way, and the other follow the suspect to make sure that the merchandise (evidence) is not thrown away.
- Take the suspect to an office or room. Make sure that there is a member of staff of the same sex as the suspect with him/her at all times.
- Ask the suspect to declare goods he/she has not paid for and to empty pockets and/or bags. If he/she refuses you have no power to search him/her.
- If the suspect asks you to search him/her do not comply.
- Call the police to prosecute. Keep the suspect under observation all the time to make sure that the stolen articles are not dumped.
- On arrival of the police, outline the circumstances to them in the presence and hearing of the suspect.
- Keep a record book to record details of all incidents in a locked cupboard. Record all details of the offence, including date, time, names and offices held by witnesses, name, address, age and full description of suspect, full description of stolen items, full description of the arrest and the numbers of police officers present.

Do not:

- Leave suspect on his/her own.
- Lock suspect in a room.
- Let suspect take pills or medicine, or smoke.
- Let suspect get between you and the door.
- Get into conversation with the suspect.
- Accept payment for any goods.
- Accuse the suspect.
- Question the suspect in public.

If you have any doubts regarding theft, take no action because if a person is arrested wrongfully they may take legal action against you. If the suspect physically threatens you it is wise to let the suspect escape and to inform the police, who are able to arrest a person on suspicion of theft, and to both search and detain the suspect.

Statements and evidence

Evidence, which is the means of proving or disproving the truth of a matter under judicial examination, is used to prove whether or not a crime has been committed, and also whether the accused committed the crime. Evidence must prove that the person is guilty of theft *'beyond all reasonable doubt'*. Therefore, to make a prosecution, the person who saw and heard the theft has to give direct evidence, sometimes on oath in court.

There are three types of evidence:

1 Oral evidence from an eye witness.
2 Documentary evidence – for example, a written statement of events, photograph or official records.
3 Real evidence, which is any article involved in a crime, including goods stolen.

In Scotland, under common law, there has to be corroboration of evidence – two pieces of evidence which support each other. This can be provided by:

1 Two or more direct eye witnesses.
2 One eye witness supported by indirect or circumstantial evidence such as goods stolen or CCTV evidence.
3 Sufficient indirect evidence to conclude the guilt of the accused.

In England, under the Police and Criminal Evidence Act 1984, the rules for evidence are similar to those in Scotland, except that it is not always necessary to have corroboration. However, corroboration does strengthen the case.

Box 10.2 Dealing with young people

In both England and Scotland it is rare for children under the age of 14 to be prosecuted for shoplifting. However, in Scotland, the age at which a child can be found guilty of an offence is 8 years old – in England it is 10 years old. In Scotland, children under 16 years charged with a criminal offence will have their case dealt with by a Children's Panel, who can order custodial and other types of sentence. Children have the right of appeal to a higher court.

In England, the penalty for theft ranges from a verbal or written caution to 10 years' imprisonment. In Scotland, all arrests and their circumstances are referred to the Procurator Fiscal's office by the arresting officers. At this level lies the decision to proceed further, to issue a caution, send a report to the Reporter of the Children's Panel or to prosecute in court.

Retail loss prevention

The cost of crime prevention in the year 2000 was estimated to be £626 million – up 13 per cent on the expenditure of the previous year. Table 10.2 shows the breakdown of expenditure.

This figure masks the true cost of crime prevention, because prevention of crime costs must include other measures which are useful in reducing crime, such as employee recruitment methods and screening; investment in staff retention and reduction in employment of part-time staff; and training in retail crime and security plus supervisory and management skills. Retailers know that motivated, trained and retained staff can reduce customer and staff theft, in addition to spotting and dealing efficiently with external threats to security.

There are three main categories of methods for retail crime prevention which retailers can employ to combat customer and staff theft, fraud and external threats to security:

Table 10.2 Expenditure on crime prevention

Type of prevention	Percentage of expenditure
Security staff	57
Cash collection	17
Theft protection	11
Hardware, leasing and maintenance	8
Burglary protection	7

Source: British Retail Consortium (2001).

1 Human.
2 Mechanical.
3 Electronic.

A range of examples of each category is shown in Table 10.3.

There are a wide variety of methods of deterrent available within each category and many are used to counteract a variety of methods of crime. Many of the human deterrents – for example: store layout; policies, procedures and audits; display security; credit and employment checks during recruitment; staff awareness and training in security – are no more than good retail management practice and are cheap to deploy. One research study found, for instance, that regular public posting of loss levels reduced crime (Oliphant and Oliphant, 2001). Other deterrents require retailers to act together to drive down crime through the sharing of crime/criminal information and security best practice. For example, Retail Crime Partnerships allow retailers to identify local criminals through photographs, radio links and CCTV.

A different level of deterrence involves retailers joining with other agencies in tackling underlying issues such as drug use. In Scotland, it is estimated that 50 per cent of retail crime is drug related, and the frequency of drug-related crime, together with its potential for associated violence and threats, further impacts on one of the generators of staff crime – poor recruitment procedures and high staff turnover. 'There is a direct link between drug use, theft from shops and violence and intimidation towards employees, which poses problems for the recruitment and retention of staff' (Clarke, 2001). Charities such as Drug Abuse Resistance Education are aimed at reducing drug usage and associated crime, and Drug Courts provide an alternative way to deal with drug-related offenders. Another example of collaboration in retail crime prevention is the Thumbprint Signature Programme, which aims to reduce fraud by requiring

Table 10.3 Human, mechanical and electronic loss deterrents

Human	Mechanical	Electronic
Employee screening	Mirrors	Loop alarms
Honesty testing	Screens and grilles	Electronic article
Security training	Shutters	surveillance tags
Supervisory and	Cages	Scanners
management training	Locks	Lighting
Security staff and plain	Lockers	CCTV
clothes police	Bells	Dummy cameras
Staffing levels	Security cases	Radio links
Procedures for storage/	Chains	Secure payment
disposal of risk items	Display cabinets	applications (online
such as invoice/receipt	Security doors/glass	fraud)
pads, delivery details		Burglar alarms
and addresses, scrap		
credit card vouchers		
Staff alertness and		
reporting procedures		
Audits		
Public posting of loss		
levels		
Monitoring overages,		
shortages and voids		
Design of unit and shop		
layout		
Cash collection and		
routing methods		
Banking procedures		
Exit and alarm procedures		
Integrity shoppers		
Goods reception and		
display procedures		
Searches		
Risk assessments		
Rewards		
Drug courts		
Co-operative efforts such		
as Retail Crime		
Partnerships and retail		
crime conferences		

people to voluntarily attach their thumbprint to cheques and transaction slips (see Box 10.3).

Civil recovery is an initiative widely used in the United States and Canada, in which retailers obtain compensation from those who commit crimes such as theft, fraud and criminal damage. Commitment

---

Box 10.3   Using thumbprints to combat fraud

The Thumbprint Signature Programme, launched in summer 2002 in Fife, is an example of collaborative effort aimed at combating cheque and credit card fraud. Town centre managers, Fife Community Safety Panels, Fife Constabulary and Fife retailers collaborated to introduce the programme at outlets in all the main shopping and business areas. Customers are asked to provide a thumbprint on the back of a cheque or the store copy of a transaction slip. This creates a permanent record of identity of the presenter, without leaving an ink mark on the user's thumb. If the customer declines, the business can ask for a secondary means of identification, or can refuse to take payment.

A similar initiative reduced payment fraud by 87 per cent in the first few months after it was launched in Inverness. Associated crimes, such as theft of handbags, purses and wallets, decreased by 50 per cent.

---

of any crime also involves a 'tort', or wrongdoing under civil law, for which the person or organization affected by the crime can claim damages. Shortly after the offender is arrested, the retailer sends out a civil demand, which includes the circumstances of the crime, legal position and a claim for damages. These can include the cost of goods, investigation, security relating to the arrest and costs of the civil demand process itself. The offender also faces criminal prosecution. Civil recovery seems poised for growth in the UK as a means of deterring retail crime, with a National Civil Recovery Programme set up by a group of large retailers in England and Wales and a pilot scheme running within Scotland.

New shopping centres and new retail units have the opportunity for customized security solutions. 'Secured by Design' is a scheme intended to provide adequate security based on police crime prevention experience of the particular locality of the retail development, with architectural liaison officers charged with approving developments to the 'Secured by Design' standard. Considerations include boundary definition through walls, fences, landscaping or psychological barriers such as changes in road surface, rumble strips and use of colour to delineate 'private' areas. Landscaping can be used to enhance security, for example through densely planted thorny bushes to deter entry to certain areas. Physical security of doors, windows and locks can be designed into the plan, and higher levels of lighting applied to areas such as loading bays and fire exits, where security is especially important. There are also basic specifications for burglar alarm wiring which should be incorporated into all commercial premises.

Fifty-three per cent of intrusions occur via doors and 35 per cent via windows. Mechanical deterrents include the wide variety of grilles, shutters and screens which can be used to bar entry to the unit or sections of the unit where high-value stock is located. Mirrors can be used to enable staff surveillance of the shop-floor, or management/ security staff surveillance of staff and customers and bells can be used to warn of theft or emergency. Security can be built into new units in the form of secure locking systems for external doors, laminated glass used in glazed doors and glazed panels adjacent to door locks, locking handles and opening restrictors to accessible windows (The Scottish Office, 1996).

Electronic deterrence devices, such as mobile wireless systems, allow discrete messages to be sent between stores and security staff to warn of shoplifters or secure emergency help. In addition to combating crime, these contribute towards staff confidence in their own security. Closed-circuit television (CCTV) and point-of-sale closed-circuit television (POSCCTV) allow retailers and security providers to monitor customer, staff and stock movements. If live monitoring is not feasible, it enables investigation or proof of theft on stored film. That this is an effective means of combating retail crime is indisputable, with benefits in terms of detection and evidence of crime and in terms of enhancement of customers' perception of security. However, concerns regarding the infringement of civil liberty and misuse of information are addressed through The Data Protection Act 1998, which established eight principles of data protection with which controllers of CCTV have to comply:

1 Personal information shall be processed fairly and lawfully.
2 Personal data shall be obtained only for one or more specified and lawful purposes and shall not be further processed in any manner incompatible with that purpose or purposes.
3 Personal data shall be adequate, relevant and not excessive in relation to the purpose or purposes.
4 Personal data shall be accurate and, where necessary, kept up to date.
5 Personal data processed for any purpose or purposes shall not be kept for longer than is necessary for that purpose or purposes.
6 Personal data shall be processed in accordance with the rights of data subjects under this Act.
7 Appropriate technical and organizational measures shall be taken against unauthorized or unlawful processing of personal data and against accidental loss or destruction of, or damage to, personal data.

8 Personal data shall not be transferred to a country or territory outside
  the European Economic Area unless that country or territory ensures
  an adequate level of protection for the rights and freedoms of data
  subjects.

As a result of this Act, controllers of CCTV have to address the following
points carefully:

- Assessment of the purpose of its usage.
- Notification of its usage with the Office of the Information
  Commissioner.
- Establishment and documentation of security and disclosure policies.
- Location of cameras.
- Notification of usage.
- Access to data by data subjects.
- Retention of images.
- Access to and disclosure of CCTV images.
- Quality of the images.

A variety of electronic tagging devices have been developed to combat
theft. Sale items are tagged with tags removed or deactivated on
purchase. Pedestals are installed at exit points that trigger an alarm
should an item be taken through which has not been 'de-tagged'.
Electronic data tags, or intelligent tags, which support storage of article
information, can provide further applications aimed at improving retail
and supply chain efficiency. Although there is a range of technologies
involved (including electromagnetic, radio-frequency and acoustic
magnetic), they are all devices which signal their presence and transmit
data. Both retailers and electronic article surveillance (EAS) suppliers
envisage a future in which items for sale are data-tagged at source or
integrated during manufacture, and packaging tagged, using a range of
low-cost tags containing information about the merchandise – for
example, product and batch number, price, date and so on. Intelligent
tags will perform multiple functions in controlling retail and distribution
operations, including:

- Combating theft – for a much wider range of merchandise.
- Control of movement of goods – e.g. routing through warehouse,
  control of delivery.
- Intelligent packaging, giving data on merchandise – e.g. whether
  stored at correct temperature, whether the article has been tampered
  with.
- Inventory control – to determine location and number of items,
  including information on categories, colours.

- Provision of customer information – for household inventory control and reordering.

There are a number of technological issues to be considered in developing tags with the potential to transmit significant amounts of data, but a basic specification includes four key requirements:

1 Data must be accessible consistently, accurately and from a distance.
2 Control of data/interface/communications.
3 Data storage.
4 Energy source.

Three further key issues are tag security (elimination of mistakes in reading tag data), tag value (the added value to retailers provided by investment in electronic data tagging) and standardization (see Box 10.4). As technology issues are addressed, and more (and larger) organizations enter the electronic data tagging market, prices should come down to the level where they are applicable to FMCG organizations (Centre for Retail Research, 2002b).

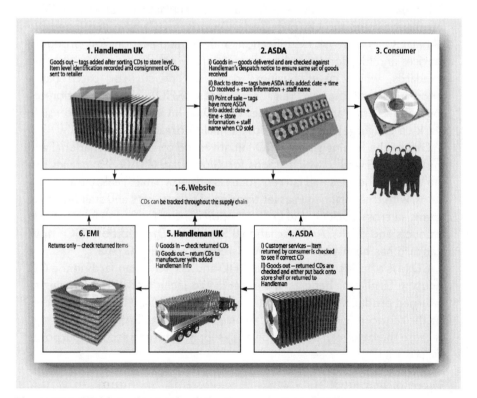

Figure 10.4 CD:id music supply chain. *Source*: e.centre (2002).

Box 10.4   Radio-frequency identification (RFID) and global standards for RFID tags

Radio-frequency identification is a data carrier technology that communicates data using radio waves. RFID works at different frequencies:

Long wave:	9–135 kHz
Short wave:	13.56 MHz
UHF:	400–1200 MHz
Microwave:	2.45 and 5.8 GHz

RFID tags consist of a semiconductor chip with memory, processing capability and transmitter connected to an antenna. RFID readers consist of an antenna and controller, which codes, decodes, checks, stores data and manages communications with tags and with the host. The tags are variable in shape and size, and can be applied directly to goods as 'smart labels'.

Although similar to bar coding, there are several key differences. The tag reader does not need to be orientated towards the tag nor to 'see' the tag. Bulk reading of tags is possible, as is the reading of individual data items from the tag. It is also possible for the user to programme data into the tag.

Standardization is a key issue for data tag manufacturers and users. EAN International and the Uniform Code Council (UCC) have developed the EAN.UCC system of identification and communication for products, services and locations based on internationally accepted and business-led standards, which cover business data (e.g. product or batch data), automatic data capture (e.g. bar codes, RFID) and application-to-application data transfer (e.g. Electronic Data Interchange and Extensible Mark-up Language), used by almost a million organizations globally.

One of the leading global RFID initiatives led by EAN International and the UCC is GTAG™, which stands for Global Tag. GTAG™ standards use the UHF frequencies and current focus is on returnable, reusable and bulk items, with trials planned in asset tracking of pallets, kegs and stainless steel drums, in cross-docking, and in distribution control for frozen foods, music products and drinks. An International Standards Organization (ISO) draft standard has been published which is consistent with GTAG™.

CD:id is a project piloting use of RFID and GTAG™ standards in the CD industry. Significant benefits are expected to include effective handling of returned products and increased security. ASDA–Wal-Mart are considering the replacement of Electronic Article Surveillance (EAS) with RFID tags because the latter can be used for both supply chain and security purposes (Figure 10.4).

Source: e.centre (2002).

Online fraud is also being tackled through electronic deterrents. One measure is the Secure Payment Application, which is the equivalent of a cardholder signature in which a pop-up window appears on screen where the buyer enters the password. This scheme, introduced by Mastercard, requires cardholders, retailers and banks dealing with the card to work together within an integrated system.

A similar system is in use by Mastercard's rival, Visa. Called 'Verified by Visa', this was first used in the United States, before being introduced to the UK. With this system, the buyer types a password into the website, then the card-holding bank verifies the identity of the cardholder and notifies the retailer to go ahead with the sale.

A third system introduced by Cahoot, Abbey National's online bank, in 2002 issued cardholders with a 'new' card for every transaction. The card is linked to the Cahoot customer's account, and the software for 'new' card generation is downloaded on to the cardholder's computer. When a purchase is made, the card is activated and a 16-digit number created for that specific transaction, while an upper limit for spending is also defined. The card number is transaction specific, so it cannot be stolen and used for another transaction. Cahoot estimated in 2002 that £1 million of fraud was prevented with this system.

As with electronic tagging, a common approach is needed. In 2002, for home shopping, banks would prefer the integration of chipcard readers within standard PCs. Meanwhile, the UK government is making theft of identity a criminal offence in response to the rise in online crime. At the same time it is considering ways of making it harder to obtain driving licences and passports by deception by, for example, issuing an electronic card alongside these documents. There is also consideration being made of government collaboration with banks to establish smart (electronic data storage) cards which could double up as official 'citizenship entitlement cards', and which would be used by the public to access entitlement to public services and act as an 'unofficial' national identity card. A further move is the establishment of a database of stolen identities to enable online checks on identity.

Summary

Retail crime has developed as a major issue for the UK retail industry only in the last decade, during which retailers and associated agencies such as the British Retail Consortium and the Scottish Grocers' Federation have developed collaborative initiatives to combat crime. Retail crime and shrinkage statistics are published annually which retailers can use as a benchmark for their own levels of crime and security.

Customer theft, accounting for 52 per cent of retail crime, is the most significant form of retail crime. Drug use, youth and male gender are three factors closely associated with customer theft, and most customer theft could be classified under three headings: organized gang theft, opportunistic theft and peer-related youth theft. Staff theft is the second most significant form of retail crime, accounting for 30 per cent. Staff theft, including staff collusion with customer and supplier thieves, is also a fast-growing sector of retail crime, and is associated with inadequate management, poor pay, high staff turnover and high rates of part-time staff – all features of many UK retail organizations. Fraud is the third largest source of crime in retailing, with cheque and card fraud in particular fast developing features of retail crime. External sources of crime including burglary, robbery/till snatches, criminal damage, arson and terrorism constitute a small percentage of overall retail crime.

The British Retail Consortium publish data on types of crime by retail sector and size of organization. Customer crime, for example, constitutes a much higher proportion of retail crime for small retailers than large multiple retailers, while the latter experience a much higher level of employee crime. Department stores and mixed retail businesses experience higher than average customer and staff theft, while the furniture, textiles and carpet sector experienced lower than average customer theft but more than average levels of fraud – particularly cheque fraud. Retailers which diversify their merchandise ranges, therefore, have to be aware that the nature and level of retail crime they experience will also change.

Retail loss deterrents can be classified under three main headings: human, mechanical and electronic. While many security measures are easy and cheap to deploy, 74 per cent of expenditure on retail security in the UK is directed towards security staff and cash collections. The published spend on deterrence does not include investment in most of the other 'human' methods of combating crime, although given the rising levels of employee crime, retailers should give consideration to measures including stricter pre-employment screening, management and security training, and boosting staff loyalty. Collaboration is a growing feature of retail security, both in securing, publishing and sharing information on retail crime, and in developing a wide variety of preventative measures.

Review questions

1 Why has retail crime long been trivialized in the UK?
2 Explain the main forms of retail crime.

3 What are the main categories of external threat to retail security and discuss their relative importance to retailers?
4 Discuss why a member of staff should take care when dealing with a suspected shoplifter.
5 Describe three human deterrents to retail crime, including at least one co-operative deterrent.

References

British Retail Consortium (2001). *8th Retail Crime Survey 2000*. British Retail Consortium, June.

Centre for Retail Research (2002a). http://www.retailing.uk.com/report2.html.

Centre for Retail Research (2002b). Electronic data tags. http://www.retailing.uk.com/report6.html, 13 February.

Clarke, M. (2001). Dealing with users. *Retail Week Crime and Security Report*, October.

DiLonardo, R. (2002). http://www.retailernews.com/1198/unise118.html.

May, J. (1996). Opening Address, Battle Against Retail Crime Conference, 13 June.

Oliphant, B. J. and Oliphant, G. C. (2001). Using a behavior-based method to identify and reduce employee theft. *International Journal of Retail and Distribution Management*, **29**(10), 442–51.

The Scottish Office (1996). *Secured by Design – Commercial*. HMSO, Scotland.

11

Merchandising in retailing

Introduction

The nature, role and coverage of retail merchandising are dimensions that are often a source of confusion for practitioners and researchers. In effect, this is because merchandising is a term that denotes two different, but related, aspects of retail management activity. Firstly, merchandising, or rather a merchandiser, can be understood as someone who has an important role to play in the buying function and who, in broad terms, typically has the responsibility for managing the financial dimensions of the process of product procurement and management. Secondly, a merchandiser, or more precisely, a visual merchandiser (the terms which will be used throughout this chapter to distinguish this role), refers to someone who is responsible for the visual presentation of products, and in many instances, the general aesthetics of the retail outlet. Both of these dimensions of merchandising will be delineated within this chapter.

From an analysis of the job descriptions of more than 50 merchandisers employed by retailers across a variety of sectors and various national markets, it is possible to identify three prominent dimensions that are crucial to the role of merchandisers. These relate to:

1 Managing the financial performance of the product range.
2 Managing space.
3 The contribution of merchandising to the process inherent to category management.

Each of these dimensions will be considered in this chapter.

Managing the financial performance of the product range

Controlling and assuring the financial health of the buying function is a key responsibility of the merchandiser. This is achieved in three ways: managing the buying budget; controlling the gross buying margin and managing the open-to-buy.

The buying budget

The buying budget exists as a complement to the buying plan. It details, on an ongoing basis, the amounts available for the buying team to spend on products. It also serves as a mechanism for monitoring and reviewing performance of the buying function on a continuous basis.

The buying budget is typically developed by both the retailer's financial team and their merchandisers. In terms of coverage, it includes all of the principal buying targets for the company. The starting point for developing a buying budget is the generation of *sales targets* for the range to be bought. Sales targets are based upon forecasted sales for the half-year period, and in most cases, for a monthly period too. The process of sales forecasting includes a full consideration of the performance, on a monthly period basis, of sales achieved in the previous year integrated with intelligence relevant to any projected prices changes and the anticipated impact of inflation/deflation upon future demand. Furthermore, it takes into account general market trends and seeks to anticipate the impact of these upon consumer demand.

Having established and verified the sales targets for the forthcoming period, the *buying spend* is then identified. This is the amount of money that will be available for the buying team to spend on ranges/products within the period. The reason why sales targets are established before the buying spend is defined is simple. No retailer wants to under- or over-buy. If the company under-buys, then customer demand will not be satisfied; customers will become disaffected and opportunities within the market will be lost. If the company over-buys, then there will be more stock available than is needed and the stock will have to be discounted in order to liquidate that asset. For this reason, then, the buying spend must be based upon a clear understanding of sales demand.

Controlling the gross buying margin

As well as estimating sales and controlling the buying spend, the buying budget is also used as an important method of monitoring and controlling the profitability of the buy. This is achieved, in the first instance, through the setting of the *gross buying margin*. The gross buying margin is calculated as follows:

$$\frac{\text{Selling price of goods} - \text{Cost price of goods}}{\text{Selling price of goods}}$$

The management of the gross buying margin is a key responsibility for merchandisers and, as a result, it is necessary for them to track margin performance on a weekly, if not daily, basis. It is common for each buying team to have a specific gross buying margin target.

For example, Table 11.1 indicates the gross buying margin for a British retailer that has a discount market positioning.

Table 11.1 Gross margin targets for a discount toiletries retailer

Product grouping	Gross margin target (%)
Baby products	27.5
Perfumery	29
Toiletries	31
Household	22
Confectionery	23
Personal electrical	31

For this retailer, all of the gross margin targets are relatively tight because the company operates within the discount market, which means that their retail prices must remain very competitive. In this case, the company has set different gross margin targets to reflect the different retail and cost pricing structures within the market, the differences in the nature of the supply base, as well as variations in volume demand within each product grouping.

For this company, the Director of Merchandising has decided that a *fixed margin policy* must be adopted. This means that all lines – for example, within the baby products area – must reach, if not exceed, the target of 27.5 per cent. While the motivation for the adoption of a fixed margin policy is driven by the desire to protect the profitability of the retailer's business, there are a number of weaknesses associated with this strict margin policy. Firstly, this approach fails to allow for a sufficient distinction to be made between differentiated and undifferentiated products. As such, there may be some products within the baby products grouping which, because of their undifferentiated, mass-appeal nature, cannot bear anything other than a highly competitive price. Secondly, buying teams which operate within the confines of a fixed margin policy may have to set uncompetitive prices in order to achieve their margin target, or they may have to negotiate aggressively with their suppliers in order to achieve their targets. These latter problems are particularly acute for buyers that operate within the discount sector. This is because their market positioning will not tolerate retail price increases, while the buying margins that they achieve with their suppliers are often as good as they can be.

In recognition of the restraints that a fixed margin policy can generate, some retailers operate a *flexible margin policy*. This means that merchandisers and buyers have the discretion to set variable margins at product level provided that the overall buying margins are achieved. This flexibility allows the merchandiser to distinguish between differentiated products, which can sustain higher margins because of their premium price positioning, and undifferentiated products which require a competitive price positioning. These latter products often generate a lower margin in order that prices can remain competitive, but rely upon a sufficient volume of demand in order to assure profitability.

While *gross margin management* has remained an important consideration for the merchandiser, it has been suggested that there has been too much emphasis upon gross margins by retailers, not least for the fact that the achievement of a gross margin is no guarantee of profitability, nor does it promise an acceptable return on equity (McGoldrick, 2002). Furthermore, Knee and Walters (1985) suggested that the fixation with gross margins failed to take full account of the impact of market-based pricing upon retail performance, assumes that all items have a similar cost structure (particularly in terms of failing to distinguishing between fixed and variable costs), and disregards elasticity in the demand for products.

Based upon the premise that an emphasis upon gross margins fails to provide an adequate indication of the profit contribution that a particular product may generate, some retailers have sought to identify the direct profitability of a product. *Direct product profitability* therefore seeks to provide a specific indication of a particular product's contribution to the retailer's profitability (Pinnock, 1986) According to McGoldrick (2002), direct product profitability is the balance between the gross margin of a product and its direct product costs. These direct product costs arise as part of the process of managing the movement of the product from the supplier to the final customer. As such, these costs are typically derived from four key areas – warehousing, transportation, in-store stocking and merchandising – as well as from the head office, which manages and controls the process of product movement.

In defence of the use of direct product profitability, Harris and Walters (1992) suggested that it focuses attention upon all the revenues that are generated by a product item, as well as the costs associated with supplying them. As such, they contend that direct product profitability can provide very different insights into the actual profitability of a product compared to the indications provided by a review of gross margins.

While various applications of direct product profitability have been commonly used by retailers, especially within the grocery and DIY sectors, it must also be recognized that there are a number of difficulties associated with applying direct product profitability principles. For example, the process of establishing and applying direct profitability measures has been found to be complex and expensive (Borin and Farris, 1995). Furthermore, given that the process tends to focus attention exclusively upon the measure of a product's profitability, it has been criticized for encouraging more of a product rather than a customer need orientation among buying teams (Davies and Rands, 1992).

Regardless of whether or not the merchandiser decides to adopt the principles of direct product profitability, it is incumbent on them to manage the costs that are attributable to the buying process. Generally, these costs will relate to mark-downs, transport and stock financing charges, as well as costs associated with supplier selection and product development, including packaging development and the like. It is common for a cost target to be set for a product category and for these targets to be expressed as a percentage of sales.

The *net buying margin* is the difference between the gross margin and the costs associated with the buying process. Again, it is common for the merchandiser to establish a net buying margin in order to monitor and control the costs associated with the buying process and to assure an acceptable net buying margin level. At this stage, however, it is important to remember that the net buying margin usually accounts for all costs accrued to the point when the product reaches the retail outlet. The net buying margin does not take into account the costs associated with retail operations.

Acting on performance target information

Each of these activities is concerned with measuring the performance of the buying process. However, measurement ought never to be an end in itself, but instead should also serve to provide a direction for taking action if the target performance, and particularly under-performance, requires it. If the range is under-performing, the merchandiser may advise the following:

- *Reconfiguration of the product mix.* This may require the buying team to focus their attention upon identifying the reasons for the poor performance of certain products or groups of products in the range. As a result, they may choose to alter the balance of the buy. For example, for a wine buyer, the sales performance may indicate that the choice needs to refocus upon cheaper lines or it may require that the range needs to be more inclusive of newly launched brands.

- *Reviewing the product pricing and margin mix.* In certain circumstances it may be necessary to reduce the retail price of under-performing lines. For those retailers that enjoy a powerful position within the supply chain, it may be that this is not at the expense of margin, since any price reduction will be adsorbed by the suppliers. Where this is not possible, it is vital that the merchandiser accurately calculates the volume of sales that would be required at the new, lower selling price in order to maintain margin performance.

- *Redefining the sales and profit forecast.* This may be the only course of action available to buyers in situations where there is no obvious action that can be undertaken in order to remedy the problem of under-performance.

- *Gross margin under-performance.* Under-performance with respect to gross margin does not necessarily require remedial action. In circumstances where sales are higher than expected and costs are lower, it may be the case that gross margin deficits are compensated by improved sales and better cost management performance. Furthermore, other than revising the gross margin projection, the merchandiser may direct a change in merchandise mix, whereby high-demand products, with higher gross margins, assume a proportionately greater role within the assortment. In certain circumstances, in order to protect the gross margin, merchandisers may elect to renegotiate the cost price with their suppliers or they may decide to increase the selling price. In difficult situations, it may be necessary for the merchandiser to countenance both forms of action.

Managing the open to buy

It is very unusual for a buying team to commit all of their orders at one point in time within the year or season. The proportion of spend and the timing of the buying commitment will depend upon the sector within which the retailer operates, as well as the type of product being bought and the amount of money that is available for the buy. However, in most sectors, the process of buying stock is often an ongoing activity. Within the grocery sector, for example, it is common for the buying team to commit a sizeable proportion of their budget to the ordering of staple lines (i.e. those products where demand is constant and relatively consistent). However, a proportion of the buying budget will also be set aside to pay for newly launched lines and to top up orders for ongoing lines which have perhaps enjoyed an unexpected increase in sales.

Within the fashion sector, it was traditionally the case that the majority of the buying budget would be committed at the beginning of the season and that any remaining budget would be used in order to replenish the availability of high-demand lines. However, as the fashion market has become more dynamic, with customers constantly demanding new products to be available on an ongoing basis, it has become common practice for merchandisers to retain a significant proportion of the budget back in order that it can be spent throughout the season. This retention of buying funds therefore means that the buying team can easily replenish best-selling lines in order to maximize demand. Furthermore, it allows for greater flexibility in the buying process, in that the latest fashion looks can be incorporated as near to the point and time of sale as possible.

The process which allows for the ongoing process of buying is called the *open to buy*. Risch (1987) defined open to buy as the difference between the planned purchases for a season or period and the values of goods that had already been committed by the retailer.

Management of the open to buy budget is usually the responsibility of the merchandiser. Successful management of the open to buy budget requires that the merchandiser accurately monitors the level of stock committed and received by the business and the levels which are committed but have not as yet been received. Furthermore, the merchandiser must also keep a close eye upon consumer demand on stock throughput so that they can reorder best-selling lines, as well as introduce new lines which are predicted to enjoy significant customer demand. In many cases, it is the careful management of the open to buy which allows for the replenishment of high-demand lines as these emerge, as well as the purchase of newly launched products which may very quickly generate high demand and contribute most to the overall profitability of the buy.

It is common for the open to buy to be managed on a monthly basis. The open to buy budget is comprised of the required stock holding (which is the sum of all products that are required in order to cover size/colour options in order to meet customer demand and assure a strong merchandise presentation) plus the estimated sales for the period plus mark-down allowances minus current stock holdings and stock currently on order.

Table 11.2 details the open to buy budget for the shoe department of a major department store chain.

Table 11.2 Open to buy for the shoe department for a major department store chain

Open to buy for September 2002	Retail prices (£)
Required holding stock	1 050 000
Estimated sales for September 2002	560 000
Mark-down allowances	20 000
Total stock required	1 630 000
Current holding stock	1 200 450
Stock on order as at 1 September 2002	55 000
Total open to buy budget	374 550

Risch (1987) identified that the open to buy assists the buying team in two important ways. Firstly, it serves as an important planning and control device. Secondly, it acts as an important diagnostic tool in the valuation of merchandising activities.

As a planning and control device, the open to buy balances stock levels with sales demand. As such, it helps prevent an over- or an under-bought situation. In so doing, this minimizes the volume of lost sales as a result of an out-of-stock situation. Furthermore, a carefully managed open to buy budget ought to control the amount spent on goods within the financial limitations of the periodic merchandise budget. This should then reduce the number of mark-downs, increase sales and therefore protect, if not enhance, the gross margin target that have been set. Finally, the open to buy process allows the retailer to retain funds in order to reorder fast-selling lines, take advantage of cost price reductions provided by a supplier, as well as trial new lines as they appear on the market.

As a diagnostic tool, Risch (1987) suggests that the open to buy allows the retailer to identify planning errors, such as in relation to inaccurate sales forecasts. Furthermore, it helps identify buying errors with respect to a failure in recognizing emerging fashion trends and allows the retailer to take prompt corrective action. This approach also minimizes the difficulties associated with timing errors, such as in relation to the late delivery of goods within a season.

In conclusion, a comment provided by a Senior Merchandiser for a DIY store group provides an interesting insight into the responsibilities associated with managing the open to buy budget:

> Managing the open to buy budget requires keen analytical skills. Merchandisers need to monitor actual sales and at the same time try to predict future sales. It involves tracking the

flow of goods into the business and making sure that the product winners and losers are correctly identified. It is about delaying the ordering or reordering decision to the very last possible moment so that the products that come into the business are the correct ones that will sell quickly and at the highest price. It is complex and can be very rewarding. But it is not for the faint hearted.

Management of space

Space has been identified as one of a retailer's most expensive resources. As such, space management decisions ought to be founded upon the principle of achieving the best profitability on this key asset (Harris and Walters, 1992). However, prior to a consideration of the issues associated with the effective management of space in store, it is important to first consider the basic principles that merchandisers adopt in order to allocate stock to stores.

Stock allocation

Whether a retailer has five outlets or 500, it is unlikely that they will operate stores that are totally the same either in terms of their architecture or the nature of their business. Each will differ in terms of their size and shape, their customer base and the competitive environment in which they operate. As such, it is inevitable that the retailer must develop some set of stock allocation principles that will ensure that the correct type and amount of stock is allocated to the various and varying stores at a rate that matches local demand.

A variety of allocation processes have been developed by merchandisers who, with product allocators, are vested with the responsibility for stock assignment and distribution throughout a store network. The most common stock allocation methodology that is used by retailers is that of store grading.

Store grading requires that the store network is divided into subsets or clusters. The number of clusters is dependent upon the number of stores in the network and the differences that exist between and among these stores. For retailers that operate more than 50 or so stores, it is common for them to grade their stores into four or five cluster groupings. Stores that share the same cluster grouping are those that possess similar characteristics, normally in terms of their sales turnover, store size and location (such as city centre, out-of-town and local neighbourhood stores). The grading that a store receives directly

Table 11.3 Store grading and product allocation for a UK fashion retailer

Store classification	Store type/location	Product allocation features
AA	Major city centre stores – Central London/Manchester/ Glasgow/Edinburgh	• Full merchandise range • Full range of services • Trial merchandise • Emphasis upon specialist/ premium ranges
A	City centre/out-of-town stores – Birmingham/Bluewater	• Full merchandise range • Full range of services • 70% of trial merchandise • 70% of specialist/premium ranges
B	Smaller city stores – such as Cardiff, Aberdeen	• 85% of merchandise range • Some services • Limited trial merchandise
C	Large town stores	• 75% of merchandise range
D	Medium town stores	• 65% of merchandise range
E	Small town stores	• 50% of merchandise range

determines the breadth and the depth of products that are subsequently allocated to them. Table 11.3 provides an example of the allocation procedures that have been adopted by a leading UK fashion retailer chain.

While grading systems, such as the one described above, are the most common method of product allocation used by merchandisers, many retailers also have come to recognize their need to include greater degrees of flexibility in their allocation procedures so as to maximize the sales and profit potential within their markets. As such, the most successful retailers, while broadly adopting the rigidity implied by the grading system identified above, will also allow merchandisers the freedom to allocate, albeit on a restricted basis, product lines to outlets regardless of their classification status. Decisions of this kind are very much motivated by the desire to exploit market potential where these arise and are a recognition that, in certain cases, the application of rigid allocation classifications does not fully acknowledge the variety that exists with respect to differences in consumer demand between similar types of outlet.

It is also important to note that store gradings may change in response to changes in consumer buying patterns and changes in the competitive environment. It is not uncommon for a retailer, especially within the food sector, to regrade a store (usually upwards if the store is commercially important to the company), in response to the entry of a new competitor in the market who may offer a more comprehensive product range. In these circumstances, the regrading of the store is clearly a defensive position in response to the threat of competitor attack.

The drivers of space management

Having allocated stock to stores, it is also the responsibility of the merchandising team to ensure that the stock is presented in a manner that is attractive to the consumer, is cost efficient and maximizes the profit potential of the space available.

Decisions relevant to the management of space are influenced by a variety of key drivers. Firstly, the nature of the sector within which the retailer operates has a direct bearing upon the amount of space that is available. In certain circumstances, the amount of space that is required in order to display and facilitate the sale of stock may be minimal. For example, those stores that sell by sample, such as Argos, or luxury brand retailers, often require a minimal amount of space by virtue of the nature of their trading format (as in the case for Argos) or because of their premium market position (for example, Chanel). In other instances, the demands of a wide and deep product range, such as is the case for department stores, DIY and grocery retailers, requires that considerable amounts of space are available in order to adequately display goods, meet customers' demands and accommodate their service expectations.

As a result of the drive to assure greater efficiency and maintain and improve net margins, there has been a general shift in the retail sector towards the minimization of stock holding, especially at store level, in order to reduce financing, administration, handling and storage costs. As a result of this policy, retailers are now seeking to convert stockroom space into selling space and hold stock higher up in the supply chain, drawing it into stores nearer to the time of sale.

Given the importance of effective and efficient space management, a number of key principles have emerged with respect to best practice in the area. These include the need to ensure that:

- sufficient space is allocated across the product assortment in order to meet forecasts with respect to sales, volume and profit targets;
- the best-selling and the most profitable lines are allocated space which maximizes their contribution potential;

- customer service levels are met through maximum product availability;
- displays are not undermined between replenishment cycles.

Davidson et al. (1988) identified that space management decisions are taken at three levels: strategic, tactical and operational. Each level fulfils different business objectives, operates within different time-scales and has different time horizons.

In most cases, the merchandising team will have little involvement in space management decisions at the strategic level, but they will, however, have to operate within the constraints and opportunities afforded by strategic-level decisions. In essence, strategic space management decisions are concerned with the number, location and design of locations. Decisions at this level invariably require significant capital investment and, as such, are a long-term commitment on the part of the retailer.

Tactical space management decisions are generally store based, and relate to issues of store design, layout, allocation of space and location to key product categories. Implicit within these latter decisions is the need to identify how the retailer's market positioning, sales and profitability targets, the expectations of customers, as well as format conventions, should impact upon the space allocation decisions. While these decisions are perhaps not as irrevocable as strategic decisions, it is important to remember that many tactical space management decisions, such as those relevant to the location of certain departments, may involve considerable cost. This is especially true of departments that rely upon specialist equipment, such as frozen foods, or require stockroom space, such as occasional furniture.

A merchandising team is likely to be closely involved in tactical space management decisions. In many cases, it will be their expertise in sales and profit forecasting, as well as merchandise presentation, handling and storage, that will be drawn upon in order to make these tactical decisions.

It is at the operational level of space management that the influence of a merchandising team is clearly evident. Those operational decisions are essentially micro-level in nature and are concerned with the amount of space that is given over to specific products and brands. A variety of approaches have been developed in order to effectively manage the allocation of space to products. These are discussed below.

Productivity ratios seek to allocate space and a particular location to a product based upon the sales or profit that it is expected to generate. In the broadest of terms, productivity ratios will directly apportion space to the proportion of sales that the product will generate. Therefore, if a product generates 8 per cent of sales within a product category, it will be given 8 per cent of the available space. This has been described as the 'share-of-shelf = share-of-market rule' (Borin and Faris, 1995). This approach is supported by the leading brand manufacturers, especially in the grocery sector, who recognize that this approach serves to reinforce their market leadership status. As a means of securing maximum space and the best location within store, the leading brand manufacturers are prepared to pay 'over-riders' to their stockists, which are cash payments for the maintenance of space and location agreements. Many smaller manufacturers perceive this to be an unfair practice and argue that its continuance undermines their ability to access customers and improve their market share.

McGoldrick (2002) suggested that there are a number of reasons as to why retailers ought not to allocate space and locations solely upon the level of sales that a product generates. In particular, he noted that this approach fails to recognize the relationship between the velocity of sales and their visual appeal. Furthermore, the fastest selling lines may not in fact be the most profitable, while displays that are dominated by fast-selling lines may give the impression of a narrow choice of product and of a predictable assortment. Finally, the market possibilities of newly launched products may be undermined by virtue of their lack of sales history, which may preclude a significant space allocation.

The *balanced stock model approach* seeks to balance issues of sales participation and profitability contribution with considerations relevant to the demand for the product, its characteristics and the associated display requirements. A number of computer packages have been developed, such as SpaceMax, Spacemaster and Spaceman (Pearson, 1993), which correlate these various demands and produce, in turn, a planogram. A planogram is a pictorial representation of a stock display and, according to McGoldrick (2002), brings together the numerical and visual dimensions of developing a stock layout plan in a way that ought to maximize sales and profitability, while still maintaining the visual integrity of the offer.

These space management computer packages are not solely available within the grocery sector. Lea Greenwood (1998) identified that fashion yield was a commonly used space management system that was used by clothing retailers in order to manage the visual presentation of stock, while maximizing their profitability. A major advantage of such packages resides in their ability to produce images that can be cost-effectively reproduced and sent to stores for replication.

A number of factors impact upon space allocation and location management decisions. Of the *external factors* that influence this decision making, the nature of the relationship with a supplier is crucial. For example, if the product category is dominated, in market share terms, by a small number of powerful manufacturer brands, any decision upon the allocation and location of space to these products will be determined by the demands of the supplier. As part of the terms of trade, which incorporate their agreement to supply to a retailer, a manufacturer may insist that their brand range is given particular prominence as evidenced by the number of product facings or the shelf location that the brand is given. The decision to comply with the manufacturer's demands may be further compounded by the amount of money that they are prepared to contribute to make their brand successful – such as through offering point-of-sale promotional material, contributions towards fixture costs, or promotional offers and discounts that they may provide. The merchandising team may also consider the degree of media advertising that is available to support the manufacturer's brand. This may be sufficient reason to provide a generous space allocation.

Internal factors that may influence the allocation of space to products include considerations relevant to product attributes and their visual appeal. In circumstances where the product is perhaps fragile or of a non-standard shape, these features alone may determine the space allocation decisions. The composition of the product range may also determine the allocation, in that products that have a clear relationship are often grouped together. For example, in Sainsbury's supermarkets in the UK, newspapers, magazines, books, CDs and greetings cards are all grouped together because these are regarded as leisure/event products, and their location near to the store entrance/exit indicates their impulse nature.

Many retailers also recognize that space management and location decisions must be customer focused and should contribute to the customer service orientation of their business. As a result, retailers such as Boots the Chemist and Marks & Spencer site their sandwich shops close to exits in order that lunch-time shoppers can purchase food quickly and easily. There are some instances, however, where it would seem that retailers are not always fully customer-centred in their stock location decisions. For example, department store retailers are often criticized for locating their children's wear departments on the top floor, which causes considerable inconvenience for parents trying to access these areas with young children. In many cases, the retailers adopt this strategy because children's wear is not the most profitable merchandise category. Furthermore, by placing children's wear on the highest floor, the retailer is trying to manipulate the movement of families within stores to make sure that they are exposed to as much of the store and its merchandise as possible.

Merchandise allocation and the product life cycle

It would be wrong to assume that a product or brand retains the same level of importance to the retailer throughout its life cycle and that the space that it is allocated will remain static through time. Much rather, it is likely that the space allocation will alter as the demand and profitability of the product changes through time.

At the point of *introducing* a product, or a range of products, the amount of space that is allocated will be dependent upon the importance of the product to the retailer in terms of the product's exclusivity, its relevance to the retailer's market positioning, the likely customer demand and the communication strategy that will accompany its launch. The amount of space allocated will depend upon the retailer's assessment of the strength of the product in relation to these dimensions.

If the launch of the product or product range has been successful and demand enables it to enter into the *growth stage*, then it is expected that the product will enjoy a greater space allocation, in order that volume sales can be achieved. This enables scale economies to be accrued and allows for the opportunities inherent to the line to be exploited, particularly if competition is limited.

At the *maturity stage*, it is common for retailers to aim to maximize cash flow and to maintain market penetration. At this stage, it may be possible to move these products to secondary locations without undermining sales levels because customer awareness and loyalty are high. It typically will be the case that, at this stage, the overall space allocation will be reduced from the levels achieved at the growth stage. This will be motivated, in part, by the desire to provide space and opportunity to products that have reached the introduction and growth stages.

When the *decline stage* of a product or range is reached, the amount of stock ought to have reduced and therefore the space that is allocated will also decline markedly. Indeed, not only will the space levels change, but it is possible that the location of the range will change to a tertiary area which has comparatively less customer traffic. Alternatively, at this point, the retailer may choose to place the range in an area of high traffic in order to clear any residual stock quickly and efficiently.

A review of the impact the product life cycle has upon the amount and location of space that is allocated to products underlines the elasticity that is inherent to the processes of space management. Indeed, as McGoldrick (2002) identified, the successful management of space necessitates strong quantitative qualities as well as sound commercial judgement on the part of the merchandising team. Without these

Box 11.1   External observations on space allocation for the Autograph Collection at Marks & Spencer

When Marks & Spencer launched their Autograph Collection in the late 1990s, it was clear that the company was trying to address, head on, the criticism that it was no longer an innovative or design-led fashion retailer. By commissioning a number of leading designers to design, anonymously, for their Autograph Collection, Marks & Spencer sought to create a premium brand that incorporated leading-edge design at a relatively competitive price.

At the time of the initial launch of the Autograph Collection (which was solely a female range), only a small number of Marks & Spencer stores were selected to stock the range. These stores included the company's flagship store at Marble Arch, London, as well as their other large and important stores in cities such as Glasgow, Manchester and Leeds. Within each store, a designated sales area was identified and a new, more upmarket shop fit was developed to accommodate the Autograph Collection. In most cases, the sales area was isolated from the rest of the store by some form of partitioning. The overall space given over to the launch of the range was more than the usual amount given by Marks & Spencer to a newly launched range. Indeed, extra space was provided for sofas and coffee tables, while the layout and changing rooms were spatially more generous than normal for a Marks & Spencer store. This liberal allocation of space was motivated by the company's desire to create a different, more luxurious environment which would reflect the Autograph Collection's premium positioning.

After the initial launch and success of Autograph, Marks & Spencer sought to further develop the opportunities that the Autograph Collection appeared to provide. The number of lines available was extended and, soon after, an Autograph Menswear line was launched. This growth stage required that further space be allocated to the range for menswear, although this was typically sited adjacent to the existing menswear departments.

In 2002, Marks & Spencer announced that the Autograph Collection would not be extended beyond 25 of their 302 stores. Instead, the range has been consolidated and, for the moment, the space that has been allocated to the range will be maintained. What is not clear is whether Marks & Spencer will maintain the amount of space allocated to this premium range if sales start to decline.

required skills, the profitability as well as the image of the retailer is likely to be severely undermined. External observations on the space management principles adopted by Marks & Spencer during the various life stages of their Autograph Collection are reviewed in Box 11.1.

The contribution of merchandising to category management

> We have only just adopted category management and it is really a different way of doing business. In the past, we thought on a product-by-product, supplier-by-supplier basis. It was about us developing a sales plan and pushing to reach the targets. With category management everything is much more unified. Put simply, it is about seeing the relationships between and among the company, our suppliers and all our products and managing these collectively.
> Merchandise Director, UK Grocery Retailer

The above quote gets to the heart of the defining principles of category management. McGoldrick (2002) suggests that the origin of category management can be attributed to the collaboration that was established between Wal-Mart and Procter & Gamble, which resulted in a new internal product management approach within Wal-Mart and a new sort of relationship between Wal-Mart and their major supplier.

Varley (2001) defines the process of adopting category management as 'the establishment of a group of products as a category, which essentially have similar demand patterns, are reasonable substitutes for one another and can be viewed from a marketing viewpoint as a sensible strategic business unit on which to base a marketing plan' (p. 46). Similarly, the IGD (1997) suggests that category management is a strategic approach to product management, which emphasizes the importance of trade relationships in order to maximize sales and profits through the satisfaction of consumer need.

While category was promoted throughout the late 1990s as a revolutionary new approach to product management, it has to be acknowledged that category management is not commonly used in all sectors of retailing. It is most prevalent within the grocery sector, although DIY and department stores have adopted it within certain product areas. It is least common within the fashion sector, and this is typically explained by the fact that product life cycles are significantly shorter, that – certainly within the UK market – manufacturer brands are less powerful and, as a result, retailer–supplier relationships are less stable and are more likely to be short term.

A category management approach typically results in the formation of a category management team. This team, lead by a category manager, is comprised of buyers, merchandisers, marketing promotions specialists, as well as product designers, technologists, logistics specialists and those responsible for the presentation of the category in the stores. In addition, the category team may also incorporate the inputs from specialists employed by their most important suppliers. Typically, the number of suppliers involved in these sorts of relationship within the category team will be small and, if more than one is involved, these will be mutually exclusive in terms of the products that they supply. It is impossible for a retailer to work with a large number of suppliers within a category team for two main reasons. The first is that the rivalry between and among suppliers would be detrimental to the collaborative principles of category management. Secondly, a large number of participants would be difficult to co-ordinate and manage and, as a result, would undermine the category management approach.

There are three main reasons for the development of an inclusive category team structure, which brings together the retailer and their suppliers. Firstly, it helps to create a clear focus upon the needs of the customer rather than solely the requirements of retailers and suppliers. Secondly, it encourages retailers and suppliers to consider themselves as partners that collaborate in order to profitably satisfy the needs of consumers, rather than as combatants that try to exert the greatest amount of power over the other. Finally, the improved integration that category management promotes between retailer and supplier typically generates efficiencies and operational improvements which can improve the overall profitability of the procurement process.

Adopting a category management approach

A variety of proximate approaches have been identified in the literature with respect to the process of adopting a category management strategy. Fernie and Sparks (1998) identified a three-stage process, which begins with the *category definition* stage, which involves defining, from the prospective of the consumer, which products will constitute and contribute to the category. The second is the *category planning* stage, which involves determining the performance measures for the category, identifying the category's product mix and formulating a marketing strategy to support the category. The third phase is the *category implementation* stage, which involves the assignment of responsibilities to supply chain partners in terms of managing, controlling and monitoring category performance.

McGoldrick (2002) identified an eight-stage process for creating and managing a category management approach. This commenced with the process of defining the category and also included the process of identifying the nature of the merchandise assortment, defining all management and control responsibilities to supply chain partners, as well as a strategy for monitoring category performance.

As such, there is sufficient coverage elsewhere in the literature in terms of delineating the broad stages of category management implementation and development. However, what is less well defined in the literature is the identification of the actual activities and processes inherent to defining the boundaries of the category and the decisions that are relevant to assembling the product mix within the category. This stage in the development of the category requires significant analytical skills and it is invariably the responsibility of the merchandiser to establish the category in this way and at this stage.

Given the importance of this particular stage to the category development process, the key actions inherent to defining and assembling a product mix for a category are detailed below.

Stage 1: Analysis of consumer demand trends within the category

As a starting point, it is necessary for the merchandiser to define the broad parameters of the category in terms of its scope and coverage. This is achieved by considering the range of products that customers may need in order to solve a particular problem or satisfy a particular need. For example, a merchandiser may begin by identifying the products that customers may need for laundering and caring for clothes washing in the home.

Initially, a review of internal sales data is crucial, since such a review will serve to identify the range of products that customers currently purchase. Furthermore, by analysing the sales histories of these products, the merchandiser is then able to establish patterns of demand and identify product sales trends. However, a review of internal intelligence alone provides a narrow and insufficient review of general market trends. Therefore, it is important for merchandisers to augment this information with external data, such as in the form of competitor reports which may consider, in particular, the breadth and depth of the product ranges that other retailers provide within the category area. Other important sources, such as trade publications, will identify other products that customers currently use, but which perhaps are not part of the retailer's current offer, while market intelligence agencies should identify imminent and recent product launches in the area.

At this stage, the inclusion of primary consumer research is also vital. By commissioning consumer research, which seeks to outline customers' attitudes and behaviours with respect to particular product areas, the merchandiser may obtain a clearer insight into how and why customers purchase particular products within the category. Crucial to this stage is the provision of a competent understanding of customers' need requirements, as well as some insights into what motivates their decision to purchase one product or brand over another. This research may consider the extent to which existing customers are satisfied with the company's current product range and offers an opportunity to identify gaps in the current merchandise mix.

Assembling the internal sales information, alongside the external data and the results of the primary research, the merchandiser is then able to define the broad parameters of the category, as illustrated in Figure 11.1. Having defined the scope of the category, the merchandiser is then able to progress to the next stage, which involves the review of the category mix options.

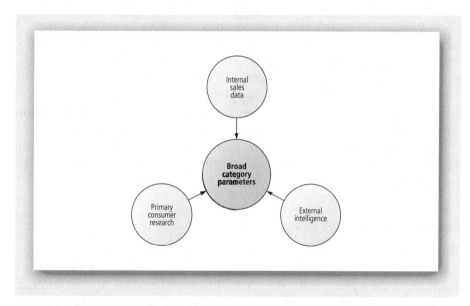

Figure 11.1 The process of defining the broad category parameters.

Stage 2: Reviewing the category mix options

Drawing from the information obtained in the first stage, the merchandiser will seek to identify *all* of the products that the customer may expect to be included within a particular category. For each product type, brands that complement the retailer's market positioning will be considered, as will opportunities for own-brand development. Furthermore, the various variants for each product, such as in terms of pack size, product ingredients, product use and price level, will also be reviewed.

Having generated an inventory of product options for a category, it is then necessary for the merchandiser to evaluate each. The criteria that merchandisers use for this evaluation will depend upon a number of factors, including the sector within which the retailer operates, their market positioning, the product expectations of their customers, as well as the nature of the particular category. However, it would be expected that an evaluation would focus primarily upon some consideration of likely consumer demand for each, as well as an estimation of gross margin contribution, and an evaluation of the competitive advantage that the inclusion of each product could provide for the retailer.

Having sketched the potential product options within the proposed category, it is necessary for the merchandiser to collaborate closely with the relevant manufacturers and suppliers. This consultation requires that the supply base reviews the feasibility of consistently and profitably supplying the various product options within a category. It is at this stage that the importance of excellent retailer–supplier relations becomes apparent. As Varley (2001) suggests, the success of category management is ultimately dependent upon the extent to which retailers and suppliers can form strategic alliances that serve to support a competent evaluation of commercial oppor-tunities based upon an efficient and cost-effective supply chain.

The sum of this information then enables the manufacturer to begin the process of assembling the range of products that is to be included in the category.

Stage 3: Assembling the category

Based upon the information obtained from the first research stage, and the product-specific analysis undertaken as part of the second stage, it is then the responsibility of the merchandiser to recommend to the category management team the make-up of the category in terms of its overall coverage and structure. With a competent understanding of the nature of customer demand, the availability of supply and the financial performance requirements of the category, the category management teams can then begin to identify the specific products to be included in the category.

This process usually commences with the identification of all possible product options within a subcategory. From this, considera-tion is then given to those product options that better match customer requirements in relation to function, price, size, use, quality and brand. These products are then selected for further scrutiny. The products that are finally selected for inclusion are chosen on the basis that these:

- collectively satisfy the product requirements of the majority of customers in terms of product function, pack size, quality, retail price and brand;
- present the customer with an impression of sufficient and reasonable choice;
- share similar characteristics to be reasonable substitutes for each other;
- are likely to have, if not similar, then certainly predictable, demand patterns;
- satisfy the business's requirements in terms of profitability and sales levels.

Table 11.4 lists the category composition for the home laundry category for a UK supermarket retailer. The category was developed by using the three stages identified above. It is interesting that as part of their review of the category, the company reduced the total number of product options in their range by 57 options, despite the fact that they had also introduced the stain removal and accessories subcategories for the first time. As a result of this initiative, home laundry sales increased by 17 per cent in the first year and the gross margin for the category improved by 4.9 per cent.

According to the Senior Merchandiser responsible for the category, the improvement in performance can be attributed to:

- reduced product duplication resulting in improved scale economies;
- improved buying terms as a result of a more concentrated buy;
- reduced operational costs related to storage, handling, etc., as a result of the elimination of 57 product options;
- the introduction of new, premium price lines with significant volume demand.

It would be wrong to suggest that the involvement of the merchandiser in the category development process ends at this stage. Much rather, the merchandiser's role is significant in the process of managing the profitability of the category, and will be involved in setting performance measures, as well as in the operationalization of the category at store level, through the allocation of stock to stores and the allocation of space to specific products within the category. The nature and extent of the ongoing involvement of the merchandiser in the category development process is clearly delineated by the comments of a Merchandise

Table 11.4 Category composition for home laundry for a UK supermarket retailer

Category name: Home laundry

Detergents (Automatic)
Washing powders	12 variants by biological/non-biological/pack size/brand
Washing tablets	12 variants by biological/non-biological/pack size/brand
Washing capsules	12 variants by biological/non-biological/pack size/brand
Liquid	8 variants by biological/non-biological/pack size/brand

(Twin-tub)
Washing powders	3 variants by biological/non-biological/pack size

(Hand-wash)
Washing powders	2 variants by non-biological/pack size
Travel wash	2 variants by brand

Fabric conditioner
Liquid	8 variants by brand/pack size
Tumble dryer	2 variants by brand
Spray – easy iron	2 variants by brand

Home dry cleaning   2 variants by brand

Fabric fresheners
Spray	1 variant by brand
Steam iron liquid	2 variant by brand

Stain removal
Bottle	16 variants by type
Soap	2 variants by brand
Cream	1 variant by brand
Impregnated textile	1 variant by brand

Water softeners
Tablet	1 variant by brand
Powder	1 variants by brand

Fabric dyes
Liquid	18 variants by colour/brand
Powder	16 variants by colour/brand

Starch
Spray	4 variants by size/brand

Accessories
Clothes Brush	2 variants by size
De-fuzzer	2 variants by brand
De-piller	1 variant by brand

Equipment
Clothes lines	3 variants by size
Clothes pegs	3 variants by size/colour
Peg carriers	2 variants by material
Clothes hangers	10 variants by material/type/colour
Laundry bags	8 variants by material/size/use
Clothes carriers	6 variants by size/colour

Director for a food retailer who provided information in support of the development of this chapter. He said:

> The success of category management is predicated upon the extent to which there is a capable and experienced merchandiser within the category team. Without a strong merchandiser, then the chances are the coverage of the category will be wrong and the financial projections will never be reached. The merchandiser is the financial custodian. Without them, the buying function may exist, but it is unlikely to ever be profitable.

These observations are relevant not only to the role of the merchandiser in terms of the delivery of a successful category management strategy, but are also pertinent to the wider contribution of the merchandiser to a retail organization. It has been the intention of the first stage of this chapter to clearly highlight the key financial responsibilities of the merchandiser. The purpose of the following section of this chapter will be to consider another aspect of merchandising, namely that of visual merchandising. In certain circumstances, it may be the case that the merchandiser, who has financial management responsibilities as delineated above, will also have an active involvement in the visual presentation of stores and of stock.

However, in larger retail organizations, the responsibility for visual merchandising will be delegated to a particular team that possesses strong design and creative skills. The key considerations inherent to the process of visual merchandising are presented below.

The dimensions of visual merchandise management

Visual merchandising is concerned with the creation of a store environment which, on the one hand, consistently represents the values of the retailer and their brand to consumers and, on the other, satisfies the needs and expectations that the consumer has of the retailer. Indeed, as Lea Greenwood (1998) noted, the purpose of visual merchandising is at once to convey the retailer's corporate positioning to the market, as well as to reflect the aspirations of prospective customers.

The processes inherent to the creation and management of a store environment are many and complex. Indeed, a veritable science of store atmospherics has emerged which seeks to manipulate the visual, aural, olfactory and tactile dimensions of the store environment in order to influence customer's perceptions and subsequent behaviour (Kotler, 1973). As a result, a variety of studies have been undertaken by academics into this interesting dimension of retailing, and these include consideration of the psychological effect that store design has upon consumers' decision making in stores (Green, 1986), the role that store atmospherics has in relation to brand development and positioning (Sherry, 1998), as well as more recent studies which have suggested that a primary purpose of store atmospherics is to entertain consumers in a theatrical way (Kim, 2001).

The development and implementation of a visual merchandise strategy is a costly activity and requires significant capital investment by retailers. For example, Mintel (1999) estimated that, in the UK, the store design and shopfitting sector was worth £1.5 billion each year.

Given the complexity of the store design process, and limited space available in this text, it is impossible to provide details of all the dimensions of visual merchandising here. Therefore, the remainder of this chapter will consider:

- The relationship between visual merchandising and consumer behaviour.
- The key business objectives of visual merchandising.
- The principles of store layout.
- The common methods of in-store display used by retailers.

Visual merchandising and consumer behaviour

The investments made by retailers in store atmospherics are predicated upon a clear assumption. That assumption is that the environmental context within which customers shop can have a significant impact upon their purchasing behaviour. Furthermore, it is based upon the assumption that significant and worthwhile proportions of customers' decisions are unplanned and are made at the point of purchase within the store.

A variety of studies, such as those undertaken by The Point of Purchasing Advertising Institute (POPAI) Dupont Surveys in 1977 and 1986 identified that two-thirds of purchase decisions are actually made within the store. Their study classified purchasing decisions into four categories, as follows:

- *Specifically planned* – the customer knows which product and brand that they want before entering the store and do not deviate from this position when buying.
- *Generally planned* – the customer knows which product they want, but has no specific brand in mind when they shop.

- *Substitute purchase* – the customer purchases a different product from their declared intention.
- *Unplanned purchase* – the customer buys a purchase without prior intention.

Based upon the results of their 1986 study, it was found that 33.9 per cent of purchases were specifically planned, 10.6 per cent were generally planned, 2.9 per cent were substitute purchases and 52.6 per cent were unplanned purchases.

A number of models have been developed in order to explain consumer behaviour. Among the most important are those provided by Nicosia (1969), Howard and Sheth (1969), and Engel et al. (1990). Each of these models indicates that there is an opportunity for external agents, such as retailers, to influence the buying decision-making process, in terms of stimulating the buying process or influencing the final decisions that buyers make. As such, it is by virtue of their desire to positively affect customers' decision making that retailers decide to make considerable investments in the area of visual merchandising.

The key business objectives of visual merchandising

Lea Greenwood (1998) identified that the key business objectives of visual merchandising were to: attract customers' attention; encourage customers to increase the time and money they spend in store; differentiate the retailer from the competition; as well as reinforce the messages integral to the company's marketing communications strategy. Schimp (1990) maintained that the role of visual merchandising is to:

- create awareness among consumers about a product and provide relevant information about it;
- remind customers about the benefits of a product and of its availability;
- encourage a customer to buy a particular product or brand;
- maximize the utilization of space, while at the same time making the buying experience as easy as possible for consumers;
- reinforce the retailer's communications campaign;
- assist the customer in locating, evaluating and selecting a product.

Within this context, Harris and Walters (1992) identified that visual merchandising should serve to:

- reinforce the marketing positioning of the company within the competitive environment;

- encourage interest and comparison among customers and prompt the customer to make a purchase;
- co-ordinate the merchandise into a coherent proposition, which provides an integrated communications message.

Similarly, Varley (2001) suggests that visual merchandising has a crucial role to play in communicating and differentiating the retail offer to consumers, and maintains that the image that the visual dimensions of the store generates must be consistent with the retailer's overall positioning in the market.

The principles of store layout

An important dimension of visual merchandising is the design of the store layout. The layout that the retailer adopts is dependent upon a number of factors and these include:

- the sector in which the retailer operates – for example, a food retailer will adopt a different layout scheme from that of an exclusive fashion retailer;
- the architecture of the store itself.
- the market positioning of the retailer – for example, a discount retailer will adopt a layout which maximizes the use of space and ensures that as much product is available on the shop floor as possible.

Like most aspects of retailing, most companies adopt a standardized approach to store layout which is managed and controlled by a visual merchandising team at their head office. This ensures that the layout plans that are used within a retail chain are consistently applied and that a corporate store format is developed (Lea Greenwood, 1998).

There are four principle store layout formats. The first is the *grid layout*. The grid layout is used primarily by food retailers, as well as retailers that operate large-scale, warehouse-style formats, such as DIY and electrical goods retailers. The grid layout involves the organization of gondola fixtures on a row-after-row basis. Merchandise rows are separated by aisles which allow for customer movement. At the end of each gondola, where customers enter from one row to the next, the selling areas are usually classified as 'hot spots', where promotional lines are displayed. These are described as 'hot spots' by virtue of the fact that a large number of customers are exposed to these areas. Furthermore, because of the widespread adoption of 'hot spot' areas by retailers, it would appear that customers are conditioned to expect that the merchandise displayed in these areas will be of particular interest.

According to Varley (2001), the grid layout maximizes the use of space available and provides a logical organization of the various product categories on offer. In many cases, the grid layout tries to expose customers to as much merchandise as possible. Within food retailing, this is achieved by placing high-demand products, such as bread and milk, in the centre of the store, at the middle of the aisle. This technique seeks to manipulate the movement of customers throughout the store and ensures that they are exposed to as much of the store as possible.

This approach to store layout has some negative dimensions. For example, some customers can feel frustrated by the manipulation that the grid layout provides. Furthermore, this layout can also be criticized for being inflexible and a monotonous experience for shoppers.

An alternative approach to store layout is the *free-flow layout*. This layout is used within fashion stores and involves the presentation of merchandise fixtures on a more random basis. This approach enables the customers to move easily between fixtures and allows them to browse as they select merchandise. McGoldrick (2002) noted that, while this approach was more visually appealing, a free-flow layout allows for a less intensive use of space, is cost intensive and, if the merchandise is not presented in a co-ordinated manner, then the overall effect may be of confusion.

Boutique layouts are similar to the free-flow layout, but departments or sections are laid out to produce the feeling of a 'shop-in-a-shop'. This approach is often adopted by brands within department stores on the basis that it helps to promote a unified identity for the brand. For certain fashion brands sold under wholesale arrangements, the adoption of a boutique layout is a precondition to supply. This is because these fashion brands want to protect their distinctive identity and ensure that no other brand infringes on their business. While this layout approach allows for the targeting of specific groups of consumers and allows for a variety of different brand experiences for customers, it has to be acknowledged that it does not provide for an economical use of selling space.

The Swedish furniture retailer IKEA is famous for its adoption of the *controlled flow layout*. This involves the creation of a layout which tightly controls the movement of customers through the store by creating a one-way racetrack system from which the customer cannot deviate. This system seeks to expose as many customers to as much merchandise as possible. Like all layout forms which seek to rigidly control the movement of people, customers can feel frustrated by the lack of freedom of movement that this approach involves.

Whatever the store layout method that a retailer adopts, it is clear that all must ensure that a balance is struck between ensuring the optimum use of space with the need to provide flexibility and interest for customers.

Methods of in-store display

Many retailers allocate considerable amounts of resource to the display and presentation of their products. Indeed, retailers, such as the upmarket department store retailer, Harrods, have developed such a reputation for innovative displays that many customers are attracted to the store in order to view their latest displays. Window displays have been found to be a crucially important marketing communications device, and studies have found that the positive impact of a window display can serve as the primary reason as to why a customer chooses to enter a store for the first time (Lochhead and Moore, 1999).

Given the importance of window displays to the process of generating and communicating a brand identity, many retailers have decided to centralize the process of constructing, implementing and controlling window displays by investing the responsibility to the visual merchandising team based at head office. As a means of assuring the consistency of window display presentation, many retailers now opt to use large-scale photographs of their products, rather than the products themselves, in their store windows. An increasing number, however, now augment these photographs with actual products so as to avoid the impression of a display that is sterile, predictable and lacking in detail.

The display of merchandise takes two forms. Standard merchandise displays are used for the presentation of products en masse. Special merchandise displays are used to showcase specific products (that are perhaps either seasonal or are on promotion) within a discrete space within the store. The details of each form are presented below.

Standard merchandise displays

Every product that is offered for sale within a retail outlet is subject to some display principle. The method of display may be to use shelving or it may be in the form of a hanging fixture. In most cases, the organization of display would exhibit some form of internal logic, such as in terms of price, size, colour or use. The organizational logic that retailers use is usually based upon an understanding of how the customer actually selects the product. As such, an understanding of the customer's principle selection criteria is crucial. If the retailer has no clear idea of how the customer interacts with a product, then there is every possibility that the manner in which they organize their display may hinder, rather than assist, the product selection process.

For example, the fashion retailer Next presents its men's formal shirt range on the basis of the product's primary feature. For example, all long-sleeved shirts are presented separately from short-sleeved shirts and double-cuff shirts arranged separately from their single-cuff range. The company also distinguishes between shirts that are made from 100 per cent cotton and those that are made from mixed fibres. Within each grouping, the shirts are presented in size order, from the smallest to the largest in their range. The underlying principle behind Next's approach to product display is to make product selection and evaluation as easy for its customers as possible. By simplifying the display process, Next believes that it is providing an important and valued service to its customers.

Special merchandise displays

For merchandise that a retailer wants to highlight or promote in particular, there are a number of display options available. These are detailed below.

- *Event displays*. This is perhaps the most commonly used display format. Merchandise that has some connection to an event, holiday or festival is displayed together in order to maximize the impact of the range. Events may include Christmas, Easter, Valentine's Day or Mother's Day. Often located near to store entrances, the purpose of these displays is to showcase the range of merchandise that the retailer has to support the event. These displays are often used as a means of giving ideas and inspiration to customers.
- *Table-top displays*. These involve the presentation of merchandise on table tops with the aim of encouraging customers to interact with the product range and, in some cases, to select for purchase from the display. The Italian knitwear retailer, Benetton, has successfully pioneered this technique.
- *Hot spots*. These are displays of promotional merchandise presented in areas of high customer density. Often, the merchandise is 'blocked', one on top of the other, to give the impression of product availability and to ensure maximum promotional impact.
- *Lifestyle displays*. These sorts of displays utilize props that are associated with a particular lifestyle in order to create an association between the product range and a lifestyle image. The American fashion retailer, Ralph Lauren, uses lifestyle displays of artefacts typically associated with English country living so as to connect his

Polo brand with an English country lifestyle. Indeed, the Ralph Lauren flagship store in New York takes the lifestyle display to another level in that the store has the feel and aura of an English Gentleman's Club.

- *Brand displays*. These present the goods that are included in a brand range collectively in order to showcase to customers the breadth of the range. For example, in Debenhams department stores, the company presents edited displays from their Designers at Debenhams Range at the foot of escalators and at their stores' entrances.

Increasingly, retailers are recognizing the importance of effective visual merchandising as a means of generating differentiation within the market. Its importance is clearly evident in the observations made by the Managing Director of a major UK fashion chain:

> The reason for people shopping has changed in the past 10 years. It is not always just a chore but is for many an enjoyable leisure activity. For this reason, retailers need to invest in visual merchandising in order that the theatre and fun of retailing can be established. In the future, the visual dimensions will be as important as the products themselves.

Summary

This chapter reviewed the role of the merchandiser within retail organizations and found that the term may either refer to activities associated with the financial management and control of the buying function, or may refer to the management of the visual presentation of stock.

In terms of merchandising from a financial management perspective, the chapter noted that it is the responsibility of the merchandiser to manage the buying budget and ensure that the profitability of the buying function is maintained through the management of gross buying margin. Furthermore, the actions that the merchandiser may suggest in response to poor margin performance were also identified.

The principle of open to buy is important within the procurement process since it provides the buying team with the opportunity to commit to merchandise as late in the day as possible. In sectors such as fashion, this is especially important since it allows the buyer to respond to trends as they emerge in the market.

The chapter also considered the issues relevant to the management of space within retailing and reviewed the various strategies that retailers may adopt in order to allocate stock to stores. The drivers of space management were also identified, and consideration was also given to the relationship between a product's life cycle and the amount of space it is allocated in store.

The principles of category management were also introduced and the contribution of the merchandiser to the development of a category assortment was explained.

The chapter also reviewed the processes inherent to the management of the visual presentation of goods within retail outlets. Consideration was given to the relationship between visual merchandising and consumer behaviour, and it was noted that a sizeable proportion of consumer decisions are made within the store.

The key business objectives of visual merchandising were introduced, as were the principles relevant to store layout decisions. The chapter concluded by considering the most popular methods of managing displays within a retail setting.

Review questions

1 What actions might a merchandiser recommend in order that a retailer might better reach its gross margin targets?
2 Describe what is meant by 'open to buy'. Explain why retailers adopt this approach.
3 How does the life cycle of a product affect the amount of space that a product is allocated in store?
4 Outline the role that merchandisers may have in the process of category management development.
5 Identify how visual merchandising may assist retailers in the achievement of their key business objectives.
6 Detail the various options that retailers have when it comes to the selection of a layout for the store. Identify the factors that may influence their layout decision.
7 Describe the options that retailers have available to them for the display and promotion of their merchandise.

References

Borin, N. and Farris, P. (1995). A sensitivity analysis of retailer shelf management model. *Journal of Retailing*, **71**(2), 153–71.

Davidson, W. R., Sweeney, D. J. and Stampfl, R. W. (1988). *Retailing Management*. John Wiley, New York.

Davies, G. and Rands, J. (1992). The strategic use of space by retailers: a perspective from operations management. *International Journal of Logistics Management*, **3**(2), 63–76.

Engel, J. F., Blackwell, R. D. and Miniard, P. (1990). *Consumer Behaviour.* Dryden Press, Orlando.

Fernie, J. and Sparks, L. (eds) (1998). *Logistics and Retail Management.* Kogan Page, London.

Green, W. R. (1986). *The Retail Store: Design and Construction.* Van Nostrand, New York.

Harris, D. and Walters, D. (1992). *Retail Operations Management – A Strategic Approach.* Prentice-Hall, Hemel Hempstead.

Howard, J. A. and Sheth, J. N. (1969). *The Theory of Buyer Behaviour.* John Wiley, New York.

IGD (1997). *A Guide to Category Management.* Institute of Grocery Distribution, Watford.

Kim, Y. (2001). Experiential retailing. *Journal of Retailing and Consumer Services*, **8**(5), 287–9.

Knee, D. and Walters, D. (1985). *Strategy in Retailing.* Philip Allen, Oxford.

Kotler, P. (1973). Atmospherics as a marketing tool. *Journal of Retailing*, **49**(4), 48–64.

Lea Greenwood, G. (1998). Visual merchandising – a neglected area in UK retail fashion marketing. *International Journal of Retail and Distribution Management*, **26**(8), 324–9.

Lochhead, M. and Moore, C. M. (1999). A Christmas fit for a Princes' Square. In *European Cases in Retailing* (Dupuis, M. and Dawson, J., eds), pp. 247–56. Blackwell, Oxford.

McGoldrick, P. (2002). *Retail Marketing*, 2nd edn. McGraw-Hill, London.

Mintel (1999). Retail store design. *Retail Intelligence*, August, 1–112.

Nocosia, F. M. (1969). *Consumer Decision Process.* Prentice-Hall, New Jersey.

Pearson, R. (1993). Space management. *Progressive Grocer*, **72** (December), 31–2.

Pinnock, A. (1986). *D.P.P. IGD Unified D.P.P. Model.* ISBN 0907316 45X.

POPAI (1977). *The 1977 Supermarket Consumer Buying Habits Study.* POPAI, New York.

POPAI (1986). *The 1986 Supermarket Consumer Buying Habits Study.* POPAI, New York.

Risch, E. H. (1987). *Retail Merchandising.* Merrill, Columbus, OH.

Schimp, T. A. (1990). *Promotion Management and Marketing Communications.* Dryden Press, Orlando.

Sherry, J. F (1998). The soul of the company store. In *The Concept of Place in Contemporary Markets* (Sherry, J. F., ed.), pp. 109–46. NTC Business Books, Chicago.

Varley, R. (2001). *Retail Product Management – Buying and Merchandising*, 1st edn. Routledge, London.

Part 4

Managing the Future

12

The internationalization of retailing

Introduction

In the first chapter of this book, the world's largest retailers were listed and comparisons were made between the internationalization of the retail industry and other sectors. Many of the world's largest retailers are US in origin and several operate solely in their domestic market (Albertson, Kroger and Target). Consolidation in the retail industry is low compared with other sectors and the share of foreign to total assets is correspondingly low. This is indeed the case, but there has been considerable change in retail markets during the 1990s and the early part of the twenty-first century which will lead to further restructuring of global markets in the future. The catalyst for much of this change has been the rise of Wal-Mart as the world's dominant retailer. Its sales of $245 billion for the fiscal year to 31 January 2003 not only makes it over three times larger than Carrefour, its nearest retail competitor, but the world's largest company. Yet in the late 1990s, Wal-Mart's sales in international markets was around 9 per cent of total sales. By 2010, this figure is expected to rise to 25 per cent, which will add another $75 billion alone – this equates to Carrefour's total sales in 2002. This chapter will focus upon international operations of companies such as Wal-Mart; however, it is necessary to discuss other forms of internationalization and the conceptual framework within which retail internationalization (RI) research takes place.

Internationalization of concepts

The internationalization of 'know-how', concepts and formats was highlighted by Kacker (1998), who detailed the range of 'technologies' which could be transferred from one market to another. Early examples of copying operational practices and applying them to their domestic market are 'fact-finding' missions undertaken by Simon Marks in the 1920s to the US for Marks & Spencer and the early post-war forays by Alan Sainsbury which led to the introduction of US-style self-service supermarkets into Sainsbury's in the early 1950s. Such 'tours' continue to the present day, aided and abetted by the advances of modern technology, which allow managers to scour the globe for ideas to incorporate into their retail offer. This alerts us to one of the key differences between the internationalization of manufacturing and retailing innovations. Whilst you can patent a new product you cannot patent a retail format or operational procedure. First mover advantage is important in retailing, but new ideas will be copied and perfected so constant innovation is imperative to maintain competitive advantage.

This has become more evident with the internationalization of retail businesses. As the large retailers open more subsidiaries in new markets, best practice principles can be applied across the world. The transfer of people, merchandise and operational procedures can greatly benefit different parts of the chain. This dissemination of ideas also takes place in an informal way through meetings of trade associations hosting conferences on themes which affect 'national' retailers. The efficient consumer response (ECR) annual events discussed in Chapter 7 provide another good example where case studies of the application of ECR principles can equip retailers with the wherewithal to capitalize upon efficiency savings.

Most academic attention on the internationalization of concepts has focused upon the 'export' of retail formats into new markets, thereby linking this form of internationalization with retail operations strategy. Much of the transfer of such formats relates to the expansion of US companies seeking expansion opportunities because of saturation at home. For example, Costco's move into Latin America and Europe with its warehouse clubs and US developers' attempts at entering the European market with the factory outlet concept (McArthur Glen, Value Retail, Prime). Conversely, the hypermarket concept developed in France and championed by Carrefour was successful in Latin America and Asia but failed in the US, where the format was not innovative enough to take trade away from the existing competition (Dupuis and Prime, 1996). Since the 1980s, however, Wal-Mart experimented with a super hypermarket concept which was eventually rolled out as supercentres in the 1990s. This enabled Wal-Mart to bolt-on a food offering to their traditional discount department stores. The company's expansion into Europe and Asia is enhanced by this move in that acquisition targets tend to be hypermarket operators rather than discount department stores, such as Woolco in Canada.

Sourcing of products and services

The first step to internationalization for many retailers is often through their buying decisions. Large clothing firms have been sourcing products 'offshore' for some time, securing the benefits of low-cost manufacturing in countries of the Pacific Rim, Eastern Europe and North Africa. Marks & Spencer, renowned for its 'Buy British' sources, succumbed to the pressure of high costs and increased competition by switching to lower cost markets in the late 1990s. It was shown in Chapter 7 how The Limited, which has its store operations entirely within the US, revolutionized the US apparel market through the flying of stock from its Hong Kong supply base to its warehouse in Columbus for onward distribution to its stores. This reduction in time to market through co-ordinated supply chain management enables buyers to source the globe for ideas, designs and products.

This is not confined to fashion markets. Food retailers, especially the 'big box' companies which are forming a super league of global players, are introducing new 'ethnic' products in the continents throughout the world. The global consumer is acquiring global tastes as travel and media exposure places increasing demands on the retailer to provide a cosmopolitan retail offer.

In order to enhance their buying power, companies have joined buying alliances and web exchanges to foster co-ordination in international sourcing. In the grocery sector, initial alliances were dominated in Europe by voluntary trading groups and consumer co-operatives, but by the late 1980s multiple retail groups became affiliated to particular alliances to co-ordinate marketing and logistics activities.

The retail industry has followed in the footsteps of other sectors in utilizing a range of 'international' services. As companies play on the international stage, they draw upon an international labour pool, the world's financial markets and the services of professional service providers (logistics, IT, accountancy and legal, for example). Just as the soccer associations in England and Scotland looked to a 'foreigner' to lead them to better times, Marks & Spencer and Safeway turned to a Belgian and an Argentine respectively to turn around their ailing businesses.

Internationalization of store development

The academic literature on retail internationalization (RI) tends to focus on retail operations as evidenced by the key themes promulgated in textbooks by Alexander (1997) and Sternquist (1998). See also the *International Marketing Review* (2000, nos 4/5). The starting point for research in this area was Stan Hollander's seminal work, *Multinational Retailing*, published in 1970. Hollander charted the international flows of retail investment up until this time, indicating that Sears Roebuck, FW Woolworth and other famous names of their time did have international aspirations going back to early in the twentieth century. Hollander's work has therefore provided a benchmark for later research into RI when the scale of investment increased in the last decades of the century.

Much of the research into RI focuses upon four main themes:

- Motives for internationalization.
- Direction of growth.
- Method of market entry.
- Degree of adaption to new markets.

Motives for internationalization

McGoldrick (1995) provides a framework within which decisions to internationalize are taken. The classic push–pull factors are at either end of the spectrum – with inhibitors and facilitators influencing the nature of the strategic decision (Figure 12.1). In the earlier section on the internationalization of retail concepts, the spread of warehouse clubs and factory outlet centres to new markets can be attributed to saturation (a push factor) in the domestic US market and the attraction of the UK for political and cultural reasons (pull factor). The history of early internationalization in the post-Hollander era is marked by push factors and often a reactive approach to internationalization. It is not surprising that European retailers dominate the literature on RI in that their small domestic markets (Ahold, Delhaize) or tight regulations constraining format development (Carrefour) have forced them to seek growth opportunities in international markets.

The so-called proactive retailers who have embraced internationalization and have been 'pulled' towards new markets were invariably the subjects of case histories. These companies had a differentiated retail offer, a strong brand image and were either category killers (Toys 'R' Us, IKEA) or specialist clothing retailers (The Gap, Benetton, high fashion

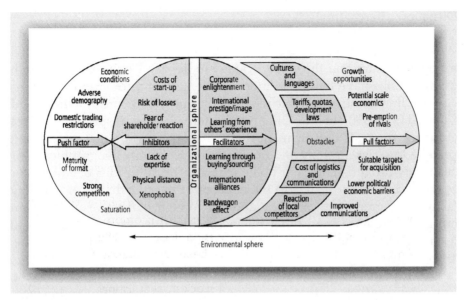

Figure 12.1 Driving forces of internationalization. *Source*: McGoldrick (1995).

houses such as Armani and Donna Karan). Despite all of the time and effort deployed by academics in studying these companies, the impact of specialist retailers in terms of international sales is minimal. Until recently, supermarket chains and department store operators were viewed as reactive to RI; food products, in particular, were deemed to be 'culturally' grounded.

These arguments are now beginning to look rather hollow. The facilitators listed in Figure 12.1 are encouraging consolidation in the food/mass merchandise sector. The creation of major political trading blocks in America, Europe and Asia has opened new markets and removed prohibitive regulation in the movement of goods and people across national boundaries. Consumers, whilst retaining local tastes, are becoming more geocentric in experimenting with 'international' products, especially from the country of origin of the foreign retailer. Europe provides a potential battleground for international development. The adoption of a common currency and an enlarged 'Greater Europe' of over 500 million people by 2010 offer market attractions for international retailers. It is the 'powerhouse' retailers with their large-scale formats – hypermarkets, discount warehouses – which will dominate the international scene in the future. Wal-Mart is beginning to transform the food/general merchandise sector. How long before Home Depot follows the Wal-Mart route and creates global consolidation in the DIY market?

Direction of growth

With the motivations for RI clear, retailers then have to decide which markets to enter and the entry strategy to deploy. Commercial research organizations have tended to monitor the flow of international activity, superseding earlier academic research by Burt (1993) and Robinson and Clarke-Hill (1990) in the UK and Western Europe respectively. Most evidence suggests that firms in the early stages of internationalization prefer a low-risk strategy and favour markets that are geographically or culturally proximate to their home market. The latter idea of cultural or business proximity relates to the concept of psychic distance, whereby 'a firm's degree of uncertainty about a foreign market resulting from cultural differences and other business difficulties presents barriers to learning about the market and operating there' (O'Grady and Lane, 1996, p. 330).

This explains why US retailers target the UK as a bridgehead to the European market in that a common language and similar business practices are deemed 'culturally proximate' in terms of country selection. Indeed, 31 per cent of all foreign retailers entering the UK originated from the USA (Davies and Finney, 1998).

The pattern of international investment shows that early internationalization is to near neighbours in order that the venture can be more easily managed and controlled. Hence, retailers from:

- the UK favour Ireland and, to a lesser extent, the Netherlands and France;
- France target Spain;
- Germany target Austria;
- Japan target Hong Kong and Singapore;
- Australia target New Zealand;
- the USA target Canada and Mexico.

As retailers gain experience (sometimes negative experience), they reshape their international strategies. But with the development of NAFTA, EU and ASEAN markets, the main players are represented in two or more of these major trading blocs, thereby seeking opportunities for growth as and when they arise.

Method of market entry

The literature on entry strategies in retailing mirrors that of the research undertaken on manufacturing concerns. The main difference is one of scale and investment required for international expansion. The step-by-step approach in manufacturing goes from the low-cost, low-risk exporting of goods through licensing to foreign direct investment (FDI). International management gurus such as Ohmae and Porter have then discussed the type of management structure which evolves beyond the FDI stage to create a support function in key world markets.

Retailers also evaluate low-risk to high-risk stages in their entry strategies. Initial low-investment strategies to glean better knowledge of the market can occur through minority shareholdings or franchise agreements. In the case of minority shareholdings, several of the buying alliances in Europe involve cross-shareholdings of 'partners', which open the door for greater collaboration or even merger activity in the future. When Sainsbury first ventured into the US in 1987, it took a 40 per cent share of Shaws and only took full control of it a decade later. Tesco's foray into the US in 2001, with its shareholding in the Safeway (US) Internet project, also gives the company experience of the American market to assess its options for further investment. In March 2002, Wal-Mart secured a 6.1 per cent stake in Seiju, the fourth largest supermarket group in Japan, with an option to raise the stake to 66.7 per cent. This will allow Wal-Mart to study the notoriously difficult Japanese market before committing further investment.

Franchising has been a popular method of market entry for companies in domestic as well as international markets. Akin to licensing in manufacturing, the advantages of franchising are the speed of market entry, the availability of local management knowledge and expertise, and the low costs of entry, as costs are borne by the franchisee. The problem with franchising is the policing of the franchise network. It is important that franchisees conform to the strict rules laid down by the franchiser in terms of merchandising, brand image and store design. Franchising is particularly popular with niche retailers with a strong brand image. Body Shop, for example, has over 13 000 franchise outlets in around 50 countries. Benetton, with 5500 shops in 120 countries, sells and distributes its products through agents who develop a given market area. These agents then set up a franchise agreement with the owners of stores who sell Benetton products. It is interesting to note, however, that Benetton is building 100 megastores throughout the world. These large 7500 square metre units will house the full Benetton range *and* will be managed in-house to monitor the success of this new venture.

Box 12.1 and Figure 12.2 illustrate the market development and entry strategies of fashion design houses. In the context of this discussion on franchising, fashion design houses use this method of market entry in stage 4 in their market expansion (Figure 12.2). These design houses, such as Versace, Nicole Fahri, Donna Karan, Calvin Klein and Christian

---

Box 12.1   Market entry strategies of fashion design retailers

Figure 12.2 shows the four stages of international market development adopted by fashion design houses. In stage 1, wholesaling plays a key role in establishing the brand at low cost. Limited couture and ready-to-wear (RTW) collections were distributed to elite department stores (Harrods, Saks Fifth Avenue) and, once established, made available to other provincial department stores and bespoke independent fashion retailers. Stage 2 involves the opening of flagship stores within capital cities, typically in premium shopping streets (Bond Street, London; Fifth Avenue, New York; Rue Saint Honaire, Paris). These stores, because of the high rental and operating costs, tend to be 'loss leaders' that promote the brand for stage 3, which is the promotion of diffusion lines. The diffusion brand is aimed at the middle market and has been the catalyst for designer retailers' growth in international markets. This is why so many of these famous family companies have achieved stock market listings in the 1990s – they needed the capital to fund wholesaling and franchising agreements and to open new company-owned stores in international markets. The fourth and final stage of expansion is the development of diffusion stores throughout countries, spreading out from the capital cities to provincial cities. Agreements are often made to allow a franchisee to operate a chain of fashion designer stores on behalf of the brand owner, for example Calvin Klein's plan to allow CK diffusion stores to be opened under a franchise agreement.

Lacroix, have developed chains of diffusion stores within the major cities of Europe, America and Asia. While the flagship stores highlight their ready-to-wear collections and generally are owned and controlled by the design house, the diffusion stores can be operated under a franchise agreement to avoid the high start-up costs and risks associated with managing a national chain of stores. Moore et al. (2000, p. 932) quote a foreign operations director for an American diffusion brand who states that:

> We, like most fashion designers, are relatively small and our resources are finite, so it is a division of labour. Our partners run the diffusion chains and we supply the product and, most important of all, create the brand image through our advertising which has a high cost in terms of time and money.

The example of fashion design retailing shows a complex web of relationships in entering new markets from wholesaling through

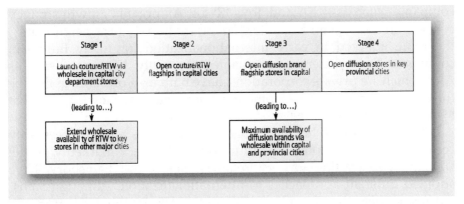

Figure 12.2 **The four stages of fashion designer foreign market development.** *Source*: Moore et al. (2000).

franchising to operating company-owned stores. The foreign direct investment (FDI) decision poses a further set of options for the international retailer. Do you grow organically or do you acquire a going concern? Do you operate a wholly owned subsidiary or do you partner with a host company in the target market and form a joint venture? In many markets there is no option. In China and India, for example, the government will insist that a joint venture is the only route to entering their markets.

Much of the evidence from the international marketing/management literature indicates that approaches to FDI differ according to 'country culture'. US and UK companies, for example, prefer an acquisition strategy that gives them speed of entry to a new market, the purchasing of a going concern, albeit the possible problems of integrating the management culture of the target company with the predator. This strategy is underpinned by a corporate culture which demands quick results to appease institutional investors who are short term in their stock market perspective. Japanese and German companies, in contrast, prefer the organic growth strategy and are willing to build up market penetration in new markets over a long time period through developing their own sites. This again is related to country culture, with Japanese institutions looking for long-term returns even at the expense of short-term losses.

In retailing there is some evidence to support this hypothesis, in particular in mass merchandise or 'big box' retailing. In order to achieve market growth, Wal-Mart and Tesco have adopted an acquisition strategy to move into new markets during the last 10 years. In the case of niche retailers, however, an organic growth strategy is more prevalent for companies such as Gap, Body Shop and the category killer companies such as IKEA and Toys 'R' Us. An organic growth strategy is also pursued when companies 'boundary hop' to near neighbours – the route adopted in early internationalization for many European companies. Several German companies, especially discounters such as Aldi, which are private corporations, have built up a presence in Europe through the gradual development of new sites, acknowledging that losses will be made in the short run.

It should be noted, however, that such strategies are not necessarily country specific, as company cultures can also vary markedly. In the UK, the two leading grocery retailers, Tesco and Sainsbury, have adopted different approaches to internationalization. Although Sainsbury was first to internationalize in the US in the late 1980s, its minority shareholding typified its cautious approach. In order to increase its market penetration in Scotland, Tesco bought the Wm Low chain in 1994 and then moved to Ireland with the purchase of Power Supermarkets in 1997. Sainsbury has preferred an organic growth strategy, building its presence in Scotland and Northern Ireland with the incremental development of new sites. Now, a large part of Tesco's capital investment programme (over 40 per cent) is in overseas markets, especially in Eastern Europe and Asia. Meanwhile, institutional investors have questioned Sainsbury's continued presence in overseas markets when it has been losing market share to Tesco in the UK. Its withdrawal from the Egyptian market in 2001 is indicative of its renewed focus on the domestic market. While most academic research has investigated the motivations and entry strategies of international retailers, Alexander and Quinn (2002) have explored the divestment and strategic withdrawal strategies of retailers from international markets, using Marks & Spencer and Arcadia as case studies. Marks & Spencer illustrate the 'hype' associated with some of the research into retail internationalization. In 1998, Davies and Finney based a chapter on internationalization, in a contribution edited by one of the authors of this textbook, strongly on Marks & Spencer, which was championed as a retail leader within the UK on internationalization. The company was in 33 countries and 'no other company anywhere has this diversity of international expression' (p. 138), a reference to the numerous entry strategies deployed by the company. The strong performance in the UK had in many ways concealed the poor trading performance of the international division. When Marks & Spencer began to experience serious problems in the late 1990s with strong competition in its home market, it was no surprise that a planned withdrawal from international markets ensued, with the closure of its stores in North America and Europe leaving a rump of mainly franchised operations from the Marks & Spencer empire (see Box 12.2).

Box 12.2   The rise and fall of Marks & Spencer's international aspirations

Marks & Spencer's initial foray into international markets was the exporting of its unique private label brand, St Michael. The expatriate and military (NAAFI) markets were the main focus of this business and its success in exporting to around 50 countries earned it the Queen's Award for Export on five occasions. This business was eventually to lead to franchise agreements which were to become a key element of M&S' international strategy.

Its first store-based international entry was in Canada in 1972 with a 50 per cent shareholding in three clothing chains. Although it took full ownership of these chains in the late 1970s, the Canadian operation never made a profit and M&S cut back store numbers in the 1990s, finally closing the business in 1999. The successful UK format of clothing and food was not popular in Canada and adjustments to the merchandising mix could not save the operation.

M&S also entered the Continental Europe market in the 1970s with its first store in Paris in 1975, and then developing company-owned stores in Belgium and Ireland with a further wave of activity in the 1990s in Spain, the Netherlands and Germany. It was in the late 1980s and early 1990s that M&S undertook expansion into the USA and South-East Asia, with the acquisition of the Brooks Brothers menswear chain and King Supermarkets in the US and the opening of company-owned stores in Hong Kong from 1988.

Franchising was a key element of the company's strategy, utilizing master franchises throughout the world. With the exception of Hong Kong, this was a favoured strategy for 'peripheral' markets in Europe so that, in 1999, M&S had 54 franchise stores across 12 European countries. This method of marketing was also used in the East Asian market and was to produce greater profit than the Brooks Brothers chain of company-owned stores.

As late as 1997, the company announced an ambitious expansion plan which included further growth in its international operations to make M&S a global retailer. But its plans were poorly received in the City and market factors began to work against the company. The Asian crisis led to problems with the Hong Kong business and other Far East franchises. The German market was proving problematic with the higher price points of M&S products and the difficulties of accepting the M&S brand (a feature also evident in Spain). With increased competition at home in both its core clothing and food markets, M&S began to scale back its operations in the Far East and Europe. By 2000, international activities represented 25 per cent of the company's retail floorspace, 17.2 per cent of its retail turnover but less than 1.25 per cent of its pre-tax profits. It is interesting to note that in its most profitable year (1997) pre-tax profits were only 8.3 per cent of the total.

The announcement in March 2001 that the company was selling its USA businesses and closing most of its European stores (except Ireland) came as no surprise in the light of its plummeting share price and falling profits from 1997 to 2000. It was also turning its Hong Kong stores into a franchise operation, thereby turning the clock back 30 years to where M&S' international operations had begun.

The obituaries are being written, including a journalistic contribution (Bevan, 2001). It is clear that management wanted M&S to be a global player but the strategy was ad hoc, with little synergy between acquired businesses and a mistaken belief that the St Michael brand could be transferred to international markets with similar success to that in the UK.

Sources: after Alexander and Quinn (2002); Burt et al. (2002).

Degree of adaptation to new markets

The general international management literature has used Levitt's ideas on globalization of markets, published in the *Harvard Business Review* in 1983, as the benchmark for the standardization versus customization debate when companies take their products into international markets. Levitt argued that consumers have the same needs and aspirations around the world and companies should recognize this in their product and service offerings. This view is supported by specific sectors of service businesses – hotel chains, credit card companies and car rental operators – in addition to well-known global brands such as Coca-Cola and McDonald's. Nevertheless, these companies have had to adapt their product to specific markets and the communications message has to be conveyed in different ways in new markets. In fast-moving consumer goods (FMCG) markets, adaptation for specific country markets has been deemed necessary because of the 'culturally grounded' nature of tastes. But is this necessarily the case? In Japan, Carrefour entered the market as a low-cost operator trying to appeal to Japanese tastes when the consumer wanted to buy French goods and enjoy a French shopping experience. In retailing the degree of adaptation to specific markets is largely driven by the image of the store brand and whether values associated with the brand can be transferred across international boundaries. In our earlier example of fashion design houses, the spreading of these brands to a global market has been highly successful. To reinforce the Levitt approach to global markets, communication strategies ensure global advertising campaigns promote a standard brand image across markets.

While fashion houses may be unique in their approach, category specialists and brand differentiated niche players also exhibit a high degree of standardization in their retail offer. The brand image, store name and well-tried format is much the same for IKEA, Toys 'R' Us, Body Shop, The Gap and Benetton in the markets in which they are represented. Some degree of adaptation is necessary in the range, but this could be due to physical constraints on site acquisition or the need to adapt colours/sizes for different markets. Benetton, for example, offers the same range of products in all markets, but until 2001 allowed 20 per cent of its ranges to be customized to meet the needs of specific country markets (smaller sizes for Far East countries, different colour ranges for the Middle East). In order to communicate one image throughout the world, Benetton has streamlined its brands so that all garments are sold under the United Colours of Benetton and Sisley brands, and customization has been reduced to between 5 and 10 per cent for different markets.

For the mass merchandisers and hypermarket operators, approaches differ according to the scale of operation and management style of companies. The larger 'big box' operators which focus on fewer, large-scale formats – hypermarkets and warehouse clubs – have tried to create a global brand identity. Wal-Mart has four large-scale formats, three of which have an international dimension. These are the Wal-Mart Discount Department Stores, Supercenters and SAMs Clubs. In view of the scale of Wal-Mart's operations, it clearly has a desire to be the McDonald's of retailing. Carrefour and Tesco have also adopted large-scale formats and a global brand approach to internationalization. Conversely, Ahold and J Sainsbury, which operate smaller retail formats, have retained the local brand names of companies which they have acquired. In the USA, both companies dominate grocery retailing in the North-East USA, with Giant, Stop & Shop, Bi-Lo, Tops, Finast and Edwards owned by Ahold, and Shaws and Star Markets by J Sainsbury.

Towards a conceptual framework

As RI gathered pace in the 1980s and 1990s, academics provided conceptual frameworks within which to base their empirical research. Much of the early work drew upon research from the manufacturing sector, most notably Dunning's (1998) eclectic paradigm. This model shows that the nature of international expansion is a function of a series of advantages: *ownership specific*, where the product (retail offer) gives competitive advantage; *location specific*, where the host country can yield cost or market opportunities (Eastern Europe, Asia); or *internalization*, where management innovation or other corporate advantages can lead to success. This borrowing of concepts has led to criticisms that the internationalization of retailing differs fundamentally from that of manufacturing. This is true in terms of the scale of capital flows and the degree of complexity in an FMCG environment compared with the industrial sector; however, methods of entry and values associated with an international brand are comparable. Early models discussed stages of international expansion, which mirrors much of the literature in international marketing textbooks on entry strategies. Furthermore, authors such as Treadgold (1989, 1990) and Salmon and Tordjman (1989) provided taxonomies of retail international development strategies which 'borrow' from the initial work of Levitt on globalization of markets.

The problem with most of these models is that they were derived at a time when RI was small scale in terms of global impact. The retail internationalists of the time were niche players, mainly clothing chains with strong franchise agreements. The 1990s and the early part of the twenty-first century have witnessed true internationalization so many of these initial works, although valuable then, tend to discuss early internationalization. In the late 1990s, two US works have made a more relevant contribution to our knowledge of this complex subject. Sternquist (1997) produced her strategic international retail expansion (SIRE) model to explain the international expansion of US retailers (Figure 12.3). Her model integrates the eclectic paradigm (left side of the diagram), stages theory and the global versus multinational strategy literature. She observed that multinational retailers' expansion is slower than global retailers, that they adapt rather than standardize, and that they concentrate their expansion within a geographical area before moving to a new country or region. The other model is by Vida and Fairhurst (1998), and it draws on behavioural work in international marketing. They acknowledge that RI is a complex issue but the internal driving forces behind internationalization are the firm's ownership advantages and management perceptions of specific markets, i.e. knowledge, experience and attitudes towards markets. Clearly, as managers move up the learning curve through experience of international markets, they become more ambitious and less cautious than their first move into a new market. Their model considered *antecedents*, which encapsulate the environment within which a decision is taken, the *process* whereby expansion or withdrawal is decided and the *outcomes*, which considered the strategic options on entry method and selection of market.

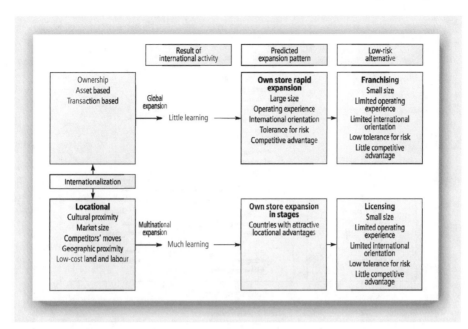

Figure 12.3 Model of strategic international retail expansion (SIRE). *Source:* Stern-quist (1997).

In more recent work, Alexander and Myers (2000) have integrated previous research into a framework which encapsulates the internationalization process from the corporate perspective. In Figure 12.4, they illustrate the drivers of change in the market of origin. Here the retailer has asset-based advantages (Dunning) through innovation of format and retail brand. Its ability to internationalize these assets will largely be determined by the internal facilitating competencies within the retail organization (Vida and Fairhurst). On the basis of the internal competencies, strategic decisions will be taken on market selection, entry method and the approach to be adopted in an international retailing strategy. As the retailer gains experience within the international environment, the internal facilitating competencies are upgraded to accommodate the lessons learnt from its operations in new geographical markets.

In Figure 12.5, Alexander and Myers (2000) have produced a 2 × 2 matrix in an attempt to explain international retail strategies. They use the extension of the retail concept along the *x*-axis and the firm's perspective on internationalization on the *y*-axis. They measure the latter in terms of a company's ethnocentricity or geocentricity. An enthnocentric approach is one whereby the retailer adapts a domestic orientation to its international strategy. The geocentric approach is to adopt a one-market view of the world where like-minded consumers

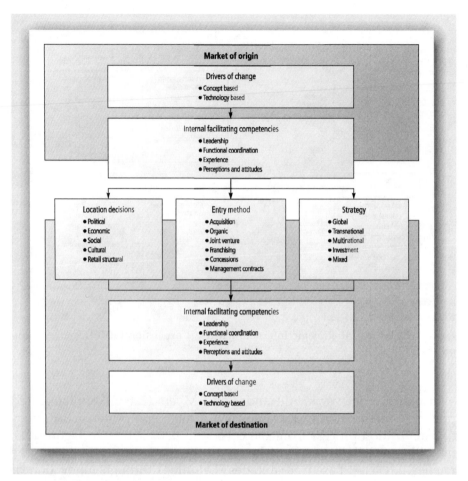

Figure 12.4 Operational organization. *Source:* **Alexander and Myers (2000).**

will demand the retail offer with limited adaptation in specific markets. In Figure 12.5, they classify the proximal retailer as one which provides a similar retail offer to customers in adjacent countries – the boundary hopping which typified much of the early internationalization strategies of retailers. This would equate with the domestic market extension concept applied to manufacturing companies.

The other quadrants in the matrix are much more controversial in terms of a typology of strategies. They argue that the multinational retailer has considerable global reach but remains psychologically rooted within the competitive market of the domestic market, whereas the global retailer may embrace change rather than replicate an existing formula. The difference between a transnational and a global retailer is the scale of operations, in that a transnational only operates in a limited number of markets. On the basis of this taxonomy, they classify Ahold

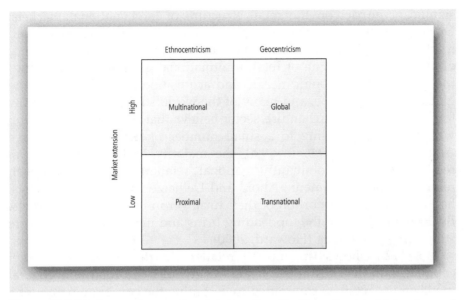

Figure 12.5 Market and operational internationalization. *Source*: Alexander and Myers (2000).

as a global retailer, Wal-Mart and The Gap as multinationals, and Zara as a transnational. Burt (2002), in a more recent contribution, acknowledges problems with taxonomies of this nature; however, he classifies global retailers as high fashion retailers and specialist chains and multinational retailers as grocery chains such as Ahold which adapt their strategy to individual country markets. Much of the confusion about these taxonomies is due to their relative simplicity. In the matrix in Figure 12.5, a 2 × 2 grid is shown. In the marketing literature a broader definition of a firm's view on internationalization would be given. For example, a polycentric approach would equate with a multinational approach. Here, a company recognizes that country markets are very different and that market success requires a more 'hands-off' approach by the corporate parent to allow local management to develop the retail offer accordingly.

The reshaping of the global retail market

Retail internationalization is a relatively recent topic of interest for researchers and much of the work presented here, including the development of conceptual models, has tended to discuss the international strategies of companies of modest size. IKEA, Toys 'R' Us and Benetton are truly global companies, but they are not going to have any significant impact on the retail structure of large national markets. During the 1990s and the early part of the twenty-first century, retail markets throughout the world have been transformed by the emergence of an elite super league of retail multinational groups. The growth of these companies through merger and acquisition has transformed the global retail landscape, and many of the world's largest retailers in the food and general merchandise sector believe that further consolidation will take place, leading to a small number of mega-groupings (see Aggarwal et al., 2000). In 1990, the majority of US and European retailers were predominantly national retailers. Of the European retailers, only Tengelmann, Ahold and Delhaize, all with US interests, had a significant proportion of their turnover in international markets. By 2000, only two of the top leading firms and nine of the top 50 were still domestic retailers (Howard, 2000).

Table 12.1 shows the top 10 retailers in the world by market capitalization in 2002. Four of these companies are food and general merchandise retailers committed to becoming the corporate parent of a large mega-group. It can be argued that the rise of Wal-Mart to be the world's largest company, and its international aspirations, has been the key driver for consolidation in the markets of the US, Latin America, Europe and Asia. It is therefore necessary to glean an overview of Wal-Mart's international aspirations in order to assess the response from competitors such as Carrefour, Ahold and Tesco.

When Sam Walton opened his first Wal-Mart Discount City store in 1962, he did not realize that his company would become the largest in the world 40 years later. The rise has been meteoric (see Figure 12.6). Yet most of this growth was achieved in its large domestic market as it

Table 12.1 Top 10 world retailers ranked by market capitalization, February 2002

Rank	Firm	Market cap. ($ billion)
1	Wal-Mart	268.9
2	Home Depot	121.6
3	Target	40.9
4	Walgreen	39.6
5	Lowe's	36.1
6	Carrefour	32.0
7	Tesco	24.1
8	Ahold	23.1
9	Kohl's	23.0
10	Safeway (US)	21.6

Source: Wrigley (2002b).

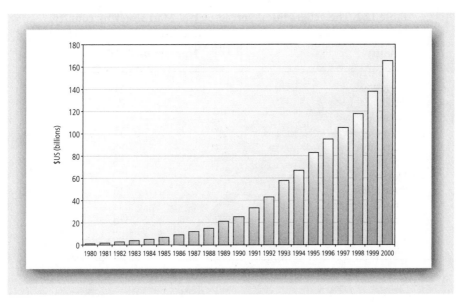

Figure 12.6 Wal-Mart net sales, 1980–2000. *Source*: **Wal-Mart 2000 Annual Report.**

rolled out four key formats: Discount Department Stores, SAMs Clubs, Supercenters and its most recent format, Neighborhood Markets. Its initial moves into the international market were to its near neighbours (confirming the proximate principle), Mexico in 1991 and Canada in 1994, before entering the higher-risk, more distant markets in Asia and Latin America. Even though it entered Europe through two small acquisitions in Germany in 1997/1998 and the UK through the purchase of ASDA, international sales only accounted for 9 per cent of the group's total turnover in 1999. Table 12.2 shows the spread of Wal-Mart stores prior to its entry into the Japanese market in early 2002.

As can be seen in Figure 12.7, however, Wal-Mart's forecasted sales for 2010 are estimated to approach $700 million and international expansion is a major element of this growth strategy. To envisage the sheer scale of this growth, if international sales were to grow from the 2001 figure of 17 per cent to 27 per cent of total sales by 2010, the international division would account for the equivalent to all of Wal-Mart's sales in 2001! Former CEO of Wal-Mart Stores, Randy Mott, spoke of the large number of countries on Wal-Mart's shopping list in 2000. These included Poland, France, South Africa, Turkey, Thailand, Chile, Venezuela, Malaysia, Hungary, the Czech Republic, Spain, Italy, Australia and Japan. To date, only Japan has been added to the list of countries in Table 12.2.

The strength of Wal-Mart is largely based on its strong retail proposition. It is a discount operation with wide assortments and good

Table 12.2 The geographical spread of Wal-Mart stores by country

Country	Number of Wal-Mart stores
Argentina	11
Brazil	20
Canada	174
China	11
Germany	95
Korea	6
Mexico	499
Puerto Rico	15
United Kingdom	241
United States	3118
Total Wal-Mart stores	4190

Source: Wal-Mart Stores, Inc., press release, 20 February 2001.

customer service and community support. It is a huge operation with a small-town focus which goes back to its roots in small-town America. Its every day low pricing (EDLP) strategy can be achieved through the economies of scale in its buying, its innovative Retail Link information system and its high inventory turnover because of efficient logistics.

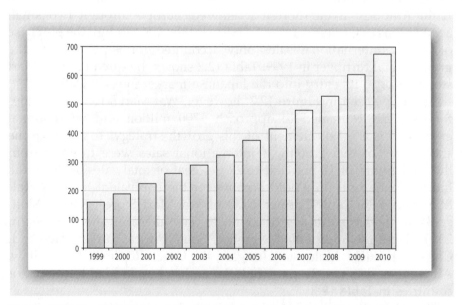

Figure 12.7 Future Wal-Mart sales. *Sources*: **Lehman Bros. and** *Discount Store News* **estimates.**

Moreover, Wal-Mart has a unique organizational culture embodied in the spirit of its founder, Sam Walton. Employees are known as 'associates' who are empowered to be innovative and to try out their own ideas. Team spirit is engendered amongst associates with the 'morning cheer' and the motivation to win in the marketplace. To maintain community spirit and good customer relations, Wal-Mart contributes to local causes, has a 'greeter' to welcome customers to the store and operates an aggressive hospitality '3-metre' rule, i.e. if a customer comes within 3 metres an associate is obligated to help.

Wal-Mart's successful formula propelled it to become the leading retailer in the US, and its acquisition of Woolco in Canada also led the company to achieve market share gains with the demise of once famous names, such as Eatons. Steve Arnold and colleagues have written extensively about the impact of Wal-Mart when it enters new markets in North America. He has argued that Wal-Mart has a 'market spoiler' effect upon the markets which it enters – that is, it changes store choice attributes towards its own positioning and low price emphasis. The evidence from empirical research suggests that it is difficult, if not impossible, to compete with Wal-Mart on price, head to head, so differentiation and adaptation to the new entrant is necessary. For details of such research studies, see Steve Arnold's special issue on this theme in the *International Journal of Retail and Distribution Management* in 2000, nos 4/5.

Although it has internationalized relatively late, Wal-Mart's presence or intended presence in new markets has reshaped the nature of global competition. Wal-Mart's international strategy has been strongly influenced by forming partnerships or acquiring companies that can be moulded to the 'Wal-Mart way' of doing business. For example, its move into Brazil was built upon a long-lasting personal relationship between Sam Walton and Jorge Lemann, one of the founders of the Garantia group, a major shareholder of Lojas Americanas. The relationship allowed for the cross-fertilization of ideas and Lojas Americanas executives visited the US to acquire ideas on how to develop the Brazilian business. Thus, when Wal-Mart entered Brazil in 1993 it was through a joint venture with Lojas Americanas. The development of supercentres and the introduction of SAMs Clubs had a major impact upon the structure of the retail market in Brazil. Throughout the 1990s, acquisitions changed the nature of the industry, as small and medium-sized chains were acquired and Ahold and Casino acquired shareholdings of leading groups to challenge Carrefour, the well-established market leader, and Wal-Mart Brazil.

Similar parallels can be drawn with Wal-Mart's entry into the UK market. The enlightened leadership of Archie Norman and Allan Leighton in turning around ASDA's fortunes in the 1990s has often been attributed to the borrowing of management ideas from Bentonville, headquarters of Wal-Mart. It was therefore no surprise when Wal-Mart acquired ASDA in June 1999 because of its large store portfolio, a similar retail offer and its Waltonian style of management. Although ASDA remains in third place behind Tesco and Sainsbury in the UK market, Wal-Mart is implementing changes which is causing a major shake-up of the British retail market. EDLP is a major focus of the strategy by using price as a 'market spoiler' in changing consumers' store choice variables away from convenience, quality and assortments. The rolling out of 20 supercentres and the utilization of superior Wal-Mart IT systems is allowing greater space utilization and the introduction of more non-food lines.

The impact upon other retailers in the UK market has been profound and illustrates how the global marketplace is changing. Only Tesco, another player in the super league, has competed head to head with ASDA on price. The other supermarket groups and non-food operators, which are likely to be affected by ASDA's change in product mix, have reorientated their strategies. Of relevance here is the competition's rethinking of their international strategies. The increased competition at home has resulted in Sainsbury's divesting in non-core businesses, including withdrawal from the Egyptian market, Boots concentrating on added value health care services and withdrawing from several overseas markets, and Marks & Spencer's strategic withdrawal from nearly all of its international markets (see Box 12.2). Only Kingfisher, which is undergoing a series of demergers, has major international aspirations with its B&Q format, although it could be a takeover target for Home Depot if the US giant wishes to enter the European market. What this shows us is that entry by Wal-Mart and other global companies is flushing out the companies who will continue to share global aspirations and those who clearly see their role as national champions. M&S, for example, has changed direction in the last 5 years to aspire to the latter role.

Before moving away from the UK scene, it is worth noting that the Walmartian culture has definitely borne results for ASDA. The *Sunday Times* produced a list of the top companies to work for in the UK. In 2001, ASDA was ranked fifth; in 2002, it was deemed to be the best, a testimony to a company which has retained a happy, motivated workforce in a period of extensive change.

Although Wal-Mart has achieved considerable success in the UK, the situation in the rest of Europe is problematic. Analysts have commented that, to be a truly global retailer, a company needs to have credible scale in Europe, which means a leading position in at least two of the three largest markets: Germany, France and the UK. Yet none of the main supergroups have a major presence in these key

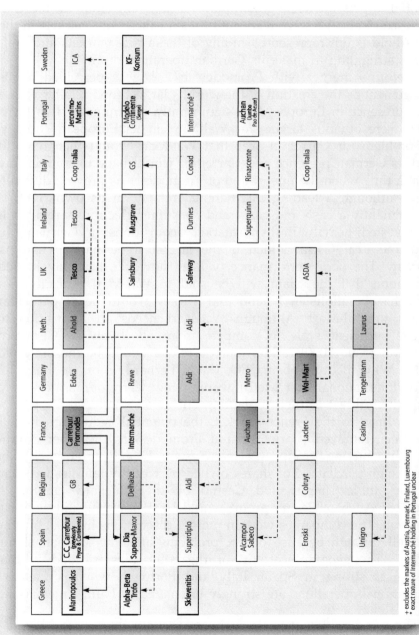

Figure 12.8 The structure of the EU food retail market and the interlinkages between firms in that market in mid-2001. *Source:* **Wrigley (2002a).**

+ excludes the markets of Austria, Denmark, Finland, Luxembourg
* exact nature of Intermarché holding in Portugal unclear

markets; indeed, the linkages that do exist involve a presence in the more peripheral, but growing, markets of Southern and Eastern Europe (see Figure 12.8).

Because of the strong planning regulations evident in most Western European markets, the main route to consolidation will be through merger and acquisition. Considerable speculation exists about the potential targets for these global players. Both Carrefour (in the UK) and Tesco (France) have pulled out of one of these key markets in the past; Ahold is not represented in any of these core markets and Wal-Mart is struggling to make its German operation profitable.

Carrefour's merger with Promodés in 1999 was perceived by its management as the creation of the world's largest food retailer with a major presence in Europe. More significantly, it eliminated two firms which were obvious targets for Wal-Mart in its European strategy. The problem for Carrefour was that Wal-Mart would then have to build its German presence and Carrefour would have to counter any bid at a time when the integration of Promodés was proving difficult. Metro, although a leading international retailer in its own right, is predominantly a cash and carry and consumer electronics retailer. It has invested heavily in hypermarket acquisitions in Germany to create the Real fascia, which is the largest hypermarket chain in Germany. The poor performance of Real, however, has only fuelled speculation that the chain will be sold to Wal-Mart, Carrefour or Tesco. Its operations in Poland and Turkey would be of particular interest to Wal-Mart. Although Wal-Mart needs an acquisition to achieve sufficient scale to compete more effectively in Germany, Aggarwal et al. (2000) reckon that Carrefour would be the preferred bidder. Why? Because their CEO, David Bernard, is on the board of Metro International and Metro would view Carrefour as less of a competitive threat to their remaining businesses than Wal-Mart.

If we turn to the French market, the potential acquisition targets have been removed (Carrefour and Promodés) as the other groups are either buying groups (Leclerc/System U and Intermarché) or have a high percentage of shares owned by wealthy families (Auchan by the Mulliez family and Casino by the Guichard family). A combined Auchan/Casino group would be a powerful international operation. The companies were in merger discussions in 2000, but the deal fell through because of tax problems affecting Auchan shareholders. The geographical 'fit' of the companies is good in that Auchan is strong in Spain, Italy and Portugal, whereas Casino's international operations are strongly orientated to Latin America and Asia.

Wal-Mart is reported to have made an approach to the Mulliez family but their advances were repelled. Such an acquisition would give Wal-Mart a presence in the largest Western European markets, a foothold in Eastern Europe, and would complement its operations in Latin America and Asia. Casino is a poorer fit for Wal-Mart because of its multiformatted portfolio. Although its Géant hypermarkets would be of interest to Wal-Mart, it would be less happy in picking up the smaller supermarkets, discount stores and convenience stores which account for most of the store portfolio.

Both these French retailers are also of interest to Ahold. The Dutch retailer has experienced faster growth than its main competitors during the 1990s; however, much of this growth has been in the US market, which contributed 60 per cent of its overall sales. The merger activity in Europe by its competitors has rekindled its interest in Europe, culminating in the acquisition (50 per cent share) of ICA, the market leader in Scandinavia, and Superdiplo, a regional chain in Spain. Ahold had acknowledged that it is seeking further prey in Europe. Ahold is not present in the main Western European markets and is reputed to have Germany low down in its pecking order. This leaves France and the UK. Auchan would also fit with the Ahold portfolio. It would mean that the combined group would be a major force in Europe, and it would strengthen their position in the emerging markets of Eastern Europe, Latin America and Asia. It may also be a more appealing option for Auchan shareholders than a bid from Wal-Mart, because Ahold has a reputation for retaining and nurturing the local management of chains which it acquires. This could be a factor if Casino became part of the equation, because the mixed portfolio of stores would be more suitable to the smaller-scale multiformatted Ahold than the 'big box' retail formats of Wal-Mart.

The UK is another market where there has been speculation that Ahold may enter, especially in the wake of the ASDA–Wal-Mart merger. A variety of possible mergers was mooted in response – a deal between Ahold and Sainsbury, the number two grocery retailer in the UK, was the most consistent deal proposed by analysts to the extent that Ahold has had to refute such speculation. Such a deal is unlikely because it would have major implications for Ahold's strategy in the US, where Sainsbury and Ahold dominate the New England market. Indeed, Ahold has had to divest stores in the past because of its acquisitions in the US and it bought out the 50 per cent voting stock of Giant not in Sainsbury's hands in 1998. A merger between Ahold and Sainsbury would undoubtedly lead the Federal Trade Commission to divest many of its stores to its competitors in the US food industry (Kroger and Safeway).

A more likely target for Ahold in the UK is Safeway. In the 1990s, Ahold was a partner with Safeway and Casino in a buying alliance and Ahold has learnt much from Safeway's distribution system to incorporate best practice principles into its Albert Heijn chain in the Netherlands. Likewise, self-scanning introduced into Safeway stores was 'borrowed' from Albert Heijn. Safeway's fortunes have improved in recent years under the leadership of Carlos Criado-Perez, a former Wal-Mart executive. Safeway's stores tend to be smaller than those of ASDA and Tesco; however, Criado-Perez is widening the store portfolio with a move into hypermarkets and an indication that it may develop a discount chain. Again, this multiformatted portfolio is more suitable for Ahold's management style than the other global competitors.

It has been suggested that Wal-Mart may have to acquire another UK company if it is to challenge Tesco for market leadership. The prospects for doing this are slim unless Safeway was to be bought and broken up, with Wal-Mart purchasing the largest stores. Wm. Morrison, which has outperformed much of the grocery sector since the ASDA acquisition, would be an excellent purchase for a retail mega-group. Unfortunately for Wal-Mart, Morrisons is strong in similar areas to ASDA. Furthermore, this company has cherished its independence and the family has control of the key stock in any takeover bid. This lead Wrigley (2002a) to suggest that Morrisons offers a more likely target for Ahold than Sainsbury.

Of the key retail mega-groups, Tesco is the smallest despite its prominent position in the UK market; however, it has moved very quickly into international markets since its move into Hungary in 1994. It is likely that around 30 per cent of its sales will come from its international operations by 2003/2004. In contrast to Ahold, Tesco's strategy is strongly focused upon the large hypermarket format and it intends to reinforce its presence in the markets in which it has built up market share, namely Eastern Europe and Asia. Its joint venture with Safeway in the US also shows a willingness to enter new markets with its e-commerce expertise, where it has no store operations. But is Tesco big enough to challenge Wal-Mart in global markets? Would a Carrefour–Tesco merger present a more realistic challenge to Wal-Mart by creating a powerful mega-group which would have a major presence in all global markets except the US. Even then, Aggarwal et al. (2000) estimate that a move by Carrefour into the US is a distinct probability in the 2000s. Now that Wal-Mart's Supercenters are gaining acceptability, Carrefour would have the expertise to succeed in the US where it had failed in the late 1980s. To go head to head with Wal-Mart, a merger with Target would be a possibility, giving Target the benefit of Carrefour's food offer.

Carrefour's ability to remain at number two to Wal-Mart has been questioned, however, primarily because of the difficulties in integrating Promedés into the Carrefour banner, especially in Spain. The

Table 12.3 Alternative corporate models of globalized retail operation

'Aggressively industrial'	'Intelligently federal'
Low format adaptation	Multiple/flexible formats
Lack of partnerships/alliances in emerging markets	Partnerships/alliances in emerging markets
Focus on economies of scale in purchasing, marketing, logistics	Focus on back-end integration, accessing economies of skills as much as scale, and best practice knowledge transfer
Centralized bureaucracy, export of key management and corporate culture from core	Absorb, utilize/transfer, best local management acquired
The global *'category killer'* model	The *umbrella organization/corporate parent* model

Source: Wrigley (2002a).

merger has pushed up its gearing ratio, reducing its financial manoeuvrability for expansion on all fronts. Carrefour's international success was built upon its 'first mover' advantage into new markets but the large retail groups have also moved into Latin America and Asia, thereby reducing Carrefour's return from these areas. Wrigley (2002a) maintains that the spectacular growth of Ahold in the late 1990s/early 2000s will see it overtake Carrefour in the global league table.

He also discusses which global model of retail operation is likely to win in the future. Table 12.3 outlines the two corporate models which he proposes. The 'intelligently federal' model is the one adopted by Ahold. Here there is more a 'hands-off' approach to acquisition, with a high degree of retention of the local brand and management skills. The umbrella organization model is flexible, with a focus on local partnerships, format adaption and best practice knowledge transfer. The 'aggressively industrial' model, by contrast, is a more centralized organizational culture which has low format adoption and a category killer approach to internationalization. This is the Wal-Mart approach to international expansion, with Tesco also adopting such an approach with its internationalization based on the hypermarket format. Carrefour lies somewhere between the two models with a more decentralized management structure but a multiformat international strategy.

Summary

This chapter has devoted much time to the new evolving landscape of international retailing. Largely ignored in the literature until very recently, the aspirations of Wal-Mart, Carrefour, Ahold and Tesco can be applied to the conceptual context sketched out in the early part of the chapter. Here we discussed internationalization of concepts, including the transfer of know-how, ideas and best practice as identified in the 'intelligently federal' model discussed above. Although most research focuses upon retail operations, it was pointed out that internationalization is also about managing an international supply chain and international labour force. Tesco's focused strategy in Eastern Europe and Asia is related to managing the supply chain in these markets. With regard to store development, the four key areas of research into retail internationalization were discussed – motives for internationalization, direction of growth, method of market entry and the degree of adaptation to new markets. Early internationalization invariably leads to a cautious, near neighbour approach as retailers take their format to new markets. Then, with experience, they become more ambitious in higher-risk, more distant markets where the joint venture is sometimes the only method of market entry. The degree of adaptation is tied up with the nature of the retail offer. In differentiated, high brand image formats such as category killers or niche fashion brands, the format is replicated throughout global markets. This was illustrated in Box 12.1 with the case of fashion design retailers which promote their image with the development of diffusion lines and franchising of stores in provincial areas.

The next section discussed the conceptual framework within which retail internationalization research was framed. Much of the early work drew heavily on models derived from the international management literature, which focused upon the manufacturing sector with taxonomies of international strategies being produced in the late 1980s. Although these have been revisited over the last decade or so, the 1990s witnessed a new global retail landscape. The so-called internationalists of the 1980s are either niche players on the global scene or they have reorientated their strategies to focus upon their domestic market (see Box 12.2 and the case of Marks & Spencer).

This is why we focused upon the reshaping of the global retail market in the final section. The meteoric rise of Wal-Mart with its grandoise international expansion plans has created change in the markets which it has entered and redefined the nature of global competition. Whether Ahold, Carrefour or Tesco can take on the might of the world's largest company remains to be seen.

Review questions

1 Comment upon the main reasons for retailers 'going international'.
2 Discuss the main marketing strategies deployed by retailers, stressing the advantages and disadvantages of acquisitions as a preferred strategy.
3 To what extent can Levitt's ideas of globalization of markets be applied to the retail sector?
4 Critically review the main theoretical models which have been developed to explain retail internationalization.
5 Chart the growth of Wal-Mart's international developments and discuss the impact which Wal-Mart has had on the nature of global competition.
6 Which of the alternative corporate models of globalized retail operations, proposed by Wrigley, do you think will have most success in the future?

References and further reading

Aggarwal, R., Brodier, A., Spillard, L. and Webb, S. (2000). *Global Retailing, The Future*. IGD, Letchmore Heath.

Alexander, N. (1997). *International Retailing*. Blackwell, Oxford.

Alexander, N. and Myers, H. (2000). The retail internationalisation process. *International Marketing Review*, **17**(4/5), 334–53.

Alexander, N. and Quinn, B. (2002). International retail divestment. *International Journal of Retail and Distribution Management*, **30**(2), 112–25.

Arnold, S. J. and Fernie, J. (2000). Wal-Mart in Europe: prospects for the UK. *International Marketing Review*, **17**(4/5), 416–32.

Bevan, J. (2001). *The Rise and Fall of Marks & Spencer*. Profile Books, London.

Burt, S. L. (1993). Temporal trends in the internationalisation of British retailing. *International Review of Retail, Distribution and Consumer Research*, **3**(4), 391–410.

Burt, S. L. (2002). International retailing. In *Retail Marketing* (McGoldrick, P. J., ed.). McGraw-Hill, Maidenhead.

Burt, S. L., Mellahi, K., Jackson, T. P. and Sparks, L. (2002). Retail internationalisation and retail failure: issues from the case of Marks & Spencer. *The International Review of Retail Distribution and Consumer Research*, **12**(2), 191–219.

Colla, E. and Dupuis, M. (2002). Research and managerial issues on global retail competition: Carrefour/Wal-Mart. *International Journal of Retail and Distribution Management*, **30**, 103–11.

da Rocha, A. and Dib, L. A. (2002). The entry of Wal-Mart in Brazil and the competitive responses of multinational and domestic firms. *International Journal of Retail and Distribution Management*, **30**(1), 61–73.

Davies, R. and Finney, M. (1998). Internationalisation. In *The Future for UK Retailing* (Fernie, J., ed.), Chapter 7, pp. 134–45. Financial Times Retail and Consumer, London.

Dunning, J. (1988). The eclectic paradigm of international production: a restatement and some possible extensions. *Journal of International Business Studies*, **19**(1), 1–31.

Dupuis, M. and Prime, N. (1996). Business distance and global retailing: a model for analysis of key success/failure factors. *International Journal of Retail and Distribution Management*, **24**(11), 30–8.

Fernie, J. and Arnold, S. J. (2002). Wal-Mart in Europe: prospects for Germany, the UK and France. *International Journal of Retail and Distribution Management*, **30**(2), 92–102.

Hollander, S. (1970). *Multinational Retailing*. Michigan State University Press, East Lansing, MI.

Howard, E. (2000). European retailers approach to Asian markets. In *Retail Investment in Asia/Pacific: Local Responses and Public Policy Issues* (Davies, R. and Yahagi, J., eds). OXIRM, Oxford.

Kacker, M. (1998). International flows of retailing know-how. Bridging the technology gap in distribution. *Journal of Retailing*, **64**(1), 41–67.

Levitt, T. (1983). The globalisation of markets. *Harvard Business Review*, **61**, May–June, 92–102.

McGoldrick, P. J. (1995). Introduction to international retailing. In *International Retailing: Trends and Strategies* (McGoldrick, P. J. and Davies, G., eds), Chapter 1, pp. 1–14. Pitman, London.

Moore, C. M., Fernie, J. and Burt, S. L. (2000). Brands without boundaries: the internationalisation of the designer retailer's brand. *European Journal of Marketing*, **34**(8), 919–37.

O'Grady, S. and Lane, H. (1996). The psychic distance paradox. *Journal of International Business Studies*, **27**(2), 309–33.

Robinson, T. and Clarke-Hill, C. (1990). Directional growth by European retailers. *International Journal of Retail and Distribution Management*, **18**(5), 3–14.

Salmon, W. J. and Tordjman, A. (1989). The internationalisation of retailing. *International Journal of Retailing*, **4**(2), 3–16.

Sternquist, B. (1997). International expansion of US retailers. *International Journal of Retail and Distribution Management*, **25**(8), 262–8.

Sternquist, B. (1998). *International Retailing*. Fairchild, New York.

Treadgold, A. (1989). Retailing without frontiers. *Retail and Distribution Management*, November/December, 8–12.

Treadgold, A. (1990). The developing internationalisation of retailing. *International Journal of Retail and Distribution Management*, **18**(2), 4–11.

Vida, I. and Fairhurst, A. (1998). International expansion of retail firms: a theoretical approach for further investigation. *Journal of Retailing and Consumer Services*, **5**(3), 143–51.

Wrigley, N. (2002a). The landscape of pan-European food retail consolidation. *International Journal of Retail and Distribution Management*, **30**(2), 81–91.

Wrigley, N. (2002b). Retail TNCs and the challenge of e-commerce. Paper presented at the Association of American Geographers' Annual Conference, Los Angeles, March.

13

Electronic commerce and retailing

Introduction

Non-store shopping is not new. Traditional mail order goes back over a century. The 'big book' catalogues have experienced slow decline with the advent of more upmarket 'specialogues'. Nevertheless, the tradition of selling to friends and family continues with party plans, most notably Ann Summers, and door-to-door selling through Avon and Betterware catalogues. These 'low tech' forms of selling have accounted for around 4–5 per cent of all retail sales in the UK and the US for many years, but this was forecast to change dramatically in the new millennium when 'higher tech' options would dominate the market-place. *Déjà vu*? When one of the authors of this text took over as Editor of the *International Journal of Retail and Distribution Management*, two early features in 1990 focused upon the status of e-commerce schemes in the US and Europe. After many false dawns and dot.com collapses, Amazon.com reported a quarterly profit for the first time in 2001. A considerable shakeout of the industry has occurred since 2000, with the prospect of a more stable pattern of development occurring until 2010. This chapter will discuss growth of e-commerce, the evolving market and consumer responses to online retailing. The challenges faced by the grocery sector will be discussed in some depth, especially the 'killer costs' of picking and delivering to customers' homes. Finally, the status of the business-to-business market will be reviewed.

The growth of e-commerce

Whilst it is generally accepted that e-commerce has grown considerably in the 1990s and the early part of this century, accurate, reliable figures are difficult to ascertain because of the need to agree upon a widely accepted definition. Nevertheless, national statistical agencies, notably in Canada, the US and Australia, have begun to release data on the use of the Internet for e-commerce. Most research has focused upon business-to-consumer (B2C) transactions, although few companies in this sector have made a profit. It has been the business-to-business (B2B) and consumer-to-consumer (C2C) sectors which have produced real benefits to customers and hence increased profitability for the partners involved. In C2C markets, intermediaries such as eBay are online auctioneers brokering deals between bidders and sellers. Similarly B2B exchanges, such as GlobalNetXchange and WorldWide Retail Exchange, promote online auctions and collaborations between partners to reduce costs. Businesses involved in these e-commerce markets are *infomediaries* in that they are trading information and are facilitators in reducing transaction costs between buyer and seller.

The problem with the B2C model compared with C2C and B2B models is the requirement to trade goods and services which are tangible and need to be stored and transported to the final consumer. Additionally, a market presence and brand identity are necessary ingredients to wean customers away from their traditional methods of buying behaviour. Yet despite these apparent drawbacks, the 'hype' associated with this new form of trading led many analysts to discuss the notion of *disintermediation* in B2C markets. Traditional retail channels were to be disrupted as new players entered the market with online offers. Not surprisingly, conventional retailers reacted passively to the new threat in view of their investment in capital assets. Pure e-tailers, with the exception of niche players, sustained losses with numerous bankruptcies and others such as Peapod were taken over by major retail groups (Ahold in this case). With hindsight, a multichannel strategy is the obvious route to success, especially for companies with a mail order presence. Some multichannel retailers, such as Eddie Bauer, indicate that customers shopping at all channel alternatives (stores, catalogues and online sites) spend more than single- or dual-channel customers. This 'clicks and bricks' approach gives a customer greater flexibility including, in the case of clothing products, the opportunity to return goods to their nearest stores.

The market

One of the reasons for over-optimistic forecasts for e-commerce growth in the 1990s was consumer acceptance of the Internet and widespread adoption of PC usage. By 2002, it was estimated that the number of Internet users numbered 450 million, with over half of this market coming from five countries: the US, China, the UK, Germany and Japan (Table 13.1). Over 90 per cent of Internet users are English speaking, with a similar percentage of 'secure' commercial sites (those which can perform 'secure' credit card transactions) on offer. Growth has been greatest in North America, partly because of the relative cheapness of transaction costs, where telephone charges are lower than other parts of the world. In Europe, however, deregulation of national monopolies, such as in the UK, will facilitate growth in the future. The increased sophistication of mobile phones with WAP applications also offers potential opportunities.

The technology for delivering e-commerce solutions is much more sophisticated and reliable than a decade earlier. Unfortunately, forecasts

Table 13.1 The largest users of Internet worldwide: a comparison of estimates for 2002 (millions)

Country	Estimate	Country	Estimate
1. USA	149.0	21. Turkey	3.7
2. China	33.7	22. Switzerland	3.4
3. UK	33.0	23. Portugal	3.1
4. Germany	26.0	24. Belgium	2.7
5. Japan	22.0	25. Austria	2.7
6. South Korea	16.7	26. Mexico	2.3
7. Canada	14.2	27. Czech Republic	2.2
8. France	11.0	28. Norway	2.2
9. Italy	11.0	29. Finland	2.1
10. Russia	7.5	30. Argentina	2.0
11. Spain	7.0	31. Philippines	2.0
12. Netherlands	6.8	32. Malaysia	2.0
13. Taiwan	6.4	33. Chile	1.8
14. Brazil	6.1	34. Denmark	1.6
15. Australia	5.6	35. South Africa	1.5
16. India	5.0	36. Greece	1.3
17. Poland	4.9	37. New Zealand	1.3
18. Thailand	4.6	38. Singapore	1.3
19. Sweden	4.5	39. Israel	1.2
20. Hong Kong	3.9		

Source: Michalak and Jones (2003).

of online retail sales were strictly *technological* rather than behavioural based. This should present a warning to those who see WAP technology as the new medium for e-commerce in the next 5–10 years.

To give an indication of the optimism exhibited by commentators in the mid-1990s with regard to the scale of online retail sales penetration, the *Financial Times* produced a conservative estimate of sales in Europe by 2000 in 1995. The author estimated that 10–15 per cent of food sales and 20–25 per cent of non-food sales would be made by home shopping (Mandeville, 1995). In reality, online grocery sales throughout Europe were around 0.24 per cent in 2000, with non-food sales only making an impact in computer software, CDs, books and videos. The position is much the same in the US, where online sales accounted for around 1 per cent of all retail sales in 2000 and 2001 (Reynolds, 2001). This slow growth in sales can be attributed to consumers using the web for informational rather than transactional purposes, in addition to purchasing other services rather than retail. For example, Forrester Research showed that, of the $20–30 billion estimate of the online consumer market in the US in 1999, only 60 per cent accounted for the physical distribution of goods (Laseter et al., 2000). The other 40 per cent accounted for digital delivered goods, such as airline and event tickets, banking services and auctions.

Although the rise and fall of Internet retailers has brought a touch of realism to the market potential of online shopping, forecasts are still being made of up to 12.5 per cent of retail sales in both the US and UK by 2005. This seems unduly optimistic in view of some of the problems, especially fulfilment problems, which have still to be overcome. Verdict Research forecasts UK online retail sales to be 5 per cent of all retail sales by this time, with computer software, music and video and books increasing their penetration of these retail markets. Similar patterns of online purchase behaviour are evident in other geographical markets with minor variations by country – for example, apparel sales are higher in Australia and Canada than other markets, perhaps a reflection of countries with a dispersed rural population with a mail order tradition. Verdict's figures show an increase in this category's share of retail sales as a result of 'clicks and bricks' development, whilst the increase in electrical goods sales from £18 to £993 million is indicative of price being a key store choice variable and the Net offering savings to consumers.

The e-commerce consumer

Internet connectivity, as revealed in Table 13.1, depicted an English-speaking, developed country phenomenon. This concealed the different stages of development of these markets and the geodemographic profile of Internet consumers. It is generally accepted that most European countries lag behind the US, which had more than 80 per cent of households connected to the Net in 2001. As the market matures, the profile of the consumer begins to be more representative of the population it serves. In the early stages of development the profile of the e-commerce shopper was a young, male, professional living in middle class neighbourhoods. As the technology becomes more accepted, the gender and socio-economic mix have changed. CACI (2000), the market research group, has undertaken an analysis of online behaviour and buying activity of adults (over 18 years of age) in the UK. Box 13.1 provides a detailed classification of e-types, combining CACI's core database of 30 million lifestyle records with Forrester Research's UK Internet Monitor. This shows an online life cycle from infrequent online purchases (virtual virgins, chatters and gamers, and dot.com chatters) to frequent online purchases (surfing suits and wired living).

Box 13.1   Segmentation of online consumers in the UK

Group 1: Virtual virgins

Of those online, this group is least likely to have bought online. Less than two per 1000 will have made any form of online purchase last month. Their time online is half the national average and they are likely to have started using the Internet more recently than other people.

With the exception of chatting, this group do Internet activities less frequently than average. Because of their relative inexperience they are more likely to worry about security and delivery problems with online purchases and to consider the process to be difficult.

People in this group are twice as likely to be female compared to any other group. The elderly and children are more commonly found in this type than any other.

Group 2: Chatters and gamers

This group, predominantly young males, might spend as much time online as the most avid type of Internet user; however, they tend not to be buyers. Only one in five will ever have made an online purchase. They may consider shopping online to be difficult, and their fear of delivery and security problems is above average.

These people are avid chatters and gamers who use news groups and download as frequently as the most active and experienced surfers. Nearly half are under 25. The schoolchildren in this type are more likely to connect from school/university than any other e-type, although connection from home is still the most frequent.

Group 3: Dot.com dabblers

As average Internet users, these people have mixed feelings regarding the pros and cons of online shopping. Around 40 per cent will have made some form of purchase online and, with the exception of chatting, their interests spread across all forms of Internet activity.

These people may see benefits of the Internet in convenience and speed of delivery. Alternatively, a specialist product not available elsewhere may have introduced them to buying online. In any event, their enthusiasm for e-commerce is not yet complete.

Group 4: Surfing suits

Although they spend less time on the Internet than average, these people can be quite enthusiastic online purchasers. They are more likely than average to have bought books, software, hardware, holidays, groceries, insurance and tickets for events online.

Shopping online is seen to offer benefits such as range of product information, speed of ordering, price advantages and an element of fun. They are less likely to fear e-commerce.

They control their time on the Internet, and surfing, searching, e-mail and news groups tend to be preferred to chat, games or magazines.

Group 5: Wired living

These are cosmopolitan young people and the most extensive Internet users, spending four and a half hours online each week. They are more experienced than most online and on average they have been using the Internet for 3 years. Over 70 per cent will have purchased over the Internet, covering between them the full gamut of products available for purchase. Over 60 per cent of these people are educated to degree level.

These people use the web as part of their lifestyle. Preferred interests tend to be newsgroups, news and magazines, with only an average interest in games or chat.

Source: CACI (2000).

When this classification of online shopping categories is applied to 3000 retail catchment areas, a more detailed picture of online geodemographics is evident. As would be expected, London and South-East England lead the way in terms of online shopping. Nevertheless, there are 'hot spots' across the UK, with Edinburgh, Aberdeen and Bristol scoring highly despite poor overall representation in Scotland and the South-West. Areas with a poor score are North of England cities with a mixed income profile and rural towns and centres.

In Canada, Statistics Canada have undertaken a Household Internet Use Survey since 1997. This provides a comprehensive data source to monitor e-commerce trends on a longitudinal basis. Michalak and Jones (2003) have analysed data from these surveys and show that the Internet adoption rate has grown from 29.4 to 51.3 per cent from 1997 to 2000. Similar geodemographic trends are evident in Canada to those of the UK. The spatial distribution of e-commerce sales is strongly related to population and income distribution in Canada, with households in Ontario accounting for 41.8 per cent of all Internet shoppers, followed by British Columbia with around a quarter of all purchases. They note, however, that e-commerce is overwhelmingly a middle class phenomenon, with regions of Canada with lower incomes or lower population densities having much lower rates of e-commerce sales activity.

Much of this discussion on the e-shopper has focused upon the PC and the Internet as the medium of choice. For much of the 1990s, however, the development of TV shopping was often mooted as the likely channel to dominate the e-commerce market. Television shopping channels were already common in the US and by the early 1990s had entered the UK market. Penetration of cable and satellite TV was low in Europe compared with North America, but the arrival of Digital TV (DTV) was seen as the catalyst for the growth of interactive TV. Much of this optimism has failed to materialize. Digital TV services have not proven as popular as expected and operators have made losses or have gone out of business (ON Digital in the UK).

Even if DTV was to become more popular in Europe, evidence from the US suggests that the motivations for watching TV are very different from PC usage. The latter is individualistic compared with the companionship associated with the television. Pace Microtechnology, one of the companies involved in making set-top boxes for existing analogue TV sets, have undertaken research into consumer attitudes to DTV services (Ody, 1998). Most potential consumers are interested in DTV because of the enhancement of traditional features (better picture quality, sound, more channel choice) rather than to use it for shopping purposes.

It is clear that DTV is still a long way off from challenging the Internet as the medium for home shopping, especially as cheap Internet access

PCs are made available on the market. Reynolds (2002) indicates that convergence between the two technologies will take time because the two markets are sufficiently dissimilar. This is reflected in the early adopters of cable and satellite TV, who tended to be from lower income, socio-economic groups – a different market segment from the early adopters of the Internet.

Online store attributes

As online usage has increased, more research has been conducted upon the shopping service attributes of e-tailing compared with conventional store attributes. Most products and services can be obtained through alternative channels, so the e-tail offer has to provide additional benefits to the consumer which they cannot receive from traditional channels. The majority of studies indicate that such benefits are convenience, the saving of time and lower prices associated with some Internet retailers. After all, companies such as Priceline.com hoped to change the nature of the retail and service market through its 'name your price' auctions for airline seats, hotel rooms, petrol and grocery products.

Broadly, online store attributes fall into the following categories:

- Navigation and convenience.
- Merchandise mix.
- Pricing.
- Customer service.
- Security.

Navigation and convenience relate to a consumer's ability to reduce transaction costs through visiting a website rather than a retail outlet. Navigating on easy-to-use uncluttered sites will minimize the time and effort to search and buy products and services. Conversely, a time-constrained consumer will be inconvenienced by a site which is slow to navigate and difficult to use.

This relates to the merchandise on offer with regard to the overall assortment, variety and product information. One of the advantages which pure play e-tailers had over their bricks and mortar counterparts was that they developed their websites around their position in the market and the product assortment on offer. Many conventional retailers with a large number of stock-keeping units (SKUs) and a variety of product categories found it difficult to make available the same product range on their online stores.

Conceptually, pricing should be a key online shopping attribute in that consumers should have a reduction in search costs, more product information and a greater opportunity to compare prices. In practice, the importance of price as a choice attribute is not unlike the situation with conventional store choice. Price is only one of a multitude of factors which influence patronage behaviour. Reynolds (2002) reports that much of the research on online pricing is inconclusive and at times contradictory. Nevertheless, price is clearly an important variable for specific online product categories where consumers know what they want and are prepared to buy at the cheapest price. This explains the relative success of online retailers selling books, CDs and computer equipment.

Customer service or the overall service quality experience embraces some of the other attributes discussed in this section – convenience, navigation and security. Here we will focus more upon the service process. Customers surfing a website invariably need help about product selection and services available. Having traded off the inconvenience of going to the store, customers need to know how/ when to pay, when the goods will be delivered and what after-sales service is available for returning goods or complaining about elements of poor service. The problems associated with e-fulfilment are the main ones to resolve before e-tailing can be an established, profitable channel of distribution.

Security was a major negative factor in deterring consumers from buying online in the early years of e-commerce development. Consumers were initially concerned about credit card and other forms of payment fraud. More recently, issues about the disclosure of personal as well as financial information, and possible theft of goods in transit to the customer's address, are of concern to customers. Americans, in particular, are not enamoured by a deluge of junk e-mails to parallel that of the junk mail revolution of earlier decades.

Longitudinal surveys undertaken by various authors in the late 1990s have shown how the e-tailing market has matured both in terms of the customer base and the range of online offerings. In the US, the peak period of demand for Internet retailing is between Thanksgiving and Christmas. Lavin (2002) draws upon consumer surveys undertaken by consultancy companies during Christmas 1998 and 1999 and her own primary research of retailers' websites during the same period. She comments that the profile of the web shopper had changed, e-tailers had worked to meet rising consumer expectations and the 'first to market' advantage of early adopters had been eroded away. The customer of 1998 was predominantly male, technologically proficient and relatively affluent. More significantly, they were not mainstream shoppers and had low expectations for their online purchase experience. She equates this with the innovator and early adopter stages of the adoption life cycle. A year later, with a rapidly growing market, the profile of the online customer had changed to a more balanced gender and age, with overall lower average incomes. These are more likely to be mainstream shoppers with higher expectations from their purchase experiences. This early majority segment raised the stakes for online providers. Considerable investment was made to upgrade sites, advertise on traditional media to attract customers and in logistical infrastructure to ship products to customers' homes. Despite this, the 1999 Christmas period was notorious for failure to meet the Christmas deadline, partly due to consumers delaying purchase to the last minute but also to sheer volume of business in the network.

In the UK, Ellis-Chadwick et al. (2002) completed a longitudinal study of Internet adoption by UK multiple retailers from 1997 to 2000. Again, as in Lavin's study, the primary research was largely based on reviewing retail websites over this 4-year period to ascertain how Internet business models were being developed. They report a six-fold increase in the number of retailers offering online shopping to their customers. Companies have moved from offering purely informational services to a fully serviced transactional e-shop. In the case of the well-established retailers, they have been more creative in linking their sites to other companies with complementary products – for example, birthday.co.uk to Thorntons, suppliers of chocolates, and Wax Lyrical, a specialist candle retailer.

These studies, and other more sector-specific research investigations, indicate that retailers are responding to the choice attributes identified earlier. However, as the market matures, consumers tend to behave in a similar fashion to dealing with traditional retail outlets. The basics of convenience, product range, customer service and price will always feature in a consumer's 'evoked set' of attributes. Above all, retailers have become brands and customer loyalty has been established through continually high levels of service. It is not surprising therefore that traditional retailers with strong brand equity can gain even more leverage through a sound web strategy. They have the trust of the consumer to begin with and the capital to invest in the necessary infrastructure. Many dot.com pure players needed to build a brand and tackle the formidable challenge of delivering to customers' homes. This is why it has taken Amazon.com so long to register a profit. Nevertheless, Amazon.com has strong brand presence, and research by Brynjolfsson and Smith (2000) indicates that the company can charge higher prices because of this brand equity or what they term 'heterogeneity of trust'. In their survey of online pricing in specific markets, they showed that Amazon.com had a market share of around 80 per cent in books, yet charged a 10 per cent premium over the least expensive book retailer in their research.

The grocery market

Despite the fact that online grocery sales account for less than 1 per cent of retail sales in most country markets, this sector has attracted most attention from researchers and government bodies, including the DTI in the UK (DTI, 2001). Grocery shopping impacts upon all consumers. We all have to eat! However, our populations are getting older, so shopping is more of a chore; conversely, the younger, time-poor, affluent consumers may hate to waste time buying groceries. The relatively slow uptake of online grocery shopping in the US can be attributed to the lack of online shopping availability in that only about one-third of supermarket operators offer some type of home shopping service.

Morganosky and Cude (2002) have undertaken one of the few studies on the behaviour of online grocery shoppers. Their research was based on a longitudinal study of consumers of Schnucks Markets, a St Louis-based chain of supermarkets operating in Illinois, Missouri and Indiana. The first two surveys in 1998 and 1999 asked Schnuck's online shoppers to complete a questionnaire online on the completion of their order. The final survey re-contacted respondents from the 1999 survey to track their shopping behaviours in 2001. The results here did have some parallels with other surveys of non-food online shopping, most notably more sophisticated consumers who had moved on from being 'new' users to experienced online shoppers. This is further reflected in their willingness to buy most or all of their groceries online and to improve their efficiency at completing the shopping tasks. The main difference noted from this research compared with other work is the profile of the consumer, who remained relatively stable over the time period. Online grocery shoppers bought for the family. They were younger, female and better educated with higher incomes. The final survey showed that customer retention rates were good. The main reason for defections was the relocation to another part of the US where the same online service was not available.

Although similar empirical research has not been carried out in the UK, trade sources indicate that the online consumer has become more experienced and is buying more online. The two main e-grocers in the UK, Tesco and Sainsbury, claim that their online customers spend more than their conventional customers. Tesco also explodes the myth that online customers would not buy fresh products because of the so-called 'touch and feel' factor. Indeed, the opposite is true – of the top 10 selling lines, seven are fresh, with skinless chicken breasts at number one (Jones, 2001). Tesco, however, is one of the few success stories in e-grocery (see Box 13.2). In Europe, grocery retailers are powerful 'bricks and mortar' companies, and the approach to Internet retailing has been reactive rather than proactive. Most Internet operations have

Box 13.2   Tesco.com: the world's largest Internet grocery retailer

In 2002, Tesco.com's service was available to 95 per cent of the British population from 273 of its stores. Other important facts are:

- 85 000 orders per week;
- 40 000 lines;
- 19 out of the top 20 lines are fresh foods;
- basket size is £85 online compared with £21 in-store;
- 80 per cent of shoppers are women, of which 54 per cent are AB1;
- 30 per cent of customers shop nowhere else online;
- young families with children aged 3–9 are the largest segment;
- Wednesday night is the busiest for ordering.

The company has come a long way since its pilot trials began in December 1996. Significantly, turnover has grown from £52 million in 2000 to £350 million in 2002 and is now contributing to the group's profitability. The secret of its success has been the way in which it has developed the business incrementally. Tesco.com realized within the first 2 years of operation that customers wanted the full range of Tesco products so the warehouse model was ruled out, not only because of limited product offering, but the economics of delivery outside of the London conurbation. In effect, they determined that the extended drive time to a Tesco store would increase from 15 to 25 minutes for a home shopper.

As Tesco Direct was rolled out throughout the country, the company began to reduce operating costs in its ordering and picking operation. Initially, Tesco.com accepted orders through different media – fax, telephone, CDs – but soon realized the complexities of customers' systems. The move to an Internet ordering system streamlined this process. Within the store, the warehouse picking system was refined and semi-automated to further reduce costs.

With costs coming down, Tesco.com has also been able to increase its revenue through expanding its product range and transferring its model to international markets. In 2001, it bought a 35 per cent stake in groceryworks.com, the online division of the US Safeway chain. Portland, Oregon and San Francisco are the first two target markets for the US service. Within its own international operations it now operates an online operation for 70 per cent of the Irish population from its Tesco stores and launched an e-homeplus service from its store in Ansan, near Seoul, in South Korea.

While development of the non-food offer has been a strategy of the store-based operation, the online service gives customers more choice than they can ever experience in even the largest store. In the UK, it can match Amazon's range of books and carries stock of every CD, DVD, video and computer game on UK release. The scope for further growth is immense. Tesco's popular Clubcard enables it to tailor offers to its own customers, test promotions with suppliers, and achieve synergies between its store and online operations.

been small and few pure players have entered the market to challenge the conventional supermarket chains.

The situation is different in the US, where a more fragmented, regionally orientated grocery retail structure has encouraged new entrants into the market. In the late 1980s, this came in the form of Warehouse Clubs and Wal-Mart Supercenters; by the 1990s, dot.com players began to challenge the traditional supermarket operators (Table 13.2 identifies the key players, along with Tesco for comparison). Unfortunately, these pure players have either gone into liquidation, scaled down their operations or they have been taken over by conventional grocery businesses.

Why have pure players failed? Laseter et al. (2000) identify four key challenges:

1 Limited online potential.
2 High cost of delivery.
3 Selection variety trade-offs.
4 Existing entrenched competition.

Ring and Tigert (2001) came to similar conclusions when comparing the Internet offering with the conventional 'bricks and mortar' experience. They looked at what consumers would trade away from a store in terms of the place, product, service and value for money by shopping online. They also detailed the 'killer costs' of the pure play Internet grocers, notably the picking and delivery costs. The gist of the argument presented by these critics is that the basic Internet model is flawed.

Even if the potential is there, the consumer has to be lured away from existing behaviour with regard to store shopping. Convenience is invariably ranked as the key choice variable in both store patronage and Internet usage surveys. For store shoppers, convenience is about location and the interaction with staff and the store experience. Internet users tend to be trading off the time it takes to shop. However, as Wilson-Jeanselme (2001) has shown, the 58 per cent net gain in

Table 13.2 The major existing and former e-grocers

	Tesco UK	Webvan USA	Streamline USA	Peapod USA
Background	The biggest supermarket chain in the UK	Started as a pure e-grocer in 1999	Started as a pure e-grocer in 1992	Started home delivery service before the Internet in 1989
Investments in e-grocer development	US $58 million	Approx. US $1200 million	Approx. US $80 million	Approx. US $150 million
Main operational mode	Industrialized picking from the supermarket	Highly automated picking in distribution centre (DC)	Picking from the distribution centre, reception boxes, value adding services	Picking from both DC and from stores
Current status	The biggest e-grocer in the world. Expanding its operations outside the UK. Partnering with Safeway and Groceryworks	Operations ceased July 2001	Part of operations were sold to Peapod in September 2000. The rest of operations ceased in November 2000	Bought by global grocery retailer Royal Ahold. Second biggest e-grocer in the world

Source: Tanskanen et al. (2002).

convenience benefit is often eroded away by 'leakages' in the process of ordering to ultimate delivery. Furthermore, the next two key store choice variables in the US tend to be price and assortment. With the exception of Webvan, pure players offered a limited number of stock-keeping units (SKUs) compared with conventional supermarkets. Price may have been competitive with stores but delivery charges push prices up to the customer. In the highly competitive US grocery market, customers will switch stores for only a 3–4 per cent differential in prices across leading competitors. Ring and Tigert (2001) therefore pose the question:

> What percentage of households will pay substantially more for an inferior assortment (and perhaps quality) of groceries just for the convenience of having them delivered to their home? (p. 270)

Tanskanen et al. (2002) argue that e-grocery companies failed because an electronic copy of a supermarket does not work. They claim that e-grocery should be a complementary channel rather than a substitute and that companies should be investing in service innovations to give value to the customer. Building upon their research in Finland, they maintain that the 'clicks and bricks' model will lead to success for e-grocery. Most of the difficulties for pure players relate to building a business with its associated infrastructure. Conventional retailers have built trust with their suppliers and customers. The customer needs a credible alternative to self-service and the Finnish researchers suggest that this has to be achieved at a local level, where routine purchases can be shifted effectively to e-grocery. To facilitate product selection, web-based information technology can tailor the retail offer to the customer's needs. The virtual store can be more creative than the restrictions placed on the physical stocking of goods on shelves; however, manufacturers will need to provide 'pre-packaged' electronic product information for ordering on the web.

E-fulfilment

Regardless of the nature of the 'accepted' e-grocery model of the future, the 'last mile' problem continues to pose difficulties for e-grocers. In many ways, the initial pure players in the US have pioneered the various fulfilment models (see Table 13.2). Webvan raised $360 million of share capital in October 1999 partly to fund the construction of 26 giant warehouses, each greater than 300 000 square feet, in 26 cities. The model is a hub and spoke logistics system in each of these regions. The highly automated warehouses stocked around 50 000 SKUs, and orders were picked and moved by conveyor belt to loading trucks which transported product to 10–12 substations in the region. Here, loads were broken down into customers' orders for onward delivery by company trucks. Webvan could not generate sufficient volume to cover the fixed costs of the investment in its warehouse infrastructure and ceased operations in July 2001. Stream-line, the other innovative US pure player, did offer value-added services. It was the pioneer of unattended reception whereby the Stream Box was accessed by keypad entry systems in the garage. The company also offered to automatically replenish inventory of key value items for customers, in addition to other services such as dry cleaning, video rental and shoe repairs. This fragmentation of offering did not build up a customer base quickly enough before the company ran out of cash in 2000.

In the UK, much of the early experimentation with online grocery focused upon the London region because of the high density of drops which could be achieved. Tesco opted for the store fulfilment model while its main competitors, Sainsbury and ASDA, developed picking centres. Waitrose, a major South-East England chain, developed its Waitrose @ work, delivering to the workplace of key businesses along the M4 corridor.

Discussions on the main fulfilment models can be found in Chapter 7. It is necessary to note here, however, that the store-based fulfilment model, as advocated by Tesco, offers the best *short-term* solution to meeting growing market demand for online grocery retailing. Even then, the so-called 'killer costs' of order processing, picking and delivery for groceries in the UK are between £8 and £20 per order depending on the system operated and utilization of vehicle fleets (DTI, 2001). As the delivery to the customer is around £5 per order, it is clear that unless the order value is high, retailers will make a loss in every delivery that they make.

The potential solution to this 'last mile' problem is to have some form of unattended reception facility at home/collection or to persuade customers to accept more flexible 'time windows' for attended deliveries. Indeed, Tesco was trialling differential cost structures for attended delivery in 2002 so that customers would have a reduced delivery charge – £3.99 for deliveries determined by Tesco and more expensive charges, £6.99, for time slots fixed by the customer. To achieve the cost savings required, it will be necessary to change customer attitudes to existing forms of home delivery. Whether this can be achieved is debatable, especially as it throws up another series of challenges, such as potential crime threats in the e-tailing channel.

For example, what security measures will be necessary to protect reception boxes from burglary and how will attended deliveries be accounted for when the recipient is not at home and the goods are stolen?

The business-to-business (B2B) market

> B2B exchanges are virtual, Internet-enabled information, communication and transaction marketplaces, where buyers and sellers meet, trade, interact and transact. They are technological enablers, nothing more, nothing less.
> (Corsten and Hofstetter, 2001, p. 53)

The advent of e-commerce has had a major impact on business-to-business (B2B) channels of distribution because of the potential cost savings that could be achieved in the sourcing of products, a high proportion of the overall manufacturing cost. Not surprisingly, the creation of B2B exchanges has been particularly successful in highly concentrated global market sectors with a streamlined number of buyers and sellers, for example in the automobile, chemical and steel industries.

The FMCG sector has been a laggard in new developments. This was partly due to the large number of participants, the proliferation of e-marketplaces, and therefore a multiplicity of different standards and data formats. By the late 1990s, B2B exchanges began to take shape in the form of private exchanges, consortium exchanges and mega-exchanges. Private exchanges are exclusive marketplaces restricted to a retailer or manufacturer's suppliers or customers. For example, the more proactive retailers developed B2B Internet exchanges as an extension of their EDI platforms, created a decade earlier. This has enabled companies such as Tesco, Sainsbury and Wal-Mart to establish their own private exchanges with suppliers to share data on sales, product forecasting, promotion tracking and production planning. There are major benefits from pooling EDI platforms into a smaller number of B2B platforms. For example, it is easier to standardize processes for communication, reduce development costs and give members access to a larger customer base.

In order to achieve critical mass of transaction volumes, consortium exchanges were created with key companies in the FMCG sector becoming equity members. In the grocery sector, four major exchanges dominate the market:

- WorldWide Retail Exchange (WWRE) and GlobalNetXchange (GNX), which are retail-derived exchanges (see Box 13.3).
- Transora and CPG market (CPG), which were founded by suppliers and therefore are orientated towards manufacturers.

Clearly, there is potential for further integration between these exchanges to create mega-exchanges, and GNX and Transora have intentions to form integrated exchange which would facilitate collaboration across the FMCG supply chain.

Since these services were offered in 2000, some progress has been made in facilitating transactions across these exchanges. Most retailers will claim that they have recouped their investment in consortia exchanges (Box 13.3). However, recent ECR Europe conferences

---

Box 13.3   Profiles of GNX and WWRE

GlobalNetXchange – www.gnx.com

- Founding equity partners include Carrefour, Metro AG, Sainsbury's, Karstadt Quelle, Sears Roebuck, Pinault-Printempts-Redoute, Kroger, Coles Myer, Oracle and Pricewaterhouse Coopers.
- There are 30 retail members.
- In 2001, GNX customers conducted more than 2600 online auctions, with a total value of approximately US $2.1 billion (£1.4 billion).
- GNX's main areas of business are online auctions, collaborative supply chain management programmes, collaborative product development (own-brand) and a perishables exchange.

WorldWide Retail Exchange – www.wwre.org

- WWRE has 60 retail members with combined sales of more than US $845 billion (£579 billion).
- Members include Ahold, Delhaize, Dixons, Gap, Kingfishers, John Lewis, Kmart, Casino, Boots Company, Toys 'R' Us, Tesco, Safeway Inc., Safeway plc (UK), C&A Europe, Target and Marks & Spencer.
- WWRE claims to have saved its members more than US $270 million (£185 million) through online negotiations.
- WWRE aims to reduce costs and improve efficiencies throughout the supply chain, employing product and service solutions.

Source: Retail Week, 10 May 2002.

suggest that performance has not matched initial expectations. Although the Global Commerce Initiative established draft standards for global Internet trading, many issues need to be resolved before ECR's vision of a seamless data flow across the world is realized. One major problem here is that Wal-Mart is such a large organization it is setting its own standards faster than consortia can agree their technical specifications.

Much of the initial focus on consortia exchanges was collaboration on non-merchandise stock – office equipment, store fittings, stationery, etc. In practice, the buying of such products requires product specifications to be agreed in advance and these products do not necessarily have straightforward specifications. Indeed, for these products, it is the complexity of dealing with thousands of SKUs for all product categories which has resulted in retailers routing selected projects through consortia exchanges rather than their own private exchanges. Thus, staple products, ideal for own-label development, are more suitable for consortia buying than ready meals, which have specifications unique to a particular retailer.

Although there have been teething difficulties with all of these B2B exchanges, the scope for growth and potential savings for supply chain participants are high. E-marketplaces bring in an element of discipline into buyer–seller negotiations for relatively standardized goods and services, in addition to speeding up the transaction process. As the market matures, consortia exchanges will provide more services to attract members to use their exchanges to further reduce supply chain costs.

Summary

This chapter has charted the major changes which have occurred in e-commerce in recent years and the impact which these changes have had on the retail sector. The growth and size of the market were illustrated showing how optimistic projections of Internet retailing have not materialized to date because forecasts were strongly based on the availability of technological media rather than their rate of acceptability by the consumer. Nevertheless, the e-commerce consumer has changed in a relatively short period of time. The initial adopter tended to be a young, male professional living in a middle class neighbourhood. As the technology became more acceptable, the gender bias was slowly removed and the socio-economic mix changed. Evidence from a series of empirical longitudinal studies confirmed these trends, with the exception of grocery shoppers, who tend to be better-off suburban housewives with a young family.

Online retailers have had to respond to a more discerning consumer as sales volumes began to grow. To lure customers away from traditional shopping patterns, these retailers have to embrace many of the same attributes evident in store choice models – convenience, product range, customer service and price. The best 'pure players' such as Amazon.com have built up a reputation for their high levels of customer service and therefore achieved a high degree of brand loyalty.

It has been the strong established players, however, who have capitalized on the failure of many dot.com companies. An Internet presence has allowed them to capitalize on their existing brand equity in addition to having the required investment to develop the necessary infrastructure. A 'clicks and bricks' approach has proven to be the most successful model to date in that synergies can be achieved through a multichannel strategy.

The one retail sector which has attracted most interest, despite the fact that its percentage of online sales is under 1 per cent in most country markets, is the grocery sector. The potential market is large but success remains elusive to all but a few companies. In the US, in particular, the demise of Webvan and Streamline show that you can have the 'ideal' online model but without sufficient market demand, losses are inevitable. Tesco is one of the few success stories here, primarily because it has grown the business incrementally and developed a store-based delivery model. Even for Tesco, the 'last mile' problem still requires a solution. Order processing, picking and delivering groceries are the 'killer costs' of online grocery retailing. Some solutions were discussed, such as the use of some form of unattended delivery (reception boxes at home or collection points) or the acceptance by consumers of more flexible delivery times.

The final part of the chapter discussed B2B markets in order to ascertain how e-commerce could bring benefits to retailers through better information exchange with their suppliers. It was shown that private exchanges and consortia exchanges had been developed in the late 1990s/early 2000s to build upon EDI platforms of a decade earlier. In some ways, the 'hype' of the benefits from consortia exchanges had not been realized. Agreements over standardization of data formats continue to be an issue which hinders progress towards a seamless integration of data across global supply chains. Nevertheless, retailers that are affiliated to consortia acknowledge that they have recouped their investment costs through faster, more organized transactions for a range of goods and services which have straightforward specifications.

Review questions

1 Despite the 'hype' of the 1990s, online retail sales account for less than 1 per cent in most markets. Discuss.
2 Comment upon the changing profile of the e-commerce consumer from empirical research in the UK and North America.
3 Discuss the key choice attributes for shopping online and compare these with conventional store attributes.
4 Evaluate the main factors which led to the demise of pure e-grocery players in the US grocery market.
5 Assess the possible solutions to overcoming the problems in e-grocery.
6 Critically review the development of B2B exchanges.

References

Brynjolfsson, F. and Smith, M. (2000). Frictionless commerce? A comparison of internet and conventional retailers. *Management Science*, **46**(4), 563–85.

CACI (2000). *Who's Buying Online?* CACI Information Solutions, London.

Corsten, D. and Hofstetter, J. S. (2001). After the type: the emerging landscape of B2B exchanges. *ECR Journal*, **1**(1), 51–9.

Department of Trade and Industry (DTI) (2001). @ *Your Home, New Markets for Customer Service and Delivery*. Retail Logistics Task Force, Foresight, London.

Ellis-Chadwick, F., Doherty, N. and Hast, C. (2002). Signs of change? A longitudinal study of Internet adoption in the UK retail sector. *Journal of Retailing and Consumer Services*, **9**(2), 71–80.

Jones, D. (2001). Tesco.com: delivering home shopping. *ECR Journal*, **1**(1), 37–43.

Laseter, T., Houston, P., Ching, A., Byrne, S., Turner, M. and Devendran, A. (2000). The last mile to nowhere. *Strategy and Business*, **20**, September.

Lavin, M. (2002). Christmas on the Web: 1998 v 1999. *Journal of Retailing and Consumer Services*, **9**(2), 87–96.

Mandeville, L. (1995). *Prospects for Home Shopping in Europe*, FT Management Report. Pearson, London.

Michalak, W. and Jones, K. (2003). Canadian e-commerce. *International Journal of Retail and Distribution Management*, **31**(1), 5–15.

Morganosky, M. A. and Cude, B. (2002). Consumer demand for online food retailing: is it really a supply side issue? *International Journal of Retail and Distribution Management*, **30**(10), 451–8.

Ody, P (1998). Non-store retailing. In *The Future for UK Retailing* (Fernie, J. ed.), Chapter 4. FT Retail and Consumer, London.

Reynolds, J. (2001). The new etail landscape: the view from the beach. *European Retail Digest*, **30**, 6–8.

Reynolds, J. (2002). E-tail marketing. In *Retail Marketing* (McGoldrick, P. J., ed.), 2nd edn, Chapter 15. McGraw-Hill, London.

Ring, L. J. and Tigert, D. J. (2001). Viewpoint: the decline and fall of Internet grocery retailers. *International Journal of Retail and Distribution Management*, **29**(6), 266–73.

Tanskanen, K., Yroyla, M. and Holmstron, J. (2002). The way to profitable Internet grocery retailing – 6 lessons learned. *International Journal of Retail and Distribution Management*, **30**(4), 169–78.

Verdict Research (2000). *Electronic Shopping, UK*. Verdict, London.

Wilson-Jeanselme, M. (2001). Grocery retailing on the Internet: the leaking bucket theory. *European Retail Digest*, **30**, 9–12.

Index